Programming.NET
Components

Programming .NET Components

Juval Löwy

O'REILLY®

Beijing · Cambridge · Farnham · Köln · Paris · Sebastopol · Taipei · Tokyo

Programming .NET Components
by Juval Löwy

Published by O'Reilly & Associates, Inc., 1005 Gravenstein Highway North, Sebastopol, CA 95472.

O'Reilly & Associates books may be purchased for educational, business, or sales promotional use. Online editions are also available for most titles (*safari.oreilly.com*). For more information, contact our corporate/institutional sales department: (800) 998-9938 or *corporate@oreilly.com*.

Editor:	John Osborn
Development Editor:	Brian MacDonald
Production Editor:	Mary Anne Weeks Mayo
Cover Designer:	Ellie Volckhausen
Interior Designers:	David Futato and Bret Kerr

Printing History:

April 2003:	First Edition.

ISBN: 0-596-00347-1

[M]

To my daughter, Abigail

Table of Contents

Preface

I've been fortunate in my career to have lived through most generations of Microsoft component technologies. In the mid 1990s, I developed DLLs and exported their functions, and used MFC extension DLLs to expose classes. I experienced first hand the enormous complexity involved in managing a set of interacting applications comprising 156 DLLs and deployed as a single unit, as well as the maintenance and versioning issues raised by their use of ordinal numbers. I helped design COM-like solutions to those problems and remember the excitement I felt when I heard about COM for the first time and generated my first GUID using a command-line utility.

I learned how to write class factories and IDL interfaces long before the release of ATL, and I tried to use RPC before DCOM abstracted it away. I designed component-based applications using COM and experienced what it takes to share design ideas with other developers who aren't familiar with its requirements. I programmed with MTS and learned the workarounds involved in its use, and I marveled at the elegance and usefulness of COM+ when it came to architecting large-scale enterprise frameworks.

My understanding of component-oriented programming has evolved and grown over that time, just as the component-based technologies themselves have done. I have often asked myself, what are the fundamental principles of using components, and in what ways do they differ from traditional object-oriented programming? I have tried to learn from my mistakes and to abstract and generalize the good ideas and techniques I have encountered or developed on my own. I believe that I have identified some core principles of component-oriented design that transcend any technologies available today and that result in components that are easier to reuse, and extend and maintain over the long term.

With the advent of the .NET Framework, Windows developers finally have a first-class technology at their disposal that aims at simplifying the task of developing and deploying component-based applications. .NET is the result of much soul-searching by Microsoft and, in my view, improves on the deficiencies of previous technologies—especially COM. .NET incorporates and enforces proven methodologies and approaches while retaining their core benefits.

To me, .NET is fundamentally a component technology that provides an easy and clean way to generate binary components, in compliance with what I regard as sound design principles. .NET is engineered from the ground up to simplify component development and deployment, and to support interoperability between programming languages. .NET components are used for building component-based applications, from standalone desktop applications to web-based applications and services.

Of course, .NET is more than just a new component technology; it's actually a brand name for a set of technologies. .NET provides several specialized application frameworks, including Windows Forms for rich Windows clients, ADO.NET for data access, ASP.NET for web applications, and Web Services for exposing and consuming remote objects that use the SOAP and other XML-based protocols. Visual Studio .NET supports the development of .NET applications in Visual Basic, Managed C++ and C#, as well as more than a dozen other languages. Microsoft server products will increasingly support ".NET-connected" applications in coming years. In the context of this book, whenever I use the term ".NET," I'm referring to the .NET Framework in general and the component technology it embodies in particular.

Scope of This Book

This book covers the topics and skills you need to design and develop component-based .NET applications. However, to make the most of .NET, it helps to know its origins and how it improves on the shortcomings of past technologies. In addition to showing you how to perform a certain task, the book often explains the rationale behind it in terms of the principles of component-oriented programming. Armed with such insights, you can optimize your application design for maintainability, extensibility, reusability, and productivity. While the book can be read without prior knowledge of COM, I occasionally use COM as a reference model when it helps explain why .NET operates the way it does. You'll not only learn .NET component programming and the related system issues, but also relevant design options, tips, best practices, and pitfalls. The book avoids many implementation details of .NET and largely confines its coverage to the possibilities and the practical aspects of using .NET as a component technology: how to apply the technology and how to choose among the available design and programming models.

In addition, the book contains many useful utilities, tools, and helper classes I've developed since .NET was introduced three years ago. These are aimed at increasing your productivity and the quality of your .NET components. After reading the book, you will be able to start developing .NET components immediately, taking full advantage of .NET development infrastructure and application frameworks.

Here is a brief summary of the chapters and appendixes in this book:

Chapter 1, *Introducing Component-Oriented Programming*

Provides the basic terminology used throughout the book. It contrasts object-oriented programming with component-oriented programming and then enumerates the principles of component-oriented programming. These principles are the "why" behind the "how" of .NET, and understanding them is a prerequisite to correctly building component-based applications.

Chapter 2, *.NET Component-Oriented Programming Essentials*

Describes the elements of .NET, such as the CLR, .NET programming languages, the code-generation process, assemblies, and building and composing those assemblies. The chapter ends by explaining how .NET maintains binary compatibility between clients and components, and the implications of this solution for the programming model. If you are already familiar with the fundamentals of the .NET Framework, feel free to skim over or entirely skip this chapter.

Chapter 3, *Interface-Based Programming*

Dedicated to working with interfaces. It explains how to separate an interface from its implementation in .NET, how to implement interfaces, and how to design and factor interfaces that cater to reuse, maintainability, and extensibility.

Chapter 4, *Lifecycle Management*

Deals with the way .NET manages objects, and the good and bad implications this has for the overall .NET programming model. The chapter explains the underlying .NET garbage collection mechanism and shows component developers how to dispose of resources held by instances of a component.

Chapter 5, *Version Control*

Begins by describing .NET version control policy and the ways you can deploy and share their components. After dealing with the default policy, the chapter shows how to provide custom version binding and resolution policies to address application- or even machine-specific needs. The chapter also discusses how to develop applications that support multiple versions of .NET itself.

Chapter 6, *Events*

Shows how to publish and subscribe to events in a component-based application. After discussing the built-in support provided by .NET, the chapter presents a number of best practices and utilities, which are designed to make the most of the basic event support and to improve it.

Chapter 7, *Asynchronous Calls*

Describes .NET's built-in support for invoking asynchronous calls on components, the available programming models, their tradeoffs, when to use them, and their pitfalls.

Chapter 8, *Multithreading and Concurrency Management*

Explains in depth how to build multithreaded components. No modern application is complete without multiple threads, but multithreading comes with a hefty price—the need to synchronize access to your components. The chapter shows how to create and manage threads, and how to synchronize access to objects, using both the little-known synchronization domains and the manual synchronization locks. The chapter ends with a rundown of various multithreading services in .NET, such as the thread pool and timers.

Chapter 9, *Serialization and Persistence*

Shows how to persist and serialize an object state. Serialization is useful when saving the state of an application to a file and in remote calls. The chapter demonstrates the use of automatic and custom serialization and shows how to combine serialization with a class hierarchy.

Chapter 10, *Remoting*

Demystifies .NET support for remote calls. It starts by explaining application domains and the available remote object types and activation modes. After a discussion of the remoting architecture, the chapter shows how to set up a distributed component-based .NET application, both programmatically and administratively. The chapter concludes by explaining how to manage the lifecycle of remote objects using leasing and sponsorship.

Chapter 11, *Context and Interception*

Describes a powerful and useful, but undocumented facet of .NET: its ability to provide ways to define custom services via contexts and call interception. The chapter explains contexts and how they are used to implement component services, as well as the interception architecture and how to extend it. It ends with a walkthrough of a real life productivity-oriented custom service.

Chapter 12, *Security*

Addresses the rich topic of .NET code-access security. Unlike Windows security, .NET security is component-based, not user-based. As such, it opens new possibilities for component developers. The chapter shows how to administer security using the .NET configuration tool and how to provide additional security programmatically. The chapter also shows how to use .NET role-based security and how to install a custom authorization mechanism.

Appendix A, *Interface-Based Web Services*

Shows how to enforce a core principal of component-oriented programming (separation of interface from implementation) when using .NET web services, both on the service and the client side. The appendix presents a simple workaround that can add the missing support to Visual Studio.NET.

Appendix B, *Custom Security Principal*

Demonstrates how to replace the default identity authorization building block in .NET. Because .NET uses Windows accounts for authorization by default, it isn't applicable for many Internet and enterprise applications. The appendix presents a generic custom mechanism that uses identities and roles stored in a database.

Appendix C, *Reflection and Attributes*

Explains .NET reflection and how to develop and reflect custom attributes. If you aren't familiar with reflection, I recommend reading this appendix before the rest of the chapters.

Some Assumptions About the Reader

I assume you, the reader, are an experienced developer and that you feel comfortable with object-oriented concepts such as encapsulation and inheritance. I also assume you have basic familiarity with either C# or Visual Basic.NET. Although the book uses C# for the most part, it's just as pertinent to Visual Basic.NET developers. In cases in which the translation from C# to Visual Basic.NET isn't straightforward or when the two languages differ significantly, I've provided either Visual Basic.NET matching sample code or an explicit note. If you're experienced with COM, this book will port your COM understanding to .NET. If you've never used COM before, you'll find the coverage of the principles of component-oriented programming especially useful.

Conventions Used in This Book

The following typographic conventions are used in this book:

Italic is used for:

- Definition of a technical term, online links, and filenames

`Constant width` is used for:

- Code samples, statements, namespaces, classes, assemblies, interface directives, operators, attributes, reserved words

`Bold constant width` is used for:

- Code emphasis

 This icon designates a note, which is an important aside to the nearby text.

 This icon designates a warning relating to the nearby text.

Whenever I wish to make a point in a code sample , I do so with the static `Assert` method of the `Debug` class:

```
int num = 1+2;
Debug.Assert(num == 3);
```

The `Assert` method accepts a Boolean statement, and throws an exception when the statement is false.

The book follows the recommended naming guidelines for .NET. (For information on recommended .NET coding techniques, see the article entitled "Coding Techniques" in the online documentation for Visual Studio .NET.) I use "camel casing" for public member variables and properties; this means the first letter of each word in the name is capitalized. For local variables and method parameters I use "Pascal casing" in which the first letter of the first word of the name is not capitalized. The recommended guidelines don't specify what to do in the case of private members, so in the book, I prefix such variables with m_:

```
public class SomeClass
{
  public int Num;
  private int m_Num;
}
```

I use ellipses between curly braces to indicate the presence of code that is necessary but unspecified:

```
public class SomeClass
{...}
```

In the interest of clarity and space, code examples often don't contain all the using statements needed to specify all the namespaces the example requires; instead, such examples include only the new namespaces introduced in the preceding text.

Comments and Questions

Please address comments and questions concerning this book to the publisher:

O'Reilly & Associates, Inc.
1005 Gravenstein Highway North
Sebastopol, CA 95472
(800) 998-9938 (in the United States or Canada)
(707) 829-0515 (international/local)
(707) 829-0104 (fax)

There is a web page for this book, which lists errata, examples, or any additional information. You can access this page at:

http://www.oreilly.com/catalog/pnetcomp

To comment or ask technical questions about this book, send email to:

bookquestions@oreilly.com

You can also contact the author at:

juval.lowy@idesign.net

For more information about books, conferences, Resource Centers, and the O'Reilly Network, see the O'Reilly web site at:

http://www.oreilly.com

Acknowledgments

Shortly after the unveiling of .NET in the summer of 2000, John Osborn from O'Reilly and I started discussing a book that would explore the uses of .NET as a component-based application development platform. This book is the result of John's sponsorship and support.

I am grateful to my friend and colleague Chris W. Rea for reviewing the book as I was writing it and for providing valuable insight and feedback as I drafted chapters. I am grateful as well to the following industry experts and fellow authors: Billy Hollis, Jimmy Nilsson, Nicholas Paldino, Ingo Rammer, and Pradeep Tapadiya, who gave generously of their time to read each of my chapters and comment extensively on their clarity and accuracy. I feel privileged to have had your help. A special thanks to Pradeep for answering some of my toughest technical questions. Thanks also to Ron Jacobs from Microsoft for reviewing this and my previous book, and to Dennis Angeline from Microsoft for explaining the intricacies of the CLR versioning.

Finally, to my family: my wife Dana, who knew that writing a book entailed time away from the family but still encouraged me to write. I dedicate this book to my three-year-old daughter Abigail for all the times she invited me to play with her and I said: "Daddy has to work on his book." Perhaps she will read this book one day. Technologies will have changed by then, but I am sure the principles of component-oriented programming will be just as valid as ever.

CHAPTER 1

Introducing Component-Oriented Programming

Over the last decade, component-oriented programming has established itself as the predominant software development methodology. The software industry is moving away from giant, monolithic, hard-to-maintain code bases. Practitioners have discovered that by breaking a system down into binary components, they can attain much greater reusability, extensibility, and maintainability. These benefits can, in turn, lead to faster time to market, more robust and highly scalable applications, and lower development and long-term maintenance costs. Consequently, it's no coincidence that component-oriented programming has caught on in a big way.

Several component technologies, such as DCOM, CORBA, and Java Beans now give programmers the means to implement component-oriented applications. However, each technology has its drawbacks; for example, DCOM is too difficult to master, and Java doesn't support interoperation with other languages.

.NET is the newest entrant, and as you will see later in this chapter and in the rest of the book, it addresses the requirements of component-oriented programming in a way that is unique and vastly easier to use. This is little surprise because the .NET architects learned from the mistakes of previous technologies, as well as from their successes.

In this chapter, I'll define the basic terms of component-oriented programming and summarize the core principles and corresponding benefits of component-oriented programming. These principles apply throughout the book, and I'll refer to them in later chapters when describing the motivation for a particular .NET design pattern. Component-oriented programming is different from object-oriented programming, although the two methodologies have things in common. You could say that component-oriented programming sprouted from the well of object-oriented programming methodologies. Therefore, this chapter also contrasts component-oriented programming and object-oriented programming, and briefly discusses .NET as a component technology.

Basic Terminology

The term *component* is probably one of the most overloaded and therefore most confusing terms in modern software engineering, and the .NET documentation has its fair share of inconsistency in its handling of this concept. The confusion arises in deciding where to draw the line between a class that implements some logic, the physical entity that contains it (typically a DLL), and the associated logic used to deploy and use it, including type information, security policy, and versioning information (called the *assembly* in .NET). In this book, a component is a .NET class. For example, this is a .NET component:

```
public class MyClass
{
    public string GetMessage()
    {
        return "Hello";
    }
}
```

Chapter 2 discusses DLLs and assemblies, and explains the rationale behind physical and logical packaging, as well as why it is that every .NET class is a binary component, unlike traditional object-oriented classes.

A component is responsible for exposing business logic to clients. A *client* is any entity that uses the component, although typically, clients are simply other classes. The client's code can be packaged in the same physical unit as the component, in the same logical unit but in a separate physical unit, or in separate physical and logical units altogether. The client code should not have to make any assumptions about such details. An *object* is an instance of a component, a definition that is similar to the classic object-oriented definition of an object as an instance of a class. The object is also sometimes referred to as the *server* because the relationship between client and object, often called the *client-server* model. In this model, the client creates an object and accesses its functionality via a publicly available entry point, traditionally a public method but preferably an interface, as illustrated by Figure 1-1. Note that in the figure an object is an instance of a component; the "lollipop" denotes an interface.

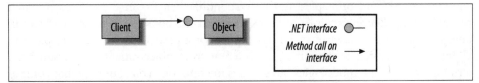

Figure 1-1. A client accessing an object

I'll discuss .NET interface-based programming in detail in Chapter 3. For now, it's important to emphasize that while .NET doesn't enforce interface-based programming, as you will see shortly, you should strive to do so with your own code whenever possible. To emphasize this practice, I represent the entry points of the components that appear in my design diagrams as interfaces rather than mere public methods.

 Although the object depicted in Figure 1-1 is drawn like a COM object with its characteristic lollipop icon, use of this icon isn't restricted to COM, but is accepted as the standard UML symbol for an interface, regardless of the component technology and development platform that implement it.

Interface-based programming promotes *encapsulation*, or the hiding of information from the client. The less a client knows about the way an object is implemented, the better. The more the details of an implementation are encapsulated, the greater the likelihood that you can change a method or property without affecting the client code. Interfaces maximize encapsulation because the client interacts with an abstract service definition instead of an actual object. Encapsulation is *key* to successfully applying both object-oriented and component-oriented methodologies.

Another important term originating from object-oriented programming is *polymorphism*. Two objects are said to be polymorphic with respect to each other when both derive from a common base type (such as an interface) and implement the exact set of operations defined by the base type. If a client is written to use the operations of the base type, the same client code can interact with any object that is polymorphic with the base type. When polymorphism is used properly, changing from one object to another has no effect on the client; it simplifies maintenance of the application to which the client and object belong.

Component-Oriented Versus Object-Oriented Programming

If every .NET class is a component, and if both classes and components share so many qualities, then what is the difference between traditional object-oriented programming and component-oriented programming? In a nutshell, object-oriented programming focuses on the relationship between classes that are combined into one large binary executable. Component-oriented programming instead focuses on interchangeable code modules that work independently and don't require you to be familiar with their inner workings to use them.

Building Blocks Versus Monolithic Applications

The fundamental difference between the two methodologies is the way in which they view the final application. In the traditional object-oriented world, even though you may factor the business logic into many fine-grained classes, once these classes are compiled, the result is monolithic binary code. All the classes share the same physical deployment unit (typically an EXE), process, address space, security privileges, and so on. If multiple developers work on the same code base, they have to share source files. In such an application, a change made to one class can trigger a massive relinking of the entire application and necessitate retesting and redeployment of all other classes.

On the other hand, a component-oriented application comprises a collection of interacting binary application modules—that is, its components and the calls that bind them (see Figure 1-2).

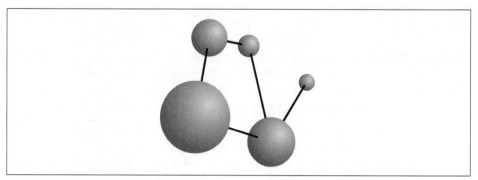

Figure 1-2. A component-oriented application

A particular binary component may not do much on its own. Some may be general-purpose components such as communication wrappers or file-access components. Others may be highly specialized and developed specifically for the application. An application implements and executes its required business logic by gluing together the functionality offered by the individual components. Component-enabling technologies such as COM, J2EE, CORBA, and .NET provide the "plumbing" or infrastructure needed to connect binary components in a seamless manner, and the main distinction between these technologies is the ease with which they allow you to connect those components.

The motivation for breaking down a monolithic application into multiple binary components is analogous to that for placing the code for different classes into different files. By placing the code for each class in an application into its own file, you loosen the coupling between the classes and the developers responsible for them. A change made to one class may require recompilation only of the source file for that class, although the entire application will have to go through relinking.

However, there is more to component-oriented programming than simple software project management. Because a component-based application is a collection of binary building blocks, you can treat its components like Legos, adding and removing them as you see fit. If you need to modify a component, changes are contained to that component only. No existing client of the component requires recompilation or redeployment. Components can even be updated while a client application is running, as long as the components aren't currently being used.

In addition, improvements, enhancements and fixes made to one component are immediately available to all applications using that component, on the same machine or perhaps across the network.

A component-oriented application is easier to extend as well. When you have new requirements to implement, you can provide them in new components, without having to touch existing components not affected by the new requirements.

These factors enable component-oriented programming to reduce the cost of long-term maintenance, a factor essential to almost any business, which explains the widespread adoption of component technologies.

Component-oriented applications usually have a faster time to market because you can select from a range of available components, either from inhouse collections or from third-party component vendors, and thus avoid repeatedly reinventing the wheel. For example, consider the rapid development enjoyed by many Visual Basic projects, which rely on libraries of ActiveX controls for almost every aspect of the application.

Interfaces Versus Inheritance

Another important difference between object-oriented and component-oriented applications is the emphasis the two models place on inheritance and reuse models.

In object-oriented analysis and design, you often model applications as complex hierarchies of classes, which are designed to approximate as much as possible the business problem being solved. Existing code is reused by inheriting from an existing base class and specializing its behavior. The problem is that inheritance is a poor way to reuse. When you derive a subclass from a base class, you must be intimately aware of the implementation details of the base class. For example: what is the side effect of changing the value of a member variable? How does it affect the code in the base class? Will overriding a base class method and providing a different behavior break the code of clients that expect the base behavior?

This form of reuse is commonly known as *white box reuse* because you are required to be familiar with the details of its implementation. White box reuse simply doesn't allow for economy of scale in large organizations' reuse programs or easy adoption of third-party frameworks.

Component-oriented programming promotes *black box reuse* instead, which allows you to use an existing component without caring about its internals, as long as the component complies with some predefined set of operations or interfaces. Instead of investing in designing complex class hierarchies, component-oriented developers spend most of their time factoring out the interfaces used as contracts between components and clients.

 .NET does allow components to use inheritance of implementation, and you can certainly use this technique to develop complex class hierarchies. However, you should keep your class hierarchies as simple and as flat as possible, and focus instead on factoring interfaces. Doing so promotes black-box reuse of your component instead of white-box reuse via inheritance.

Finally, object-oriented programming provides few tools or design patterns for dealing with the runtime aspects of the application, such as multithreading and concurrency management, security, distributed applications, deployment, or version control. Object-oriented developers are more or less left to their own devices when it comes to providing infrastructure for handling these common requirements. As you will see throughout the book, .NET supports you by providing a superb component-development infrastructure. Using .NET, you can focus on the business problem at hand instead of the software infrastructure needed to build the solution.

Principles of Component-Oriented Programming

Systems that support component-oriented programming and the programmers that use them adhere to a set of core principles that continues to evolve. The most important of these include:

- Separation of interface and implementation
- Binary compatibility
- Language independence
- Location transparency
- Concurrency management
- Version control
- Component-based security

Often, it's hard to tell the difference between a true principle and a mere feature of the component technology being used. Component programming requires both systems that support the approach and programmers that adhere to its discipline. As the supporting technologies become more powerful, no doubt software engineering will extend its understanding of what constitutes component-oriented programming and embrace new ideas. The following sections discuss these seven important principles of component-oriented programming.

Separation of Interface from Implementation

The fundamental principle of component-oriented programming is that the basic unit in an application is a binary-compatible interface. The interface provides an abstract service definition between a client and the object. This principle contrasts with the object-oriented view of the world that places the object rather than its interface at the center. An *interface* is a logical grouping of method definitions that acts as the *contract* between the client and the service provider. Each provider is free to provide its own interpretation of the interface—that is, its own implementation. The interface is implemented by a black-box binary component that completely encapsulates its interior. This principle is known as *separation of interface from implementation*.

To use a component, the client needs to know only the interface definition (the service *contract*) and be able to access a binary component that implements that interface. This extra level of indirection between the client and the object allows one implementation of an interface to be replaced by another without affecting client code. The client doesn't need to be recompiled to use a new version. Sometimes the client doesn't even need to be shut down to do the upgrade. Provided the interface is immutable, objects implementing the interface are free to evolve, and new versions can be introduced. To implement the functionality promised by an interface inside a component, you use traditional object-oriented methodologies, but the resulting class hierarchies are usually simpler and easier to manage.

Another effect of using interfaces is that they enable reuse. In object oriented-programming, the basic unit of reuse is the object. In theory, different clients should be able to use the same object. Each reuse instance saves the reusing party the amount of time and effort spent implementing the object. Reuse initiatives have the potential for significant cost reduction and reduced product-development cycle time. One reason why the industry adopted object-oriented programming so avidly was its desire to reap the benefits of reuse.

In reality, however, objects are rarely reusable. Objects are often specific to the problem and the particular context they were developed for, and unless the objects are "nuts and bolts," that is, simple and generic, the objects can't be reused even in very similar contexts. This reality is true in many engineering disciplines, including mechanical and electrical engineering. For example, consider the computer mouse you use with your workstation. Each part of this mouse is designed and manufactured specifically for your make and model. For reasons of branding and electronics, parts such as the body case can't be used in the manufacturing of any other type of mouse (even very similar ones), whether made by the same manufacturer or others. However, the interface between mouse and human hand is well defined, and any human (not just yourself) can use the mouse. Similarly, the typical USB interface between mouse and computer is well defined, and your mouse can plug into almost any computer adhering to the interface. The basic units of reuse in the computer mouse are the interfaces the mouse complies with, not the mouse parts themselves.

In component-oriented programming, the basic unit of reuse is the interface, not a particular component. By separating interfaces from implementation in your application, and using predefined interfaces or defining new interfaces, you enable that application to reuse existing components and enable reuse of your new components in other applications.

Binary Compatibility Between Client and Server

Another core principle of component-oriented programming is *binary compatibility* between client and server. Traditional object-oriented programming requires all the parties involved—clients and servers—to be part of one monolithic application. During compilation, the compiler inserts the address of the server entry points into the client code. Component-oriented programming revolves around packaging code into components, i.e., binary building blocks. Changes to the component code are contained in the binary unit hosting it; you don't need to recompile and redeploy the clients. However, the ability to replace and plug in new binary versions of the server implies binary compatibility between the client and the server, meaning that the client's code must interact at runtime with exactly what it expects as far as the binary layout in memory of the component entry points. This binary compatibility is the basis for the contract between the component and the client. As long as the new version of the component abides by this contract, the client isn't affected. In Chapter 2, you will see how .NET provides binary compatibility.

Language Independence

Unlike traditional object-oriented programming, in component-oriented programming, the server is developed independently of the client. Because the client interacts with the server only at runtime, the only thing that binds the two is binary compatibility. A corollary is that the programming languages that implement the client and server should not affect their ability to interact at runtime. *Language independence* means exactly that: when you develop and deploy components your choice of programming language should be irrelevant. Language independence promotes the interchangeability of components, and their adoption and reuse. .NET achieves language independence through an architecture and implementation called the Common Language Runtime (CLR), which is discussed further in Chapter 2.

Location Transparency

A component-based application contains multiple binary components. These components can all exist in the same process, in different processes on the same machine, or on different machines on a network. Recently, with the advent of web services, components can also be distributed across the Internet.

The underlying component technology is required to provide a client with *location transparency*, which allows the client code to be independent of the actual location of the object it uses. Location transparency means there is nothing in the client's code pertaining to where the object executes. The same client code must be able to handle all cases of object location (see Figure 1-3), although the client should be able to insist on a specific location as well. Note that in the figure, the object can be in the same process (e.g., Process 1 on Machine A), in different processes on the same machine (e.g., Process 1 and Process 2 on Machine A), on different machines in the same local network, or even across the Internet (e.g., Machines B and C).

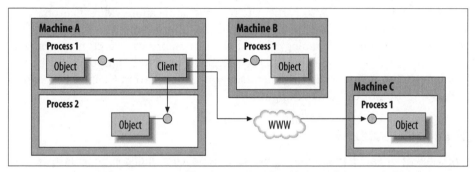

Figure 1-3. Location transparency enables client code to be oblivious of the actual object location

Location transparency is crucial to component-oriented programming for a number of reasons. First, it lets you develop the client and components locally (which leads to easier and more productive debugging), yet deploy the same code base in distributed scenarios. Second, the choice of using the same process for all components, or multiple processes for multiple machines, has a significant impact on performance and ease of management versus scalability, availability, robustness, throughput, and security. Organizations have different priorities and preferences for these tradeoffs, yet the same set of components from a particular vendor or team should be able to handle all scenarios. Third, the location of components tends to change as the application's requirements evolve over time.

To minimize the cost of long-term maintenance and extensibility, you should avoid having client code make any assumptions regarding the location of the objects it uses and avoid making explicit calls across processes or across machines. .NET remoting is the name of the technology that enables remote calls in .NET. Chapter 10 is dedicated to .NET remoting and discusses .NET support for location transparency.

Concurrency Management

A component developer can't possibly know in advance all the possible ways in which a component will be used and particularly whether it will be accessed concurrently by multiple threads. The safest course is for you to assume that the component will be used in concurrent situations and to provide some mechanism inside the component for synchronizing access. However, this approach has two flaws. First, it may lead to deadlocks; if every component in the application has its own synchronization lock, a deadlock can occur if two components on different threads try to access each other. Second, it's an inefficient use of system resources for all components in the application to be accessed by the same thread.

The underlying component technology must provide a *concurrency management* service—way for components to participate in some application-wide synchronization mechanism, even when the components are developed separately. In addition, the underlying component technology should allow components and clients to provide their own synchronization solutions for fine-grained control and optimized performance. .NET concurrency management support is discussed in Chapter 8 as part of developing multithreaded .NET applications.

Versioning Support

Component-oriented programming must allow clients and components to evolve separately. Component developers should be able to deploy new versions (or just fixes) of existing components without affecting existing client applications. Client developers should be able to deploy new versions of the client application and expect it to work with older versions of components. The underlying component technology should support *versioning*, which allows a component to evolve along different paths, and for different versions of the same component to be deployed on the same machine, or *side by side*. The component technology should also detect incompatibility as soon as possible and alert the client. .NET's solution to version control is discussed in Chapter 6.

Component-Based Security

In component-oriented programming, components are developed separately from the client applications that use them. Component developers have no way of knowing how a client application or end user will try to use their work. A benign component could be used maliciously to corrupt data or transfer funds between accounts without proper authorization or authentication. Similarly, a client application has no way to know whether it's interacting with a malicious component that will abuse the credentials the client provides. In addition, even if both the client and the component have no ill intent, the end application user can still try to hack into the system or do some other damage (even by mistake).

Version Control and DLL Hell

Historically, the versioning problem has been the source of much aggravation. Early attempts at component technology using DLL and DLL-exported functions created the predicament known as *DLL Hell*. A typical DLL Hell scenario involved two client applications, say A1.0 and B1.0, each using Version C1.0 of a component in the *mydll. dll* file. Both A1.0 and B1.0 install a copy of the *mydll.dll* in some global location such as the System directory. When Version A1.1 is installed, it also installs Version C1.1 of the component, providing new functionality in addition to the functionality defined in C1.0. Note that *mydll.dll* can contain C1.1 and still serve both old and new client application versions because the old clients aren't aware of the new functionality, and the old functionality is still supported. Binary compatibility is maintained via strict management of ordinal numbers for the exported functions (a source for another set of problems associated with DLL Hell). The problem starts when Application B1.0 is reinstalled. As part of installing B1.0, Version C1.0 is reinstalled, overriding C1.1. As a result, A1.1 can't execute.

Interestingly enough, addressing the issue of DLL Hell was one of the driving forces behind COM. Even though COM makes wide use of objects in DLLs, COM can completely eliminate DLL Hell. However, COM is difficult to learn and apply, and consequently can be misused or abused, resulting in problems similar to DLL Hell.

Like COM in its time, .NET was designed with DLL Hell in mind. .NET doesn't eliminate all chances of DLL Hell but reduces its likelihood substantially. The default .NET versioning and deployment policies don't allow for DLL Hell. However, .NET is an extensible platform. You can choose to override the default behavior for some advanced need or to provide your own custom version control policy, but you risk DLL Hell.

To lessen the danger, a component technology must provide a security infrastructure to deal with these scenarios, without coupling components and client applications to each other. In addition, security requirements, policies, and events (such as new users) are among the most volatile aspects of the application lifecycle, not to mention the fact that security policies vary between applications and customers. A productive component technology should allow for the components to have as few security policies and as little security awareness as possible in the code itself. It should also allow system administrators to customize and manage the application security policy without requiring you to make changes to the code. .NET's rich security infrastructure is the subject of Chapter 12.

.NET Adherence to Component Principles

One challenge facing the software industry today is the skill gap between what developers should know and what they do know. Even if you have formal training in computer science, you may lack effective component-oriented design skills, which are

.NET Versus COM

If you're a seasoned COM developer, .NET might seem to be missing many of the elements you have taken for granted as part of your component development environment. If you have no COM background, you can skip this section. If you are still reading, you should know that the seemingly missing elements remain in .NET, although they are expressed differently:

- There is no base interface such as IUnknown that all components derive from. Instead, all components derive from the class System.Object. Every .NET object is therefore polymorphic with System.Object.

- There are no class factories. In .NET, the runtime resolves a type declaration to the assembly containing it and the exact class or struct within the assembly. Chapter 2 discusses this mechanism.

- There is no reference counting of objects. .NET has a sophisticated garbage collection mechanism that detects when an object is no longer used by clients and then destroys it. Chapter 4 describes the .NET garbage collection mechanism and the various ways you can manage resources held by objects.

- There are no IDL files or type libraries to describe your interfaces and custom types. Instead, you put those definitions in your source code. The compiler is responsible for embedding the type definitions in a special format in your assembly, called *metadata*. Metadata is described in Chapter 2.

- Component dependencies are captured by the compiler during compilation and persisted in a special format in your assembly, called a *manifest*. The manifest is described in Chapter 2.

- Identification isn't based on globally unique identifiers (GUIDs). Uniqueness of type (class or interface) is provided by scoping the types with the namespace and assembly name. When an assembly is shared between clients, the assembly must contain a *strong name*—i.e., a unique digital signature generated by using an encryption key. The strong name also guarantees component authenticity, and .NET refuses to execute a mismatch. In essence, these are GUIDs, but you don't have to manage them any more. Chapter 6 discusses shared assemblies and strong names.

- There are no apartments. By default, every .NET component executes in a free-threaded environment, and it's up to you to synchronize access. Synchronization can be done either by using manual synchronization locks or by relying on automatic .NET synchronization domains. .NET multithreading and synchronization are discussed in Chapter 8.

primarily acquired through experience. Today's aggressive deadlines, tight budgets, and a continuing shortage of developers precludes, for many, the opportunity to attend formal training sessions or to receive effective on-the-job training. Nowhere is the skill gap more apparent than among developers at companies who attempt to adhere to component development principles. In contrast, object-oriented concepts are easier to understand and apply, partly because they have been around much longer, so a larger number of developers are familiar with them, and partly because of the added degree of complexity involved with component development compared to monolithic applications.

A primary goal of the .NET platform is to simplify the development and use of binary components and to make component-oriented programming accessible. As a result, .NET doesn't enforce some core principles of component-oriented programming, such as separation of interface from implementation, and unlike COM, .NET allows binary inheritance of implementation. Instead, .NET merely enforces a few of the concepts and enables the rest. Doing so caters to both ends of the skill spectrum. If you understand only object-oriented concepts, you will develop .NET "objects," but because every .NET class is consumed as a binary component by its clients, you can gain many of the benefits of component-oriented programming. If you understand and master how to apply component-oriented principles, you can fully maximize the benefit of .NET as a powerful component-development technology.

This duality can be confusing. Throughout the book, whenever applicable, I will point out the places where .NET doesn't enforce a core principle and suggest methods to stick with it nonetheless.

Developing .NET Components

A component technology is more than just a set of rules and guidelines on how to build components. A successful component technology must provide a development environment and tools that will allow you to rapidly develop components. .NET offers a superb development environment and semantics that are the product of years of observing the way you use COM and the hurdles you face. All .NET programming languages are component-oriented in their very nature, and the primary development environment (Visual Studio.NET) provides views, wizards, and tools that are oriented toward developing components. .NET shields you from the underlying raw operating services and provides instead operating system-like services (such as filesystem access or threading) in a component-oriented manner. The services are factored to various components in a logical and consistent fashion, resulting in a uniform programming model. You will see numerous examples of these services throughout this book. The following sections detail key factors that enable .NET to significantly simplify component development.

The .NET Base Classes

When you develop .NET components, there is no need for a hard-to-learn component development framework such as the Active Template Library (ATL), which was used to develop COM components in C++. .NET takes care of all the underlying plumbing. In addition, to help you develop your business logic faster, .NET provides you with more than 8,000 base classes (from message boxes to security permissions), available through a common library available to all .NET languages. The base classes are easy to learn and apply. You can use the base classes as-is or derive from them to extend and specialize their behavior. You will see examples of how to use these base classes throughout the book.

Attribute-Based Programming

When developing components, you can use attributes to declare their special runtime and other needs, rather than coding them. This is analogous to the way COM developers declare the threading model attribute of their components. .NET offers numerous attributes, allowing you to focus on the domain problem at hand. You can also define your own attributes or extend existing ones. Appendix C discusses reflection and custom attributes.

Component-Oriented Security

The classic Windows NT security model is based on what a given user is allowed to do. This model emerged at a time when COM was in its infancy, and applications were usually standalone and monolithic. In today's highly distributed, component-oriented environment, there is a need for a security model based on what a given piece of code, a component, is allowed to do, not only on what its caller is allowed to do.

.NET allows you to configure permissions for a piece of code and to provide evidence proving the code has the right credentials to access a resource or perform sensitive work. Evidence is tightly related to the component's origin. System administrators can decide that they trust all code that came from a particular vendor but distrust everything else, from downloaded components to malicious attacks. A component can also demand that a permission check be performed to verify that all callers in its call chain have the right permissions before it proceeds to do its work. Chapter 12 is dedicated to .NET's rich security infrastructure.

Simplified Deployment

Installing a .NET component can be as simple as copying it to the directory of the application using it. This is in contrast to COM, which relies on the Registry for component deployment to let it know where to look for the component file and how to treat it. .NET maintains tight version control, enabling side-by-side execution of new and old versions of a shared component on the same machine. The net result is a zero-impact install; by default, you can't harm another application by installing yours, thus ending DLL Hell. The .NET motto is: it just works. If you want to install components to be shared by multiple applications, you can install them in a storage area called the *Global Assembly Cache* (GAC). If the GAC already contains a previous version of your assembly, it keeps it, for use by clients that were built against the old version. You can purge old versions as well, but that isn't the default. .NET shared deployment and version control is discussed in Chapter 2.

CHAPTER 2

.NET Component-Oriented Programming Essentials

Regardless of what you use .NET components for, you need to be familiar with the essentials of .NET as a component technology and deployment platform. This chapter introduces basic concepts such as the assembly, metadata, and the Common Language Runtime (CLR). You will see how to compose client or class library assemblies and how to consume a binary component in one assembly by a client in another. The chapter then discusses how .NET achieves binary compatibility, demonstrating how .NET supports this important component-oriented principle presented in the previous chapter. Although I use C# to demonstrate the key points in this chapter and elsewhere in the book, the discussion (unless explicitly stated otherwise) is always from a language-agnostic perspective. The information is applicable to every .NET language, so the focus is on the concept, not the syntax. If you are already familiar with .NET essentials, feel free to skip this chapter and move on to Chapter 3.

Language Independence: The CLR

The .NET CLR provides a common context within which all .NET components execute, regardless of the language in which they are written. The CLR manages every runtime aspect of the code, providing it with memory management, a secure environment to run in, and access to the underlying operating system services. Because the CLR manages these aspects of the code's behavior, code that targets the CLR is called *managed code*. The CLR provides absolute language interoperability, allowing a high degree of component interaction during development and runtime. .NET can this because the CLR is based on a strict type system, which all .NET languages must adhere to. All constructs (such as class, struct, primitive types) in every .NET language must compile to CLR-compatible types to qualify as a .NET language. The gain in language interoperability comes at the expense of the languages and compilers Windows and COM developers have been using for years. The problem is that existing compilers produce code that doesn't target the CLR, doesn't comply with the CLR type system, and therefore can't be managed by the CLR. To program .NET components, you must use one of the new .NET language compilers released with the .NET Framework and Visual Studio .NET. The first release of Visual Studio.NET ships with three new CLR-compliant languages: C#, Visual Basic.NET, and Managed C++. (A fourth language, JScript.NET, is available in a limited fashion for ASP.NET applications.) The second version (1.1) contains J# (Java for .NET). Third-party compiler vendors are also targeting the CLR, with more than 20 additional languages, from COBOL to Eiffel.

Intermediate Language and the JIT Compiler

One detail that often confuses .NET novices is how the transformations are made from high-level languages (such as C# or Visual Basic.NET), to managed code, to machine code. Understanding this process is also key to understanding how .NET provides support for language interoperability (that is, the core principle of language independence), and it has implications for binary compatibility. Although this book tries to steer away from most underlying implementation details and instead focus on how to best apply .NET, a brief overview of the CLR code generation process goes a long way to demystify it all. In addition, understanding the .NET code-generation process is key to dealing with some specific security issues; this is discussed further in Chapter 12.

Compiling .NET managed code is a two-phase process. First, the high-level code is compiled into a language called *intermediate language* (IL). The IL constructs look more like machine code than a high-level language, but the IL does contain some abstract concepts such as base classes and exception handling, which is why the language is called intermediate. The IL is packaged in either a DLL or an EXE. As in traditional Windows programming, an EXE assembly can be run directly by a user, while a DLL assembly must be loaded into an already running process. Because the machine's CPU can't execute IL and can execute only native machine code, further compilation into actual machine code is required. This compilation takes place at runtime by the *Just-in-Time (JIT)* compiler. As the name suggests, the JIT compiler is responsible for compiling IL code into machine code at runtime, only when that IL code is required.

When the high-level code is first compiled, the high-level language compiler does two things: first, it stores the IL in the EXE or the DLL, and then it creates a machine code stub for every class method. The stub calls into the JIT compiler, passing its own method address as a parameter. The JIT compiler retrieves the corresponding IL from the DLL or EXE, compiles it into machine code, and replaces the stub in memory with the newly generated machine code. The idea is that when a method that is already compiled calls into a method that isn't yet compiled, it actually calls the stub. The stub calls the JIT compiler, which compiles the IL code into native machine code. .NET then repeats the method call to actually execute the method. Subsequent calls into that method execute as native code, and the application pays the compilation penalty only once per method actually used.

Methods that are never called are never compiled. When the compiler generates an EXE file, its entry point is the WinMain( ) method. It has only native machine code, which loads the .NET runtime libraries (including the JIT compiler) and then calls into the EXE's Main( ) IL method. This triggers compiling the IL in the Main( ) method into native code in memory, and the .NET application starts running. Once compiled into native code, native code can call other native code freely. When the program terminates, the native code is discarded, and the IL will need to be recompiled into native machine code by the JIT compiler the next time the application runs.

JIT compilation provides a number of important benefits. As you will see later in this chapter, JIT compilation offers .NET developers late-binding flexibility combined with compile-time type safety. JIT compilation is also key to .NET component binary compatibility. In addition, if all the implementations of the .NET runtime on different platforms (such as Windows XP and Linux) expose exactly the same standard set of services, .NET applications can be ported between different platforms very easily.

You might be concerned with the JIT compilation performance penalty. However, this concern should be mitigated by the fact that the JIT compiler can generate code that runs faster than code generated by traditional static source code compilers. For example, today the JIT compiler looks at the exact CPU type (such as Pentium II or Pentium III), and it takes advantage of the added instruction sets offered by each CPU type. In contrast, traditional compilers have to generate code that targets the lowest common denominator, such as the 386-instruction set, and therefore can't take advantage of newer CPU features. Future versions of the JIT compiler could be written to keep track of the way an application uses the code (frequency of branch instructions used, forward-looking branches, etc.) and then decide to recompile in order to optimize the way the particular application (or even a particular user!) is using the components. The JIT compiler can also optimize the machine code it generates based on actual available machine resources, such as memory or CPU speed. Note that these advanced options aren't implemented yet, but the mechanism has at least the potential of providing all that. In general, JIT compiler optimization is a tradeoff between the additional compilation time required and the increased application performance that results, and its effectiveness depends on the application calling patterns and usage. In the future, this cost can be measured during application installation or looked up in a user preferences repository.

.NET Programming Languages

The IL is the common denominator for all .NET programming languages. At least in theory, equivalent constructs in two different languages should produce identical IL.

As a result, the traditional performance and capability attributes that previously distinguished between programming languages don't apply when comparing .NET

Native Image Compilation

As an alternative to JIT compilation, developers can compile their IL code into native code using a utility called the *Native Image Generator* (*Ngen.exe*). Native images are stored automatically in a special global location called the *Native Images Cache*, a dedicated per-machine global storage. When searching for an assembly to load, the assembly resolver first checks the Native Image Cache for a compatible version, and if one is found, the native image version is used. You could use *Ngen.exe* to generate native images during deployment and installation to take advantage of potential optimizations done on a per-machine basis. The primary motivation for using *Ngen.exe* is to avoid the JIT compiler's performance penalty. The penalty may be a reason for concern in a client application. You don't want a user-interface application to take more than a second or two to load, nor do you want the end user to wait after selecting a menu item or clicking a button for the first time. For example, the Windows Forms framework is installed in native image form. However, using native images renders most of the benefits of JIT compilation (discussed in this chapter) useless.

Another *Ngen.exe* liability is that it adds a step to your installation program. Deploying .NET applications can be as easy as copying the EXEs and DLLs to the customer machine, and you lose that simplicity with *Ngen.exe*. I recommend using *Ngen.exe* only after careful examination of your case and being convinced that there is a performance bottleneck in your application specifically caused by the JIT compiler. The easiest way to verify that is to run your profiling and test suite against both a JIT-compiled version and a native image version of the application, and compare the measurements.

languages. However, that doesn't imply that it doesn't matter which language you choose (see the later sidebar "Choosing your .NET Language: C# Versus Visual Basic.NET").

The fact that all .NET components, regardless of language, execute in the same managed environment, and the fact that all constructs, in every language, must compile to a predefined CLR compatible type, allows a high degree of language interoperability. Types defined in one language have a equivalent native representation in all others. You can use the existing set of CLR types that are supported by all languages or define new custom types. The CLR also provides a uniform exception-based error-handling model. An exception thrown in one language can be caught and handled in another. You can use the predefined set of CLR exception classes or derive and extend them for a specific use. You can fire events from one language and catch them in another. Because the CLR knows only about IL, security permissions and security demands travel across language barriers. The CLR has no problem, for example, verifying that the calling client has the right permissions to use an object even if they were developed in different languages.

.NET Components Are Language-Independent

As explained in Chapter 1, a core principle of component-oriented programming is language independence. When a client calls methods on an object, the programming language that develops the client or the object should not be taken into account and should not affect the client's ability to interact with the object. Because all .NET components are compiled to IL before runtime, regardless of the higher-level language, the result is language independent by definition. At runtime, the JIT compiler links the client calls to the component entry points. This sort of language independence is similar to the language independence supported by COM. Because the .NET development tools can read the metadata accompanying the IL, .NET also provides development-time language independence, which allows you to interact with or even derive from components written in other languages. For example, all the .NET framework base classes were written in C# but are used by both C# and Visual Basic.NET developers.

Packaging and Deployment: Assemblies

.NET assemblies are a result of trying to improve the ways previous technologies packaged and deployed components. To make the most of .NET assemblies, it's best to first understand the rationale behind them. Understanding the "why" will make the "how" a lot easier.

DLLs and COM Components

Microsoft's first two attempts at component technologies (first, raw DLLs exporting functions, and then later, COM components) used raw executable files for storing binary code. In COM, component developers compiled their source code, usually into a DLL or sometimes into an EXE, and then installed these executables on the customer machine. Higher-level abstractions or logical attributes shared by all the DLLs had to be managed manually by both the component vendor and the client-side administrator. For example, even though all DLLs in a component-oriented application should be installed and uninstalled as one logical operation, developers had to write installation programs to repeat the same registration code for every DLL used or to copy them one by one. Most companies didn't invest enough time in developing robust installation programs and procedures, and this in turn resulted in orphaned DLLs bloating the client's machine after uninstallation. Even worse, after installing a new version, the application might still try to use the older versions of DLLs.

Another attribute that should have applied logically to all DLLs that are part of the same application was a version number. Imagine a particular vendor providing a set of interacting components in two DLLs, both labeled Version 1.0. When a new version (1.1) of these components is available, the vendor has to manually update the

Choosing your .NET Language: C# Versus Visual Basic.NET

Visual Studio.NET ships with five CLR-compliant languages: C#, Visual Basic.NET, J#, JScript.NET, and Managed C++. JScript.NET and Managed C++ are used mostly for porting and migration purposes, and it's safe to assume that the majority of .NET developers will choose to disregard them. J# is for former J++ developers. The real question is: as a .NET developer, should you choose C# or Visual Basic.NET? The official Microsoft party line is that all .NET languages are equal in performance and ease of use, and therefore choosing a language should be based on personal preference. According to this philosophy, if you come from a C++ background, you will naturally pick up C#; if you come from a Visual Basic 6 background, you will select Visual Basic.NET.

I believe that basing the decision merely on your current language isn't the best approach, and that you have to look not only at where you come from, but also where you are headed. The development community today is roughly divided into two types of development-tool users: rapid application developers and enterprise (or system) developers. The two types address different business needs and use different tools. Rapid development today is easier in Visual Basic 6.0 than with C++ tools such as MFC. In contrast, because of its inherently simpler model, Visual Basic 6.0 doesn't lend itself to developing large, maintainable applications. In addition, Visual Basic 6.0 has built-in limitations that impede scalability (lack of multithreading or object pooling support). C++ developers, on the other hand, have access to unlimited power, but mastering ATL or MFC can take years. Applying component-oriented analysis and design methodologies in a large application requires a great deal of skill and time and results in unmaintainable code if done poorly. The two developer communities are therefore distinct not only because of the different languages they use, but primarily because of the different types of applications each develops and the methodologies each used.

Even in the first version of .NET, fresh out of the box, C# offers features Visual Basic. NET doesn't, and vice versa. For example: C# has native support for automatic disposal of resources (the *using* statement) to expedite releasing of resources and easing the development of scalable applications. C# also has native compiler support for automatic generation of documentation pages and development-time tips. C# further provides event accessors and offers operator overloading. All these features are absent from Visual Basic.NET. On the other hand, Visual Basic.NET has better dynamic compilation and simpler syntax for hooking up event handlers to methods. It also allows for nonstructured error handling statements, unlike the rigid C# statements. I believe that these differences aren't accidental. Visual Basic.NET developers aren't exempt from documentation; the Visual Basic.NET product managers at Microsoft had other features with higher priorities on their list for the first release of Visual Basic.NET. These priorities include features that cater more to rapid application development and less to long-term maintenance of intricate enterprise applications.

—continued—

I believe that in the future, the two languages will continue to evolve on different paths, each adding features and capabilities that better fit its target users. C# will better serve the enterprise market (by offering features such as generics and iterators), and Visual Basic.NET will be the ideal tool for rapid development, offering features such as edit-and-continue and improved IntelliSense. When you choose which .NET language, you should base the decision on what you intend to use it for, rather than on your current background. If you are a C++ developer and you intend to specialize in rapid development, it would be wise to choose Visual Basic.NET. If you are a VB6 developer and you target the enterprise market, even with no C++ background, you should bite the bullet and choose C#.

version number of both DLLs to 1.1. A change to the version number of one DLL doesn't trigger an automatic change in the other DLL, even though logically, both are part of the same deployment unit.

A third logical attribute typically associated with a set of DLLs from the same vendor is their security credentials—what were the DLLs allowed to access, what were the DLLs allowed to share with other applications, etc. The client application administrator needed to manage the way he trusted these components and had to repeat this process for all DLLs, even though they shared the same security credentials. Client-side developers and system administrators used clumsy tools such as DCOM-CFG to manage these attributes in a fragile and error-prone manner.

Why not simply put all components that logically comprise a single deployment unit into the same DLL? The answer is simple: doing so will result in monolithic applications, sacrificing many of the benefits of component-oriented programming. In contrast, when components are deployed in separate DLLs, the client application pays a time penalty for loading a DLL only when it requires its component. Moreover, the memory footprint of the components of an application is kept to a minimum because only the DLLs actually used are kept in memory. If the client application needs to download the DLLs dynamically, it pays the download latency penalty only for those it requires.

.NET Assemblies

Clearly there's a need to separate the logical attributes shared by a set of components (such as version, security, and deployment) from their physical packaging (the file that actually contains each component) while avoiding the problems of traditional DLLs. The result is the .NET concept of the *assembly*: a single deployment, versioning, and security unit. The assembly is the basic packaging unit in .NET. It's called an assembly because it assembles multiple physical DLLs into a single logical unit. An assembly can be a class library (DLL) or a standalone application (EXE) and can contain multiple physical modules, each with multiple components.Think of an assembly as a logical DLL: a meta DLL that can contain more than one physical DLL (see Figure 2-1).

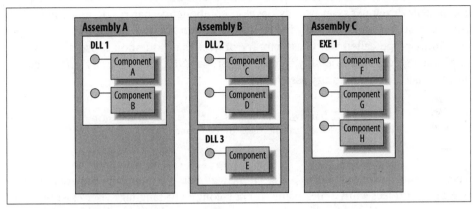

Figure 2-1. Assemblies as logical packaging units

The physical DLLs in an assembly are also referred to as *modules*. For example, in Figure 2-1, Assembly A contains a single module while Assembly B contains two. An assembly can be either a single executable (EXE or DLL) file or a collection of modules. However, an assembly usually contains just one file (a single DLL or a single EXE). Nevertheless, even when an assembly contains only a single DLL, the assembly still offers the component developer significant versioning, sharing, and security advantages. These are described later on in this book.

.NET doesn't promote the use of multiple modules unnecessarily. In fact, presently Visual Studio.NET won't generate multimodule assemblies. To do that, you have to step outside the visual environment, compile your code using a command-line compiler, and then use the *Assembly Linker* (*AL.exe*) command-line utility. *AL.exe* offers switches you can use to incorporate more than one DLL into your assembly. Please see the MSDN Library for more information on using *AL.exe*.

An assembly can contain as many components as required. All code in the assembly is IL code. An assembly can also contain resources such as icons, pictures, or localized strings.

 Applications that display a user interface shouldn't store their resources in the same assembly as the code using those resources. For localization, it's better to generate a separate satellite assembly that contains only resources. You can then generate one such satellite resource assembly per locale (culture) and load the resources from the assembly corresponding to the locale of the specific customer site. Visual Studio.NET automates most of this process when localizing Windows Forms applications, but it provides only the localization infrastructure for ASP.NET applications.

Assemblies and Visual Studio.NET

.NET components can reside in either EXE- or DLL-based assemblies. However, as a component developer, you usually develop components that reside in a single DLL assembly. Such a DLL assembly is called a *class library*. Visual Studio.NET has a special project type called the Class Library project that you should use as a starting point for a server-side assembly. The Visual Studio.NET Class Library project generates a single DLL class library assembly.

 All the .NET framework base classes are available in the form of class libraries, and they can be used by component and client application developers.

To add a binary component to a class library all you have to do is declare a class in one of the project source files using a .NET-compliant language. For existing Class Library projects, Visual Studio .NET provides an Add Class option and an Add New Item dialogue window.

To create a new C# Class Library, select New Project on the Visual Studio .NET Start Page. When the New Project dialogue window appears, select Visual C# Projects and Class Library, as shown in Figure 2-2. Name the library MyClassLibrary in the Name box, specify a location for the project files in the Location box and click OK. These actions create a project named MyClassLibrary, which should be visible in the Solution Explorer window along with a number of files, including one named *Class1.cs*. *Class1.cs* defines a single class named Class1 in the default MyClassLibrary project namespace. There is no connection between namespaces and assemblies: a single assembly can define multiple namespaces, and multiple assemblies can all contribute components to the same namespace.

To prepare for Example 2-1, rename *Class1.cs* to *MyClass.cs* in the Solutions Explorer window and modify the code in the *MyClass.cs* file (comments excluded) to the following:

```
namespace AssemblyDemo
{
   public class MyClass
   {
      public MyClass(){ }
      public string GetMessage()
      {
         return "Hello";
      }
   }
}
```

Any client regardless of the assembly in which it resides (be it a class library or an application assembly) can use the MyClass component, but first the client developer needs to import the definitions of the types and components in the class library to the

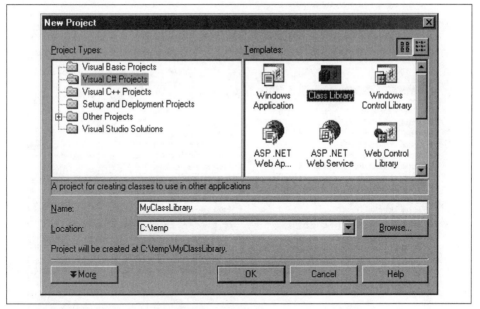

Figure 2-2. Visual Studio.NET Class Library project

client assembly. This import process is called *adding a reference* to the class library assembly. In the client project, select Project → Add Reference to bring up the Add Reference dialog box (see Figure 2-3).

The Add Reference dialog allows client developers to add a reference to predefined .NET class library assemblies or browse to a specified location and select the class library to add. The client developer can also add a reference to a class library project already defined in the client solution.

 The Add Reference dialog is misleading. The dialog allows you only to add references to other assemblies, yet it refers to assemblies as components (under the Component Name column). There is no way in .NET to add a reference to an individual component inside an assembly. Adding a reference is strictly an assembly-level operation.

To demonstrate how you can add a reference and use a component in a class library, follow these steps:

1. Create a new C# Windows Application project.

2. Add a reference to the MyClassLibrary assembly.

3. Add a using statement for the AssemblyDemo namespace.

4. Add a button to the form.

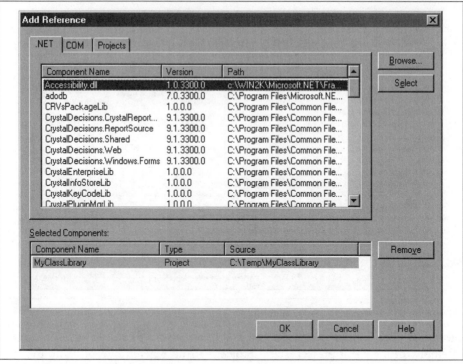

Figure 2-3. The Add Reference dialog

5. Add an event handler to the button's Click event.

6. Use the component in the referenced assembly as if it's defined in the client assembly.

The resulting client-side code should look similar to Example 2-1. Notice that although the MyClass component resides in another assembly, it can be referenced as if local to the client code.

Example 2-1. Using a component defined in another assembly

```
using System;
using System.Windows.Forms;
using AssemblyDemo;

public class ClientForm : Form
{
   static void Main( )
   {
      Application.Run(new ClientForm( ));
   }
   private void OnClicked(object sender,EventArgs e)
   {
```

Example 2-1. Using a component defined in another assembly (continued)

```
    MyClass obj = new MyClass();
    string msg = obj.GetMessage();
    MessageBox.Show(msg);
  }
  /* Rest of the client code  */
}
```

The ClientForm client creates an object of type MyClass using the new operator and retrieves the message string. The client then uses the static method Show() of the class MessageBox to display a message box with the message. The MessageBox class is part of the .NET framework and is defined in the System.Windows.Forms namespace, in the System.Windows.Forms assembly. Note that Example 2-1 includes the using System.Windows.Forms and using AssemblyDemo statements at the beginning of the file. Without these statements, you need to use *fully qualified type names* (names that include the containing namespace as part of the type declaration). The important thing about Example 2-1 is the fact that nothing in the client's code indicates that the components it uses come from other assemblies. After adding the references, it's as if these components are defined in the client's assembly. As C/C++ programmers will notice, no header, *def*, or *lib* files are required.

Client and Server Assemblies

The client of a component in a class library assembly can reside in the same assembly as the component, in a separate class library, or in a separate application assembly. Figure 2-4 shows one typical topology of a client application assembly using class libraries. If the client is in the same class library assembly as the component or if the client is in the same application assembly as the component, the client developer can simply declare an instance of the component and use it, just as in Example 2-1. However, if the component is in one class library and the client is in another assembly (be it in another class library or in an EXE assembly), the client developer first needs to add a reference to the class library. Once you've added references to them, the client assembly can use as many class libraries as required.

 You can't reference components in an EXE assembly. Client developers need to use .NET remoting (the subject of Chapter 10) to interact with components in an EXE assembly.

Managing Component Visibility in Assemblies

A set of interoperating components often includes components that are intended only for private, internal use by other components in the same assembly. These components aren't intended for outside use and should not be shared with your clients.

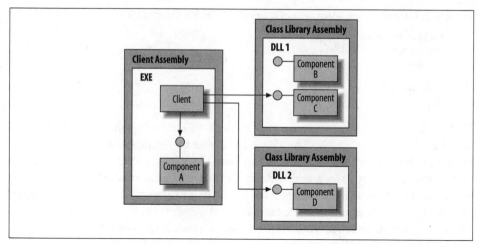

Figure 2-4. A typical client and server topology

In .NET there are two kinds of components: *public* and *internal*. .NET supports a special component-oriented visibility modifier called internal in C# (and Friend in Visual Basic.NET):

```
internal class MyClass
{
   public MyClass(){ }
   public string GetMessage()
   {
      return "Hello";
   }
}
```

An *internal* component can be accessed only by clients inside its own assembly. If client code in one assembly tries to use an internal component from a different assembly, it won't compile. In the case of a multimodule class library, any client in any module can still access the internal component because both reside in the same assembly.

 Under COM, there is no easy way of making components private; a COM client can always hunt through the Registry, find the CLSID of your private component, and use it.

If you wish to make the component available to outside clients, use the public visibility modifier:

```
public class MyClass
{
   public MyClass(){ }
   public string GetMessage()
   {
```

```
        return "Hello";
    }
}
```

.NET makes exposing components explicit: if you don't provide any visibility modifier, the default modifier is `internal`. The `public` or `internal` visibility modifiers can also be applied to any other types defined in the assembly, such as interfaces.

Another form of component used by outside entities besides object instantiation and method calls is *inheritance*. You may want to allow the creation of objects defined in their assembly and the calling of public methods but prevent developers of other assemblies from deriving from their component and accessing protected internal methods and members. To support this need, .NET adds the component-oriented `protected internal` visibility modifier on top of the classic object-oriented inheritance visibility modifiers (`public`, `protected`, and `private`). For example, examine this class definition:

```
public class MyClass
{
    public MyClass(){ }
    public string GetMessage()
    {
        return DoWork();
    }
    protected internal string DoWork()
    {
        return "Hello";
    }
}
```

To subclasses outside the assembly, the `DoWork()` method appears as an inaccessible private method, yet `MyClass` developers can extend it internally by subclassing and defining new types that take advantage of the protected member.

Assembly Metadata

Given that client assemblies add references to component assemblies, and that no source file sharing (like C++ header files) is involved, how does the client-side compiler know what types are in the assembly? How does the compiler know which types are public and which are internal? How does it know what the method signatures are? This classic component-oriented programming problem is raised by the fact that the client application is trying to use a binary component. The solution .NET introduces is called *metadata*.

Metadata is a comprehensive, standard, mandatory, and complete way of describing what is in an assembly. Metadata describes what types are available in the assembly (classes, interfaces, enums, structs, etc.) and their containing namespaces, the name of each type, its visibility, its base class, which interfaces it supports, its methods, each method's parameters, and so on. The assembly metadata is generated automati-

COM Type Libraries Versus Metadata

The COM developers usually provided type libraries to fix the types discovery problem. The COM type library included the definitions of the interfaces the components implemented and a list of the components themselves. Type libraries had many problems, but foremost among them was the low affinity between what type libraries described and what the binaries actually contained. The binaries could contain types not listed in the type libraries, and the type libraries could list components not present in the binary. The type library was limited in its description of the actual method signatures and often presented a dumbed-down version of the actual interfaces and method parameter semantics. Type libraries could be used to marshal method calls across context and process boundaries, but that in turn imposed some restrictions on the method parameters. For unusual custom types, type-library marshaling was powerless, and developers had to build custom proxy/stub pairs. Finally, type libraries could be embedded in the binary or handed to the client separately, creating a development and deployment pitfall. Even with all these shortcomings, for the first time, type libraries provided client developers with a way to interact with binary components without involving source files. .NET takes the type library concept to a whole new level because metadata provides all the information type libraries provides with precise type affinity, as well as additional type information from base classes to custom attributes. Fundamentally, however, they serve the same purpose.

cally by the high-level compiler directly from the source files. The compiler embeds the metadata in the physical file containing the IL (either a DLL or an EXE). In the case of a multifile assembly, every module with IL must contain metadata describing the types in that module. In fact, a CLR-compatible compiler is required to generate metadata, and the metadata must be in a standard format.

Metadata isn't just for compilers. .NET makes it possible to read metadata programmatically, using a mechanism called *reflection*. Reflection is particularity useful from a software engineering standpoint in the context of *attributes*—a way for you to add information to the metadata describing their types. Both reflection and attributes are addressed in Appendix C. In general, metadata is pivotal for .NET as a component technology and as a development platform. For example, .NET uses metadata for remote call marshaling across execution boundaries. *Marshaling* involves forwarding the call the client made in one execution context (such as a process or machine) to another where the object resides, invoking the call in the other execution context and sending the response back to the client. Marshaling typically uses a *proxy*—an entity that exposes the same entry points as the object. The proxy is the entity responsible for marshaling the call to the actual object. Because of the metadata's exact and formal description of the object's types and methods, .NET is able to construct proxies automatically to forward the call. Chapter 10 discusses the link between remoting and metadata. Visual Studio.NET uses metadata as well. IntelliSense is implemented using reflection. The code editor simply accesses the metadata associated with the type the developer uses and displays the content for auto-completion or type information.

You can view the metadata of your assembly with the *ILDASM* utility. For example, run *ildasm.exe* and open the MyClassLibrary DLL assembly, which contains the class MyClass defined in the AssemblyDemo namespace:

```
namespace AssemblyDemo
{
   public class MyClass
   {
      public MyClass()
      {}
      public string GetMessage()
      {
         return "Hello";
      }
   }
}
```

The ILDasm utility displays the metadata view as shown in Figure 2-5.

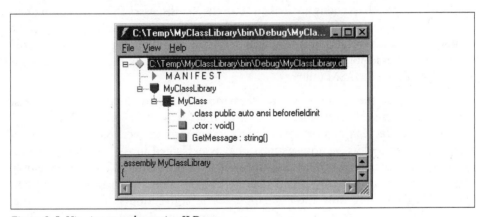

Figure 2-5. Viewing metadata using ILDasm

ILDasm uses various icons to distinguish between classes, structs, methods, properties, etc. See the MSDN documentation for a complete description of ILDasm.

Assembly Manifest

Just as metadata describes the types in an assembly, the *manifest* describes the assembly itself, providing the logical attributes shared by all the modules and all components in the assembly. The manifest contains the assembly name, version number, locale, and an optional strong name uniquely identifying the assembly (discussed in Chapter 6). The manifest contains the security demands to verify for this assembly (discussed in Chapter 12). In addition, the manifest contains the names and hashes of all the files that make up the assembly. Under COM, a malicious party (or even a benevolent party by mistake) could swap an original DLL or EXE file with another and cause damage. In .NET, every manifest contains a cryptographic hash of the different modules in the assembly. When the assembly is loaded, the .NET runtime recalculates the cryptographic hash of the modules at hand. If the hash generated at runtime is different from that found in the manifest, .NET assumes foul play. .NET refuses to load the assembly and throws an exception. Like the metadata, the manifest is generated automatically by the high-level compiler directly from the source files of all modules in the assembly. Unlike metadata, there is no need to duplicate and embed the manifest for every module in the assembly, and only one copy of it is embedded in one of the assembly physical files. Any CLR-compatible compiler must generate a manifest, and the manifest has to be in a standard format. The manifest is also the way .NET captures information about other referenced assemblies. This information is crucial to ensure version compatibility and ensure the assembly gets to interact with the exact trusted set of other assemblies it expects. For every other assembly referenced by this assembly, the manifest contains the referenced assembly name, the assembly public key (if a strong name is available), its version number, and locale. At runtime, .NET guarantees that only these specific assemblies are used, and that only compatible versions are loaded (this chapter discusses .NET versioning policy in depth). When strong names are used, the manifest maintains trust between the component vendor and its clients because only the original vendor could have signed the referenced assembly with that strong name. You can view the manifest of your assembly with the ILDASM utility.

You can provide the compiler with information to add to the assembly manifest using special *assembly attributes*, defined in the System.Runtime.CompilerServices and System.Reflection namespaces. Typically, you provide versioning and identity information, as well as security permissions, as explained in the subsequent corresponding chapters. Although you can sprinkle these attributes all over the assembly source files, a more structured and maintainable approach is to have a dedicated source file containing only these attributes. The convention is to name this file *AssemblyInfo.cs* in a C# project and *AssemblyInfo.vb* in a Visual Basic.NET project. In fact, Visual Studio.NET generates an assembly information file for every new project. The Visual Studio.NET-generated assembly information file contains an initial set of assembly attributes with default values. Example 2-2 shows a typical set of assembly attributes, including description, company name, and version number.

Example 2-2. The assembly information file

```
using System.Reflection;
using System.Runtime.CompilerServices;

[assembly: AssemblyTitle("MyAssembly")]
[assembly: AssemblyDescription("Assembly containing my .NET components")]
[assembly: AssemblyCompany("My Company")]
```

Example 2-2. The assembly information file (continued)

```
[assembly: AssemblyCopyright("(c) 2003 My Company ")]
[assembly: AssemblyTrademark("")]
[assembly: AssemblyVersion("1.0.0.0")]
```

Composing Assemblies

There are many ways to compose an assembly. The only two rules are:

- Every assembly must contain a manifest.
- Every assembly module that contains the IL must embed in it the corresponding metadata for that IL.

Assemblies can optionally contain resources such as strings or images. Of course, a single class library or application assembly contains all these items in one file. A multiple files assembly, on the other hand, has much more latitude in how to compose it all. Figure 2-6 shows a few possibilities for composing assemblies.

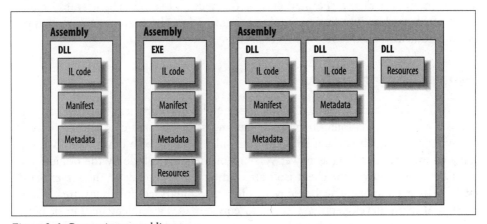

Figure 2-6. Composing assemblies

As you can see, you can compose multiple file assemblies in almost any way and use compiler switches to bind all your files together. In practice, I recommend abiding by the following composition rules:

- Always store resources in a separate satellite assembly, rather than as an embedded resource in the assembly using it. Doing so will greatly simplify localization issues. This is, by the way, the default behavior of Windows Forms.
- Avoid multiple-file class library assemblies with modules that don't contain IL.
- Minimize the code in an EXE assembly. Focus instead on visual layout, and encapsulate business logic in separate class library assemblies.

- Make sure all the components in a class library have the same lifecycle and will always have the same version number and security credentials. If you anticipate the possibility of divergence, split the assembly into two class libraries.

The Assembly Type

.NET provides a class for programmatic representation of an assembly. This is the Assembly class, defined in the System.Reflection namespace. Assembly provides numerous methods for retrieving detailed information about the assembly (location, files, etc.) and the types it contains, and methods for creating new instances of types defined in the assembly. You typically access an assembly object using a static method Assembly. For example, to get the assembly the current code is running from, use the static GetExecutingAssembly method:

```
Assembly assembly = Assembly.GetExecutingAssembly();
```

Using other static methods, you can access the assembly that called their assembly, the assembly in which a specified class is defined, and so on. The Assembly type is most often used with reflection to obtain information about an assembly or implement certain advanced remote call scenarios.

Binary Compatibility

As explained in Chapter 1, one of the core principles of component-oriented programming is binary compatibility between client and server. Binary compatibility enables binary components because it enforces both sides to abide by a binary contract, typically an interface. As long as newer versions of the server abide by the original contract between the two, the client isn't affected by changes made to the server. COM was the first component technology to offer true binary compatibility free of DLL Hell, and many developers have come to equate COM's implementation of binary compatibility (and the resulting restrictions, such as immutable COM interfaces) with the principle itself. The .NET approach to binary compatibility is different from that of COM, and so are the implications of the programming model. To understand these implications and why they are different from COM's implications, this section first briefly describes COM's binary compatibility and then discusses .NET's way of supporting binary compatibility.

COM Binary Compatibility

COM provides binary compatibility by using interface pointers and virtual tables. In COM, the client interacts with the object indirectly by using the interface pointer. The interface pointer actually points to another pointer called the *virtual table pointer*. The virtual table pointer points to a table of function pointers. Each slot in the table points to where the corresponding interface's method code resides (see Figure 2-7).

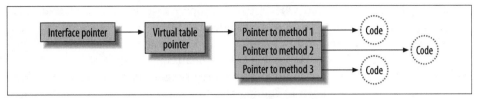

Figure 2-7. COM binary compatibility

When the client uses the interface pointer to call a method (such as the second method of the interface), all the compiler builds into the client's code is an instruction to jump to the address that the second entry in the virtual table points to. In effect, this address is given as an offset from the table's starting point. At runtime, the loader patches this jump command to the actual address because it already knows the table memory location. All that the COM client records in its code is the offset from the virtual table start address. At runtime, any server that provides the same in-memory table layout in which the table entries point to methods with exactly the same signature is considered binary compatible. This is, by the way, exactly the definition of implementing a COM interface. This model yields the famous COM Prime Directive: *Thou Shalt Not Change a Published Interface*. Any change to the virtual table layout will break the existing client's code. The virtual table layout is isomorphic to the interface definition. For example, the second method in the interface is the second entry in the virtual table. The virtual table must have the exact same number of entries as the interface has methods. Any change to the interface's definition must result in the recompiling and redeploying of all clients as well; otherwise, the clients are no longer binary-compatible with the server.

.NET Binary Compatibility

.NET provides binary compatibility using metadata. The high-level client code (such as C# or Visual Basic.NET) is compiled to IL. The client code can't contain any offsets from memory addresses because those offsets depend on the way the JIT compiler structures the native code. At runtime, the JIT compiler compiles and links the IL to native machine code. The original IL contains only requests to invoke methods or access fields of an object, based on that type's metadata. It's as if instead of a traditional method call in native code, the IL contains only a token identifying the method to invoke. Any type that provides these methods or fields in its metadata is binary-compatible because the actual binary layout in memory of the type is decided at runtime by the JIT compiler, and there is nothing pertaining to this layout in the client's IL.

The main benefit of .NET metadata-based binary compatibility is that every class is a binary component. This, in turn, simplifies developing components tremendously compared with COM. There's no need for complex frameworks such as ATL because .NET supports components natively. .NET can bridge the skill gap (mentioned in Chapter 1) between what most developers can do and what traditional component technologies demand. If you understand only object-oriented programming, you can do that and still gain some component-oriented programming benefits, relying on .NET to manage binary compatibility and versioning. If you understand the core issues of component-oriented programming, you can maximize productivity and potential while gaining the full benefits of component-oriented applications. Unlike COM, .NET binary compatibility isn't limited to interface-based programming. Any .NET type, be it class or a struct, is compatible with its clients. Any entry point, be it an instance method, object field, static method, or static field is binary-compatible. The other main benefit of metadata-based binary compatibility is that is gives you the flexibility of late binding with the safety of early binding because the code never jumps to the wrong address, and yet you don't bake actual entry point addresses or offsets into the client's code. For example, consider the following .NET interface:

```
public interface IMyInterface
{
   void Method1( );
   void Method2( );
}
```

The interface is defined and implemented in a server assembly, and its client resides in a separate assembly. The client is compiled against the interface definition, and the compiler provides type safety by enforcing correct parameter types and return values. However, the same client will function just fine (without recompiling) if you change the order of the methods in the interface:

```
public interface IMyInterface
{
   void Method2( );
   void Method1( );
}
```

or if you add a new method:

```
public interface IMyInterface
{
   void Method3( );
   void Method1( );
   void Method2( );
}
```

If the client doesn't use one of the methods, you can remove it, and the client will be unaffected. In the past, this level of flexibility was available only with late binding scripting languages, which interpreted the code instead of compiling it. All these changes are forbidden in COM interfaces because they contradict the prime directive of not changing published interfaces. In general, .NET lets you remove unused methods and add new methods (or fields). Adding new methods was the prime reason for defining new interfaces in COM (which in turn complicated the COM programming model). NET also lets you change the order of methods. However, you can't change method parameters or remove methods that clients expect to use.

Binary Inheritance

An interesting side effect of metadata-based binary compatibility is that it allows binary inheritance of implementation. In traditional object-oriented programming, the subclass developer had to have access to a source file describing the base class in order to derive his class from it. In .NET, types are described using metadata, so the subclass developer needs to access the metadata only of the base class. The compiler reads the metadata from the binary file and knows which methods and fields are available in the base type. In fact, even when both the base class and the subclass are defined in the same project, the compiler still uses the metadata in the project to compile the subclass. This is why in .NET, the order in which classes are defined doesn't matter, unlike C++, which often requires forward type declarations or a particular order of listing the included header files. All .NET framework base classes are available to you to derive and extend using binary inheritance. Note that inheritance is a double-edged sword. Inheritance is a form of white-box reuse: it tends to couple the subclass to the base class, and it requires intimate knowledge of the base class functionality. COM didn't allow binary inheritance of implementation (only of interfaces) partly because the COM architects were aware of these liabilities. The .NET architects wanted to support inheritance as part of bridging the skill gap. However, I strongly advise against abusing inheritance. Try to keep your class hierarchies as simple and as flat as possible, and use interface-based programming as much as possible.

CHAPTER 3

Interface-Based Programming

As explained in Chapter 1, separation of interface from implementation is a core principle of component-oriented programming. When you separate interface from implementation, the client is coded against an abstraction of a service (the interface), not a particular implementation of it (the object). As a result, changing an implementation detail on the server side (or even switching to a different service provider altogether) doesn't affect the client. This chapter starts by presenting .NET interfaces and describing what options are available to .NET developers when it comes to enforcing the separation of interface from implementation. The chapter then addresses a set of practical issues involving the definition and use of interfaces, such as how to implement multiple interfaces or how to combine interfaces and class hierarchies. The chapter ends with a discussion of interface design and factoring guidelines.

Separating Interface from Implementation

In both C# and Visual Basic.NET, the reserved word interface defines a CLR reference type that can't have any implementation, can't be instantiated, and has only public members. Saying that an interface can't have implementation means that it's as if all the interface's methods and properties were abstract. Saying it can't be instantiated means the same as if the interface were an abstract class (or MustInherit in Visual Basic.NET). For example, this interface definition:

```
public interface IMyInterface
{
   void Method1( );
   void Method2( );
   void Method3( );
}
```

is almost equivalent to this class definition:

```
public abstract class MyInterface
{
    abstract public void Method1( );
    abstract public void Method2( );
    abstract public void Method3( );
}
```

In traditional object-oriented programming, you typically use an abstract class to define a service abstraction. The abstract class serves to define a set of signatures that multiple classes will implement after deriving from the abstract class. When different service providers share a common base class, they all become polymorphic with that service abstraction, and the client can potentially switch between providers with minimum changes. There are a few important differences between an abstract class and an interface:

- An abstract class can still have implementation: it can have member variables or nonabstract methods or properties. An interface can't have implementation or member variables.

- A .NET class can derive from only one base class, even if that base class is abstract. A .NET class can derive from as many interfaces as required.

- An abstract class can derive from any other class or interfaces. An interface can derive only from other interfaces.

- An abstract class can have nonpublic (protected or private) methods and properties, even if they are all abstract. In an interface, by definition, all members are public.

- An abstract class can have static methods and static members and define constants. An interface can have none of those.

- An abstract class can have constructors. An interface can't.

These differences are deliberately in place, not to restrict interfaces, but rather to provide for a formal public contract between a service provider (the classes implementing the interface) and the service consumer (the client of the classes). Disallowing any kind of implementation details in interfaces (such as method implementation, constants, static members, and constructors) enables .NET to promote loose coupling between the service providers and the client. Because there is nothing in the contract that even hints at implementation, by definition, the implementation is well encapsulated behind the interface, and service providers are free to change their implementation without affecting the client. You can even say that the interface acts like a binary shield, isolating each party from the other.

Because interfaces can't be instantiated, .NET forces clients to choose a particular implementation to instantiate. Having only public members in an interface complements the contract semantics nicely: you would not want a contract with hidden clauses or "fine print." Everything the contract implies should be public and well defined. The more explicit and well defined a contract is, the less likely it is that there will be conflicts down the road regarding exactly what the class providing the service is required to do. The class implementing the interface must implement all the interface members without exception because it has committed to providing this exact service definition. An interface can extend only other interfaces, not classes. By deriving a new interface from an existing interface, you define a new and specialized contract, and the class implementing an interface must implement all members of the base interface(s). A class can choose to implement multiple interfaces, just as a person can choose to commit to multiple contracts.

To implement an interface, all a class has to do is derive from it. Example 3-1 shows the class MyClass implementing the interface IMyInterface.

Example 3-1. Defining and implementing an interface

```
public interface IMyInterface
{
   void Method1( );
   void Method2( );
   void Method3( );
}

public class MyClass : IMyInterface
{
   public void Method1( ){...}
   public void Method2( ){...}
   public void Method3( ){...}
   //other class members
}
```

As trivial as Example 3-1 is, it does demonstrate a number of important points. First, interfaces have visibility; an interface can be private to its assembly (using the internal visibility modifier) or it can be used from outside the assembly (with the public visibility modifier) as in Example 3-1. Second, even though the methods the interface defines have no visibility modifiers, they are by definition public, and the implementing class has to declare its interface methods as public. Third, there is no need to use new or override to qualify the method redefinition in the subclass because an interface method by its very nature can't have any implementation, and therefore has nothing to override. If you aren't familiar with the new or override keywords, see the sidebar "C# Inheritance Directives" later in this chapter.

Finally, the class must implement all the methods the interface defines, without exception. If the class is an abstract class, it can redefine the methods without providing concrete implementation.

Example 3-2 shows how to define and implement an interface in Visual Basic.NET. In Visual Basic.NET, you need to state which interface method a class method corresponds to. As long as the signature (the parameters and return value) matches, you can even use a different name. In addition, because the default visibility in Visual Basic.NET is public, unlike C#, adding the public visibility qualifier is optional.

Example 3-2. Defining and implementing an interface in Visual Basic.NET

```
Public Interface IMyInterface
    Sub Method1( )
    Sub Method2( )
    Sub Method3( )
End Interface

Public Class SomeClass
    Implements IMyInterface

    Public Sub Method1( ) Implements IMyInterface.Method1
    ...
    End Sub

    Public Sub Method2( ) Implements IMyInterface.Method2
    ...
    End Sub

    Public Sub Method3( ) Implements IMyInterface.Method3
    ...
    End Sub
End Class
```

To interact with an object using an interface, all a client has to do is instantiate a concrete class that supports the interface and assign that object to an interface variable, similar to using any other base type. Using the same definitions as in Example 3-1, the client code might be:

```
IMyInterface obj;
obj = new MyClass( );
obj.Method1( );
```

Interfaces promote loose coupling between clients and objects. When you use interfaces, there's a level of indirection between the client's code and the object implementing the interface. If the client wasn't responsible for instantiating the object, there is nothing in the client code that pertains to the object hidden behind the interface shield. There can be many possible implementations of the same interface, such as:

```
public interface IMyInterface
{...}
public class MyClass : IMyInterface
{...}
public class MyOtherClass : IMyInterface
{...}
```

When a client obtains an interface reference by creating an object of type MyClass, the client is actually saying to .NET "give me the *interpretation* of MyClass to the way IMyInterface should be implemented."

Treating interfaces as binary contracts, which shields clients from changes made to the service providers, is exactly the idea behind COM interfaces, and logically, .NET interfaces have the same semantics as COM interfaces. If you are an experienced

COM developer or architect, working with interfaces is probably second nature to you, and you will feel right at home with .NET interfaces.

However, unlike COM, .NET doesn't enforce separating interface from implementation. For example, using the definitions of Example 3-1, the client's code can also be:

```
MyClass obj;
obj = new MyClass();
obj.Method1();
```

Because of the way the server in Example 3-1 implements the interface (as public members), nothing prevents the client from programming directly against the object providing the service, instead of the interface. I believe this is because .NET tries to make component-oriented programming accessible to all developers, including those who have trouble with the more abstract concepts of interface-based programming (see the section ".NET Adherence to Component Principles" in Chapter 1). The fact that something is possible, of course, doesn't mean you should go ahead and do it. Disciplined .NET developers should always enforce the separation, to retain the benefits of interface-based programming.

The following example is a simple technique that allows server developers to provide the separation. The server implementing the interface can actually prevent clients from accessing the interface methods directly using *explicit interface implementation*. Implementing an interface explicitly means qualifying each interface member name with the name of the interface that defines it:

```
public interface IMyInterface
{
   void Method1();
   void Method2();
}
public class MyClass : IMyInterface
{
   void IMyInterface.Method1(){...}
   void IMyInterface.Method2(){...}
   //Other methods and members
}
```

Note that the interface members must be defined at the class's scope as private implicitly; you can't use any explicit visibility modifier on them, including private. The only way clients can invoke the methods of explicitly implemented interfaces is by accessing them via the interface:

```
IMyInterface obj;
obj = new MyClass();
obj.Method1();
```

To explicitly implement an interface in Visual Basic.NET, you need to explicitly have the method visibility set to Private:

```
Public Interface IMyInterface
   Sub Method1()
```

```
        Sub Method2()
    End Interface

    Public Class SomeClass
        Implements IMyInterface

        Private Sub Method1() Implements IMyInterface.Method1

        End Sub

        Private Sub Method2() Implements IMyInterface.Method2
        ...
        End Sub
    End Class
```

You should avoid mixing and matching explicit and implicit interface implementations, as in the following fragment:

```
//Avoid mix and match:
public interface IMyInterface
{
    void Method1();
    void Method2();
}
public class MyClass : IMyInterface
{
    void IMyInterface.Method1(){...}
    public void Method2(){...}
    //Other methods and members
}
```

Although .NET lets you mix and match implementation methods, for consistency, you should avoid doing so. This is because such an approach forces the client to adjust its references depending on whether a particular method is accessible via an interface or directly via the object.

Assemblies with Interfaces Only

Because interfaces can be implemented by multiple parties, it's good practice to put them in a separate assembly from that of the servers. A separate assembly that contains only interfaces allows concurrent development of the server and the client, once the two parties have agreed on the interfaces. Such assemblies also extend the separation of interface from implementation to the code-packaging units.

Working with Interfaces

Now that you have learned the importance of using interfaces in your component-based application, it's time to examine a number of practical issues regarding working with interfaces and tying them to the rest of your application. You will also see the support Visual Studio .NET offers component developers when it comes to adding implementation to your classes for predefined interfaces.

 When you name a new interface type, you should prefix it with a capital I, followed by a capital letter of the domain term, such as IAccount, IController, ICalculator, etc. Use the I prefix even if the domain term itself starts with an I (such as IInternetManager, IImage, etc.). In spite of the fact that .NET tries to do away with the old Windows and C++ Hungarian naming notations (prefixing a variable name with its type), the I prefix is a direct legacy from COM, and that tradition is maintained in .NET.

Interfaces and Type Safety

Interfaces are abstract types, and as such, can't be used directly. To use an interface, you need to cast into an interface reference an object that supports it. Casting has some implications on safety pitfalls, described next. Before doing so, I'll define two concepts. First, casting from a class instance to an interface is called an *implicit cast* because the compiler is required to figure out which type to cast the class to:

```
IMyInterface obj;
obj = new MyClass( );
obj.Method1( );
```

When you use implicit casts, the compiler enforces type safety. If the class MyClass doesn't implement the IMyInterface interface, the compiler refuses to generate the code and produces a compilation error. The compiler can do that because it can read the class's metadata and can tell in advance that the class doesn't derive from the interface. However, there are a number of cases where you use the second concept instead: an *explicit cast*. The first is for readability. Sometimes you want to convey to readers of the code explicitly what interface you expect to get back:

```
IMyInterface obj;
/* Some code here */
obj = (IMyInterface) new MyClass( );
obj.Method1( );
```

Explicit casts to an interface is at the expense of type safety. Even if the class doesn't support the interface, the compiler will compile the client's code, and .NET will throw an exception at runtime when the cast fails.

The second case in which explicit casts are used is with class factories. In object-oriented programming, clients often don't create objects directly but rather get their instances from some class factory.* A *class factory* is a known object in the system,

---

* See the Abstract Factory design pattern in *Design Patterns*, by Erich Gamma, Richard Helm, Ralph Johnson, and John Vlissides (Addison-Wesley).

which clients ask to create objects they require, instead of creating them directly. The advantage of using a class factory is that only the factory is coupled to the actual component types that provide the generic interfaces. The clients only know about the interfaces. When you need to switch from one service provider to another, you need to modify only the factory (actually, instantiate a different type of a factory), and the clients aren't affected. When using a class factory that returns some generic base type (usually object) explicit casts are unavoidable:

```
IClassFactory factory;
/* Some code to initialize the class factory */
IMyInterface obj;
obj = (IMyInterface)factory.GetObject();//GetObject() returns System.Object
obj.Method1();
```

The third case that mandates explicit casts is when you have one interface the class implements, and you want to use it to get a reference to another interface the class also supports. Consider the code in Example 3-3. Even when the client uses an implicit cast to get hold of the first interface, it must do an explicit cast to obtain the second.

Example 3-3. Defining and using multiple interfaces

```
public interface IMyInterface
{
    void Method1();
    void Method2();
}
public interface IMyOtherInterface
{
    void Method3();
}

public class MyClass : IMyInterface,IMyOtherInterface
{
    public void Method1(){...}
    public void Method2(){...}
    public void Method3(){...}
}
//Client side code:
IMyInterface obj1;
IMyOtherInterface obj2;

obj1 = new MyClass();
obj1.Method1();

obj2 = (IMyOtherInterface)obj1;
obj2.Method3();
```

In all these examples that use an explicit cast, you must incorporate error handling, in case the type you are trying to cast from doesn't support the interface. You can, of course, use try and catch statements to handle the exception, but you can also use the as operator to do a safe cast. The as operator performs the cast if it's legal and assigns a value to the variable. If a cast isn't possible, instead of throwing an exception, the as operator assigns null to the interface variable. Example 3-4 shows how to use the as operator to perform a safe cast that doesn't result in an exception in case of an error.

Example 3-4. Using the as operator to cast safely to the desired interface

```
SomeType obj1;
IMyInterface obj2;

/* Some code to initialize obj1 */

obj2 = obj1 as IMyInterface;
if(obj2 != null)
{
    obj.Method1();
}
else
{
    //Handle error in expected interface
}
```

 Interestingly enough, using the as operator to find out whether a particular object supports a given interface is semantically identical to COM's QueryInterface() method. Both mechanisms allow clients to defensively obtain an interface from an object and handle the situation when it doesn't support it.

In the general case, always program defensively on the client side, using the as operator as shown in Example 3-4. Never assume an object supports an interface. Keeping that thought in mind leads both to robust error handling and to separation of interface from implementation, regardless of whether or not the server is using explicit interface implementation. Make a habit on the client side to use the server via an interface and thus enforce the separation manually.

Interface Methods, Properties, and Events

An interface isn't limited only to defining methods. An interface can also define properties, indexers, and events. Example 3-5 shows the syntax for defining all of these in an interface and the corresponding implementation.

Example 3-5. An interface can define methods, properties, indexers and events

```
public delegate void NumberChangedEvent(int num);

public interface IMyInterface
{
```

Example 3-5. An interface can define methods, properties, indexers and events (continued)

```
    void Method1( ); //A method:
    int  SomeProperty{ get; set; }//A property:
    int  this[int index]{ get; set;}//An indexer:
    event NumberChangedEvent NumberChanged;//An event
 }

public class MyClass : IMyInterface
{
    public void Method1( ){...}
    public int  SomeProperty
    {
      get
      {...}
      set
      {...}
    }
    public int  this[int index]
    {
      get
      {...}
      set
      {...}
    }
    public event NumberChangedEvent NumberChanged;
}
```

Interfaces and Structs

An interesting use of interfaces with properties involves structs. In .NET, a struct (a Structure in Visual Basic.NET) can't have a base struct or a base class because it's a value type. However, .NET does permit structs to derive from one or more interface. The reason is that sometimes you want to define abstract data storage, and there are a number of possible implementations for the actual structure. By defining an interface (preferably with properties only, but it can have methods as well), you can pass around the interface instead of the actual struct and gain the benefits of polymorphism, even though structs aren't allowed to derive from a common base struct. Example 3-6 demonstrates the use of an interface (with properties only) as a base type for structs.

Example 3-6. Using an interface as a base type for structs

```
public interface IMyBaseStruct
{
    int    SomeNumber{ get; set; }
    string SomeString{ get; set; }
}

struct MyStruct : IMyBaseStruct
{
    public int SomeNumber
```

Example 3-6. Using an interface as a base type for structs (continued)

```
    { get{...} set{...} }
    public string  SomeString
    { get{...} set{...} }
    //Rest of the implementation
}
struct MyOtherStruct : IMyBaseStruct
{
    public int SomeNumber
    { get{...} set{...} }
    public string  SomeString
    { get{...} set{...} }
    //Rest of the implementation
}
//A method that accepts a struct, without knowing exactly the type
public void DoWork(IMyBaseStruct storage){...}
```

Implementing Multiple Interfaces

A class can derive from as many interfaces as required (see Example 3-3), but a class is limited to only one base class at the most. When a class derives from a base class and from interfaces, the base must be listed first in the derivation chain, a requirement the compiler enforces:

```
public interface IMyInterface
{}
public interface IMyOtherInterface
{}
public class MyBaseClass
{}
public class MySubClass : MyBaseClass,IMyInterface,IMyOtherInterface
{}
```

Even such a trivial example raises a number of questions: what if both interfaces define identical methods? What are the available ways to resolve such collisions? What if the base class already derives from one or more of the interfaces? The following section addresses these questions.

Interface Method Collisions

When a class derives from two or more interfaces that define an identical method, you have two options: the first is to channel both interface methods to the same actual method implementation. The second is to provide separate method implementations. For example, consider two interfaces that define the identical method Method1( ):

```
public interface IMyInterface
{
    void Method1( );
}
```

```
public interface IMyOtherInterface
{
    void Method1( );
}
```

If you want to channel both interface methods to the same method implementation, all you have to do is derive from the interfaces and implement the method once:

```
public class MyClass : IMyInterface,IMyOtherInterface
{
    public void Method1( ){...}
    //Other methods and members
}
```

Regardless of which interface the client of `MyClass` chooses to use, calls to `Method1( )` will be channeled to that single implementation:

```
IMyInterface obj1;
IMyOtherInterface obj2;

obj1 = new MyClass( );
obj1.Method1( );

obj2 = (IMyOtherInterface)obj1;
obj2.Method1( );
```

To provide separate implementations, use explicit interface implementation by qualifying the method implementation with the name of the interface that defines it:

```
public class MyClass : IMyInterface,IMyOtherInterface
{
    void IMyInterface.Method1( ){...}
    void IMyOtherInterface.Method1( ){...}
    //Other methods and members
}
```

Now, when the client calls an interface method, that interface specific method is called. You can even have separate explicit implementations for some of the common methods and channel the others to the same implementation. However, as mentioned before, for consistency, it's better to avoid mixing and matching.

Interfaces and Class Hierarchy

In component-oriented programming, you focus on defining and implementing interfaces. In object-oriented programming, you model your solution by using class hierarchies. How do the two concepts interact? The answer depends on the way you override or redefine the interface methods at the different levels of the class hierarchy. Consider the code in Example 3-7, which illustrates that when defining an interface only at the root of a class hierarchy, each level must override its base class declarations to preserve semantics.

Example 3-7. Overriding an interface in a class hierarchy

```
using System.Diagnostics;//For the Trace class

public interface ITrace
{
    void TraceSelf( );
}
public class A : ITrace
{
    public virtual void TraceSelf( ){Trace.WriteLine("A");}
}
public class B : A
{
    public override void TraceSelf( ){Trace.WriteLine("B");}
}
public class C : B
{
    public override void TraceSelf( ){Trace.WriteLine("C");}
}
```

In a typical class hierarchy, the top-most base class should derive from the interface, providing polymorphism to all subclasses with the interface. The top-most base class must also define all the interface members as virtual so that subclasses can override them. Each level of the class hierarchy then override its preceding level (using the override inheritance qualifier), as shown in Example 3-7. When the client uses the interface, it gets the desired interpretation of the interface. For example, if the client code is:

```
ITrace obj  = new B( );
obj.TraceSelf( );
```

the object traces "B" to the output window as expected.

Things are less obvious if the subclasses use the new inheritance qualifier. The new modifier gives subclass behavior only when dealing with an explicit reference to a subclass, such as:

```
B obj = new B( );
```

In all other cases, the base class implementation is used. If the code in Example 3-7 was written as:

```
public class A : ITrace
{
    public virtual void TraceSelf( ){Trace.WriteLine("A");}//virtual is optional
}
public class B : A
{
    public new void TraceSelf( ){Trace.WriteLine("B");}
}
public class C : B
```

```
    {
        public new void TraceSelf( ){Trace.WriteLine("C");}
    }
```

then this client code:

```
ITrace obj  = new B( );
obj.TraceSelf( );
```

now traces "A" to the output window instead of "B." Note that this is exactly why the new inheritance visibility modifier is available in the first place. Imagine a client that somehow depends on the base class's particular implementation. If a new subclass is used instead of the base class, the new modifier ensures that the client will get the implementation it expects. However, this nuance makes sense only when you're dealing with clients that aren't using interface based-programming but rather program directly against the objects:

```
A obj = new B();
obj.TraceSelf();//Traces "A"
```

You can still support such clients and provide interface-based services to the rest of the clients. To achieve that, each class in the hierarchy can reiterate its polymorphism with the interface by explicitly deriving from the interface (in addition to having the base class derive from the interface). Doing so (as shown in Example 3-8) makes the new modifier yield the same results as the override modifier for the interface-based clients:

```
ITrace obj = new B();
obj.TraceSelf();//Traces "B"
```

Note that using virtual at the base class level is optional.

In general, you should use code such as Example 3-7, with the override visibility modifier, virtual interface members being the top-most base class. Such code is readable and straightforward. Code such as Example 3-8 makes for an interesting exercise but is of rare practical use.

Example 3-8. Defining an interface explicitly at each level of a class hierarchy

```
using System.Diagnostics;//For the Trace class

public interface ITrace
{
   void TraceSelf();
}
public class A : ITrace
{
   public virtual void TraceSelf(){Trace.WriteLine("A");}//virtual is optional
}
public class B : A,ITrace
{
   public new void TraceSelf(){Trace.WriteLine("B");}
}
public class C : B,ITrace
{
   public new void TraceSelf(){Trace.WriteLine("C");}
}
```

Unfortunately, you shouldn't combine explicit interface implementation and class hierarchy. The reason is that in a class hierarchy, you often call your base class implementation of a virtual method. Because with explicit interface implementation, the implementation is private, there's no way to refer to the base class implementation in a subclass:

```csharp
public class A : ITrace
{
    void ITrace.TraceSelf()
    {
        Trace.WriteLine("A");
    }
}
public class B : A,ITrace
{
    void ITrace.TraceSelf()
    {
        Trace.WriteLine("B");
        base.TraceSelf();//Does not compile
    }
}
```

Implementing a Skeletal Interface

As a component developer, you occasionally need to implement on your class an interface defined by another party. Instead of copying and pasting the interface definition, or typing it in, you can use Visual Studio.NET to generate a skeletal implementation of the interface. A *skeletal* implementation is a do-nothing implementation of the interface: methods don't modify parameters, and they return default values. A skeletal implementation is required to at least get the code compiled as a starting point for your implementation of an interface. To have Visual Studio.NET generate a skeletal interface implementation, you first add the interface to the class derivation chain. When you finish typing the interface name (such as IMyInterface), IntelliSense asks in a tool tip:

```
Press TAB to implement stubs for interface IMyInterface.
```

If you press the Tab key, VS.NET creates a skeletal implementation of the interface on your class and scopes it with a collapsible #region directive. For example, for this interface definition:

```csharp
public interface IMyInterface
{
    void Method1();
    int Method2(int num);
    string Method3();
}
```

Visual Studio.NET generates this skeletal implementation:

```csharp
public class MyClass : IMyInterface
{
    #region Implementation of IMyInterface
    public void Method1()
```

```
    {
    }
    public int Method2(int num)
    {
        return 0;
    }
    public string Method3()
    {
        return null;
    }
    #endregion
}
```

So that it can be compiled, the skeleton returns a default value from methods that have a return value.

You can also have VS.NET generate the skeletal implementation with the Class View. Go to the Class View window, expand the Classes tree item, and find your class. Expand the class's Bases and Interfaces tree item, go to the Interfaces tree item, and find the interface you wish to implement. Right-click on the interface and select from the pop-up context menu Add → Implement Interface, as shown in Figure 3-1.

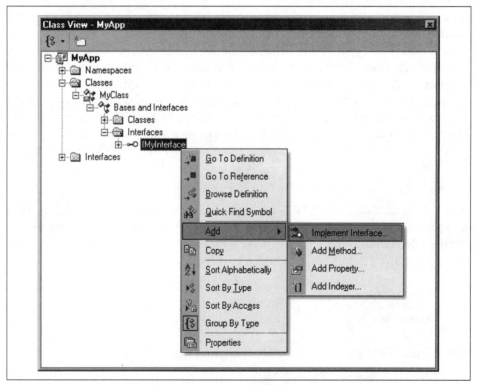

Figure 3-1. Using Visual Studio.NET to provide a skeletal interface implementation

Visual Basic.NET has only IntelliSense-level skeletal interface implementation, and it doesn't generate a region around the skeleton.

Designing and Factoring Interfaces

Syntax aside, how do you go about designing interfaces? How would you know which methods to allocate to which interface? How many members should each interface have? Answering these questions has little to do with .NET and a lot to do with abstract component-oriented analysis and design. An in-depth discussion of how to decompose a system into components and how to discover interface methods and properties is beyond the scope of this book. Nonetheless, here are a few pieces of advice to guide you in your interface design efforts.

Method Factoring

An interface is a grouping of logically related methods and properties. What constitutes "logically related" is usually domain-specific. You can think of interfaces as different facets of the same entity. Once you have identified (after a requirements analysis) all the operations and properties the entity supports, you need to allocate them to interfaces. This is called *interface factoring*. When you factor an interface, always think in terms of reusable elements. Because in a component-oriented application the basic unit of reuse is the interface, would this particular interface factoring yield interfaces that can be reused by other entities in the system? What facets of the entity could be logically factored out and used by other entities?

Suppose you wish to model a dog. The requirements are that a dog be able to bark and fetch and have a veterinarian clinic registration number and a property for having received shots. You can define the IDog interface and have different kinds of dogs, such as poodle and German shepherd implement the IDog interface:

```
public interface IDog
{
    void  Fetch();
    void  Bark();
    long  VetClinicNumber{ get; set; }
    bool  HasShots{ get; set; }
}
public class Poodle : IDog
{...}

public class GermanShepherd : IDog
{...}
```

However, such a composition of the IDog interface isn't well factored. The reason is, even though all the interface members are things a dog should support, Fetch and Bark are more logically related to each other than to VetClinicNumber and HasShots.

Fetch( ) and Bark( ) involve one facet of the dog, as a living active entity, while VetClinicNumber and HasShots involve a different facet, one that relates it as a record of a pet in a veterinarian clinic. A better approach is to factor out the VetClinicNumber and HasShots properties to a separate interface called IPet:

```
public interface IPet
{
    long  VetClinicNumber{ get; set; }
    bool  HasShots{ get; set; }
}
public interface IDog
{
    void  Fetch( );
    void  Bark( );
}
```

Because the pet facet is independent of the canine facet, you could have other entities (such as cats) reuse the IPet interface and support it:

```
public interface IPet
{
    long  VetClinicNumber{ get; set; }
    bool  HasShots{ get; set; }
}
public interface IDog
{
    void  Fetch( );
    void  Bark( );
}
public interface ICat
{
    void  Purr( );
    void  CatchMouse( );
}

public class Poodle : IDog,IPet
{...}
public class Siamese  : ICat,IPet
{...}
```

This factoring, in turn, allows you to decouple the clinic management aspect of the application from the actual pet types (be it dogs or cats). Factoring operations and properties into separate interfaces is usually done when there is a weak logical relation between methods. However, sometimes identical operations are found in several unrelated interfaces, and these operations are logically related to their respective interfaces. For example, both cats and dogs need to shed fur and feed their offspring. Logically, shedding is just a dog operation as is barking, and is also just a cat operation, as is purring. In such cases, you can factor interfaces into a hierarchy of interfaces instead of separate interfaces:

```
public interface IMammal
{
    void  ShedFur( );
    void  Lactate( );
```

```
   }
   public interface IDog : IMammal
   {
      void  Fetch();
      void  Bark();
   }
   public interface ICat : IMammal
   {
      void  Purr();
      void  CatchMouse();
   }
```

Factoring Metrics

As you can see, proper interface factoring results in more specialized, loosely coupled, fine-tuned, and reusable interfaces, and subsequently, those benefits apply to the system as well. In general, interface factoring results in interfaces with fewer members. When you design a system, however, you need to balance out two opposed forces. If you have too many granular interfaces, the overall cost of interacting with all those interfaces will be prohibitive. On the other hand, if you have only a few complex, poorly factored interfaces, the cost of interacting with those interfaces will be the prohibitive factor. Because these interface-factoring issues are independent of the component technology used, I can extrapolate from my own and others' experiences of factoring and architecting large-scale COM applications and share a few rules of thumb and metrics I have collected about interface factoring.

Interfaces with just one member are possible, but you should avoid them. Because an interface is a facet of an entity, that facet must be pretty dull if you can express it with just one method or property. Examine that single method: is it using too many parameters? Is it too coarse, and therefore, should it be factored into several methods? Should you factor this method or property into an already existing interface?

The optimal number of interface members (in my opinion and experience) is between three and five. If you design an interface with more members, say six to nine members, you are still doing relatively well. However, try to look at the members to determine whether any can be collapsed into each other, since it's quite possible to over-factor methods and properties. If you have an interface with 12 or more methods, you should definitely find ways to factor the members into either separate interfaces or a hierarchy of interfaces. Your coding standard should set some upper limit never to be exceeded, regardless of the circumstances; one possible number is 20.

Another rule involves the ratio of methods to properties among interface members. Interfaces allow clients to invoke abstract operations, without caring about actual implementation details. Properties are what are known as *just-enough-encapsulation*. It's much better to expose a member variable as a property than to give direct access to it, because then you can encapsulate the business logic of setting and reading that variable value in the object, instead of spreading it over the clients. A better approach would be not to bother clients with properties at all. Clients should invoke methods and let the object worry about how to manage its state. As a result, interfaces should have more methods than properties with a ratio of at least 2:1. The one exception is interfaces that do nothing except define properties; such interfaces should have properties only, with no methods.

I don't think that defining events as interface members is a good idea, and you should avoid it as much as possible. Leave it up to the object to decide if it needs an event member variable or not. There is more than one way to manage events, as you'll see in Chapter 6.

Is .NET Well-Factored?

After writing down the rules of thumb and metrics for interface factoring, I was curious to see how the various interfaces defined by the .NET frameworks look in light of these points. I examined more than 300 interfaces defined by .NET. I excluded from the survey the COM interoperation interfaces redefined in .NET because I wanted to look at native .NET interfaces only. I also excluded from the results the outliers—interfaces with zero members (9) and interfaces with more than 20 members (8). I consider an interface with more than 20 members to be a poorly factored one, not to be used as an example. On average, a .NET framework interface has 3.75 members, with a methods-to-properties ratio of 3.5:1. Less than 3% of the members are events. These metrics nicely reaffirm the rules of thumb outlined in this section; you could say that on average, .NET interfaces are well factored.

A final word of caution about factoring metrics: rules of thumb and generic metrics are only tools to help you gauge and evaluate your particular design. There is no substitute for domain expertise and experience. Always be practical, apply judgment, and question what you do in light of the metrics.

CHAPTER 4

Lifecycle Management

Traditionally, most defects in implementation that aren't business-logic specific can be traced back to memory management and object lifecycle issues. These defects include memory leaks, cyclic reference counts, the failure to release an object, the failure to free allocated memory, accessing objects already deallocated, accessing memory or objects not yet allocated, and so on. Writing impeccable code is possible, but it takes years of experience, iron discipline, a mature development process, quality commitment from management, and strict coding and development standards, such as code reviews and quality control. Most software organizations today lack most of these ingredients. To cope with this reality, .NET aims at simplifying component development to bridge the skill gap and increase the quality of the resulting code. .NET relieves you of almost all the burden of memory allocation for objects, memory deallocation, and object lifecycle management. This chapter describes the .NET solution for memory and object lifecycle management, and its implications for the programming model, including the pitfalls and the workarounds component developers need to apply.

The Managed Heap

.NET components aren't allocated off the raw memory maintained by the underlying operating system. Instead, in each physical process that hosts .NET, the .NET runtime preallocates a special heap called the *managed heap*. The heap is used like traditional operating system heaps: to allocate memory for objects and data storage. Every time a .NET developer uses the new operator on a class:

```
MyClass obj = new MyClass();
```

.NET allocates memory off the managed heap.

The managed heap is just a long strip of memory. .NET maintains a pointer to the next available address in the managed heap. When .NET is asked to create a new object, it allocates the required space for the object and advances the pointer as you can see in Figure 4-1. (Figure 4-1 is adapted with permission from Figure 1 in

"Garbage Collection: Automatic Memory Management in the Microsoft .NET Framework," by Jeffrey Richter (*MSDN Magazine*, November 2000.)

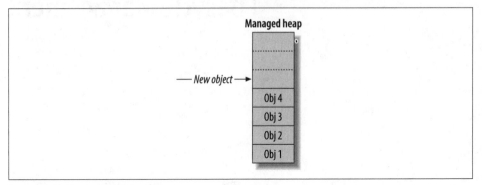

Figure 4-1. The managed heap

This allocation method is orders of magnitude faster than raw memory allocation. In unmanaged environments such as C++, objects are allocated off the native operating system heap. The operating system manages its memory by using a linked list of available blocks of memory. Each time the operating system has to allocate memory, it traverses that list looking for a big-enough block. After a while, the memory can get fragmented, and consequently the list gets very long. Memory fragmentation is a major source of performance problems because of the time it takes to traverse the list for allocation requests, combined with added memory page faults and disk access penalty.

Traditional Memory Deallocation Schemas

Deallocation of memory and the destruction of objects are also different in .NET compared with raw C++ or COM. In C++, the object destructor is called when a stack-based object goes out of scope:

```
{//beginning of a C++ scope
    MyClass object;
    //use object;
}//End of scope, C++ calls the object destructor
```

The object destructor is also called in C++ when the delete operator is used:

```
//in C++:
MyClass* pObject = new MyClass;
//using pObject, then de-allocating it
delete pObject;
```

COM uses reference counting, and it's up to the client to increment and decrement a counter associated with each object. Clients that share an object have to call AddRef( ) to increment the counter. New COM objects are created with a reference count of one. When a client is done with an object, it calls `Release()` to decrement the counter:

```
//COM pseudo code:
IMyInterface* pObject = NULL;
::CoCreateInstance(CLSIF_MyClass,IID_IMyInterface,&pObject);
//using pObject, then releasing it
pObject->Release();
```

When the reference count reaches zero, the object destroys itself:

```
//COM implementation of IUnknown::Release()
ULONG MyClass::Release()
{
   //m_Counter is this class counter
   m_Counter--;
   if(m_Counter == 0)
      delete this;

   // Should return the counter:
   return m_Counter;
}
```

.NET Garbage Collection

In .NET programming, exiting a scope doesn't destroy an object, and unlike COM, .NET doesn't use reference counting of objects. .NET has a sophisticated garbage collection mechanism that detects when an object is no longer used by clients and then destroys it. To do so, .NET must keep track of accessible paths in the code to objects. In the abstract, when the JIT compiler compiles the IL code, it updates a list of *roots*—top-level primordial application starting points, such as static variables and methods (`Main`, for example), but also internal .NET entities that should be kept alive as long as the application is running. Each root is the top-most node in a tree-like graph. .NET keeps track of each new object it allocates off the managed heap and the relationship between this object and its clients. Whenever an object is allocated, .NET updates its graph of objects and adds a reference in the graph to that object from the object that created it. Similarly, .NET updates the graph every time a client receives a reference to an object and when an object saves a reference to another object as a member variable. The JIT compiler also injects code to update the graphs each time the execution path enters or exits a scope.

The entity responsible for releasing unused memory is called the *garbage collector*. When garbage collection is triggered (usually when the managed heap is exhausted, but also if garbage collection is explicitly requested by the code), the garbage collector deems every object in the graphs as garbage. The garbage collector then recursively traverses each graph, going down from the roots, looking for *reachable* objects. Every time the garbage collector visits an object, it tags it as reachable. Because the graphs represent the relationships between client and objects, when the garbage collector is done traversing the graphs, it knows which objects were reachable and which were not. Reachable objects should be kept alive. Unreachable objects are considered garbage, and therefore, destroying them harms no one. This algorithm handles cyclic references between objects as well (Object A references Object B that references Object C that references back to Object A). When the garbage collector reaches an object already marked as reachable, it doesn't continue to look for other reachable objects from that tagged object.

Next, the garbage collector scans the managed heap and disposes of the unreachable objects by compacting the heap and overriding them with reachable objects (see Figure 4-2). The garbage collector moves reachable objects down the heap, writing over the garbage, and thus frees more space at the end for new object allocations. In addition, the garbage collector purges all unreachable objects from the graphs.

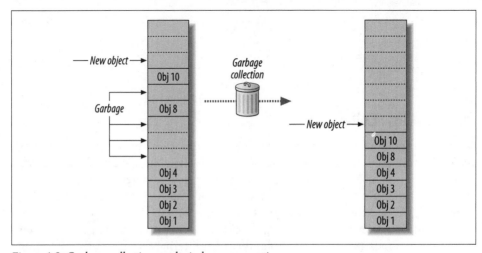

Figure 4-2. Garbage collection results in heap compaction

However, compacting the heap by moving down reachable objects means that any client that has a reference to those objects now holds an invalid reference. The garbage collector compensates for that by patching up all the references to the moved objects in the client code. Another problem faced by the garbage collector is that it must ensure that the application code doesn't change the structure of the object graphs or the state of the heap during the cleanup. The only safe way to cope with that is to suspend all application threads during garbage collection. So how does .NET know when it's safe to suspend a thread? The thread might be in the middle of some allocation or data structure modification (such as adding an element to a linked list). To handle this, the JIT compiler inserts *safe points* into the code—points in the execution path (such as those returning from a method call) that are safe for thread suspension. The garbage collector actually hijacks the thread by inserting a different return address from the safe point: an address that includes a call to suspend that thread. When garbage collection is done, .NET sends the thread back to its original return address to continue normal execution.

Even though garbage collection is usually triggered in .NET by heap exhaustion, application shutdown also triggers garbage collection.

Object Finalization

.NET objects are never told when they become garbage; they are simply overwritten when the managed heap is compacted. This presents you with a problem: if the object holds expensive resources such as files, connections, communication ports, data structures, etc., how can it dispose and release these resources? To address this problem, .NET provides *object finalization*: if the object has specific cleanup to do, it should implement a method called Finalize( ), defined as:

```
void Finalize( )
{
    /* Object cleanup here */
}
```

When the garbage collector decides that an object is garbage, it checks the object metadata. If the object implements the Finalize( ) method, the garbage collector doesn't destroy the object. Instead, the garbage collector marks the object as reachable (so it will not be overwritten by heap compaction), and then the garbage collector moves the object from its original graph to a special queue called the *finalized queue*. The queue is essentially just another object graph, and the root of the queue keeps the object reachable. The garbage collector then proceeds with collecting the garbage and compacting the heap. Meanwhile, a separate thread iterates over all the objects in the finalized queue, calling the Finalize( ) method on each, and letting the objects do their cleanup. After calling Finalize( ), the garbage collector removes the object from the queue.

Explicit Garbage Collection

You can trigger garbage collection with the static method Collect( ) of the GC class, defined in the System namespace:

```
public sealed class GC
{
    public static void Collect( );
    /* Other methods and members */
}
```

However, I recommend avoiding explicit garbage collection. Garbage collection is an expensive operation, which involves scanning object graphs, thread context switches, thread suspension and resumption, potential disk access, and extensive use of reflection to read object metadata. The reason to initiate garbage collection is often because you want to have their objects' Finalize( ) methods called to dispose of resources the objects hold. Instead, use deterministic finalization, which will be discussed later on.

Finalize( ) Method Implementation

There is much more to object finalization than meets the eye. In particular, you should note that calling `Finalize( )` is nondeterministic in time because it takes place only with the next garbage collection (actually, only with the one after that). This may postpone the release of resources the object holds and threaten scalability and performance of the application. In my opinion, nondeterministic finalization is the Achilles heel of .NET. There are, however, ways to provide deterministic object finalization, addressed later.

To end this section, here are a number of points to be mindful of when implementing a `Finalize( )` method:

- When you implement `Finalize( )`, it's important to call your base class `Finalize( )` method as well, to give the base class a chance to perform its cleanup:

  ```
  protected void Finalize( )
  {
     /* Object cleanup here */
     base.Finalize( );
  }
  ```

  Note that the canonical .NET type `System.Object` has a do-nothing, protected `Finalize( )` method, so you can always call it, whether or not your base classes actually provide their own `Finalize( )` method.

- Make sure to define `Finalize( )` as a protected method. Avoid defining `Finalize( )` as a private method because that precludes your subclasses from calling your `Finalize( )` method. Interestingly enough, .NET uses reflection to invoke the `Finalize( )` method and isn't affected by the visibility modifier.

- Avoid making a blocking call because you prevent finalization of all other objects in the queue until your blocking call returns.

- Finalization must not rely on thread affinity to do the cleanup. *Thread affinity* is the assumption by a component designer that an instance of the components will always run on the same thread (although different objects can run on different threads). `Finalize( )` will be called on a garbage collection thread, not on any user thread. You will then be unable to access any of your resources that are thread-specific, such as thread local storage or thread-relative static variables.

- Finalization must not rely on a specific order (i.e., Object A should release its resources only after Object B does). The two objects may be added to the finalization queue in any order.

- It's important to call the base class implementation of `Finalize( )` even in the face of exceptions; you do so by placing the call in a `try/finally` statement:

```
protected virtual void Finalize()
{
  try
  {
    /* Object cleanup here */
  }
  finally
  {
    base.Finalize();
  }
}
```

Because these points are generic enough to apply to every class, the C# compiler has built-in support for generating template Finalize() code. In C#, you don't need to provide a Finalize() method; instead, provide a destructor. The compiler converts the destructor definition to a Finalize() method, surrounding it in an exception handling statement and calling your base class Finalize() method automatically on your behalf. For example, for this C# class definition:

```
public class MyClass
{
  public MyClass(){ }
  ~MyClass()
  {
    //Your destructor code goes here
  }
}
```

here's the code that is actually generated by the compiler:

```
public class MyClass
{
  public MyClass(){ }
  protected virtual void Finalize()
  {
    try
    {
      //Your destructor code goes here
    }
    finally
    {
      base.Finalize();
    }
  }
}
```

If you try to define both a destructor and a Finalize() method, the compiler generates a compilation error. You will also get an error if you try to explicitly call your base class Finalize() method. Finally, in the case of a class hierarchy, if all classes have destructors, the compiler-generated code calls every destructor, in order, from the lowest subclass to the top-most base class.

Deterministic Finalization

.NET tries to simplify the management of object lifecycles by relieving you of the need to explicitly deallocate the memory occupied by their objects. However, simplifying the object lifecycle comes with potential penalties in system scalability and throughput. If the object holds onto expensive resources such as files or database connections, those resources are released only when Finalize( ) (or the C# destructor) is called. This is done at an undetermined point in the future, usually when certain memory exhaustion thresholds are met. In theory, releasing the expensive resources the object holds may never happen, thus severely hampering system scalability and throughput.

There are a few solutions to the problems rising from nondeterministic finalization. These solutions are called *deterministic finalization* because they take place at a known, determined point in time. In all deterministic finalization techniques, the object has to be explicitly told by client when it's no longer required. This section describes these solutions and contrasts them.

The Open/Close Pattern

To provide deterministic finalization, you must first implement methods on your object allow the client to explicitly order cleanup of expensive resources the object holds. Use this pattern when the resources the object holds onto can be reallocated. If this is the case, the object should expose methods such as Open( ) and Close( ).

An object encapsulating a file is a good example. The client calls Close( ) on the object, allowing the object to release the file. If the client wants to access the file again, it calls Open( ), without recreating the object.

Many classes in the .NET framework use this pattern, such as files, streams of all types (disk I/O, memory, network), database connections, or communication ports.

The main problem with Close( ) is that it makes sharing the object between clients a lot more complex than COM's reference counting. The clients have to coordinate which one is responsible for calling Close( ) and when it should be called; that is, when is it safe to call Close( ) without affecting other clients that may still want to use this object? As a result, the clients are coupled to one another. There are additional problems. Some clients may interact only with the object using one of the interfaces it supports. In that case, where should you implement Open( ) and Close( )? On every interface the object supports? On the class directly as public methods? Whatever you decide is bound to couple the clients to your specific object-finalization mechanism. If the mechanism changes, the change triggers a cascade of changes on all the clients.

The Dispose Pattern

The more common case is when disposing of the resources the object holds amounts to destroying the object and rendering it unusable. In that case, the convention is for the object to implement a method called Dispose( ), defined as:

```
void Dispose( );
```

When a client calls Dispose( ), the object should dispose of all its expensive recourses, and the disposing client (as well as all other clients) shouldn't try to access the object again. In essence, you put in Dispose( ) the same cleanup code you put in Finalize( )(or the C# destructor), except you don't wait until garbage-collection time for the cleanup.

If the object's base class has a Dispose( ) method, the object should call its base class implementation of Dispose( ) to dispose of resources the base class holds. The problems with Dispose( ) are similar to those of Close( ). Sharing the object between clients couples the clients to one another and to the object-finalization mechanism. Again, it's unclear where should you implement Dispose( ).

The IDisposable Pattern

A better design approach to deciding where and how you should implement Dispose( ) is to factor the method to a separate interface altogether. This special interface (found in the System namespace), called IDisposable, is defined as:

```
public interface IDisposable
{
    void Dispose( );
}
```

In the object's implementation of IDisposable.Dispose( ), the object disposes of all the expensive resources it holds:

```
public interface IMyInterface
{
    void MyMethod( );
}
public class MyClass : IMyInterface,IDisposable
{
    public void MyMethod( )
    {...}
    public void Dispose( )
    {
        //do object cleanup, call base.Dispose( ) if it has one
    }
    //More methods and resources
}
```

Having the Dispose( ) method on a separate interface allows the client to use the object's domain-specific methods and then query for the presence of IDisposable and always call it, independent of the object's actual type and actual finalization mechanism:

```
IMyInterface obj;
obj = new MyClass();
obj.MyMethod();

//Client wants to dispose whatever needs disposing:
IDisposable disp = obj as IDisposable;
if(disp != null)
{
    disp.Dispose();
}
```

Note the defensive way in which the client calls Dispose( ), using the as operator. The client doesn't know for certain whether the object supports IDisposable. The client finds out in a safe manner because if the object doesn't support IDisposable, as returns null. However, if the object does support IDisposable, the client would like to expedite disposing of the expensive resources the object holds. The clear advantage of IDisposable is that it further decouples the client from the object finalization mechanism and provides a standard way to implement Dispose( ). The disadvantage is that it's still complicated to share objects between clients because the clients have to coordinate among themselves who is responsible for calling IDisposable.Dispose( ) and when to call it; thus the clients are coupled to each other. In addition, a class hierarchy should implement IDisposable in a consistent manner: implement it at each level of the class hierarchy and have every level call its base level's Dispose( ).

Disposing and Error Handling

Whether the object provides IDisposable or just Dispose( ) as a public method, the client should scope the code using the object and then dispose of the resources it holds in a try/finally block. The client should put the method calls in the try statement and put the call to Dispose( ) in the finally statement. The reason is that calling methods on the object may cause an error that throws an exception. Without the try/finally block, the client's call to dispose of the resources is never reached. This pattern is demonstrated in Example 4-1.

Example 4-1. Using Dispose() with error handling

```
MyClass obj;
obj = new MyClass();
try
{
    obj.SomeMethod();
}
finally
{
    IDisposable disp;
    disp = obj as IDisposable;
```

Example 4-1. Using Dispose() with error handling (continued)

```
if(disp != null)
{
   disp.Dispose();
}
}
```

The problem with this programming model is that the code gets messy if multiple objects are involved because each one can throw an exception, and you should still clean up after using them. To automate calling Dispose() with proper error handling, C# supports the using statement, which automatically generates a try/finally block using IDisposable. For example, for this class definition:

```
public class MyClass: IDisposable
{
   public void SomeMethod(){...}
   public void Dispose(){...}
   /* Expensive resources here  */
}
```

If the client code is:

```
MyClass obj;
obj = new MyClass();

using(obj)
{
   obj.SomeMethod();
}
```

the C# compiler converts that code to code semantically equivalent to:

```
MyClass obj;
obj = new MyClass();

try
{
   obj.SomeMethod();
}
finally
{
   if(obj != null)
   {
      IDisposable disp;
      disp  = obj;
      disp.Dispose();
   }
}
```

You can even stack multiple using statements to handle multiple objects:

```
MyClass obj1;
MyClass obj2;
MyClass obj3;
```

```
obj1 = new MyClass();
obj2 = new MyClass();
obj3 = new MyClass();

using(obj1)
using(obj2)
using(obj3)
{
    obj1.SomeMethod();
    obj2.SomeMethod();
    obj3.SomeMethod();
}
```

The using statement has one liability: the compiler-generated code uses a type-safe implicit cast from the object to IDisposable. As a result, the type in the statement must derive from IDisposable, and the C# compiler enforces that. This precludes using the using statement with interfaces in the general case, even if the implementing type supports IDisposable:

```
public interface IMyInterface
{
    void SomeMethod();
}
public class MyClass: IMyInterface,IDisposable
{
    public void SomeMethod(){}
    public void Dispose(){}
}
IMyInterface obj;
obj = new MyClass();
using(obj)//This line does not compile now
{
    obj.SomeMethod();
}
```

Two workarounds allow for combining interfaces with the using statement. The first is to have all interfaces in the application derive from IDisposable:

```
public interface IMyInterface : IDisposable
{
    void SomeMethod();
}
public class MyClass: IMyInterface
{
    public void SomeMethod(){}
    public void Dispose(){}
}
IMyInterface obj;
obj = new MyClass();
using(obj)
{
    obj.SomeMethod();
}
```

The disadvantage is, of course, that the interface is now less factored.

Having all interfaces derive from IDisposable is analogous to having every COM interface derive from IUnknown so that the interface would have the reference counting methods.

The second workaround is to coerce the type used in IDisposable with an explicit cast to fool the compiler:

```
public interface IMyInterface
{
    void SomeMethod( );
}
public class MyClass: IMyInterface,IDisposable
{
    public void SomeMethod( ){ }
    public void Dispose( ){ }
}
IMyInterface obj;
obj = new MyClass( );
using((IDisposable)obj)
{
    obj.SomeMethod( );
}
```

In the current release of .NET, Visual Basic.NET doesn't provide a using statement, but that is likely to change in future releases. Until it does, Visual Basic.NET developers should write code similar to Example 4-1 (but in Visual Basic.NET, of course).

Dispose( ) and Finalize( )

Dispose( ) and Finalize( ) (or the C# destructor) aren't mutually exclusive, and in fact, you should actually provide both. The reason is simple: when you have expensive resources to dispose of, even if you provide Dispose( ), there is no guarantee that the client will actually call it, and there is a risk of unhandled exceptions on the client's side. Therefore, if Dispose( ) isn't called, your fallback plan is to use Finalize( ) and do the resources cleanup there. On the other hand, if Dispose( ) is called, there is no point in postponing object destruction (the deallocation of the memory the object itself occupies) until Finalize( ) is called. Recall that the garbage collector detects the presence of Finalize( ) from the metadata. If a Finalize( ) method is detected, the object is added to the finalization queue and destroyed later on. To compensate for that, if Dispose( ) is called, the object should suppress finalization by calling the static method SuppressFinalize( ) of the GC class, passing itself as a parameter:

```
public static void SuppressFinalize(object obj);
```

This prevents the object from being added to the finalization queue, as if the object's definition didn't contain a Finalize( ) method.

There are other things to pay attention to if you implementing both Dispose( ) and Finalize( ). The object should channel the implementation of both Dispose( ) and Finalize( ) to same helper method to enforce the fact that it's doing exactly the same thing in either case. The object should also handle multiple Dispose( ) calls, potentially on multiple threads. The object should also detect in every method whether Dispose( ) was already called, refuse to execute the method, and throw an exception instead. The object should also handle class hierarchies properly and call its base class's Dispose( ) or Finalize( ).

Deterministic Finalization Template

Clearly, there are a lot of details involved in implementing a bullet-proof Dispose( ) and Finalize( ), especially when inheritance is involved. The good news is that it's possible to provide a generic template for most cases. The template is shown in Example 4-2.

Example 4-2. Generic template to implement Dispose() and Finalize() on a class hierarchy

```
public class BaseClass: IDisposable
{
   private bool m_Disposed = false;
   protected bool Disposed
   {
      get
      {
         lock(this)
         {
            return m_Disposed;
         }
      }
   }

   //Do not make Dispose( ) virtual—you should prevent subclass from overriding
   public void Dispose( )
   {
      lock(this)
      {
         // Check to see if Dispose( ) has already been called
         if(m_Disposed == false)
         {
            Cleanup( );
            m_Disposed = true;
            // Take yourself off the Finalization queue
            // to prevent finalization from executing a second time.
            GC.SuppressFinalize(this);
         }
      }
   }
}
```

Example 4-2. Generic template to implement Dispose() and Finalize() on a class hierarchy

```
    protected virtual void Cleanup()
    {
        /*Do cleanup here*/

    }
    //Destructor will run only if Dispose() is not called.
    //Do not provide destructors in types derived from this class.
    ~BaseClass()
    {
        Cleanup();
    }
    public void DoSomething()
    {
        if(Disposed)//verify in every method
        {
            throw new ObjectDisposedException("Object is already disposed");
        }
    }
}

public class SubClass1 : BaseClass
{
    protected override void Cleanup()
    {

        /*Do cleanup here*/
        //Call base class
          base.Cleanup();
    }
}

public class SubClass2 : SubClass1
{

    protected override void Cleanup()
    {
        /*Do cleanup here*/
        //Call base class
          base.Cleanup();
    }
}
```

Each level in the class hierarchy implements its own resource cleanup code in the Cleanup() method. The implementation of calling either IDisposable.Dispose() or the destructor (the Finalize() method in Visual Basic.NET) is channeled to the Cleanup() method. Only the top-most base class in the class hierarchy implements IDisposable, making all subclasses polymorphic with IDisposable. On the other hand, the top-most base class doesn't provide a virtual Dispose() method so that subclasses can't override it. The top-most base class implementation of IDisposable. Dispose() calls Cleanup(). Dispose() can be called by only one thread at a time because it uses a synchronization lock (discussed in Chapter 8). This prevents a race condition in which two threads try to dispose of the object concurrently. The top-most base class maintains a Boolean flag called m_Disposed, signaling whether Dispose() was already called. The first time Dispose() is called, it sets m_Disposed to true, which prevents itself from calling Cleanup() again. As a result, calling Dispose() multiple times is harmless.

The top-most base class provides a thread-safe, read-only property called Disposed that every method in the base class or subclasses should check before executing method bodies and throw ObjectDisposedException if Dispose() is called.

Note that Cleanup() is both virtual and protected. Making it virtual allows sub-classes to override it. Making it protected prevents clients from using it. Every class on the hierarchy should implement its own version of Cleanup() if it has cleanup to do. Also note that only the top-most base class should have a destructor. All the destructor does anyway is delegate to the virtual protected Cleanup(). The destructor is never called if Dispose() is called first because Dispose() suppresses finalization. The only difference between calling Cleanup() via the destructor or Dispose() is the Boolean parameter, which lets it know whether to suppress finalization.

Here is how the mechanism shown in the template works:

1. The client creates and uses an object from the class hierarchy and then calls Dispose() on it by using IDisposable or Dispose() directly.

2. Regardless of which level of the class hierarchy the object is from, the call is served by the top-most base class, which calls the virtual Cleanup() method.

3. The call travels to the lowest possible subclass and calls its Cleanup() method. Because at each level the Cleanup() method calls its base's Cleanup() method, each level gets to perform its own cleanup.

4. If the client never calls Dispose(), the destructor calls the Cleanup() method.

Note that the template correctly handles all permutations of variable type, actual instantiation type, and casting:

```
SubClass1 a = new SubClass2();
a.Dispose();

SubClass1 b = new SubClass2();
((SubClass2)b).Dispose();

IDisposable c = new SubClass2();
c.Dispose();

SubClass2 d = new SubClass2();
((SubClass1)d).Dispose();

SubClass2 e = new SubClass2();
e.Dispose();
```

CHAPTER 5

Version Control

As presented in Chapter 1, a component technology must provide some sort of version-control support, which ensures that client applications have a deterministic way of always interacting with a compatible version of a server component. Component versioning challenges you face are closely related to the component-sharing mode you choose. *Private* components (components that reside in a location private to the application using them) are far less exposed to versioning issues because each application comes bundled with its own private set of compatible components, and you have to explicitly intervene to cause incompatibility. *Shared* components, on the other hand, can cause a lot of versioning headaches because they are stored in some globally known location and are used by multiple applications. Nonetheless, a mature component technology must allow multiple applications to share server components. A mature component technology should also allow different client applications to use different versions of the server components. Placing DLLs in global locations such as the system directory, as done in the past, proved fatal in the end, resulting in the devil's choice of either stifling innovation or suffering DLL Hell. Not surprisingly, one of the major goals set for the .NET platform was to simplify component deployment and version control. This chapter starts by presenting the principles behind .NET version control and assembly sharing. The chapter then explains how you can provide custom versioning policies for cases in which the .NET default isn't adequate. The chapter ends by describing how you should deal with versioning of .NET itself.

Assembly Version Number

Every assembly has a version number. That number applies to all components (potentially across multiple DLLs) in the assembly. You typically use an assembly-attribute called AssemblyVersion to assign the version number to the assembly, although you can also assign a version number during the link phase, using command-line utilities and switches. If you use Visual Studio.NET to generate the assembly, the *AssemblyInfo* file generated by Visual Studio.NET contains the assembly attribute `AssemblyVersion`. For example, the `AssemblyVersion` and its value may look like this:

```
[assembly: AssemblyVersion("1.2.3.4")]
```

The version number is recorded in the server assembly manifest. When a client developer adds a reference to the server assembly, the client assembly records in its manifest the name and the exact version of the server assembly it was compiled against. If the client uses the class `MyClass` from the assembly `MyAssembly` with Version 1.2.3.4, the manifest of the client records that the client requires Version 1.2.3.4 of `MyAssembly` to operate and will contain this declaration:

```
.assembly extern MyAssembly
{
  .ver 1:2:3:4
}
```

At runtime, .NET resolves the location of the requested assembly, and the client is guaranteed to get a compatible assembly. If a compatible assembly isn't found, an exception is thrown. The question is, what constitutes a compatible assembly? The rule of compatibility is straightforward: a compatible assembly must have the exact same version numbers that the client's manifest requests.

Version Number Elements

The version number is composed of four numbers: *major version number, minor version number, build number,* and *revision number*. Figure 5-1 points out these numbers in order.

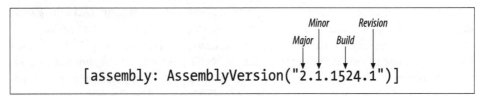

Figure 5-1. Breakdown of the assembly version number

Although you can assign any semantic to these numbers, there is a guideline or convention you should follow that conveys the meaning of version changes to the consumers of your assembly. A greater build number indicates a newer version of the same compatible assembly, and a greater revision number indicates some minor change (perhaps a minor bug fix) or changes made due to localization. As part of the product release procedures, you must verify that you have incremented the appropriate part of the version number, which reflects the nature of the new release.

Providing the Version Number

You can provide parts of the version number explicitly or let Visual Studio.NET generate them automatically. You must always provide the major version number. Any numbers not explicitly supplied are zeroed out. For example, if the assembly doesn't contain an `AssemblyVersion` attribute, the compiler assigns it the version number 0.0. 0.0. If you provide as a version number this assembly attribute:

```
[assembly: AssemblyVersion("1")]
```

the compiler generates 1.0.0.0 for the assembly version number. If you provide major and minor numbers, only the build and revision numbers are zeroed out. For example, if you provide as version number this assembly attribute:

```
[assembly: AssemblyVersion("1.2")]
```

the compiler generates 1.2.0.0 for the assembly version number. However, if you provide * for the build and revision numbers, such as

```
[assembly: AssemblyVersion("1.2.*")]
```

the compiler automatically generates build and revision numbers. For the build number, the compiler uses the number of days since January 1, 2000 local time. For revision number, the compiler uses the number of seconds since midnight, local time, divided by two. In the previous example, a possible assembly version generated by the compiler would be:

```
1.2.1078.16200
```

If you have some other schema for generating build numbers, you can use it, and choose just to mask out the revision number:

```
[assembly: AssemblyVersion("1.2.3.*")]
```

The compiler then generates only the revision number as just described. In general, the most practical way to provide a version number is to explicitly set the major and minor number, and let the compiler generate build and revision numbers:

```
[assembly: AssemblyVersion("1.2.*")]
```

Because explicit major and minor numbers, combined with masked-out build and revision numbers, are probably what you will choose to use, this schema is the default Visual Studio.NET uses when creating new projects. It thus assigns this value to the assembly version number:

```
[assembly: AssemblyVersion("1.0.*")]
```

.NET provides another assembly attribute called Assembly-InformationalVersion, used very much the same way as the AssemblyVersion attribute:

```
[assembly: AssemblyInformationalVersion ("1.2.3.4")]
```

However, the AssemblyInformationalVersion attribute is ignored by .NET when trying to resolve assembly version. This attribute is available as a complementary service for you to store some custom version number.

Assembly Deployment Models

.NET supports two assembly deployment models: private and shared. A *private assembly* implies just that: each client application maintains its own private local copy of the assembly. Deploying a private assembly is as simple as copying it to the directory of the application using it. Although during installation, client applications will typically deploy all their required private assemblies, nothing prevents copying over a new private assembly later on. This in turn allows for different lifecycles for the client and server and lets both evolve separately. When you copy a new version of a private assembly to the client directory, if the application has a previous copy of the assembly, the new copy overrides the old copy because a file directory can't have multiple files with the same name. Private assemblies are usually backward-compatible, meaning that they must support all the functionality available in the previous version. If that isn't the case, an old client application will break when it tries to access functionality in the new version that differs from the old version.

A *shared assembly* is an assembly that can be used by multiple client applications. You must install shared assemblies in a well-known global location called the *Global Assembly Cache* (GAC). The GAC can support multiple versions of the shared assembly, enabling side-by-side execution of different versions of the assembly. That means that if the older version is still present, a shared assembly doesn't have to be backward-compatible. Shared assemblies simplify complicated deployment situations, especially for framework or third-party component vendors because by installing the new version in the GAC, it's instantly available for all client applications on that machine. This chapter dedicates a separate section to generating and using shared assemblies.

The .NET entity responsible for managing assembly compatibility and for making sure a client application always gets a compatible assembly is called the *assembly resolver*. When a client application declares a type whose assembly isn't loaded yet, .NET looks in the client assembly manifest to find the exact version of the server assembly the client expects and then passes that number to the assembly resolver. The assembly resolver always tries to give the client assembly a version-compatible server assembly. The resolver first looks in the GAC (for strongly named assemblies only, as explained next) and loads the newest compatible assembly found in the GAC. If no compatible assembly is found in the GAC, the resolver looks in the client application folder. If the client application folder contains a compatible private version of the assembly (it can have only one such assembly file in its folder), the resolver loads and uses that version..NET throws an exception if no matching private assembly is found. Under no circumstance does .NET let a client application interact with an incompatible assembly.

Avoid mixing and matching private and shared server assemblies, that is, different versions of the same assembly—one used as private and some as shared. It can lead to conflicts of older and newer versions that are difficult to discern and resolve. If your deployment scenarios allow private use of assemblies, you should use it. Private assemblies allow maximum flexibility and isolation by giving each client its own version. If you need to update multiple clients, sharing via the GAC is easier. Rarely will you have to do both with different versions.

Understanding Strong Names and Shared Assemblies

As mentioned previously, an assembly can be either private or shared. A private assembly resides in the client assembly directory, whereas a shared assembly resides in the GAC. Although private assemblies are straightforward and easy to use, there are two cases in which you should consider using shared assemblies. The first case is to support side-by-side execution of different versions of the same assembly. The second case is as the name implies: simply to share assemblies between multiple client applications. Sharing allows multiple applications to take advantage of an improved compatible version as soon as is it's available, without patching up each application's private assemblies individually. Sharing also reduces disk footprint. Framework and class library vendors tend to use shared assemblies.

The client assembly can specify another location where its private assemblies are found using the .NET Configuration tool (presented later on in this chapter).

Strong Assembly Name

The GAC is likely to contain assemblies from many vendors. .NET must provide a way to uniquely identify shared assemblies. A *friendly name* such as MyAssembly isn't good enough because multiple vendors might come up with identical friendly names for their assemblies. .NET must have a way to guarantee assembly uniqueness. There are a number of ways to produce uniqueness. COM uses GUIDs—a unique 128-bit number assigned per component. Using a GUID is simple enough, but it has a fatal flaw: any party can see it, duplicate it, and swap in a new malicious component that uses the copied GUID. In short, COM GUIDs provide uniqueness because at any point in time there can be only one registered component with a given GUID on any machine; however, a GUID doesn't provide authenticity and integrity.

By contrast, for both uniqueness and authenticity, .NET-shared assemblies must contain a unique proof of their creator and original content; such a proof is called a *strong name*. .NET uses a pair of encryption keys to create a strong name. You prepare a file containing your organization's public and private keys. During compilation, the compiler uses the private key to encrypt the assembly's manifest. Recall that the manifest contains not only the assembly friendly name and version number but also a hash of all the modules comprising the assembly. The resulting encrypted blob is therefore a unique digital signature, ensuring both origin and content. The compiler then appends that signature and the public key to the manifest. During compilation, a client referencing a strongly named assembly records in its assembly manifest a token representing the public key of the server assembly, in addition to the server assembly version number:

```
.assembly extern MyClassLibrary
{
  .publickeytoken = (22 90 49 07 87 53 81 9B )
  .ver 1:2:3:4
}
```

When the client assembly triggers .NET to try to find the server assembly, .NET starts its search algorithm (first in the GAC, then in the application folder). For every assembly found with a matching friendly name, .NET verifies that the assembly has the expected strong name. Because the private key is unique and is kept safe in the organization that created it, a strong name ensures that no one can produce an assembly with an identical digital signature. Using the encryption keys, .NET maintains both uniqueness and authenticity.

Generating a strong name

.NET provides the *SN.exe* command-line utility for generating a pair of public and private encryption keys. If you try to run SN from the normal command prompt, you will get an unrecognized command error because SN isn't part of the registered environment path by default. To address this problem, Visual Studio.NET provides a dedicated command prompt, which registers .NET environment variables and path. This prompt is available in the Visual Studio .NET Tools item, under the Programs menu. Open that command prompt, and set the path to the *obj\Debug* directory of the server assembly project. Next, run this command:

```
SN -k MyCompanyKeys.snk
```

The *MyCompanyKeys.snk* file now contains a pair of keys (using *.snk* for the keys file extension is just a convention; it can be any other extension).

To sign the assembly, you need to associate the keys file with the assembly by using the AssemblyKeyFile assembly attribute:

```
[assembly: AssemblyKeyFile("MyCompanyKeys.snk")]
```

Now when the compiler builds the server assembly, it will use these encryption keys to assign a strong name to it.

Handling Large Organization Keys

An organization's strong-name private key should be kept under lock and key. If an organization's private key is compromised, less reputable parties can impersonate the organization and distribute their own components as originals. The security and reputation (as well as potential legal liability) implications can't be underestimated. Therefore, access to the private key of large organizations has to be restricted, probably to just the build team (with a backup copy in the senior manager vault). The question is, how can you perform your intermediate private builds without the private key? How can the build process combine your individual modules into a set of uniformly strongly named assemblies? To answer this need, .NET provides the AssemblyDelaySign assembly attribute. The attribute takes a Boolean value, indicating whether to sign the assembly using only the public key:

```
[assembly: AssemblyDelaySign(true)]
```

By default, Visual Studio.NET assigns false to AssemblyDelaySign attribute in a new project. You can use the -p switch of the *SN.exe* utility to extract a public key from a file containing both public and private keys:

```
SN -p  MyCompanyKeys.snk MyCompanyPrublicKey.snk

and assign a strong name with the public key only:

[assembly: AssemblyKeyFile("MyCompanyPrublicKey.snk")]
[assembly: AssemblyDelaySign(true)]
```

Signing an assembly with a public key allows you to install the assembly in the GAC and have client assembly reference it (which needs only the public key), so you can do your internal build and testing cycles. Delayed signing doesn't include a hash of the assembly files in the manifest, so you lose the benefits of a digital signature. You still need to sign the assembly with the actual private key before release.

Strong name and private assemblies

.NET distinguishes between a strongly named private assembly and a private assembly that has only a friendly name. If the private assembly has only a friendly name, .NET records the private-assembly version in the client-assembly manifest as shown earlier:

```
.assembly extern MyClassLibrary
{
  .ver 1:2:3:4
}
```

In reality .NET *ignores* version incompatibility between the client application and the private assembly, even though the version number is available in the client's manifest. If an application references a private assembly with a friendly name only, a private assembly is always the one used, and .NET doesn't look in the GAC at all. For example, imagine a client application that was compiled and deployed with Version 1.0.0.0 of a private class library assembly that doesn't have a strong name. Later on, Version 2.0.0.0 (an incompatible version, according to the .NET strict versioning rules), is available. If you copy Version 2.0.0.0 to the client application directory, it, of course, overrides Version 1.0.0.0. At runtime, .NET will try to load the new version. If the new version is backward-compatible, the client application will work just fine. .NET behaves this way because it assumes that the client application administrator knows about versions and compatibility, and that the flexibility of copying Version 2.0.0.0 is worth the risk. Note, that this has, of course, the potential of crashing the client application if Version 2.0.0.0 is incompatible with 1.0.0.0. However, unlike DLL Hell, the problem is confined to just that client application and doesn't affect other applications with their private copies of other versions of the assembly.

On the other hand, if the private assembly does contain a strong name, .NET zealously enforces its version compatibility policy. .NET records in the client manifest the token representing the public key of the private assembly and insists on a version match. In the example just discussed, the assembly resolver attempts to look up a compatible version in the GAC. If no compatible version is found in the GAC, .NET throws an exception because the private Version 2.0.0.0 is considered incompatible. The important conclusions from this are:

- Private assemblies with only friendly names must be backward-compatible.
- Private assemblies with strong names don't need to be backward-compatible because the GAC can still contain an older compatible version.
- Even if a private assembly with strong name is backward-compatible (with respect to content), if the version number isn't compatible, it results in an exception (unless the GAC contains an older compatible version).
- The private assembly deployment model is intended to work with friendly names only.

Strongly named and friendly named assemblies

An assembly with only a friendly name can add a reference to any strongly named assembly. For example, all the .NET framework classes reside in strongly named assemblies, and every user assembly can use them freely. The reverse, however, isn't true: a strongly named assembly can reference and use only other strongly named assemblies. The compiler refuses to build and assign a strong name to any assembly that uses types defined in assemblies equipped with only a friendly name. The reason is clear: a strong name implies the client can trust the assembly's authenticity and the integrity of the service provider. With a strong name, the client also assumes that it will always get this exact version. This cycle of trust is breached if the strongly named assembly can use other assemblies with potentially dubious origins and unverifiable versions. Therefore, strongly named assemblies can reference only other strongly named assemblies.

Interop Assembly and Strong Name

.NET assemblies can call methods of legacy COM components by generating an inter-operation (*interop*) assembly. The interop assembly contains metadata about the COM types, and .NET is responsible at runtime to bridge the two component technologies transparently from the .NET client perspective. To generate an interop assembly, use the COM tab on the Add Reference wizard in Visual Studio.NET. By default, the wizard generates an interop assembly with only a friendly name. If the .NET client is a strongly named assembly, it can't use that interop assembly. C# projects have built-in support to overcome this default behavior. Bring up the C# Project properties dialog. Under Common Properties → General is the "Wrapper Assembly Key File" item. If you specify the path and name of the file containing your keys, Visual Studio.NET uses those keys to automatically sign the interop assembly using the keys. Unfortunately, Visual Basic.NET has no such support in Visual Studio.NET. If your strongly named client assembly is developed in Visual Basic.NET, you must use the *TLBImp* com-command-line utility, and the /keyfile: command-line switch to specify a key filename to assign a strong name to the interop assembly:

```
tlbimp <COM TLB or DLL name> /out:<interop assembly name>
/keyfile:<snk file name>
```

Installing a Shared Assembly

Once you assign a strong name to an assembly, you can install it in the GAC. The GAC is located in a special folder called *assembly* under the Windows folder. There are a number of ways to view and manipulate the GAC. .NET installs a Windows shell extension that displays the assemblies in the GAC using the File Explorer. You can navigate to the GAC and simply drag and drop a shared assembly into the GAC folder. You can also use the File Explorer to remove assemblies from the GAC. The other option is to use a command-line utility called *GACUtil* that offers a number of switches. You typically use GACUtil in your application's installation program. The third option for managing the GAC is using a dedicated .NET administration tool called the *.NET Configuration tool*. You will see this tool used later on in this chapter to configure custom version binding policies and in Chapter 12 for specifying security policies. The .NET Configuration tool is a Microsoft Management Console snap-in, and is found after a normal .NET installation at *<Windows>\Microsoft.NET*

Framework\<version>\mscorcfg.msc or as a Control Panel applet under the Administrative Tools folder. Figure 5-2 shows the .NET Configuration tool.

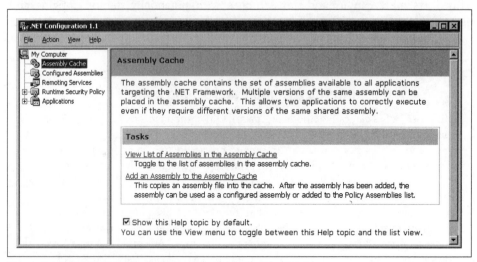

Figure 5-2. The .NET Configuration tool for managing the GAC

After launching the .NET Configuration tool, click on the Assembly Cache item in the left tree pane, and then click on "Add an Assembly to the Assembly Cache" on the right pane. This brings up a file locator dialog. Browse to where the assembly is located, and select it. If the assembly is still in its original location after a Visual Studio.NET build, select the server assembly from the *bin\debug* directory. This adds the assembly to the GAC. You can now view the assemblies in the GAC using the .NET Configuration tool. Select "View List of Assemblies in the Assembly Cache" on the right pane. Figure 5-3 shows a typical view of the assemblies in the GAC. The view contains the assembly friendly name, version number, locale, and a public key token. You would typically use this view to look up the version numbers of assemblies in the GAC, to troubleshoot some inconsistency, or just to verify all is well.

Referencing a Shared Assembly

The shared assemblies in the GAC are readily available for any client application to use. However, with the current release of Visual Studio.NET, there is no easy way to extract the server metadata from a shared assembly in the GAC to compile a client application. To build a client assembly, the client project must be given access to the server metadata. That means somewhere on the client machine (usually in the server project, if you develop both server and client) there must be a copy of the server assembly. When you use Visual Studio.NET to add a reference to a server assembly, Visual Studio.NET copies the referenced server assembly to the client directory by default. This, of course, constitutes a private server assembly for the use of the client

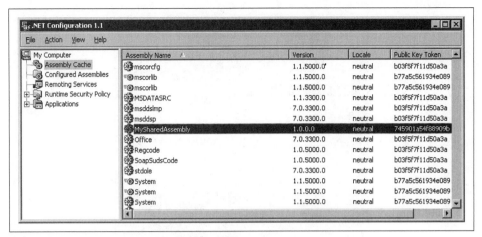

Figure 5-3. The GAC view of the .NET Configuration tool

assembly. You can manually remove that private copy of the server assembly, but there is a better way. You can instruct VS.NET to use only metadata from the server assembly and not to copy the assembly to the client directory. This enables compilation on one hand and loading the shared assembly from the GAC on the other. For example, suppose a client assembly wants to use the shared assembly *MySharedAssembly*. The file *MySharedAssembly.dll* is installed already in the GAC and is available in some other location. First, add a reference to *MySharedAssembly. dll* using the Add Reference dialog box. This copies the assembly locally to the client directory and adds an item called MySharedAssembly to the client's References folder in the Solution Explorer in Visual Studio.NET. Display the Properties window of the referenced *MySharedAssembly* assembly, and set the Copy Local property to false (see Figure 5-4); this prevents VS.NET from generating a private local copy of the server assembly.

Now you can build the client without using a local copy of the server assembly (when you set Copy Local to false, Visual Studio.NET actually removes the local copy and avoids copying it again). Now, when you run the client, the assembly resolver uses the shared assembly in the GAC.

In Visual Studio .NET, when you use the Browse... button on the .NET tab of the Add Reference dialogue to add a reference to an assembly that's already in the GAC, the Copy Local property of the reference is automatically set to false. However, when you use the Projects tab to add a reference to an assembly in a different project in the solution, Copy Local is always set to true, even when a copy of the referenced assembly is present in the GAC.

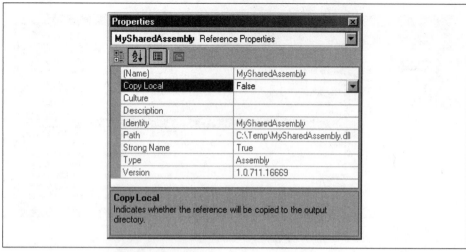

Figure 5-4. Referenced assembly properties

Verifying Shared Assembly Mode

In some cases, it's useful to programmatically verify that the server assembly is used as a shared assembly. You can take advantage of the `Assembly` type's `GlobalAssemblyCache` Boolean property. This property is set to `true` when the assembly is loaded from the GAC. You can also use the `Location` property to inform the user where the assembly is actually loaded from. Example 5-1 shows the implementation and use of the `AssertSharedAssembly` helper method. The method verifies that a given assembly is indeed loaded from the GAC. The method alerts the user and informs him where the assembly is actually loaded from. Note that for development and debugging purposes, it's sometimes necessary to verify that the assembly containing this class is loaded from the GAC and not used as a private assembly.

Example 5-1. The AssertSharedAssembly() method

```
using System;
using System.Reflection;
using System.Windows.Forms;
using System.Diagnostics;

public class MySharedClass
{
    public MySharedClass()
    {}
    public void MyMethod()
    {
        Assembly assembly = Assembly.GetExecutingAssembly();
        AssertSharedAssembly(assembly);
        //Do some work here
    }
```

Example 5-1. The AssertSharedAssembly() method (continued)

```
protected static void AssertSharedAssembly(Assembly assembly)
{
   bool shared = assembly.GlobalAssemblyCache;
   Debug.Assert(shared == true);
   if(shared == false)
   {
      string msg = @"The assembly should be used as a shared assembly.
                     It was loaded instead from: ";
      string currentDir = assembly.Location.ToString();
      msg += currentDir;
      MessageBox.Show(msg);
   }
}
}
```

Writing code that depends on the assembly deployment mode or location is wrong. Methods such as AssertSharedAssembly() should be used only during development troubleshooting—when trying to analyze what's going on and why the assembly isn't being used as a shared assembly.

Custom Version Policy

As you will see throughout the book, .NET is an extensible component technology, which means that .NET lets you override almost every key piece of its infrastructure. Specifically, .NET allows administrators to override the default assembly resolving policy and provide a custom version binding policy. Administrators can provide custom policies for individual applications that only affect the way a particular application binds to its private or shared assemblies. They can also provide machine-wide custom policies that affect the way every application on the machine binds to specific shared assemblies in the GAC. Administrators can choose to create custom policies for whatever arbitrary reason, but typically they do so when a new and improved version of a class library is available and the class library vendor guarantees backward compatibility with the older version. The administrator in that case would like to take advantage of the new version; however, the default version binding and resolving policy of .NET always tries to load the exact version the client application was compiled with. If the new version overrides a strongly named private copy of the older version, the assembly resolver throws an exception when it fails to find the old version. Even when the new version is installed in the GAC, the resolver ignores it and continues to load the older version. .NET allows administrators to redirect from the requested version to a different version. .NET also allows administrators to specify a particular location for a specific version, instead of the default location (first the GAC, then the application directory). This allows administrators to take advantage of private assemblies in other applications or redirect assembly loading from the GAC to different location altogether.

Application Custom Policy

The .NET Configuration tool has a top-level folder called Applications. To provide a custom policy to an application, you need to add it to the Application folder. Right-click the Application folder and select Add to bring up a selection dialog showing all the .NET EXE applications previously run on the machine. Select the application from that list or browse and select the application from a location on disk. Once added, you can configure a custom version policy for that application. The application will have a subfolder called Configured Assemblies (see Figure 5-5). Note in the figure that the right pane displays configured assemblies and whether custom version binding or codebase policies have been created for those assemblies.

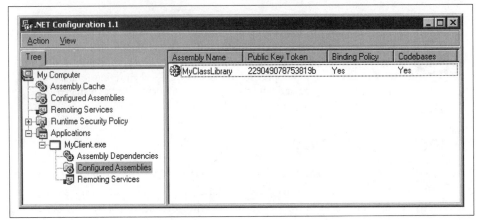

Figure 5-5. The Configured Assemblies folder

The Configured Assemblies folder contains all the assemblies used by this application that have some custom policy. To provide a custom policy for an assembly, you must add it to the folder. Right-click the Configured Assemblies folder and select Add to bring up the Configure an Assembly dialog (see Figure 5-6).

You can select either an assembly from the GAC or an assembly from a list of all assemblies used by this application (the list generated by reading the application manifest). Note that even though the list displays all assemblies and includes private ones with only friendly names, there's no point in selecting them because the resolver ignores version issues when the assembly doesn't have a strong name. You can easily tell which assemblies have a strong name: strongly named assemblies have some value in the PublicKeyToken column (see Figure 5-7).

Custom version binding policy

Once you choose an assembly, the .NET Configuration tool immediately presents you with that assembly's properties. The Binding Policy tab lets you specify a custom version binding policy (see Figure 5-8).

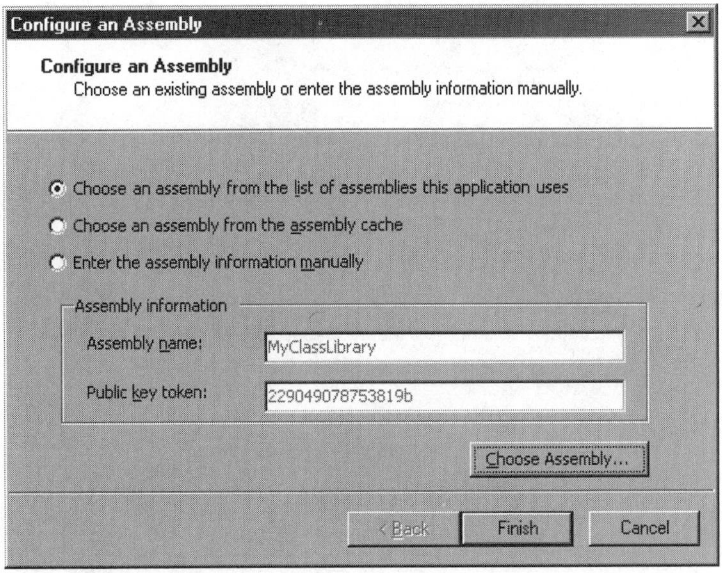

Figure 5-6. The Configure an Assembly dialog

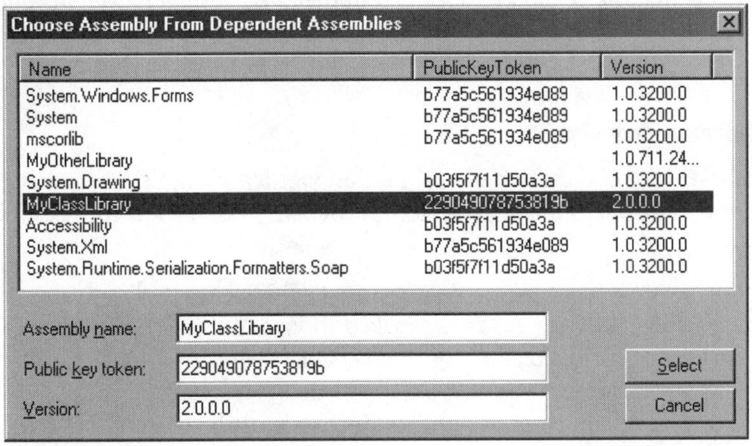

Figure 5-7. The Dependent Assemblies list

The tab contains a table listing version redirections. A *redirection* (as the name implies) instructs .NET to look for a different version than the one the application asks for. Administrators can specify redirection from a particular version to another particular version (such as from 2.0.0.0 to 2.1.0.0), or they can specify a range of redirections (such as from 1.1.0.0–1.3.0.0 to 2.1.0.0). Administrators can specify redirection from any version to any other version, including from newer version to older version (perhaps as a result of discovering a defect in a new version). The only

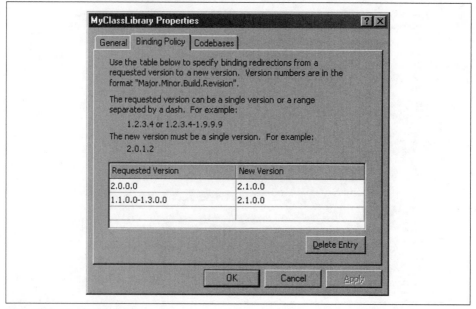

Figure 5-8. The Binding Policy tab

requirement is that the version be specified in the .NET format of *Major.Minor.Build. Revision* number. Administrators can add as many version redirections requests as needed.

Custom codebase binding policy

The Codebases tab on the assembly properties page lets administrators dictate where the assembly resolver should look for particular versions of the assembly (see Figure 5-9).

Administrators can redirect requests for private or shared assemblies to anywhere else. For example, if the assembly resolver is asked to load Version 3.2.1.0 of an assembly and there is a codebase redirection for that version, the resolver looks for that version in the redirected location, even if a suitable version is available privately or in the GAC. The only requirement is that the redirection must be given in the .NET format of *Major.Minor.Build.Revision* number, and the location must be in the form of a URL. Administrators can add as many version redirections requests as needed.

Application configuration file

When you provide an application custom policy, the configurations you make with the .NET Configuration tool are saved in the application folder in a special configuration file. That file is called <application name>.*config*, for example, *MyClient.exe. config*. The configuration file contains the custom policy in a simple XML format.

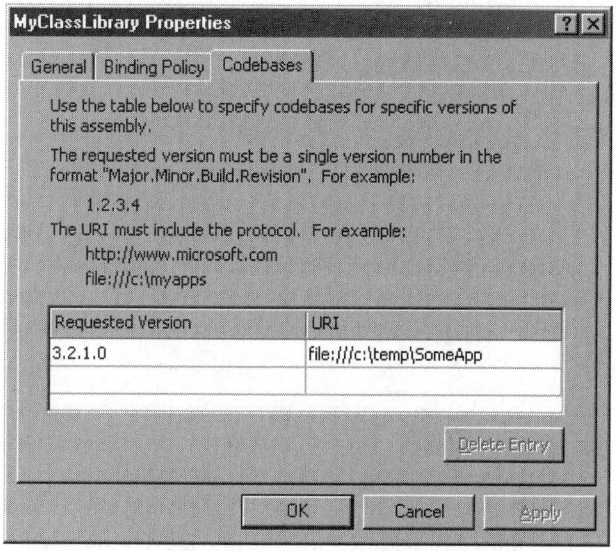

Figure 5-9. The Codebases tab

For example, here is the configuration file containing the custom version binding policies and codebase redirection shown in Figures 5-8 and 5-9:

```
<?xml version="1.0"?>
<configuration>
   <runtime>
      <assemblyBinding xmlns="urn:schemas-microsoft-com:asm.v1">
         <dependentAssembly>
            <assemblyIdentity name="MyClassLibrary"
                                    publicKeyToken="229049078753819b" />
            <bindingRedirect oldVersion="2.0.0.0" newVersion="2.1.0.0" />
            <bindingRedirect oldVersion="1.1.0.0-1.3.0.0" newVersion="2.1.0.0" />
            <codeBase version="3.2.1.0" href="file:///c:\temp\SomeApp" />
         </dependentAssembly>
      </assemblyBinding>
   </runtime>
</configuration>
```

Normally, you don't need to edit the application configuration file manually. The configuration file allows you to duplicate application custom version policies across multiple machines. First, use the .NET Configuration tool to edit that file, and then simply deploy it on every required target machine. The application configuration file also contains remoting configuration settings, described in Chapter 10.

Global Custom Policy

Administrators can also provide global custom policies for assemblies in the GAC. The .NET Configuration tool has a top-level folder called Configured Assemblies (see Figure 5-5). Administrators can add assemblies from the GAC to the Configured Assemblies folder, and then specify custom version binding and codebase policies for those assemblies. Specifying such custom policies is done exactly the same way as specifying custom policies for individual applications. Note that global custom policies affect all applications on that machine. In addition, the global custom policies take place downstream, meaning that the application applies its custom policies first, and then global custom policies are applied. For example, suppose an application was built with Version 1.0 of a class library. The application can install a custom version policy that asks to use Version 2.0 instead of 1.0. In addition, suppose that on the machine there is a global custom policy that redirects request for Version 2.0 of the class library to Version 3.0. As a result, when the application runs in the situation just described, it uses Version 3.0 of the class library.

When you provide a global custom policy, the configurations made using the .NET Configuration tool are saved in a special configuration file that affects the entire machine. This machine-wide configuration file is called *machine.config*, and it resides in the *<Windows Folder>\Microsoft.NET\Framework\<version number>\CONFIG* folder. The machine-wide configuration file contains the global custom policy in a XML format identical to that of an application configuration file. The *machine.config* file also contains configuration settings for predefined remoting channels and ASP.NET. Normally you don't need to edit *machine.config* manually. Use the .NET Configuration tool for editing, and copy the file between machines only if you need to duplicate custom global policies across multiple machines.

CLR Versioning

.NET's rigorous enforcement of version compatibility raises an interesting problem: if an application is built against Version 1.0 of .NET, when Version 1.1 of .NET is available, the application will not be able to take advantage of it. The reason is that the application's manifest contains the version number of all assemblies it relies on, including the CLR and application frameworks. The .NET assemblies are strongly named, and therefore the assembly resolver will insist on a perfect version match. To overcome the issue of version compatibility with its own assemblies, .NET provides a different set of ground rules. The issues involved are intricate. The exact version of the CLR used by components in a class library or an EXE may vary, and it depends on what they were compiled with, the available .NET versions, and the application versioning policy.

The .NET architects tried to strike a balance between allowing innovation and new versions on one hand, and supporting existing applications on the other. Ultimately, it's up to the application vendor to decide whether to support a particular CLR version. This marks a change of philosophy: Microsoft no longer guarantees absolute backward and forward compatibility because it's impractical. Instead, Microsoft pledges to make every effort to be backward-compatible and to point out where there are incompatibilities. This section describes the ground rules and the actions component vendors and application developers need to take to maintain compatibility, and if possible, take advantage of the new versions.

CLR Side-By Side Execution

Even though the CLR and the various .NET application frameworks consist of many assemblies, all are treated as a single versioning unit. Multiple versions of these units can coexist on any given machine. This is called *CLR side-by-side execution*. Side-by-side is possible because .NET is deployed in the GAC, and the GAC supports side-by-side execution of different versions of the same assembly. As a result, different .NET applications can simultaneously use different versions of .NET. It's also possible to install new versions of .NET or remove existing versions. Side-by-side coexistence reduces the likelihood of impacting one application when installing another because the old application can still use the older .NET version (provided you take certain steps, as described next). Nonetheless, CLR side-by-side execution allows you to choose when they upgrade to the next version, rather than have it ordained by the latest installed CLR version.

 If you choose to take advantage of features available in a newer version of .NET but not in older ones, your components will no longer be compatible with older versions. As a result, you must test and certify your components against each .NET version and state clearly in the product documentation which .NET versions are supported.

Version Unification

All .NET applications are hosted in an unmanaged process, which loads the CLR DLLs. That unmanaged process can use exactly one version of each CLR assembly. In addition, the version number of the CLR dictates which version of the .NET application frameworks you can use because both the CLR and its application frameworks assemblies are treated as a single versioning unit. The fact that .NET always runs a unified stack of framework assemblies is called *version unification*. Unification is required because the CLR and the .NET application frameworks aren't designed for mixing and matching, with some assemblies coming from, say, Version 1.0 and some from Version 1.1 of the .NET Framework.

Typically, a .NET application contains a single EXE application assembly, and potentially, multiple class library assemblies. Unification means that in a process containing a managed application, the EXE application assembly and the class libraries it loads use the same .NET version. It's up to the EXE to select the CLR and application frameworks version; the class libraries have no say in the matter. For example, all assemblies in the first release of .NET (.NET 1.0) have the version number 1.0.3300.0. All assemblies in the second release of .NET (.NET 1.1) are 1.1.5000.0. Imagine a machine that has both versions installed. When an EXE assembly uses .NET Version 1.1.5000.0, it makes all class libraries it loads use 1.1.5000.0, even if they are compiled with Version 1.0.3300.0. If the EXE assembly selects Version 1.0.3300.0, all the class libraries it loads will use Version 1.0.3300.0, even if they require the newer features of 1.1.5000.0. This may cause your application to malfunction. The next section describes how to explicitly indicate which CLR versions your application supports. In any case, with unification and side-by-side execution, it's possible at the same time for one application to use Version 1.0.3300.0 and another application to use 1.1.5000.0, even if they interact with each other.

 Avoid using custom version binding policies to override unification. It can lead to undetermined results.

Specifying a CLR Version

On a given machine, there can be any combination of CLR versions. Applications can implicitly rely on a default CLR version resolution policy, or applications can provide explicit configuration indicating the supported CLR versions.

Default version binding

If the application doesn't indicate to .NET which CLR versions it requires, the application is actually telling .NET that any compatible CLR version is allowed. In that case, .NET detects the CLR version the application was compiled with and uses the latest compatible CLR version on the machine. To that end, .NET is aware of which CLR version is backward-compatible with other versions (currently, all newer versions are backward-compatible). The compatibility list is maintained in the Registry. Applications that rely on this default policy are typically mainstream applications that use the subset of types and services supported by all the CLR versions. Applications that take advantage of new features or types can't use the default policy because they may be installed on machines with only older versions of the CLR. Similarly, applications that use features that are no longer supported can't use the default policy.

Specifying supported CLR versions

The default version may cause applications to run against CLR versions they were not tested for, resulting in undetermined behavior. If you don't want your application to rely on the default version binding policy, and you want it to have deterministic behavior, you can provide explicit version configuration. In such cases, the application must indicate in its configuration file which versions of the CLR it supports, using the startup tag with the supportedRuntime attribute:

```
<?xml version="1.0"?>
<configuration>
  <startup>
    <supportedRuntime version="v1.1.5000.0"/>
    <supportedRuntime version="v1.0.3300.0"/>
  </startup>
</configuration>
```

The order in which the CLR versions are listed indicates priority. .NET will try to provide the first CLR version to the application. If that version isn't available on the machine, .NET tries to use the next version down the list, and so on. If none of the specified versions is available, .NET refuses to load the application and presents a message box, asking the user to install at least one of the supported versions specified in the configuration file. Note, that the startup directive overrides any default behavior .NET can provide, meaning that even if another compatible version is available on the machine (but not listed in the configuration file), .NET will refuse to run the application. Consequently, if an application explicitly lists the supported CLR versions, it can't be deployed on a machine with a new version that isn't listed. Typically, you should not just add a CLR version to the list without going through a testing and verification cycle.

 It's likely that a future release of .NET will allow assemblies to provide the supported runtime versions as an assembly attribute. This will be instrumental only for component vendors that deploy class libraries.

Specifying required CLR version

The supportedRuntime attribute is recognized only by Version 1.1 of .NET. Microsoft intends to provide a service pack for Version 1.0 that will add the support for this tag to Version 1.0. Until such a fix is provided, applications developed with Version 1.1 of .NET have a problem if they are deployed on a machine with Version 1.0 because the supportedRuntime attribute will not be supported. However, Version 1.0 of .NET does support the requiredRuntime attribute under the startup tag:

```
<startup>
  <requiredRuntime version="v1.0.3300.0"/>
</startup>
```

When the requiredRuntime attribute is specified, .NET uses the specified CLR version number instead of what the EXE was built with. If the specified CLR version number isn't available on the machine, .NET looks in the Registry for the newest available compatible version and use that one. Developers (or system administrators) can even instruct .NET not to look in the Registry by setting the safemode attribute to true:

```
<startup>
  <requiredRuntime version="v1.0.3300.0" safemode="true"/>
</startup>
```

In this case, if the required CLR version isn't available, .NET displays an error message and refuses to load the application, even if a compatible version is available. The default value of the safemode attribute is false.

 Once Version 1.0 of .NET supports the supportedRuntime attribute, the requiredRuntime attribute will be considered deprecated and should not be used.

Visual Studio.NET and CLR versions

At present, Visual Studio.NET can build only applications targeting the highest CLR version installed on the machine (this may change in the future). Nonetheless, you can use Visual Studio.NET to edit the application configuration file for supported CLR versions. Note that the following feature is available only for application assemblies (such as console or Windows Form application) because a class library assembly doesn't have a configuration file. Bring up the Project setting dialog box, expand the Common Properties folder, and select the General item. On the right pane, expand the Application property group and select the Supported Runtimes property (see Figure 5-10).

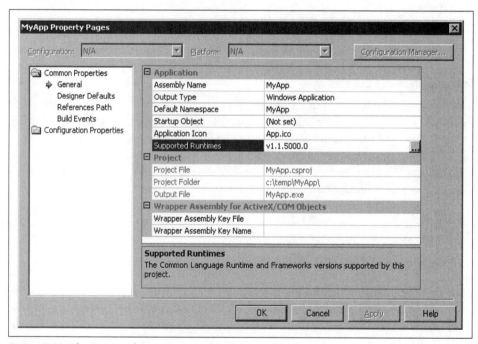

Figure 5-10. The Supported Runtimes project property

In Visual Basic.NET projects, the Supported Runtimes property is under the Build item of the Common Properties folder.

Click the ... button to bring up the .NET Framework Version dialog (see Figure 5-11).

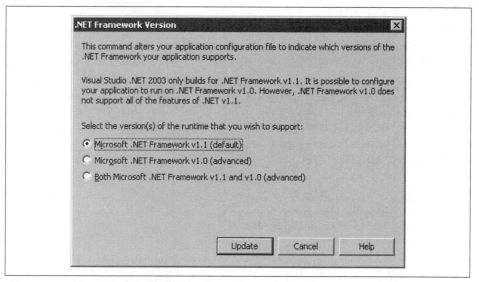

Figure 5-11. The .NET Framework Version dialog

The .NET Framework Version dialog lets you select the CLR versions you wish to support. The available options are Version 1.1 (the default) only, Version 1.0 only, or both 1.0 and 1.1. Once you make a selection and click Update, the wizard writes your selection to the file called *app.config* and places that file in the project's root directory. If your application already has a different configuration file in the *bin* folder, it will be updated as well.

If you select to support only Version 1.1 of the CLR, Visual Studio.NET adds the following entries to the configuration file:

```
<?xml version="1.0"?>
<configuration>
   <startup>
      <supportedRuntime version="v1.1.5000.0"/>
      <requiredRuntime  version="v1.1.5000.0" safemode="true"/>
   </startup>
</configuration>
```

As a result, the application always runs with Version 1.1 of the CLR, or not at all, even if the target machine has both Versions 1.0 and 1.1 of the CLR.

If you select to support only Version 1.0 of the CLR, Visual Studio.NET uses both the supportedRuntime and requiredRuntime to indicate the 1.0 CLR version:

```
<startup>
   <supportedRuntime version="v1.0.3300.0"/>
   <requiredRuntime  version="v1.0.3300.0"/>
</startup>
```

In addition, Visual Studio.NET inserts custom binding policies to all the CLR assemblies, of every possible version (0.0.0.0 to 65535.65535.65535.65535), redirecting them to the 1.0 version CLR version (1.0.3300.0):

```
<dependentAssembly>
   <assemblyIdentity name="Accessibility" publicKeyToken="b03f5f7f11d50a3a"
                                                             culture="neutral"/>
   <bindingRedirect oldVersion="0.0.0.0-65535.65535.65535.65535"
                    newVersion="1.0.3300.0"/>
</dependentAssembly>
<!-- Rest of the CLR assemblies -->
```

If you select to support both Version 1.0 and 1.1 of the CLR, Visual Studio.NET will use two supportedRuntime attributes as well as the requiredRuntime attribute:

```
<startup>
   <supportedRuntime version="v1.1.5000.0"/>
   <supportedRuntime version="v1.0.3300.0"/>
   <requiredRuntime  version="v1.0.3300.0"/>
</startup>
```

As a result, if the application is installed on a machine with Version 1.1 only, it uses 1.1. If the application is installed on a machine with both 1.0 and 1.1, it uses Version 1.1. If the application is installed on a machine with Version 1.0 only, it uses the 1.0 version.

Similar to the case in which supporting only Version 1.0 of the CLR is required, Visual Studio.NET will insert custom binding policies to all the CLR assemblies, of every possible version, redirecting them to the 1.0 version CLR. This will have the effect of always using the 1.0 version and above, even if the application is built with Version 1.1 or higher.

CHAPTER 6

Events

In a component-oriented program, an object provides services to clients by letting clients invoke methods and set properties on the object. But what if a client (or more than one client, as shown in Figure 6-1) wants to be notified about an event that occurs on the object's side? This situation is very common, and almost every application relies on some sort of event subscription and publishing mechanism.

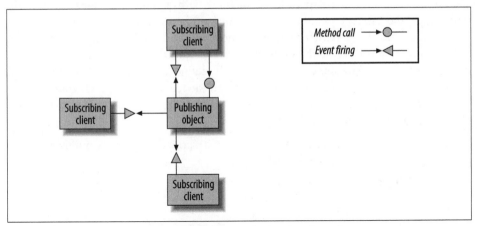

Figure 6-1. A publishing object can fire events at multiple subscribing clients

Because events are actually nothing more than method calls, there is nothing inherently special about firing events, and therefore I chose not to consider events support as a principle of component-oriented programming. However, not viewing events support as a principle doesn't mean that the component technology used should not try to ease the task of subscribing to and publishing events as much as possible. Not surprisingly, .NET event support automates the process as much as possible. This chapter starts by describing the essential concepts of .NET event support and then provides a set of practical guidelines for effectively managing events and extending the basic event support.

Delegate-Based Events

Before I describe .NET events support, here are a few terms you need to be familiar with: the object publishing the event is called the *source* or the *publisher*, and the party interested in the event is called a *sink* or a *subscriber*. The event notification is in the form of calling methods on the subscribers by the publisher. Publishing the event is also called *firing the event*. .NET offers native support for events by providing dedicated CLR types and base class implementations. .NET defines a standard way for source and sink connection setup and tear-down, a standard and concise way of firing events, and a ready-made implementation of the sink list.

.NET events support relies on delegates. Conceptually, a *delegate* is nothing more than a type-safe method reference. You can think of a delegate as a type-safe C function pointer or a function object in C++. A delegate (as the name implies) is a way you can delegate the act of calling a method to somebody else. The delegate can call static or instance methods. Consider for example, the delegate NumberChangedEvent defined as:

```
public delegate void NumberChangedEvent(int num);
```

This delegate can be used to call any method with a matching signature (a void return type and one int parameter). The name of the delegate, the name of the target methods and the parameter names of those methods are of no importance. The only requirement is that the methods being called have the exact signature (the same types) that the delegate expects. You typically define a delegate with a meaningful name (such as NumberChangedEvent) to convey to the reader of your code that this delegate is used to publish an event notifying subscribers that the value of a certain number they are monitoring has changed.

In the case of the number changed event just described, the event publisher has a public member variable of the delegate type:

```
public delegate void NumberChangedEvent(int num);

public class MyPublisher
{
   public NumberChangedEvent NumberChanged;
   /* Other methods and members  */
}
```

The event subscriber has to implement a method with the required signature:

```
public class MySubscriber
{
   public void OnNumberChanged(int num)
   {
      string msg = "New Number value is " + num.ToString();
      MessageBox.Show(msg,"MySubscriber");
   }
}
```

The compiler replaces the delegate type definition with a sophisticated class providing the implementation of the sink list. You can use the =, +=, and -= operators to manage the list of target methods. That list is actually a list of delegate objects, each referencing a single target method. The += operator adds a new subscriber (actually, just a new target method wrapped in a delegate) to the end of the list. To add a new target, you need to create a new delegate object wrapped around the target method. The -= operator removes a target method from the list (either by creating a new delegate object wrapped around the target method or using an existing delegate that targets that method). The = operator can initialize the list with the first target. When you want to fire the event, simply call the delegate, passing in the parameters. This causes the delegate to iterate over its internal list of targets, calling each target method with the parameters. Example 6-1 shows how to add two subscribers to the delegate list of sinks, how to fire the event, and how to remove a subscriber from the list.

Example 6-1. Using delegates to manage event subscription and publishing

```
MyPublisher  publisher  = new MyPublisher();
MySubscriber subscriber1 = new MySubscriber();
MySubscriber subscriber2 = new MySubscriber();

//Adding subscriptions:
publisher.NumberChanged += new NumberChangedEvent(subscriber1.OnNumberChanged);
publisher.NumberChanged += new NumberChangedEvent(subscriber2.OnNumberChanged);

//Firing the event:
publisher.NumberChanged(3);

//Removing a subscription:
publisher.NumberChanged -= new NumberChangedEvent(subscriber2.OnNumberChanged);
```

All the code in Example 6-1 does is delegate to the NumberChanged delegate the act of calling the subscribers methods. Note that you can add the same subscriber target method multiple times:

```
publisher.NumberChanged += new NumberChangedEvent(subscriber1.OnNumberChanged);
publisher.NumberChanged += new NumberChangedEvent(subscriber1.OnNumberChanged);
```

or:

```
NumberChangedEvent del = new NumberChangedEvent(subscriber1.OnNumberChanged);
publisher.NumberChanged += del;
publisher.NumberChanged += del;
```

The delegate then simply calls that subscriber a matching number of times. When you remove a target method from the list, if it has multiple occurrences, the first one found (the one closer to the list's head) is removed.

Delegates are widely used in .NET, not just for a consistent way of managing events but also for other tasks such as asynchronous method invocation (described in Chapter 7) and creating new threads (described in Chapter 8).

The event Keyword

Using raw delegates for event management is simple enough, but it has a flaw: the publisher class should expose the delegate member as public member variable so that any party can add subscribers to that delegate list. Exposing the delegate as a public member allows anyone to access it and publish the event, however, even if no event takes place on the object side. To address this flaw, C# refines the type of delegates used for events subscription and notification, using the *event* reserved word. When you define a delegate member variable as an event, even if that member is public, only the publisher class can fire the event (although anyone can add target methods to the delegate list). It's then up to the discretion of the publisher class's developer whether to provide a public method to fire the event:

```
public delegate void NumberChangedEvent(int num);

public class MyPublisher
{
    public event NumberChangedEvent NumberChanged;
    public void FireEvent(int num)
    {
        NumberChanged(num);
    }
    /* Other methods and members  */
}
```

The code that hooks up subscribers with the publisher remains the same (using the += and the -= operators) as in Example 6-1. Using events instead of raw delegates also promotes looser coupling between the publisher and the subscribers because the business logic on the object side that triggers firing the event is hidden from the subscribers.

When you type the += operator to add a target method to a delegate in Visual Studio.NET, IntelliSense presents a tool tip offering to add a new delegate of the matching type when you press the Tab key. If you don't like the default target method name, simply type in a different name. If the target method doesn't exist, IntelliSense lets you generate a handling method by that name by pressing Tab once more. This IntelliSense support works only with delegates defined as events (not mere delegates). Also worth mentioning is that there is no IntelliSense support for removing a subscription.

Events in Visual Basic.NET

The semantic of the operations for event handling in Visual Basic.NET is exactly as described for C#. The syntax however is sufficiently different to merit a few words and some sample code. Visual Basic.NET doesn't provide overloaded operators for adding and removing event-handling methods. Instead, Visual Basic.NET uses the reserved words AddHandler and RemoveHandler. Visual Basic.NET uses the AddressOf operator to obtain the address of the event-handling method. To fire the event in Visual Basic.NET, instead of using the delegate directly as in C#, you need to use the RaiseEvent operator. Example 6-2 uses Visual Basic.NET to implement the NumberChangedEvent event, demonstrating the same code as Example 6-1 (except it uses an event instead of a raw delegate).

Example 6-2. .NET events using Visual Basic.NET

```
Public Delegate Sub NumberChangedEvent(ByVal num As Integer)

Public Class MyPublisher
   Public Event NumberChanged As NumberChangedEvent
   Public Sub FireEvent(ByVal num As Integer)
      RaiseEvent NumberChanged(num)
   End Sub
End Class

Public Class MySubscriber
   Public Sub OnNumberChanged(ByVal num As Integer)
      Dim msg As String
      msg = "New Number value is " + num.ToString()
      MessageBox.Show(msg, "MySubscriber")
   End Sub
End Class

Dim publisher   As MyPublisher  = New MyPublisher()
Dim subscriber1 As MySubscriber = New MySubscriber()
Dim subscriber2 As MySubscriber = New MySubscriber()

'Adding subscriptions:
AddHandler publisher.NumberChanged, AddressOf subscriber1.OnNumberChanged
AddHandler publisher.NumberChanged, AddressOf subscriber2.OnNumberChanged

publisher.FireEvent(3)

'Removing a subscription:
RemoveHandler publisher.NumberChanged, AddressOf subscriber2.OnNumberChanged
```

Working with .NET Events

This section discusses .NET event-design guidelines and development practices that promote loose coupling between publishers and subscribers, improve availability, conform to existing conventions, and generally take advantage of .NET's rich event

.NET Loosely Coupled Events

.NET events support eases the task of managing events, and it relieves you of the burden of providing the mundane code for managing the list of subscribers. However, .NET delegate-based events still suffer from other drawbacks:

- The subscriber (or the client adding the subscription) must repeat the code for adding the subscription for every publisher object from which it wants to receive events. There is no way to subscribe to a type of event and have the event delivered to the subscriber, regardless of who the publisher is.

- The subscriber has no way to filter events that are fired (e.g., "notify me about the event only if a certain condition is met").

- The subscriber must have a way to get hold of the publisher object in order to advise it. That in turn introduces coupling between clients and objects and coupling between individual clients.

- The publisher and the subscribers have coupled lifetimes; both publisher and subscriber have to be running at the same time. There is no way for a subscriber to say to .NET: "if any object fires this particular event, please create an instance of me and let me handle it."

- There is no easy way for doing disconnected work; that is, the publisher object fires the event from an offline machine, and the event is subsequently delivered to subscribing clients once the machine is brought online. The reverse is also not possible—having a client running on an offline machine and receiving events fired while the connection is down.

- Setting up connections has to be done programmatically. There is no administrative way to set up connections between publishers and subscribers.

To offset these drawbacks, .NET supports a separate kind of events, called *loosely coupled events* (LCE). LCE support is provided in the System.EnterpriseServices namespace. Even though LCE isn't based on delegates, using LCE is easy and straightforward, and you can gain additional benefits such as combining events with transactions and security. .NET Enterprise Services are beyond the scope of this book, but you can read about it in my book, *COM and .NET Component Services*, (O'Reilly & Associates). LCE is described in depth in Chapters 9 and 10 of that book.

support infrastructure. Another event-related technique (publishing events asynchronously) is discussed in Chapter 7.

Defining Delegate Signatures

Although technically, a delegate declaration can define any method signature, in practice, event delegates should conform to specific guidelines.

First, the target methods should have a void return type only. For example, for an event dealing with a new value for a number, such a signature might be:

```
public delegate void NumberChangedEvent(int num);
```

The reason you should use a void return type is that it simply doesn't make any sense to return a value to the event publisher. What should the event publisher do with those values? The publisher has no idea why an event subscriber wants to subscribe in the first place. In addition, the delegate class hides the actual publishing act from the publisher. The delegate is the one iterating over its internal list of sinks (subscribing objects), calling each corresponding method. The returned values aren't propagated to the publisher's code. The same logic for using the void return type also suggests that you should avoid output parameters that use either the ref or out parameter modifiers because the output parameters of the various subscribers don't propagate to the publisher.

Second, some subscribers will probably want to receive the same event from multiple event-publishing sources. Because there is no flexibility in providing as many methods as publishers, the subscriber would like to provide the same method to multiple publishers. For the subscriber to distinguish between different publishers, the signature should contain the publisher's identity. The easiest and most generic way to do this is to add a parameter of type object, called the *sender* parameter:

```
public delegate void NumberChangedEvent(object sender,int num);
```

A publisher simply passes itself as the sender (using this in C# or Me in Visual Basic.NET).

Finally, defining actual event arguments (such as int num) couples publishers to subscribers because the subscriber has to expect a particular set of arguments. If you wish to change these arguments in the future, such a change affects all subscribers. To contain the impact of an argument change, .NET provides a generic event arguments container, the EventArgs class that you can use in place of a specific list of arguments. The EventArgs class definition is as follows:

```
public class EventArgs
{
    public static readonly EventArgs Empty;
    static EventArgs()
    {
        Empty = new EventArgs();
    }
    public EventArgs(){}
}
```

Instead of specific event arguments, pass in an EventArgs object:

```
public delegate void NumberChangedEvent(object sender, EventArgs eventArgs);
```

If the publisher has no need for an argument, simply pass in EventArgs.Empty, taking advantage of the static constructor and the static read-only Empty class member.

If the event requires arguments, derive a class from EventArgs, such as NumberChangedEventArgs; add member variables, methods, or properties as required; and pass in the derived class. The subscriber should downcast the generic EventArgs to the specific argument class associated with this event (NumberChangedEventArgs, in this example) and access the arguments. Example 6-3 demonstrates an EventArgs-derived class.

Example 6-3. Events arguments using an EventArgs-derived class

```
public delegate void NumberChangedEvent(object sender, EventArgs eventArgs);

public class NumberChangedEventArgs : EventArgs
{
   public int Num;//This should really be a property
}
public class MySource
{
   public event NumberChangedEvent NewNumberEvent;
   public void FireNewNumberEvent(EventArgs eventArgs)
   {
      //Always check delegate for null before using:
      if(NewNumberEvent!= null)
         NewNumberEvent(this,eventArgs);
   }
}
public class MySink
{
   public void OnNewNumber(object sender,EventArgs eventArgs)
   {
      NumberChangedEventArgs numberArg = (NumberChangedEventArgs)eventArgs;
      string msg = numberArg.Num.ToString();
      MessageBox.Show("The new number is "+ msg);
   }
}
//Client side code
MySource source = new MySource();
MySink   sink  = new MySink();
source.NewNumberEvent += new NumberChangedEvent(sink.OnNewNumber);

NumberChangedEventArgs numArg = new NumberChangedEventArgs();
numArg.Num = 4;

//Note that the source can publish without knowing the argument type
source.FireNewNumberEvent(numArg);
```

Deriving a class from EventArgs to pass specific arguments allows you to add arguments, remove unused arguments, derive yet another class from EventArgs, and so on, without forcing a change on the subscribers.

Because the resulting delegate definition is now so generic, .NET provides the EventHandler delegate:

```
public delegate void EventHandler(object sender,EventArgs eventArgs);
```

EventHandler is used extensively by the .NET application frameworks, such as Windows Forms and ASP.NET.

 The convention for the sink's event-handling method name is On<EventName>, which makes the code standard and readable.

Defining Custom Event Arguments

As explained in the preceding section, you should provide arguments to an event handler in a class derived from EventArgs and have the arguments as class members. The delegate class simply iterates over its list of subscribers, passing the argument object from one sink to the next. However, nothing prevents a particular subscriber from modifying the argument values and thus affecting all succeeding subscribers that handle the event. Usually, you should prevent subscribers from modifying these members as the event argument object is passed from one subscriber to the next. To preclude changing the arguments, either provide access to them as read-only properties or expose them as public members and apply the readonly access modifier. In both cases, you should initialize the argument values in the constructor. Example 6-4 shows both techniques.

Example 6-4. Preventing subscribers from modifying parameters in the argument class

```
public class NumberEventArgs1 : EventArgs
{
   public readonly int Num;
   NumberEventArgs1(int num)
   {
      Num = num;
   }
}
public class NumberEventArgs2 : EventArgs
{
   protected int m_Num;

   NumberEventArgs2(int num)
   {
      m_Num = num;
   }
   int Num
   {
      get
      {
```

Example 6-4. Preventing subscribers from modifying parameters in the argument class (continued)

```
        return m_Num;
      }
   }
}
```

Publishing Events Defensively

A C# publisher should always check an event delegate for null before attempting to publish. If no client has subscribed to the event, the delegate's target list will be empty and the delegate value set to null. When the publisher tries to access a nulled delegate, an exception is thrown. Visual Basic.NET developers don't need to check the value of the delegate because the RaiseEvent statement can accept an empty delegate without throwing an exception. Speaking of exceptions, the publisher has no way to know how disciplined the subscribers are. Some subscribers may encounter an exception in their handling of the event, not handle it, and cause the publisher to crash. For these reasons, you should always publish inside a try/catch block. Example 6-5 demonstrates these points.

Example 6-5. Defensive publishing

```
public class MySource
{
   public event EventHandler MyEvent;
   public void FireEvent()
   {
      try
      {
         if(MyEvent != null)
            MyEvent(this,EventArgs.Empty);
      }
      catch
      {
         //handle exceptions
      }
   }
}
```

However, the code in Example 6-5 aborts the event publishing in case a subscriber throws an exception. Sometimes you want to continue publishing even if a subscribers throws an exception. To do so, you need to manually iterate over the internal delegate list maintained by the delegate and catch any exception thrown by the individual delegates in the list. You access the internal list by using a special method every delegate supports called GetInvocationList( ), which is defined as:

```
   public virtual Delegate[ ] GetInvocationList( );
```

GetInvocationList( ) returns a collection of delegates you can iterate over, as shown in Example 6-6.

Example 6-6. Continuous publishing in the face of exceptions thrown by the subscribers

```
public class MySource
{
   public event EventHandler MyEvent;
   public void FireEvent()
   {
      if(MyEvent == null)
      {
         return;
      }
      Delegate[] delegates = MyEvent.GetInvocationList();
      foreach(Delegate del in delegates)
      {
         EventHandler sink = (EventHandler)del;
         try
         {
            sink(this,EventArgs.Empty);
         }
         catch{}
      }
   }
}
```

The problem with the publishing code in Example 6-6 is that it isn't generic, and you have to duplicate it each time you want fault isolation between the publisher and the subscribers. It's possible, however, to write a generic helper class that can publish to any delegate, pass any argument collection, and catch potential exceptions. Example 6-7 shows the EventsHelper class, which provides the static Fire() method that defensively fires any type of event.

Example 6-7. The EventsHelper class

```
public class EventsHelper
{
   public static void Fire(Delegate del,params object[] args)
   {
      if(del == null)
      {
         return;
      }
      Delegate[] delegates = del.GetInvocationList();
      foreach(Delegate sink in delegates)
      {
         try
         {
            sink.DynamicInvoke(args);
         }
         catch{}
      }
   }
}
```

There are two key elements to implementing EventsHelper. The first is its ability to invoke any delegate. This is possible using the DynamicInvoke() method that every delegate provides. DynamicInvoke() is defined as:

```
public object DynamicInvoke(object[ ] args);
```

DynamicInvoke() invokes the delegate, passing it a collection of arguments. The second key in implementing EventsHelper is passing it an open-ended number of objects as arguments for the subscribers. This is done using the C# param parameter modifier (ParamArray in Visual Basic.NET), which allows simple inlining of objects as parameters.

As a result, using EventsHelper is elegant and straightforward: simply pass it the delegate to invoke and the parameters. For example, for the delegate SomeDelegate defined as:

```
public delegate void SomeDelegate(int num,string str);
```

the following can be the publishing code:

```
public class MySource
{
    public event SomeDelegate SomeEvent;
    public void FireEvent(int num, string str)
    {
        EventsHelper.Fire(SomeEvent,num,str);
    }
}
```

When using EventsHelper from Visual Basic .NET, you need to use the matching compiler-generated member variable name concatenated with the word Event:

```
Public Delegate Sub SomeDelegate (ByVal num As Integer, ByVal str As String)
Public Class MySource
    Public Event SomeEvent As SomeDelegate
    Public Sub FireEvent (ByVal num As Integer, ByVal str As String)
        EventsHelper.Fire(SomeEventEvent, num, str)
    End Sub
End Class
```

Event Accessors

To hook a subscriber up to a publisher, you access the publisher's event member variable directly. Exposing class members in public is asking for trouble; it violates the core object-oriented principal of encapsulation and information hiding, and couples all subscribers to the exact member variable definition. To mitigate this problem, C# provides a property-like mechanism called an *event accessor*. Accessors provide a benefit similar to that of properties—hiding the actual class member, while maintaining the original ease of use. C# uses add and remove to encapsulate the actual event member variable, performing the += and -= operators, respectively. Example 6-8 demonstrates event accessors and the corresponding client code.

Example 6-8. Using event accessors

```
public class MySource
{
    protected event EventHandler m_MyEvent;
    public event EventHandler MyEvent
    {
        add
        {
            m_MyEvent += value;
        }
        remove
        {
            m_MyEvent -= value;
        }
    }
    public void FireEvent()
    {
        m_MyEvent(this,EventArgs.Empty);
    }
}
public class MySink
{
    public void OnEvent(object sender,EventArgs eventArgs)
    {
        MessageBox.Show("Event Received");
    }
}
//Client code:
MySource source = new MySource();
MySink   sink   = new MySink();

//Setup connection:
source.MyEvent += new EventHandler(sink.OnEvent);
//Fire Event
source.FireEvent();
//Teardown connection:
source.MyEvent -= new EventHandler(sink.OnEvent);
```

 In the current release of .NET, Visual Basic.NET doesn't have event accessors (only C# supports it). This may change in future releases.

Managing Large Number of Events

Imagine a class that publishes a very large number of events. This situation is common when developing frameworks. For example, the class Control in the System. Windows.Forms namespace has events corresponding to most Windows messages—a huge number, by any account. The problem with handling numerous events is that it's simply impractical to allocate a class member for each event: the class definition, documentation, CASE tool diagrams, and even IntelliSense will be unmanagable. To address this predicament, .NET provides the EventHandlerList class (found in the System.ComponentModel namespace):

```
public sealed class EventHandlerList : IDisposable
{
    public EventHandlerList();
    public Delegate this[object key] { get; set; }
    public void AddHandler(object key, Delegate value);
    public void RemoveHandler(object key, Delegate value);
    public virtual void Dispose();
}
```

EventHandlerList is a linear list that stores value/key pairs. The key is a generic object that identifies the event, and the value is an instance of System.Delegate. Because the index is an object, it can be an integer index, a string, a particular button instance and so on. You add and remove event-handling methods using the AddHandler and RemoveHandler methods, respectively. To fire an event, you access the event list using the indexer with the key object, and you get back a System.Delegate object. Downcast that delegate to the actual event delegate and fire the event.

Example 6-9 demonstrates using the EventHandlerList class when implementing a Windows Forms-like button class called MyButton. The button supports many events, such as mouse click and mouse move, all channeled to the same event list. Using event accessors, this is completely encapsulated from the clients. MyButton uses protected helper methods to fire the events.

Example 6-9. Using the EventHandlerList class to manage a large number of events

```
using System.ComponentModel;

public class MyButton
{
    EventHandlerList m_EventList;
    public MyButton()
    {
        m_EventList = new EventHandlerList();
        /* Rest of the initialization */
    }
    public event EventHandler Click
    {
        add
        {
            m_EventList.AddHandler("Click",value);
        }
        remove
        {
            m_EventList.RemoveHandler("Click",value);
        }
    }
```

Example 6-9. Using the EventHandlerList class to manage a large number of events (continued)

```
public event MouseEventHandler MouseMove
{
    add
    {
        m_EventList.AddHandler("MouseMove",value);
    }
    remove
    {
        m_EventList.RemoveHandler("MouseMove",value);
    }
}
protected void FireClick()
{
    EventHandler handler = (EventHandler)m_EventList["Click"];
    handler(this,EventArgs.Empty);
}
protected void FireMouseMove(MouseButtons button,int clicks,int x,int y,int delta)
{
    MouseEventHandler handler = (MouseEventHandler)m_EventList["MouseMove"];
    MouseEventArgs args = new MouseEventArgs(button,clicks,x,y,delta);
    handler(this,args);
}
/* Other methods and events definition */
}
```

The problem with Example 6-9 is that events such as mouse move or even mouse click are raised frequently, and creating a new string as a key for each invocation increases the pressure on the managed heap. A better approach would be to use preallocated keys, stored as class member variables:

```
public class MyButton
{
    EventHandlerList m_EventList;
    object m_MouseMoveEventKey = new object();

    public event MouseEventHandler MouseMove
    {
        add
        {
            m_EventList.AddHandler(m_MouseMoveEventKey,value);
        }
        remove
        {
            m_EventList.RemoveHandler(m_MouseMoveEventKey,value);
        }
    }
    private void FireMouseMove(MouseButtons button,int clicks,int x,int y,int delta)
    {
        MouseEventHandler handler;
        handler = (MouseEventHandler)m_EventList[m_MouseMoveEventKey];
```

```
        MouseEventArgs args = new MouseEventArgs(button,clicks,x,y,delta);
        handler(this,args);
    }
    /* Rest of the implementation  */
}
```

Writing Sink Interfaces

By hiding the actual event members, event accessors provide barely enough encapsulation. However, you can still improve this model. To illustrate: what if a subscriber wishes to subscribe to a set of events? Why should it make multiple potentially expensive calls to set up and tear down the connections? Why does the subscriber need to know about the event accessors in the first place? What if the subscriber wants to receive events on an entire interface, instead of individual methods? The next step is to provide a simple but generic way to manage the connections between the publisher and the subscribers, one that would save the redundant calls, encapsulate the event accessors and members, and allow sinking interfaces. This section describes a technique I have developed to do just that. Consider an interface that defines a set of events, the IMySink interface:

```
public interface IMySink
{
    void OnEvent1(object sender,EventArgs eventArgs);
    void OnEvent2(object sender,EventArgs eventArgs);
    void OnEvent3(object sender,EventArgs eventArgs);
}
```

Anybody can implement this interface, and the interface is really all the publisher should know about:

```
public class MySink :IMySink
{
    public void OnEvent1(object sender,EventArgs eventArgs)
    {...}
    public void OnEvent2(object sender,EventArgs eventArgs)
    {...}
    public void OnEvent3(object sender,EventArgs eventArgs)
    {...}
}
```

Next, define an enumeration of the events, an enum for each event, and mark the enum with the [Flags] attribute:

```
[Flags]
public enum EventType
{
    OnEvent1,
    OnEvent2,
    OnEvent3,
    OnAllEvents = OnEvent1|OnEvent2|OnEvent3
}
```

The [Flags] attribute indicates that the enum values could be used as a bit mask (see the EventType.OnAllEvents definition). This allows you to combine different enum values using the | (OR) bit-wise operator or mask them using the & (AND) operator.

The publisher provides two methods, Advise( ) and Unadvise( ), each of which accepts two parameters: the interface and a bit-mask flag to indicate which events to subscribe the sink interface to. Internally, the publisher could have an event delegate member per method on the sink interface or just one for all methods (it's an implementation detail, hidden from the subscribers). Example 6-10 uses an event member variable per method on the sink interface. It shows Advise( ) and Unadvise( ), as well as the FireEvent( ) method, with error handling removed for clarity. Advise( ) checks the flag and subscribes the corresponding interface method:

```
if((eventType & EventType.OnEvent1) == EventType.OnEvent1)
{
    m_Event1 += new EventHandler(sink.OnEvent1);
}
```

Unadvise( ) unsubscribes in a similar fashion.

Example 6-10. Sinking interfaces

```
public class MySource
{
    event EventHandler m_Event1;
    event EventHandler m_Event2;
    event EventHandler m_Event3;

    public void Advise(IMySink sink,EventType eventType)
    {
        if((eventType & EventType.OnEvent1) == EventType.OnEvent1)
        {
            m_Event1 += new EventHandler(sink.OnEvent1);
        }
        if((eventType & EventType.OnEvent2) == EventType.OnEvent2)
        {
            m_Event2 += new EventHandler(sink.OnEvent2);
        }
        //if ((EventType.OnEvent3...
    }
    public void Unadvise(IMySink sink,EventType eventType)
    {
        if((eventType & EventType.OnEvent1) == EventType.OnEvent1)
        {
            m_Event1 -= new EventHandler(sink.OnEvent1);
        }
        if((eventType & EventType.OnEvent2) == EventType.OnEvent2)
        {
            m_Event2 -= new EventHandler(sink.OnEvent2);
        }
        //if ((EventType.OnEvent3...
    }
```

Example 6-10. Sinking interfaces (continued)

```
    public void FireEvent(EventType eventType)
    {
        if((eventType & EventType.OnEvent1) == EventType.OnEvent1)
        {
            m_Event1(this,EventArgs.Empty)
        }
        if((eventType & EventType.OnEvent2) == EventType.OnEvent2)
        {
            m_Event2(this,EventArgs.Empty);
        }
        //if ((EventType.OnEvent3...
    }
}
```

The code required for advising or unadvising is equally straightforward:

```
MySource source = new MySource( );
IMySink  sink   = new MySink( );
//subscribe to events 1 and 2:
source.Advise(sink,EventType.OnEvent1|EventType.OnEvent2);
//Fire just event 1
source.FireEvent(EventType.OnEvent1);
```

Still, it shows the elegance of this approach for sinking whole interfaces with one call and how completely encapsulated the actual event class members are.

CHAPTER 7

Asynchronous Calls

When a method call is made on an object, typically the client is blocked while the object executes the call, and control returns to the client only when the method completes execution and returns. However, there are quite a few cases in which you want to call methods asynchronously; that is, you want control to return immediately to the client while the object executes the called method in the background, and then somehow lets the client know that the method has completed execution. Such an execution mode is called *asynchronous method invocation*, and the action is known as an *asynchronous call*. Asynchronous calls allow you to improve availability, increase throughput and performance, and scale up your application.

In the past, developers often had to handcraft a proprietary mechanism for asynchronously invoking calls on their components. One recurring mechanism was to have the object spin off a worker thread to process the client's request and immediately return control to the client. The object would later signal the client somehow when the call completed (if the client wanted to know), and the client had to distinguish between multiple method completions. These mechanisms were difficult to develop and test, and they forced developers to spend a disproportionate amount of their time reinventing the wheel instead of adding business value to the application. In addition, such solutions coupled the clients to the objects and were not consistently designed or implemented. Different vendors provided slightly different solutions, requiring at times different programming models on the client side. This predicament diminished the benefits of component-oriented programming because the component developer had to make some assumptions about the client's way of using the component, and vice versa.

The .NET mechanism for asynchronous calls is a mainstream facility used consistently and pervasively across the .NET application frameworks and base classes. .NET asynchronous calls are an essential addition to your arsenal as a component developer because implementing robust asynchronous execution on your own is a demanding task, requiring a lot of effort spent on design, implementation, and testing. By providing support for asynchronous calls, .NET lets you focus on the domain problems at hand, rather than on complicated asynchronous plumbing. Because .NET asynchronous calls are based on delegates, the chapter first takes a closer look at delegates, and then proceeds to describe how to best use .NET asynchronous calls.

Requirements for an Asynchronous Mechanism

To make the most of the various options available with .NET asynchronous calls, you first need to understand the generic requirements set for any modern component-oriented asynchronous calls support. These include the following:

- The first requirement is that the same component code should be used for both synchronous and asynchronous invocation. This allows component developers to focus on its business logic and facilitates using a standard mechanism.

- A corollary of the first requirement is that the client should be the one to decide whether to call a component synchronously or asynchronously. That in turn implies that the client will have different code for each case (whether to invoke the call synchronously or asynchronously).

- The client should be able to issue multiple asynchronous calls and have multiple asynchronous calls in progress. The client should be able to distinguish between multiple method completions.

- By that same token, the component should be able to serve multiple concurrent calls.

- When component methods have output parameters or return values, these parameters aren't available when control returns to the client. The client should have a way to get these parameters or results when the method completes.

- Similarly, errors on the component's side should be propagated to the client side. An exception thrown during the method execution should be played back to the client later on.

- The last item is less of a requirement and more of a design guideline: the asynchronous-calls mechanism should be straightforward and simple to use. For example, the mechanism should hide its implementation details such as the worker threads used to dispatch the call, as much as possible.

The client has a variety of options for handling method completion, all of which support these requirements. The client issues an asynchronous method call and then can choose to:

- Perform some work while the call is in progress, and then block until completion.

- Perform some work while the call is in progress, and then poll for completion.

- Receive notification when the method has completed. The notification will be in the form of a callback on a client-provided method. The callback should contain information identifying which method has just completed and its return values.

- Perform some work while the call is in progress, then wait for only a predetermined amount of time, and stop waiting, even if the method execution has not completed yet.

- Wait simultaneously for completion of multiple methods. The client can choose to wait for all or any of the pending calls to complete.

.NET offers all these options to clients, which can be confusing when you first start using asynchronous calls. This chapter will demonstrate each option and recommend when to use it. First, though, let's talk a little more about delegates.

Revisiting Delegates

As explained in Chapter 6, to the programmer, a delegate is nothing more than a type-safe method reference. The delegate (as the name implies) is used to delegate the act of calling a method on an object (or a static method on a class) from the client to the delegate class. For example, consider a Calculator class:

```
public class Calculator
{
    public int Add(int num1,int num2)
    {
        return num1+num2;
    }
    public int Subtract(int num1,int num2)
    {
        return num1-num2;
    }
    //Other methods
}
```

Instead of calling the Add( ) method directly, you can define a delegate called BinaryOperation :

```
public delegate int BinaryOperation(int num1,int num2);
```

You can use BinaryOperation to invoke the method:

```
Calculator calc = new Calculator( );
BinaryOperation oppDel;
oppDel = new BinaryOperation(calc.Add);//can use += as well
int result = 0;
result = oppDel(2,3);
Debug.Assert(result == 5);
```

By default, when you use a delegate to invoke methods, the delegate blocks the caller until all target methods return. In the example just shown, the caller is blocked until Add( ) returns. However, the delegate can also be used to invoke its target method asynchronously. The truth is that there isn't really anything special about delegates because delegates are actually compiled to classes. When you define a delegate type, the compiler converts the delegate declaration to a sophisticated signature-specific class definition and inserts that class instead of the delegate definition. For example, instead of this delegate definition:

```
public delegate int BinaryOperation(int num1,int num2);
```

the compiler generates this class definition:

```
public class BinaryOperation: System.MulticastDelegate
{
    public BinaryOperation(Object target,int methodPtr)
    {...}
    public virtual int Invoke(int num1,int num2)
    {...}
    public virtual IAsyncResult BeginInvoke(int num1,int num2,
                                     AsyncCallback callback,object asyncState)
    {...}
    public virtual int EndInvoke(IAsyncResult result)
    {...}
}
```

When you use the delegate simply to invoke a method, such as in this code:

```
Calculator calc = new Calculator();
BinaryOperation oppDel;
oppDel = new BinaryOperation(calc.Add);
oppDel(2,3);
```

or, in Visual Basic.NET:

```
Dim calc As New Calculator()
Dim oppDel As BinaryOperation
oppDel = New BinaryOperation(AddressOf calc.Add)
oppDel(2, 3)
```

the compiler converts the call to oppDel(2,3) to a call to the Invoke() method. The Invoke() method blocks the caller, executes the method on the caller's thread, and returns control to the caller.

> The C# compiler doesn't let you call Invoke() directly, even though it's a public method.

The compiler-generated BinaryOperation class derives from a class called MulticastDelegate, which is defined in the System namespace. The compiler also declares two methods that manage asynchronous method invocation. These methods are BeginInvoke() and EndInvoke(), and the proper use of them is the subject of this chapter.

Asynchronous Call Programming Models

To support asynchronous invocation, multiple threads are required. However, it would be a waste of system resources and a performance penalty if .NET spun off a new thread for every asynchronous method invocation. A better approach is to use a pool of already created worker threads. .NET has just such a pool, called the *.NET thread pool*. What is nice about the .NET way of supporting asynchronous calls is that it hides this interaction completely. There are quite a few programming models available when dealing with asynchronous calls, all of which comply with the general requirements set at the beginning of the chapter. In general, BeginInvoke( ) initiates an asynchronous method invocation. The calling client is blocked only for the briefest moment—the time it takes to queue up a request for a thread from the thread pool to execute the method—and then control returns to the client. EndInvoke( ) manages method completion, specifically, retrieving output parameters and return values as well error handling.

Using BeginInvoke( ) and EndInvoke( )

The compiler-generated BeginInvoke( ) and EndInvoke( ) methods take this form:

```
public virtual IAsyncResult BeginInvoke(<input and input/output parameters>,
                          AsyncCallback callback,
                          object asyncState);
public virtual <return value> EndInvoke(<output and input/output parameters>,
                          IAsyncResult asyncResult);
```

BeginInvoke( ) accepts the input parameters of the original signature the delegate defines. Input parameters include both value types passed by reference (using out or ref modifiers) and reference types. The original method's return values and any explicit output parameters are part of the EndInvoke( ) method. For example, for this delegate definition:

```
public delegate string MyDelegate(int num1,out int num2,ref int num3,object obj);
```

the corresponding BeginInvoke( ) and EndInvoke( ) methods look like this:

```
public virtual IAsyncResult BeginInvoke(int num1,out int num2,ref int num3,
                          object obj,AsyncCallback callback,
                                   object asyncState);
public virtual string EndInvoke(out int num2,ref int num3,
                               IAsyncResult asyncResult);
```

BeginInvoke( ) accepts two additional input parameters, not present in the original delegate signature: AsyncCallback callback and object asyncState. The callback parameter is actually a delegate object representing a reference to a callback method that receives the method completed notification event. asyncState is a generic object that passes in whatever state information is needed by the party handling the method completion. These two parameters are optional: the caller can choose to pass in null instead of either one of them. For example, to asynchronously invoke the Add( )

method of the Calculator class, if you have no interest in the result and no interest in a callback method or state information, you write:

```
Calculator calc = new Calculator();
BinaryOperation oppDel;

oppDel = new BinaryOperation(calc.Add);
oppDel.BeginInvoke(2,3,null,null);
```

The object itself is unaware that the client is using a delegate to asynchronously invoke the method. The same object code handles both the synchronous and the asynchronous invocation cases. As a result, every .NET class supports asynchronous invocation. Note that the class must still comply with certain design guidelines described in this chapter, even though the compiler will compile it even if it doesn't.

Because delegates can be used on both instance and static methods, clients can use BeginInvoke() to asynchronously call static methods as well. The remaining question is, how would you get the results of the method?

The IAsyncResult interface

Every BeginInvoke() method returns an object implementing the IAsyncResult interface, defined as:

```
public interface IAsyncResult
{
    object AsyncState { get; }
    WaitHandle AsyncWaitHandle { get; }
    bool CompletedSynchronously { get; }
    bool IsCompleted { get; }
}
```

You will see a few uses for the properties of IAsyncResult later on. For now, it's sufficient to know that the returned IAsyncResult object uniquely identifies the method that was invoked using BeginInvoke(). You can pass the IAsyncResult object to EndInvoke() to identify the specific asynchronous method execution from which you wish to retrieve the results. Example 7-1 shows the entire sequence.

Example 7-1. Simple asynchronous execution sequence

```
Calculator calc = new Calculator();
BinaryOperation oppDel;

oppDel = new BinaryOperation(calc.Add);

IAsyncResult asyncResult1 = oppDel.BeginInvoke(2,3,null,null);
IAsyncResult asyncResult2 = oppDel.BeginInvoke(4,5,null,null);

/*Do some work */

int result;
```

Example 7-1. Simple asynchronous execution sequence (continued)

```
result = oppDel.EndInvoke(asyncResult1);
Debug.Assert(result == 5);

result = oppDel.EndInvoke(asyncResult2);
Debug.Assert(result == 9);
```

Visual C# .NET IntelliSense doesn't detect either `BeginInvoke()` or `EndInvoke()`. You must always enter both manually.

As simple as Example 7-1 is, it does demonstrate a few key points. The most important of these is that because the primary use of `EndInvoke()` is to retrieve any output parameters as well as the method return value, `EndInvoke()` blocks its caller until the method it waits for (identified by the `IAsyncResult` object passed in) returns. The second point is that the same delegate object (with exactly one target method) can invoke multiple asynchronous calls on the target method. The caller can distinguish among the different pending calls using each unique `IAsyncResult` object returned from `BeginInvoke()`. In fact, when the caller makes asynchronous calls, as in Example 7-1, the caller must save the `IAsyncResult` objects. In addition, the caller should make no assumption about the order in which the pending calls complete. Remember: the asynchronous calls are carried out on threads from the thread pool, and because of thread context-switches (as well as internal pool management and bookkeeping), it's quite possible the second call will complete before the first one.

There are other uses for the `IAsyncResult` object besides passing it to `EndInvoke()`: you can use it to get the state object parameter of `BeginInvoke()`, you can wait for the method completion, and you can get the original delegate used to invoke the call. You will see how to do all that later on.

Although it isn't evident in Example 7-1, there are three important programming points you must always remember when using delegate-based asynchronous calls:

- `EndInvoke()` can be called only once for each asynchronous operation. Trying to call it more than once results in an exception of type `InvalidOperationException`.
- Although in general, the compiler-generated delegate class can manage multiple targets, when you use asynchronous calls, the delegate is allowed to have exactly one target method in its internal list. Calling `BeginInvoke()` when the delegate's list has more than one target will result in an `ArgumentException` being thrown, reporting that the delegate must have only one target.
- You can pass the `IAsyncResult` object to `EndInvoke()` only on the same delegate object used to dispatch the call. Passing the `IAsyncResult` object to a different delegate results in an exception of type `InvalidOperationException` stating: "The `IAsyncResult` object provided doesn't match this delegate." Example 7-2

demonstrates this point. It results in the exception, even though the other delegate targets the same method.

Example 7-2. Pass the IAsyncResult object only to the same delegate that invoked the call

```
Calculator calc = new Calculator();
BinaryOperation oppDel1;
BinaryOperation oppDel2;
oppDel1 = new BinaryOperation(calc.Add);
oppDel2 = new BinaryOperation(calc.Add);

IAsyncResult asyncResult = oppDel1.BeginInvoke(2,3,null,null);

//This will result in InvalidOperationException
oppDel2.EndInvoke(asyncResult);
```

To emphasize that the delegate can have only one target method in its list when used to invoke an asynchronous call, I recommend using the = operator to add the target method to the delegate list:

```
Binary Operation oppDel;
oppDel = new BinaryOperation(calc.Add);
```

although the += operator works just as well:

```
Binary Operation oppDel = null;
oppDel += new BinaryOperation(calc.Add);
```

Another advantage to using the = operator is that you don't need to initialize the delegate object before assigning it.

The AsyncResult class

Often, one client initiates an asynchronous call, but another calls EndInvoke(). Even when only one client is involved, it's likely to call BeginInvoke() in one code section (or method) and EndInvoke() in another. It's bad enough that you have to either save the IAsyncResult object or pass it to another client. It would be even worse if you had to do the same for the delegate object that invokes the asynchronous call, just because you needed that delegate to call EndInvoke(). Fortunately, there is an easier solution available because the IAsyncResult object itself carries with it the delegate that created it. When BeginInvoke() returns the IAsyncResult reference, it's actually an instance of a class called AsyncResult, defined as:

```
public class AsyncResult : IAsyncResult, IMessageSink
{
    //IAsyncResult implementation
    public object      AsyncState {virtual get; }
    public WaitHandle AsyncWaitHandle {virtual get; }
    public bool        CompletedSynchronously {virtual get; }
    public bool        IsCompleted {virtual get; }
```

```
        //Other properties
        public bool EndInvokeCalled {get; set; }
        public object AsyncDelegate {virtual get; }

        /* IMessageSink implementation  */
    }
```

AsyncResult is found in the System.Runtime.Remoting.Messaging namespace. AsyncResult has a property called AsyncDelegate, which, as you might guess, is a reference to the original delegate that dispatches the call. Example 7-3 shows how to use the AsyncDelegate property to call EndInvoke( ) on the original delegate.

Example 7-3. Using the AsyncDelegate property of AsynchResult to access the original delegate

```
using System.Runtime.Remoting.Messaging;

public class CalculatorClient
{
    IAsyncResult m_AsyncResult;

    public void AsynchAdd( )
    {
        Calculator calc = new Calculator( );
        DispatchAdd(calc,2,3);
        /* Do some work  */
        int result = GetResult( );
        Debug.Assert(result == 5);
    }
    protected void DispatchAdd(Calculator calc,int num1,int num2)
    {
        BinaryOperation oppDel;
        oppDel = new BinaryOperation(calc.Add);
        m_AsyncResult = oppDel.BeginInvoke(2,3,null,null);
    }
    protected int GetResult( )
    {
        int result = 0;

        //Obtain original delegate
        AsyncResult asyncResult = (AsyncResult)m_AsyncResult;
        BinaryOperation oppDel  = (BinaryOperation)asyncResult.AsyncDelegate;

        Debug.Assert(asyncResult.EndInvokeCalled == false);
        result = oppDel.EndInvoke(m_AsyncResult);
        return result;
    }
}
```

Note that because the AsyncDelegate property is of type object, you need to downcast it to the actual delegate type (BinaryOperation in Example 7-3).

Example 7-3 demonstrates using another useful property of AsyncResult—the Boolean EndInvokeCalled property. You can use it to verify that EndInvoke( ) hasn't been called:

```
Debug.Assert(asyncResult.EndInvokeCalled == false);
```

Asynchronous COM

Windows 2000 introduced *asynchronous COM* and the new [async_uuid] IDL interface attribute. This attribute caused the MIDL compiler to generate two interface definitions: one for synchronous calls and one for asynchronous calls. For every method on the normal synchronous interface, the asynchronous interface (named AsyncI<interface name>) had a method called Begin_<method name>, which dispatched the call asynchronously to the corresponding method. The Begin_<> method had only input parameters of the original method. The asynchronous interface also had a matching method, called Finish_<*method name*>, for every method on the original interface. It retrieved the output parameters and blocked the method completion. Asynchronous COM also supported a notification mechanism to signal the client upon method completion instead of polling using the Finish_<*method name*>. MIDL implemented asynchronous COM by generating a custom marshaling proxy and stub, which used threads from the RPC thread pool to dispatch the call. The major advantage of asynchronous COM was that the same component code could be used both synchronously and asynchronously, and you didn't have to waste time developing your own asynchronous method invocation mechanism. The disadvantages were that it was an esoteric mechanism and the majority of COM developers were not even aware it existed. In addition, it was supported only on Windows 2000 and above, had limitations on parameters types, and was difficult to use. However, the abstract principles of the mechanism and its design pattern (of using a tool to generate a standard solution for asynchronous support and using the same component code in both cases) were the right approach, and might have been the inspiration for the .NET architects.

Polling or Waiting for Completion

In the programming model described in the previous section, when a client calls EndInvoke( ), the client is blocked until the asynchronous method returns. This may be fine if the client has a finite amount of work to do while the call is in progress, and if, once that work is done, the client can't continue its execution without the returned value or the output parameters of the method, or even just the knowledge that the method call has completed. However, what if the client only wants to check if the method execution is completed? What if the client wants to wait for completion for a fixed timeout, do some additional finite processing, and then wait again? .NET supports these alternative programming models to calling EndInvoke( ).

The IAsyncResult interface object returned from BeginInvoke( ) has the AsyncWaitHandle property, of type WaitHandle. WaitHandle is actually a .NET wrapper around a native Windows waitable event handle. WaitHandle has a few overloaded wait methods. For example, the WaitOne( ) method returns only when the handle is signaled. Example 7-4 demonstrates using WaitOne( ).

Example 7-4. Using IAsynchResult.AsynchWaitHandle to block until method completion

```
Calculator calc = new Calculator( );
BinaryOperation oppDel;
oppDel = new BinaryOperation(calc.Add);

IAsyncResult asyncResult = oppDel.BeginInvoke(2,3,null,null);

/*Do some work */

asyncResult.AsyncWaitHandle.WaitOne( ); //This may block

int result;
result = oppDel.EndInvoke(asyncResult); //This will not block
Debug.Assert(result == 5);
```

Logically, Example 7-4 is identical to Example 7-1, which called only EndInvoke( ). If the method is still executing, WaitOne( ) will block. If by the time WaitOne( ) is called the method execution is complete, WaitOne( ) will not block, and the client proceeds to call EndInvoke( ) for the returned value. The important difference between Example 7-4 and Example 7-1 is that the call to EndInvoke( ) in Example 7-4 is guaranteed not to block its caller.

Example 7-5 demonstrates a more practical way of using WaitOne( ), by specifying the timeout (10 milliseconds in this example). When you specify a timeout, WaitOne( ) returns when the method execution is completed or when the timeout has elapsed, whichever two condition is met first.

Example 7-5. Using WaitOne() to specify wait timeout

```
Calculator calc = new Calculator( );
BinaryOperation oppDel;
oppDel = new BinaryOperation(calc.Add);

IAsyncResult asyncResult = oppDel.BeginInvoke(2,3,null,null);

while(asyncResult.IsCompleted == false)
{
   asyncResult.AsyncWaitHandle.WaitOne(10,false); //This may block
   /*Do some work */
}

int result;

result = oppDel.EndInvoke(asyncResult); //This will not block
```

When you specify a timeout, WaitOne() also accepts a Boolean flag, whose meaning is discussed in Chapter 8. Ignore that flag for now, as it bears no relevance to this discussion.

Example 7-5 uses another handy property of IAsyncResult, called IsCompleted. IsCompleted lets you find the status of the call without waiting or blocking. You can even use IsCompleted in a strict polling mode:

```
while(asyncResult.IsCompleted == false)
{
    /*Do some work */
}
```

This of course has all the adverse effects of polling (consuming CPU power for nothing), so you should generally avoid using IsCompleted this way. The AsyncWaitHandle property really shines when you use it to manage multiple concurrent asynchronous methods in progress. You can use the WaitHandle class's static WaitAll() method to wait for completion of multiple asynchronous methods, as shown in Example 7-6.

Example 7-6. Waiting for completion of multiple methods

```
Calculator calc = new Calculator();
BinaryOperation oppDel1;
BinaryOperation oppDel2;

oppDel1 = new BinaryOperation(calc.Add);
oppDel2 = new BinaryOperation(calc.Add);
IAsyncResult asyncResult1 = oppDel1.BeginInvoke(2,3,null,null);
IAsyncResult asyncResult2 = oppDel2.BeginInvoke(4,5,null,null);

WaitHandle[] handleArray = {asyncResult1.AsyncWaitHandle,asyncResult2.AsyncWaitHandle};

WaitHandle.WaitAll(handleArray);

int result;
//These calls to EndInvoke() will not block
result = oppDel1.EndInvoke(asyncResult1);
Debug.Assert(result == 5);

result = oppDel2.EndInvoke(asyncResult2);
Debug.Assert(result == 9);
```

To use WaitAll(), you need to construct an array of handles. Note that you still need to call EndInvoke() to access returned values. Instead of waiting for all the methods to return, you can choose to wait for any of them to return, using the WaitAny() static method of the WaitHandle class:

```
WaitHandle.WaitAny(handleArray);
```

Much like WaitOne(), both WaitAll() and WaitAny() have a few overloaded versions, which let you specify a timeout to wait instead of waiting indefinitely.

Using the Completion Callback Method

Instead of blocking, waiting, or polling for an asynchronously called method to complete, .NET also offers another programming model altogether: *callbacks*. The idea is simple: the client provides .NET with a method and requests that .NET call that method back when the asynchronous method completes. The client can provide a callback instance method or static method and have the same callback method handle completion of multiple asynchronous methods. The only requirement is that the callback method have the following signature:

```
<visibility modifier> void <Name>(IAsyncResult asyncResult);
```

The convention for a callback method name is to prefix it with On<>—for example, OnAsyncCallBack( ), OnMethodCompletion( ), and so on. Here is how the callback mechanism works: as explained previously, .NET uses a thread from the thread pool to execute the method dispatched via BeginInvoke( ). When the asynchronous method execution is completed, instead of quietly returning to the pool, the worker thread calls the callback method.

To use a callback method, the client needs to provide BeginInvoke( ) with a delegate that targets the callback method. That delegate is provided as the penultimate parameter to BeginInvoke( ) and is always of type AsyncCallback. AsyncCallback is a .NET-provided delegate from the System namespace, defined as:

```
public delegate void AsyncCallback(IAsyncResult asyncResult);
```

Example 7-7 demonstrates asynchronous call management by using a completion callback method.

Example 7-7. Managing asynchronous completion by using a completion method

```
public class CalculatorClient
{
   public void AsynchAdd( )
   {
      Calculator calc = new Calculator( );
      AsyncCallback callback;
      BinaryOperation oppDel;
      callback = new  AsyncCallback(OnMethodCompletion);
      oppDel   = new  BinaryOperation(calc.Add);
      oppDel.BeginInvoke(2,3,callback,null);
   }
   protected void OnMethodCompletion(IAsyncResult asyncResult)
   {
      int result = 0;

      AsyncResult resultObj = (AsyncResult)asyncResult;

      Debug.Assert(resultObj.EndInvokeCalled == false);
      BinaryOperation oppDel  = (BinaryOperation)resultObj.AsyncDelegate;
```

```
      result = oppDel.EndInvoke(asyncResult);
      Trace.WriteLine("Operation returned " + result.ToString( ));
   }
}
```

Unlike previous programming models described in this chapter when you use a completion callback method, there's no need to save the IAsyncResult object returned from BeginInvoke( ) because when .NET also calls the callback method, .NET provides the IAsyncResult object as a parameter. Note in Example 7-7 the use of a downcast of the IAsyncResult parameter to an AsyncResult class to get the original delegate that dispatched the call. You need that delegate to call EndInvoke( ). Because .NET provides a unique IAsyncResult object per asynchronous method, you can channel multiple asynchronous method completions to the same callback method, even by using the same AsyncCallback delegate:

```
      Calculator calc = new Calculator( );
      AsyncCallback callback
      callback = new  AsyncCallback(OnMethodCompletion);

      BinaryOperation oppDel1;
      BinaryOperation oppDel2;

      oppDel1   = new  BinaryOperation(calc.Add);
      oppDel1.BeginInvoke(2,3,callback,null);

      oppDel2   = new  BinaryOperation(calc.Add);
      oppDel2.BeginInvoke(4,5,callback,null);
```

Callback completion methods are by far the preferred model in any event-driven application. An *event-driven* application has methods that trigger events (or dispatch requests and post and process messages) and methods that handle these requests and fire their own events as a result. Writing an application as event-driven makes it easier to manage multiple threads, events, and messages, and allow for scalability, responsiveness, and performance. .NET asynchronous-calls management using callback completion methods fits into such an architecture like a hand in a glove. The other options (waiting, blocking, polling) are available for applications that are strict, predictable, and deterministic in their execution flow. I recommend that you use completion callback methods whenever possible.

Callback method and thread safety

Because the callback method is executed on a thread from the thread pool, you must provide for thread safety in the callback method and in the object that provides it. This means that you must use synchronization objects or locks to access the member variables of the object. You need to worry about synchronizing between the "normal" thread of the object and the worker thread from the pool, and potentially, synchronization between multiple worker threads all calling concurrently into the

---

callback method to handle their respective asynchronous method completion. You need to make sure the callback method is re-entrant and thread-safe. Thread safety and synchronization is covered in the next chapter.

Callback method visibility and binding

The callback method need not be public for .NET to call it because .NET uses reflection (discussed in Appendix C) and late binding to invoke the callback method. Late-binding invocation is unavoidable because the callback invocation is done by a worker thread object from the thread pool. That object was shipped with .NET and was never compiled against your completion method. In fact, delegates make it very easy to use late-binding invocation. Every delegate provides the DynamicInvoke( ) method, defined as:

```
public object DynamicInvoke(object[ ] args);
```

DynamicInvoke( ) takes advantage of reflection to bind to the target method and invoke it. In fact, any method invocation using a delegate internally uses DynamicInvoke( ). The worker thread simply calls DynamicInvoke( ) of the AsyncCallback delegate to invoke the callback method. For example, consider this completion method and callback delegate definition:

```
private OnAsyncCallBack(IAsyncResult asyncResult)
{...}

AsyncCallback callback;
callback = new  AsyncCallback(OnAsyncCallBack);
```

The code the worker thread uses to invoke the completion callback method is similar to this:

```
IAsyncResult asyncResult = null;
/* Some code to initialize asyncResult, such as BeginInvoke( ) */
object[ ] arg = {asyncResult};
callback.DynamicInvoke(arg);
```

The worker thread uses reflection and late binding to invoke the asynchronous method itself because it was also never compiled against the method.

Passing state information

I have ignored the last parameter to BeginInvoke( ), object asyncState, up until now when its use can be best appreciated. The asynchState object, known as a *state object* in .NET, is provided as a generic container for whatever need you deem fit. The party handling the method completion can access these container objects via the object AsyncState property of IAsyncResult. Although you can certainly use a state object with any of the .NET asynchronous models (blocking, waiting, or polling), it's most useful in conjunction with completion methods. The reason is simple: in all the other programming models, it's up to you to manage the IAsyncResult object, and managing an additional container isn't that much of an added liability. When you are using a completion callback, the container object offers the only way to pass in additional parameters to the callback method whose signature is predetermined by .NET. Example 7-8 demonstrates how you might use a state object to pass an integer value as an additional parameter to the completion callback method. Note that the callback method must downcast the AsyncState property to the actual type that Debug. Assert() expects.

Example 7-8. Passing an additional parameter using a state object

```
public class CalculatorClient
{
   public void AsynchAdd()
   {
      Calculator calc = new Calculator();
      AsyncCallback callback;
      BinaryOperation oppDel;
      int asyncState = 4;
      callback = new  AsyncCallback(OnMethodCompletion);
      oppDel   = new  BinaryOperation(calc.Add);
      oppDel.BeginInvoke(2,3,callback,asyncState);
   }
   protected void OnMethodCompletion(IAsyncResult asyncResult)
   {
      int asyncState;
      asyncState = (int)asyncResult.AsyncState;
      Debug.Assert(asyncState == 4);

      /*Rest of the callback  */
   }
}
```

Performing Asynchronous Operations Without Delegates

Delegate-based asynchronous calls like those described in the preceding sections let you asynchronously invoke any method, on any class. This technique provides valuable flexibility to a client, but requires that you define a delegate with a signature that matches the method you want to invoke. Sometimes certain operations, such as disk or network access, web requests, web service calls, or message queuing, are long in duration or even open-ended in their very nature. In such cases, you will usually opt to invoke the operations asynchronously. The designers of the .NET framework wanted to ease the task of performing such operations by building into the classes that offer them Begin<Operation> and End<Operation> methods. These methods always take a form very similar to the BeginInvoke() and EndInvoke() methods provided by a delegate class:

```
public <return type> <Operation>(<parameters>);
IAsyncResult Begin<Operation>(<input and input/output parameters>,
                                 AsyncCallback callback,
                                    object asyncState);
```

```
    public <return type> End<Operation>(<output and input/output parameters >
                                        IAsyncResult asyncResult);
```

For example, the abstract class `Stream` class defined in the `System.IO` namespace provides asynchronous `Read( )` and `Write( )` operations:

```
public abstract class Stream : MarshalByRefObject,IDisposable
{
    public virtual int Read(byte[ ]buffer,int offset,int count);
    public virtual IAsyncResult BeginRead(byte[ ]buffer,int offset,int count,
                                        AsyncCallback callback,object state);
    public virtual int EndRead(IAsyncResult asyncResult);

    public virtual void Write(byte[ ]buffer,int offset,int count);
    public virtual IAsyncResult BeginWrite(byte[ ]buffer,int offset,int count,
                                        AsyncCallback callback,object state);
    public virtual void EndWrite(IAsyncResult asyncResult);

    /* Other methods and properties */
}
```

The `Stream` class is the base class for all other stream classes, such as `FileStream`, `MemoryStream`, and `NetworkStream`. All the `Stream`-derived classes override these methods and provide their own implementation.

Another example of a class that provides its own asynchronous methods is the web service wrapper class that Visual Studio.NET automatically adds to a client project when the client adds a reference to a web service. Imagine that the `Calculator` class in the following code snippet exposes its methods, such as `Add( )`, as web services:

```
using System.Web.Services;

public class Calculator
{
    [WebMethod]
    public int Add(int num1,int num2)
    {
        return = num1+num2;
    }
    //Other methods
}
```

The wrapper class autogenerated for the client by Visual Studio .NET will contain `BeginAdd( )` and `EndAdd( )` methods that invoke the web service asynchronously:

```
using System.Web.Services.Protocols;

public class Calculator : SoapHttpClientProtocol
{
    public int Add(int num1,int num2)
    {...}
    public IAsyncResult BeginAdd(int num1,int num2,
                                AsyncCallback callback,object asyncState)
    {...}
```

```
    public int EndAdd(IAsyncResult asyncResult)
    {...}
    /* Other methods */
}
```

Using nondelegate-based asynchronous method calls is similar to using the
BeginInvoke( ) and EndInvoke( ) methods provided by a delegate class: you dispatch
the asynchronous operation using Begin<Operation> and can call End<Operation> to
block until completion, wait for the operation (or multiple operations) to complete,
or use a callback method. However, there is no uniform requirement to call
End<Operation> on the original object that dispatched the Begin<Operation> call.
With some classes (like web service wrapper classes or Stream-derived classes), you
can create a new object and call End<Operation> on it. Example 7-9 demonstrates this
technique when using a web-service wrapper class.

Example 7-9. Asynchronous web-service call with a completion callback

```
public class CalculatorWebServiceClient
{
    public void AsynchAdd( )
    {
        //Calculator here is the auto-generated wrapper class
        Calculator calc;
        calc  = new Calculator( );

        AsyncCallback callback;
        callback = new AsyncCallback(OnMethodCompletion);

        calc.BeginAdd(2,3,callback,null);
    }
    protected void OnMethodCompletion(IAsyncResult asyncResult)
    {
        //Calculator here is the auto-generated wrapper class
        Calculator calc;
        calc = new Calculator( );

        int result;
        result = calc.EndAdd(asyncResult);
        Trace.WriteLine("Operation returned " + result.ToString( ));
    }
}
```

Example 7-10 demonstrates asynchronous read operation on a FileStream object.
Note the passing of the useAsync parameter to the FileStream constructor, indicating
asynchronous operations on the stream.

Example 7-10. Asynchronous stream read with a completion callback

```
public class FileStreamClient
{
    public void AsynchRead( )
    {
```

```
    bool useAsync = true;
    Stream stream = new FileStream("MyFile.bin",FileMode.Open,FileAccess.Read,
                                              FileShare.None,1000,useAsync);

    AsyncCallback callback;
    callback = new  AsyncCallback(OnMethodCompletion);

    stream.BeginRead(m_Array,0,10,callback,null);
    stream.Close( );
}
protected void OnMethodCompletion(IAsyncResult asyncResult)
{
    bool useAsync = true;
    Stream stream = new FileStream("MyFile.bin",FileMode.Open,FileAccess.Read,
                                              FileShare.None,1000,useAsync);
    int bytesRead = stream.EndRead(asyncResult);
    stream.Close( );
    //Access m_Array
}
Byte[ ] m_Array = new Byte[2000];
```

Asynchronous Error Handling

Output parameters and returned values aren't the only elements unavailable at the time an asynchronous call is dispatched: exceptions are missing as well. After calling BeginInvoke( ), control returns to the client, but it may be some time until the asynchronous method encounters an error and throws an exception, and it may be some time after that until the client actually calls EndInvoke( ). .NET must therefore provide some way for the client to know an exception was thrown and be allowed to handle it. The .NET solution is straightforward: when the asynchronous method throws an exception, .NET catches that exception. When the client calls EndInvoke( ), .NET rethrows that exception object, letting the client handle the exception. If a callback method is provided, .NET calls the callback method immediately after the exception is thrown on the object side. For example, suppose the Calculator class has a Divide( ) method, defined as:

```
public class Calculator
{
    public int Divide(int num1,int num2)
    {
        return = num1/num2;
    }
    //Other methods
}
```

Divide( ) throws a DivideByZeroException if the denominator (num2) passed in is zero. Example 7-11 demonstrates how you might handle this error.

Example 7-11. Asynchronous error handling

```
public class CalculatorClient
{
   public void AsyncDivide( )
   {
      Calculator calc = new Calculator( );
      AsyncCallback callback;
      BinaryOperation oppDel;
      callback = new  AsyncCallback(OnMethodCompletion);
      oppDel  = new  BinaryOperation(calc.Divide);
      oppDel.BeginInvoke(2,0,callback,null);
   }
   private void OnMethodCompletion(IAsyncResult asyncResult)
   {
      AsyncResult resultObj = (AsyncResult)asyncResult;
      Debug.Assert(resultObj.EndInvokeCalled == false);
      BinaryOperation oppDel  = (BinaryOperation)resultObj.AsyncDelegate;
      try
      {
         int result = 0;
         result = oppDel.EndInvoke(asyncResult);
         Trace.WriteLine("Operation returned " + result.ToString( ));
      }
      catch(DivideByZeroException exception)
      {
         Trace.WriteLine(exception.Message);
      }
   }
}
```

 When you use a callback completion method, you must provide for error handling in the callback. The reason is that if the call to EndInvoke( ) results in an exception, and there is no error handling in place, the exception will be handled as the worker thread from the thread pool, and you will never know about it.

Asynchronous Events

The most common use for delegates in .NET is for event subscription and publishing. Example 7-12 contains a simple definition of an event source and sink.

Example 7-12. Event source and sink, using synchronous event publishing

```
public delegate void NumberChangedEvent(int num);

public class MySource
{
   public event NumberChangedEvent NumberChanged;
   public void FireEvent(int num)
   {
```

Example 7-12. Event source and sink, using synchronous event publishing (continued)

```
      NumberChanged(num);
   }
}
public class MySink
{
   public void OnNumberChanged(int num)
   {...}
}
```

Consider the following client code, which hooks sinks to the source and fires the event:

```
MySource source  = new MySource( );
MySink    sink1   = new MySink( );
MySink    sink2   = new MySink( );

source.NumberChanged += new NumberChangedEvent(sink1.OnNumberChanged);
source.NumberChanged += new NumberChangedEvent(sink2.OnNumberChanged);
source.FireEvent(3);
```

When a publisher fires an event, it's blocked until all the subscribers have finished handling the event, and only then does control return to the publisher. Disciplined and well-behaved subscribers should not perform any lengthy operation in their event-handling method because that prevents other subscribers from handling the event, not to mention blocking the publisher. The problem is, how would the publisher know if it's dealing with disciplined subscribers? The reality is, of course, that the subscriber can't tell. The solution is to fire the events asynchronously.

In the past, developers implemented an asynchronous event by publishing the event on a worker thread. The problem with a worker thread is that although it allows for asynchronous publishing, the publishing is serialized because the subscribers are notified one at a time. The proper solution is to use threads from a thread pool and try to publish to each subscriber on a different thread. This isolates the undisciplined subscribers and allows concurrent and asynchronous publishing. At this point, you probably think: what for? Why not simply use the built-in support delegates have for asynchronous invocation using threads from the pool? For example, the publisher in Example 7-12 could add a new method called FireEventAsync( ) and use BeginInvoke( ) to publish asynchronously:

```
public void FireEventAsync(int num)
{
    NumberChanged.BeginInvoke(num,null,null);//likely to raise exception
}
```

Unfortunately, you can't call BeginInvoke( ) on the event member directly because BeginInvoke( ) can be invoked only if the delegate's internal list of sink methods has just one target. As stated at the beginning of this chapter, if the delegate has more than one target, the delegate throws an exception of type ArgumentException. The workaround is to iterate over the delegate's internal invocation list, calling

BeginInvoke( ) on each one. Chapter 6 demonstrated how to access that list using the delegate's GetInvocationList( ) method:

```
public virtual Delegate[ ] GetInvocationList( );
```

GetInvocationList( ) returns a collection of delegates; each corresponds to a single target sink method, and therefore you can call BeginInvoke( ) on these delegates. Example 7-13 shows the correct implementation of the FireEventAsync( ) method. Note that you have to downcast the individual delegates to the actual delegate type. Note also that when you publish asynchronously, the publisher has no use for return value or output from the event handlers, and therefore EndInvoke( ) isn't used.

Example 7-13. Firing events asynchronously

```
public delegate void NumberChangedEvent(int num);

public class MySource
{
    public event NumberChangedEvent NumberChanged;

    public void FireEventAsync(int num)
    {
        Delegate[ ] delegates = NumberChanged.GetInvocationList( );
        foreach(Delegate del in delegates)
        {
            NumberChangedEvent sink = (NumberChangedEvent)del;
            sink.BeginInvoke(num,null,null);
        }
    }
}
```

The problem with Example 7-13 is that it isn't generic, and you have to repeat such code in every case in which you want to publish events asynchronously. Fortunately, you can come up with a generic helper method to automate asynchronous event publishing, as shown in Example 7-14.

Example 7-14. The EventsHelper class automates asynchronous event publishing

```
public class EventsHelper
{
    public static void FireAsync(Delegate del,params object[ ] args)
    {
        if(del == null)
        {
            return;
        }
        Delegate[ ] delegates = del.GetInvocationList( );
        AsyncFire asyncFire;
        foreach(Delegate sink in delegates)
        {
            asyncFire = new AsyncFire(InvokeDeleagte);
            asyncFire.BeginInvoke(sink,args,null,null);
```

Example 7-14. The EventsHelper class automates asynchronous event publishing (continued)

```
    }
  }
  delegate void AsyncFire(Delegate del,object[ ] args);

  static void InvokeDeleagte(Delegate del,object[ ] args)
  {
     del.DynamicInvoke(args);
  }
  //Synchronous publishing, discussed in Example 6-7
  public static void Fire(Delegate del,params object[ ] args)
  {...}
}
```

The technique shown in Example 7-14 is similar to that presented in Example 6-7: you use the param modifier to pass in any collection of arguments, as well as the delegate containing the subscribers list. The FireAsync( ) method iterates over the internal collection of the delegate passed in. For each delegate in the list, it uses another delegate of type AsyncFire to asynchronously call the private helper method InvokeDelegate( ). InvokeDelegate( ) simply uses the DynamicInvoke( ) method of the Delegate type to invoke the delegate.

Using EventHelper to publish events asynchronously is easy when compared to Example 7-13:

```
  public delegate void NumberChangedEvent(int num);

  public class MySource
  {
     public event NumberChangedEvent NumberChanged;

     public void FireEventAsync(int num)
     {
        EventsHelper.FireAsync(NumberChanged,num);
     }
  }
```

When using EventsHelper from Visual Basic .NET, you need to use the matching compiler-generated member variable name concatenated with the word Event, as shown in Chapter 6:

```
  Public Delegate Sub SomeDelegate (ByVal num AS Integer, ByVal str As String)
  Public Class MySource
     Public Event SomeEvent As SomeDelegate
     Public Sub FireEvent (ByVal num As Integer, ByVal str As String)
        EventsHelper.Fire(SomeEventEvent, num, str)
     End Sub
  End Class
```

> ### .NET Queued Components
>
> .NET's built-in support for asynchronous method invocation described in this chapter standardizes asynchronous calls and saves you writing a lot of error-prone plumbing code. Asynchronous calls in enterprise applications, however, often require additional support, such as disconnected work, error handling, auto-retry mechanisms, and transaction support. For such cases, .NET provides an advanced asynchronous call mechanism called Queued Components as part of its .NET Enterprise Services (`System.EnterpriseServices` namespace). Queued components use the Microsoft Message Queue (MSMQ) to queue an asynchronous call and transport it to the target server component. .NET queued components are beyond the scope of this book, but you can read about them in Chapters 8 and 10 of my book *COM and .NET Component Services*.

Asynchronous Invocation Pitfalls

By now you have probably come to appreciate the elegance of .NET asynchronous calls, and the ease with which you can turn a synchronous component and its client code into an asynchronous implementation. However, no technology is without its pitfalls. Following is a rundown of the technical pitfalls you are likely to encounter when using .NET asynchronous calls. There is also a major conceptual consequence when dealing with asynchronous calls rather than synchronous calls that deserve a dedicated section of its own at the end of this chapter.

Threading Concurrency and Synchronization

In using asynchronous method calls, you must be aware of potential problems concerning thread concurrency, state corruption, and reentrancy. An asynchronous method is invoked on a thread from the thread pool. At the same time, the called object may already be servicing a normal call from a synchronous client on another thread along with additional asynchronous calls (on different threads). A callback completion method is also a potential pitfall because it too is executed on a different thread and can have multiple threads calling it.

In general, you should invoke methods asynchronously only on thread-safe objects, that is, objects that don't allow multiple threads to access them concurrently. Even when using thread-safe objects, you must keep a watchful eye for race conditions and deadlocks. In addition, the object whose method you invoke asynchronously must not have *thread affinity* (i.e., it must not rely on always running on the same thread) or use thread-specific resources such as thread local storage or thread-relative static variables.

Thread Pool Exhaustion

.NET speeds up asynchronous calls by using threads from the thread pool. However, in the current release of .NET (Version 1.1), the pool isn't boundless. A pool with too many threads becomes a liability because the operating system wastes a lot of cycles just on thread context switches. If you have too many pending asynchronous method calls in progress, you may reach the pool's upper limit. At that point, no further asynchronous calls are dispatched, and all future asynchronous calls will in effect be serialized, waiting for worker threads to return to the pool. The default .NET thread pool is configured to use 25 threads per CPU. Avoid indiscriminate use of asynchronous calls or any long or blocking operations in the methods invoked asynchronously. Consider using your own worker thread in such cases.

Premature Access by Reference and Reference Types

If the asynchronous method signature contains value types passed by reference or reference types, even though these parameters will be part of the call to BeginInvoke( ), don't try to access these parameters before calling EndInvoke( ). Code can be especially error-prone when you use reference types as both in and output parameters. Example 7-15 demonstrates this point. In the example, the value of the X and Y member variables of the point object change silently between the call to BeginInvoke( ) and the return of EndInvoke( ). The only safe way to access the object passed as an incoming and outgoing parameter to BeginInvoke( ) is to call EndInvoke( ) first.

Example 7-15. Reference types have correct values only after the call to EndInvoke( )

```
public class MyPoint
{
   public int X;
   public int Y;
}

public delegate void MyDelegate(MyPoint obj);

public class MyClient
{
   public void Swap(MyPoint obj)
   {
      int temp = obj.X;
      obj.X = obj.Y;
      obj.Y = temp;
   }
   public void AsynchSwap( )
   {
      MyPoint point = new MyPoint ();
      point.X = 3;
      point.Y = 4;
```

```
    MyDelegate swapDel = new MyDelegate(Swap);
    IAsyncResult asyncResult = swapDel.BeginInvoke(point,null,null);

    //BeginInvoke() does not change value of reference types or value types
    //passed by reference
    Debug.Assert(point.X == 3);
    Debug.Assert(point.Y == 4);

    swapDel.EndInvoke(asyncResult);

    Debug.Assert(point.X == 4);
    Debug.Assert(point.Y == 3);
    }
}
```

Lengthy Constructors

The asynchronous invocation mechanism described in this chapter can be used only on methods. In .NET, constructors are always synchronous. This can pose a problem if a component's constructor performs operations that take a long time to complete (such as opening a database connection). In such cases, you should use the *two-phase create* pattern. First, put the trivial (and usually fast) code for initialization in the constructor, and then provide a separate method called Create() to perform the lengthy operations. This allows your clients to construct objects of your components asynchronously if they need to. A more advanced solution is to use a class factory and have the class factory expose methods such as Create() for synchronous instantiation and BeginCreate() and EndCreate() for asynchronous instantiation.

One-Way Methods

Normally, when a method is invoked asynchronously, .NET keeps track of the method completion event, the IAsyncResult object, the state object, and the exception (if one occurs). This implies that for every asynchronous method call, there is some overhead in terms of memory use and performance .NET supports defining *fire-and-forget* methods, using the OneWay attribute, which is defined in the System.Runtime.Remoting.Messaging namespace:

```
    using System.Runtime.Remoting.Messaging;

    public class MyClass
    {
        [OneWay]
        void FireandForget(int num)
        {
            /* Method body  */
        }
        /* Other class members  */

    }
```

When a one-way method is invoked asynchronously, .NET doesn't keep track of the method invocation, and there is no overhead in dispatching the call asynchronously. One-way methods semantically mean that the caller should not care what happens after calling the methods. The canonical example for fire-and-forget methods is broadcasting some event to subscribers. The event handling methods can be "fired and forgotten" because the event publisher doesn't really care what the event subscribers do with the event.

Another example involves methods such as the InvokeDeleagte( ) method of the EventsHelper class described in Example 7-14. InvokeDelegate( ) can be marked with the OneWay attribute because the client of EventsHelper doesn't care about the result of publishing the event:

```
public class EventsHelper
{
    [OneWay]
    static void InvokeDeleagte(Delegate del,object[ ] args)
    {
        del.DynamicInvoke(args);
    }
    //Rest of EventsHelper
}
```

Obviously, you should use the OneWay attribute only on methods with no output parameters and with void return type, although the compiler doesn't enforce that. One-way methods aren't asynchronous by nature, and if you want to invoke them asynchronously, you have to use a delegate. What is special about them is that after calling BeginInvoke( ), you should not call EndInvoke( ) or use a completion callback method. If you do call EndInvoke( ) on a one-way method invoked asynchronously, EndInvoke( ) returns immediately, even if the method is continuing to execute. If you use a completion callback, the callback is called immediately after BeginInvoke( ) on the same thread that called BeginInvoke( ), while the one-way method continues to execute on a thread from the pool. Any exception thrown by the one-way asynchronous method is never propagated to the client side.

Synchronous Versus Asynchronous Components

Although it's technically possible to call the same component synchronously and asynchronously, the likelihood that a component will be accessed both ways is low. The reason is that using a set of components asynchronously requires drastic changes to the workflow of the client program and, as a result, the client simply can't use the same execution sequence logic it would choose for synchronous access. Consider, for example, an online store application. Let's suppose the client (a server-side object executing the customer request) accesses a Store object, where it places the customer's order details. The Store object uses three well-factored helper components to process the order: Order, Shipment, and Billing. In a synchronous scenario, the Store object calls the Order object to place the order. Only if the Order object succeeds in processing the order (e.g., item is available in the inventory) does the Store object call the Shipment object. Only if the Shipment object succeeds does the Store object access the Billing component to bill the customer. This sequence is shown in Figure 7-1.

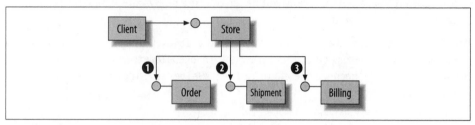

Figure 7-1. Synchronous processing of a client order

The downside to the pattern shown in Figure 7-1 is that the store must process orders synchronously and serially. On the surface, it might seem that if the Store component invoked its helper objects asynchronously, it could increase its throughput because it could process incoming orders as fast as they are submitted by the client.

The problem in doing so is that it's possible for the calls to the Order, Shipment, and Billing objects to fail independently. Because their methods are invoked in a nondeterministic order, depending on thread availability in the thread pool, overall system load, and so on, things can go wrong in many ways. For example, the Order object might discover there are no items in the inventory matching the customer request after the Billing object has already billed the customer for it.

Using asynchronous calls on a set of interacting components requires that you change your code and your workflow. To call the helper components asynchronously, the Store component should call only the Order object. The asynchronous call to the Shipment object should be done by the Order object, only if the order processing was successful (see Figure 7-2) to avoid the potential inconsistencies just mentioned. Similarly, only in the case of successful shipment should the Shipment object asynchronously call the Billing object.

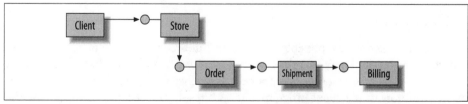

Figure 7-2. Revised workflow for asynchronous processing of a client order

In general, if you have more than one component in your asynchronous workflow, you should have each component invoke the next one in the logical execution sequence. Needless to say, such a programming model introduces tight coupling between components (they'll have to know about each other) and changes to their interfaces because you have to pass in additional parameters, which are required for the desired invocation of components downstream.

The conclusion from this simple example is that using asynchronous instead of synchronous invocation introduces major changes to the component interfaces and the client workflow. Asynchronous invocation on a component that was built for synchronous execution works only in isolated cases. When you're dealing with a set of interacting components, it's better to simply spin off a worker thread to call them and use the worker thread to provide asynchronous execution. This will preserve the component interfaces and the original client execution sequence. Of course, to do that, you need to understand .NET concurrency management and multithreading, subjects of the next chapter.

CHAPTER 8

Multithreading and Concurrency Management

In a single-threaded application, all operations, regardless of type, duration, or priority, execute on a single thread. Such applications are simple to design and build. All operations are serialized; that is, the operations never run concurrently but rather one at a time. However, there are many situations in which employing multiple threads of execution in your application will increase its performance, throughput, and scalability, and improve its responsiveness to users and clients. That said, multithreading is one of the most poorly understood and applied concepts of contemporary programming, and many developers tend to misuse the multithreading features and services available on their programming platforms.

This chapter begins with an explanation of .NET threads and shows you how to create and use them. You'll also learn how to spawn and manage multiple threads, develop multithreading-safe components, and avoid some of the common pitfalls of multithreaded programming. The second part of the chapter shows how to use .NET to synchronize the operations of multiple threads and manage concurrent attempts to access components. The chapter ends by describing several useful .NET multithreading services, including the thread pool, timers, and thread local storage.

Threads and Multithreading

In modern computing terminology, a *thread* is simply a path of execution within a process. Every application runs on at least one thread, which is initialized when the process within which the application runs is started up. The threads of an application always execute within the context provided by the application process. Typically, you find two kinds of operations in any application: CPU-bound and I/O-bound operations. *CPU-bound* operations use the machine's central processing unit (CPU) to perform intensive or repetitive computation. *I/O-bound* operations are tied to an input or output device such as a user-interface peripheral (keyboard, screen, mouse, or printer), a hard drive (or any nonmemory durable storage), a network or communication port, or any other hardware device.

It's often useful to create multiple threads within an application so that operations that are different in nature can be performed in parallel, and the machine's CPU (or CPUs) and devices can be used as efficiently as possible. An I/O-bound operation (such as disk access), for example, can take place concurrently with a CPU-bound operation (such as the processing of an image). As long as two I/O-bound operations don't use the same I/O device (such as disk access and network socket access), having them run on two different threads will improve your application's ability to efficiently handle these I/O devices and increase the application's throughput and performance. In the case of CPU-bound operations, on a single-CPU machine there is no performance advantage to allocating two distinct threads to run separate CPU-bound operations. You should definitely consider doing so on a multi-CPU machine because multithreading is the only way to use the extra processing power available through each additional CPU.

Modern applications are multithreaded almost without exception, and many of the features you take for granted would not be possible otherwise. For example, a responsive user interface implies multithreading. The application processes user requests (such as printing or connecting to a remote machine) on a different thread than the one employed for the user interface. If such requests were done by the same thread, the user interface would appear to be hung until the other requests were processed, but because the user interface is on a different thread, it can continue to respond to the user's requests. Multiple threads are also useful in applications that require high throughput. When your application needs to process incoming client requests as fast as it can, it's often advantageous to spin off a number of worker threads to handle requests in parallel.

Do not create multiple threads just for the sake of having them. You must examine your particular case carefully and evaluate all possible solutions. A decision to use multiple threads can open a Pandora's box of thread synchronization and component concurrency issues, as you'll see later in this chapter.

Components and Threads

A component-oriented application doesn't necessarily need to be multithreaded. The way in which an application is divided into components is unrelated to how many execution threads it uses. In any given application, you're as likely to have several components interacting with one another on a single thread of execution as you are to have multiple threads accessing a single component. What is special about component-oriented applications is the intricate synchronization issues inherited with the nature of component development and deployment. You will see later in this chapter how .NET addresses these challenges.

Working with Threads

In .NET, a *thread* is the basic unit of execution. .NET threads are managed code representations of the underlying threads of the operating system. Under the current version of .NET on Windows, .NET threads map one-to-one to Win32 native threads. This mapping can be changed in the future to use another implementation. For each thread, the operating system allocates registers, a program counter, a stack, and a stack pointer, and assigns it a time slot and a priority. The operating system (presently) is the one responsible for thread scheduling and thread context switches, as well as thread-manipulation requests such as suspend, resume, and sleep. .NET exposes some of the native thread properties (such as priority), It also associates managed-code properties with each thread, such as state, exception handlers, security principal (discussed in Chapter 12), name, and unique ID, as well as culture (required for localization).

The .NET class Thread defined in the System.Threading namespace represents a managed thread. The Thread class provides various methods and properties to control the managed thread.

 Calling the methods of the Thread class (be they static or instance methods) is always done on the stack of the calling thread, not on the stack of the thread represented by Thread object. The one exception to this rule occurs when the calling thread calls methods on a Thread object that represents itself.

You can get hold of the current thread your code runs on by using the CurrentThread read-only static property of the Thread class:

```
public sealed class Thread
{
    public static Thread CurrentThread { get; }
    // Other methods and properties
}
```

The CurrentThread property returns an instance of the Thread class. Each thread has a unique thread identification number called a *thread ID*. You can access the thread ID via the GetHashCode( ) method of the Thread class:

```
using System.Threading;

Thread currentThread = Thread.CurrentThread;
int threadID = currentThread.GetHashCode( );
Trace.WriteLine("Thread ID is "+ threadID.ToString( ));
```

Thread.GetHashCode( ) is guaranteed to return a value that is unique process-wide. It's worth mentioning that the thread ID obtained by GetHashCode( ) isn't related to the native thread ID allocated by the underlying operating system. You can verify that by opening the Threads debug window (under Debug→Windows) during a debug session and examining the value of the ID column (see Figure 8-1). The ID column reflects the physical thread ID. The GetHashCode( ) method simply returns a unique hash of the thread object. Having different IDs allows future .NET threads to map differently to the native operating support. If you need to programmatically access the physical thread ID your code runs on, use the static method GetCurrentThreadId( ) of the AppDomain class:

```
int physicalID = AppDomain.GetCurrentThreadId( );
int hashedID  = Thread.CurrentThread.GetHashCode( );
Debug.Assert(physicalID != hashedID);
```

App domains are described briefly later in this chapter and in greater depth in Chapter 10 within the context of .NET remoting.

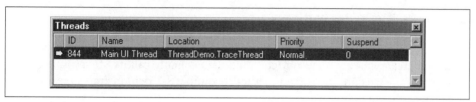

Figure 8-1. The Threads debug window

Another useful property of the Thread class is the Name string property. Name allows you to assign a human-readable name to a thread:

```
using System.Threading;

Thread currentThread = Thread.CurrentThread;
string threadName = "Main UI Thread";
currentThread.Name = threadName;
```

Only you as the developer can assign the thread name, and by default, a new .NET thread is nameless. Although naming a thread is optional, I highly recommend doing so because it's an important productivity feature. Windows doesn't have the ability to assign a name to a thread. In the past, when you debugged native Windows code, you had to record the new thread ID in every debugging session (using the Threads debug window). These IDs were not only confusing (especially when multiple threads were involved) but also changed in each new debugging session. The Threads debug window of Visual Studio.NET (see Figure 8-1) displays the value of the Name property, thus easing the task of tracing and debugging multithreaded applications. The name is a good example of a managed-code property that .NET adds to native threads.

Creating Threads

To spawn a new thread, you need to create a new Thread object and associate it with a method that is referred to as the *thread method*. The new Thread object executes the method on a separate thread. The thread terminates once the thread method returns.

The thread method can either be a static or an instance method, a public or a private one, and on your object or on another. The only requirement is that the thread method should have this exact signature:

```
void <MethodName>();
```

That is, no parameters and a void return type. You associate a Thread object with the thread method by using a dedicated delegate called ThreadStart, defined as:

```
public delegate void ThreadStart();
```

The Thread class constructor accepts as a single construction parameter an instance of the ThreadStart delegate, which targets the thread method:

```
public sealed class Thread
{
   public Thread(ThreadStart start);
   // Other methods and properties
}
```

Once you create a new thread object, you must explicitly call its Start() method to have it actually execute the thread method. Example 8-1 demonstrates creating and using a new thread.

Example 8-1. Spinning off a new thread

```
public class MyClass
{
   public void ShowMessage()
   {
      Thread currentThread = Thread.CurrentThread;
      string caption = "Thread ID = ";
      caption += currentThread.GetHashCode();
      MessageBox.Show("ShowMessage runs on a new thread",caption);
   }
}
MyClass obj = new MyClass();

ThreadStart threadStart = new ThreadStart(obj.ShowMessage);
Thread workerThread = new Thread(threadStart);
workerThread.Start();
```

Calling the Start() method is a nonblocking operation, meaning that control returns immediately to the client that started the thread, even though it may be some time later (depending on the operating-system internal-threading management) until the new thread actually starts. As a result, don't make any assumptions in your code (after calling Start()) that the thread is actually running. Although you should have only one thread method as a target for the ThreadStart delegate, you can associate it with multiple targets, in which case the new thread executes all methods in order, and the thread terminates once the last target method returns. However, there's little practical use for such a setting. In general, you should have only one target thread method.

Designing thread methods

A thread method can do whatever you want it to, but typically, it will contain a loop of some sort. In each loop iteration, the thread performs a finite amount of work and then checks some condition, letting it know whether to perform another iteration or to terminate:

```
public void MyThreadMethod( )
{
    while(<some condition>)
    {
        <Do some work>
    }
}
```

The condition is usually the result of some external event telling the thread that its work is done. The condition can be as simple as checking the value of a flag or waiting on a synchronization event. The condition is usually changed by another thread. As a result, changing and verifying the condition must be done in a thread-safe manner, using threading synchronization objects, as explained later in this chapter.

Passing thread parameters

The constructor for the thread class doesn't accept any parameters except the ThreadStart delegate, and the thread method itself takes no parameters. If you want to pass parameters to the thread method, you need to set properties on the class that provides the thread method, You could also have the method retrieve its parameters from a known location planned in advance.

Blocking Threads

The Thread class provides a number of methods you can use to block the execution of a thread, similar in their effect to the native mechanisms available to Windows programmers. These include suspending a thread, putting a thread to sleep, and waiting for a thread to die. In the past, most developers misused these mechanisms without ever realizing they were doing anything wrong. The potential for abuse exists in .NET as well. This section will outline the blocking options and why (in general) it's a bad idea to use them.

Suspending and resuming a thread

The Thread class provides the Suspend( ) method, which suspends the execution of a thread, and the Resume( ) method, which resumes a suspended thread:

```
public sealed class Thread
{
    public void Resume( );
```

```
    public void Suspend( );
    // Other methods and properties
}
```

Anybody can call Suspend( ) on a thread object, including objects running on that thread, and there is no harm in calling Suspend( ) on an already suspended thread. Obviously, only clients on other threads can resume a suspended thread. Suspend( ) is a non-blocking call, meaning that control returns immediately to the caller, and the thread is suspended later, usually at the next safe point. A *safe point* is a point in the code that's safe for garbage collection. Recall from Chapter 4 that when garbage collection takes place, .NET must suspend all running threads to compact the heap, move objects in memory, and patch client-side references. The JIT compiler identifies those points in the code that are safe for suspending the thread (such as returning from method calls or branching for another loop iteration). When Suspend( ) is called, the thread is suspended once it reaches the next safe point.

The bottom line is that suspending a thread isn't an instantaneous operation. The need to suspend and then resume a thread usually results from a need to synchronize the execution of that thread with other threads. Using Suspend( ) and Resume( ) for that purpose isn't recommended because there is no telling when it will take place. If you need to suspend the execution of a thread and then resume it later, you should use the dedicated .NET synchronization objects (described later). The synchronization objects provide a deterministic way of blocking a thread or signaling it to continue executing. In general, avoid explicitly suspending or resuming threads.

Putting a thread to sleep

The Thread class provides two overloaded versions of the static Sleep( ) method, which puts a thread to sleep for a specified timeout:

```
public sealed class Thread
{
    public static void Sleep(int millisecondsTimeout);
    public static void Sleep(TimeSpan timeout);
    // Other methods and properties
}
```

Because Sleep( ) is a static method, you can put only your own thread to sleep:

```
Thread.Sleep(20);//Sleep for 20 milliseconds
```

Sleep( ) is a blocking call, meaning that control returns to the calling thread only after the sleep period has elapsed. Sleep( ) puts the thread in a special queue of threads waiting to be awakened by the operating system. Any thread that calls Sleep( ) willingly relinquishes the remainder of its allocated CPU time slot, even if the sleep timeout is less than the reminder of the time slot. Consequently, calling sleep with a timeout of zero is a way to force a thread context switch:

```
Thread.Sleep(0);//Forces a context switch
```

If no other thread (with this priority or higher) is ready to run, control returns to the thread.

You can also put a thread to sleep indefinitely, using the Infinite static constant of the Timeout class:

```
Thread.Sleep(Timeout.Infinite);
```

Of course, putting a thread to sleep indefinitely is an inefficient use of the system services; it's better to simply terminate the thread (by returning from the thread method). If you need to block a thread until some event takes place, use .NET synchronization objects. In fact, you should generally avoid putting a thread to sleep, unless you specifically want the thread to act as a kind of timer. Traditionally, you put a thread to sleep to cope with race conditions by explicitly removing some of the threads involved in the race condition. A *race condition* is a situation in which thread T1 needs to have another thread T2 complete a task or reach a certain state. The race condition occurs when the T1 proceeds as if the T2 is ready, while in fact it may not be. Sometimes the T1 has its own processing to do, and that (in a poorly designed system) usually keeps it busy enough to avoid the race condition. Occasionally, however, the T1 will complete before T2 is ready, and an error will occur. Using Sleep() to resolve a race condition is inappropriate because it doesn't address the root cause of the race condition, usually the lack of proper synchronization between the participating threads. In that case, putting threads to sleep is at best a makeshift solution because the race condition can still manifest itself in different ways, and it isn't likely to work when more threads get involved. Avoid putting a thread to sleep, and use .NET synchronization objects instead.

A Minute for TimeSpan

Traditionally, most APIs in Windows that deal with time use some form of physical time such as seconds or milliseconds. You probably have no problem converting a minute or two to seconds. However, it's harder to convert one hour and forty-eight minutes into seconds, or two days. The TimeSpan struct addresses this by providing many methods for time conversion and representing time periods in a uniform manner. For example, if you need to represent two days, use the static method FromDays(), which returns a TimeSpan value representing two days:

```
TimeSpan TimeSpan = TimeSpan.FromDays(2);
```

Many of the methods discussed in this chapter that deal with blocking a thread have versions that accept TimeSpan instead of physical time units.

Spinning while waiting

The Thread class provides another sleep-like operation, called SpinWait( ):

```
public static void SpinWait(int iterations);
```

When a thread calls SpinWait( ), the calling thread waits the number of iterations specified, and the thread is never added to the queue of waiting threads. As a result, the thread is effectively put to sleep without relinquishing the remainder of its CPU time slot. The .NET documentation doesn't define what an iteration is, but it's likely mapped to a predetermined number (probably just one) of no-operation (NOP) assembly instructions. Consequently, the following SpinWait( ) instruction will take a different amount of time to complete on machines with different CPU clock speeds:

```
const long MILLION = 1000000;
Thread.SpinWait(MILLION);
```

SpinWait( ) isn't intended to replace Sleep( ) but is available as an advanced optimization technique. If you know that some resource your thread is waiting for will become available in the immediate future, it's potentially more efficient to spin and wait, instead of using either Sleep( ) or a synchronization object, because these force a thread context switch, which is one of the most expensive operations performed by the operating system. Even in the esoteric cases for which SpinWait( ) was designed, using it's an educated guess at best. SpinWait( ) gains you nothing if the resource isn't available at the end of the call or if the operating system preempts your thread because its time slot has elapsed or because another thread with a higher priority is ready to run. In general, I recommend that you always use deterministic programming synchronization objects, in this case) and avoid optimization techniques.

Joining a thread

The Thread class provides the Join( ) method, which allows one thread to wait for another thread to terminate. Any client that has a reference to a Thread object can call Join( ) and have the client thread blocked until the thread terminates:

```
private void WaitForThreadToDie(Thread thread)
{
    thread.Join( );
}
```

Join( ) returns regardless of the cause of death—either natural (the thread returns from the thread method) or unnatural (the thread encounters an exception). Join( ) is useful when dealing with application shutdown; when an application starts its shutdown procedure, it typically signals all the worker threads to terminate, and then the application waits for the threads to terminate. The standard way of doing this is to call Join( ) on the worker threads.

Calling Join( ) is similar to waiting on a thread handle in the Win32 world, and it's likely that the Join( ) method implementation does just that. The Join( ) method has two overloaded versions, allowing you to specify a waiting timeout:

```
public sealed class Thread
{
    public void Join( );
    public bool Join(int millisecondsTimeout);
    public bool Join(TimeSpan timeout);
    // Other methods and properties
}
```

When you specify a timeout, Join( ) returns when the timeout has expired or when the thread is terminated, whichever happens first. The bool return value is set to false if the timeout has elapsed but the thread is still running, and to true if the thread is dead.

Interrupting a waiting thread

You can rudely awaken a sleeping or waiting thread by calling the Interrupt( ) method of the thread class:

```
public void Interrupt( );
```

Calling Interrupt( ) unblocks a sleeping thread (or a waiting thread, such as a thread that called Join( ) on another thread) and throws an exception of type ThreadInterruptedException in the unblocked thread. If the code the thread executes doesn't catch that exception, the thread is terminated by the runtime. If the thread isn't sleeping (or waiting), and a call to Thread.Interrupt( ) is made, the next time the thread tries to go to sleep (or wait), .NET immediately throws in its call stack the exception of type ThreadInterruptedException. Again, you should avoid relying on drastic solutions such as throwing exceptions to unblock another thread. Use .NET synchronization objects instead to gain the benefits of structured and deterministic code flow. In addition, calling Interrupt( ) doesn't interrupt a thread that is executing unmanaged code via interop. Note that calling Interrupt( ) doesn't interrupt a thread that is in the middle of a call to SpinWait( ) because that thread is actually not waiting at all (as far as the operation system is concerned).

Aborting a Thread

The Thread class provides an Abort( ) method, which can forcefully terminate a .NET thread. Calling Abort( ) throws an exception of type ThreadAbortException in the thread being aborted. ThreadAbortException is a special kind of exception: even if the thread method uses exception handling to catch exceptions, such as:

```
public void MyThreadMethod( )
{
    try
    {
```

```
        while(<some condition>)
        {
           <Do some work>
        }
    }
    catch
    {
        //Handle exceptions here
    }
}
```

after the catch statement is executed, .NET re-throws the `ThreadAbortException` to terminate the thread. This is done so that nonstructured attempts that ignore the abort by jumping to the beginning of the thread method simply don't work:

```
//Code that doesn't work when ThreadAbortException is thrown.
public void MyThreadMethod()
{
    Resurrection:
    try
    {
        while(<some condition>)
        {
           <Do some work>
        }
    }
    catch
    {
        goto Resurrection;
    }
}
```

 Using nonstructured goto instructions is strongly discouraged in any case. Never use goto, except to fall through in a C# switch statement.

The `Abort()` method has two overloaded versions:

```
public sealed class Thread
{
    public void Abort();
    public void Abort(object stateInfo)
    // Other methods and properties
}
```

One version allows the party that calls `Abort()` to provide a generic parameter of type `object` called `stateInfo`. `stateInfo` can contain any application-specific information to the aborted thread, such as why it's being aborted. The aborted thread can access the `stateInfo` object via the `ExceptionState` public property of the `ThreadAbortException` class if the thread is using exception handling. Example 8-2 demonstrates using `Abort()` to terminate a thread. The example creates a new thread, whose thread method simply traces an incrementing integer to the Output

---

window. The thread method uses exception handling, and it traces to the Output window the information passed to it using the stateInfo parameter of Abort( ). Note that the thread that called Abort( ) uses Join( ) to wait for the thread to die. This is the recommended practice because the thread can perform an open-ended number of operations in its catch and finally exception handling statements.

Example 8-2. Terminating a thread using Abort()

```
public class MyClass
{
    public void DoWork( )
    {
     try
     {
        int i = 0;
        while(true)
        {
            Trace.WriteLine(i++.ToString( ));
        }
     }
     catch(ThreadAbortException exception)
     {
        string cause;
        cause = (string)exception.ExceptionState;
        Trace.WriteLine(cause);
     }
    }
}
MyClass obj = new MyClass( );
ThreadStart threadStart = new ThreadStart(obj.DoWork);
Thread workerThread = new Thread(threadStart);
workerThread.Start( );

/* Do some work, then:   */

workerThread.Abort("Time to go");
workerThread.Join( );
```

If Abort( ) is called before the thread is started, .NET doesn't start the thread once Thread.Start( ) is called. If Thread.Abort( ) is called while the thread is blocked (either by calling Sleep( ) or Join( ), or if the thread is waiting on one of the .NET synchronization objects), .NET unblocks the thread and throws ThreadAbortException in it. However, you can't call Abort( ) on a suspended thread. Doing so results on the calling side in an exception of type ThreadStateException, with the error message "Thread is suspended; attempting to abort". In addition, .NET terminates the suspended thread without letting it handle the exception.

The Thread class has an interesting counter-abort method—the static ResetAbort( ) method:

```
public static void ResetAbort( );
```

Calling `Thread.ResetAbort()` in a catch statement prevents .NET from rethrowing `ThreadAbortException` at the end of the catch statement:

```
catch(ThreadAbortException exception)
{
    Trace.WriteLine("Refusing to die");
    Thread.ResetAbort();
    //Do more processing or even goto somewhere
}
```

> `ResetAbort()` requires the `ControlThread` security permission. Permissions are explained in Chapter 12.

Terminating a thread by calling `Abort()` isn't recommended for a number of reasons. The first is that it forces the thread to perform an ungraceful exit. Often the thread needs to release resources it holds and perform some sort of a cleanup before terminating. You can, of course, handle exceptions and put the cleanup code in the `finally` method, but you typically want to handle the unexpected errors that way and not use it as the standard way to terminate a thread. Second, nothing prevents the thread from abusing .NET and either performing as many operations as it likes in the catch statement or jumping to a label or calling `ResetAbort()`. If you want to terminate a thread, you should do so in a structured manner using the .NET synchronization objects. You should signal the thread method to exit by using a member variable or event. Later, after presenting manual synchronization, this chapter presents a template for terminating threads using this technique, without resorting to `Abort()`.

> Calling `Thread.Abort()` has another liability: if the thread makes an interop call (using COM interop or P-Invoke), the interop call may take a while to complete. If `Thread.Abort()` is called during the interop call, .NET doesn't abort the thread; it lets the thread complete the interop call, only to abort it when it returns. This is another reason why `Thread.Abort()` isn't guaranteed to succeed (or succeed immediately).

Thread States

.NET manages a state machine for each thread and moves the thread between states. The `ThreadState` enum defines the set of states a .NET managed thread can be at:

```
[Flags]
public enum ThreadState
{
    Aborted          = 0x00000100,
    AbortRequested   = 0x00000080,
    Background       = 0x00000004,
    Running          = 0x00000000,
    Stopped          = 0x00000010,
```

```
    StopRequested    = 0x00000001,
    Suspended        = 0x00000040,
    SuspendRequested = 0x00000002,
    Unstarted        = 0x00000008,
    WaitSleepJoin    = 0x00000020
}
```

For example, if a thread is in the middle of a Sleep( ), Join( ), or a wait call on one of the synchronization objects, the thread is in the ThreadState.WaitSleepJoin state. .NET throws an exception of type ThreadStateException when it tries to move the thread to an inconsistent state, for example, by calling Start( ) on a thread at the ThreadState.Running state or trying to abort a suspended thread (ThreadState. Suspended). The Thread class has a public read-only property called ThreadState you can access to find the exact state of the thread:

```
public ThreadState ThreadState { get; }
```

The ThreadState enum values can be bit-masked together, so testing for a given state is typically done as follows:

```
Thread workerThread;
//Some code to initialize workerThread, then:
ThreadState state = workerThread.ThreadState;

if((state & ThreadState.Suspended) == ThreadState.Suspended)
{
    workerThread.Resume( );
}
```

However, I don't recommend ever designing your application so that you rely on the information provided by the ThreadState property. You should design so that your code doesn't depend on the thread being in a particular state. In addition, by the time you retrieve the thread's state and decide to act upon it, the state may have changed. If your thread transitions between logical states (specific to your application) such as beginning or finishing tasks, use .NET synchronization objects to synchronize transitioning between those states. The only exception to this is the knowledge that the thread is alive, required sometimes for diagnostics or control flow. For that reason, the Thread class has the Boolean read-only public property IsAlive that you should use instead of the ThreadState property:

```
public bool IsAlive { get; }
```

For example, there is little point in calling Join( ) on a thread if the thread isn't alive:

```
Thread workerThread;
//Some code to start workerThread, then:
if(workerThread.IsAlive)
{
    workerThread.Join( );
}
Trace.WriteLine("Thread is dead");
```

Therefore, in general, you should avoid accessing Thread.ThreadState.

Foreground and Background Threads

.NET defines two kinds of managed threads: background and foreground. The two thread types are exactly the same, except .NET keeps the process alive as long as there is at least one foreground thread running. Put differently, a background thread doesn't keep the .NET process alive once all foreground threads have exited.

New threads are created as foreground by default. To mark a thread as a background thread, you need to set the Thread object's IsBackground property to true:

```
public bool IsBackground { get; set; }
```

When the last foreground thread in a .NET application (actually, in an application domain, discussed later on) terminates, .NET shuts down the application. The .NET runtime tries to terminate all the remaining background threads by throwing ThreadAbortException in them. Background threads are a poor solution for application shutdown. Instead of designing the application correctly to keep track of what threads it created (and which threads are still running and need to be terminated when the application shuts down), a quick and dirty solution is to let .NET try to terminate all background threads. Normally, you shouldn't count on .NET to kill your background threads for you. You should have a deterministic, structured way of shutting down your application by doing your own bookkeeping and explicitly controlling the lifecycle of your threads, taking steps to shut down all threads on exit.

Thread Priority and Scheduling

Each thread is allocated a fixed time slot to run on the CPU and assigned a priority. In addition, a thread is either ready to run or waiting for some event to occur, such as a synchronization object being signaled or an elapsed sleep timeout. The underlying operating system schedules for execution those threads that are ready to run based on the thread's priority. Thread scheduling is *preemptive*, meaning that the thread with the highest priority always gets to run. If a thread T1 with priority P1 is running, and suddenly thread T2 with priority P2 is ready to run, and P2 is greater than P1, the operating system will preempt (pause) T1 and allow T2 to run. If multiple threads with the highest priority are ready to run, the operating system will let each run its CPU time slot and then preempt it in favor of another thread with the same priority, in a round-robin fashion.

The Thread class provides the Priority property of the enum type ThreadPriority, which allows you to retrieve or set the thread priority:

```
public ThreadPriority Priority { get; set; }
```

The enum ThreadPriority provides five priority levels:

```
public enum ThreadPriority
{
    Lowest,
    BelowNormal,
```

```
        Normal,
        AboveNormal,
        Highest
    }
```

New .NET threads are created by default with a priority of `ThreadPriority.Normal`. Developers often abuse thread-priority settings as a way to control the flow of a multithreaded application to work around race conditions. Tinkering with thread priorities generally isn't an appropriate solution and can lead to some adverse side effects and other race conditions. For example, imagine two threads that are involved in a race condition. By increasing one thread's priority in the hope that it will run at the expense of the other and win the race, you often just decrease the probability of the race condition because the thread with the higher priority can still be switched out or perform blocking operations. In addition, does it make sense to always run that thread at a higher priority? That can paralyze other aspects of your application. You could of course increase the priority only temporarily, but then you would address just that particular occurrence of the race condition and remain exposed to future occurrences.

You may be tempted to always keep that thread at a high priority and increase the priority of other affected threads. Often, increasing one thread's priority causes an inflation of increased thread priorities all around because the normal balance and time-sharing governed by the operating system is disturbed. The result can be a set of threads, all with the highest priority, still involved with race conditions. The major adverse effect now is that .NET suffers because many of its internal threads (such as threads used to manage memory, execute remote calls, and so on) are suddenly competing with your threads. In addition, preemptive operating systems (such as Windows) will dynamically change threads' priorities to resolve priority inversions situations.

A *priority inversion* occurs when threads with lower priority run instead of threads with a higher one. Because .NET threads are currently mapped to the underlying Windows threads, these dynamic changes propagate to the managed threads as well. Consider, for example, three managed threads T1, T2, and T3, with respective priorities of `ThreadPriority.Lowest`, `ThreadPriority.Normal`, and `ThreadPriority.Highest`. T3 is waiting for a resource held by T1. T1 is ready to run to release the resource, except that T2 is now running, always preventing T1 from executing. As a result, T2 prevents T3 from running, and priority inversion takes place because T3 has a priority greater than that of T2.

To cope with priority inversions, the operating system not only keeps track of thread priorities but also maintains a scoreboard showing who got to run and how often. If a thread is denied the CPU for a long time (a few seconds), the operating system dynamically boosts that thread's priority to a higher priority, letting it run for a couple of time slots with the new priority, and then sets the priority back to its original value. In the previous scenario, this allows T1 to run, release the resource T3 is waiting for, and then regain its original priority. T3 will be ready to run (because the resource is now available) and will preempt T2. The point of this example and the other arguments is that you should avoid controlling the application flow by setting thread priorities. Use .NET synchronization objects to control and coordinate the flow of your application and to resolve race conditions. Set threads priorities to values other than normal only when the semantics of the application requires it. For example, if you develop a screensaver, its threads should run at priority `ThreadPriority.Lowest` so that other background operations, such as compilation, network access, or number crunching, can take place and not be affected by the screen saver.

Synchronizing Threads

For all its advantages, introducing multithreading into your application opens up a Pandora's box of synchronization and concurrency management issues. With multithreading, you have to worry that threads will deadlock themselves while contesting for the same resources, you must take steps to synchronize access to objects by concurrent multiple threads, and you need to be prepared to handle method reentrancy.

When it comes to programming components that are likely to be used by you or by others in multithreaded applications, you must ensure they are *thread-safe*. A thread-safe component is one that is equipped with mechanisms to prevent multiple threads from accessing its methods and corrupting its state. Imagine a linked list component, which provides methods for adding and removing elements from a list. When the component adds or removes an element, the component keeps the list in a temporarily inconsistent state, while node references are updated and written to reflect the change. If a client asks to add an element to the list on one thread T1, and that thread is preempted by another thread (T2) during the request, T1 can leave the list in an inconsistent state, and T2 can crash trying to access the list. To make the list thread-safe, you should make sure that only one thread can access it at a time and that all other threads are barred until the current thread has finished.

With multithreaded applications, you must also concern yourself with avoiding deadlocks. In its simplest form, a *deadlock* occurs when one thread T1, which owns thread-safe resource R1, tries to access another thread-safe resource R2 at the same time a second thread T2, which owns R2, tries to access R1 (see Figure 8-2).

 There are many ways to create a deadlock. Some are complex, involving multiple threads with multiple resources and synchronization objects. There are some defensive programming techniques to reduce the likelihood of deadlocks (such as always acquiring and releasing the resources in the same order), but by far the best is to simply avoid them by design in the first place. You must analyze the behavior of your application's threads well before coding your first thread.

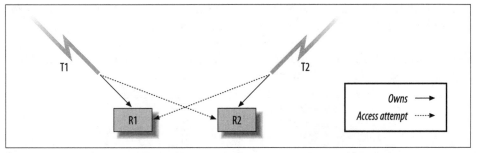

Figure 8-2. A deadlock between two threads

Multithreading defects are notoriously hard to isolate, reproduce, and eliminate. They often involve rare race conditions, and fixing one problem often introduces another. Traditionally, writing robust, high-performance multithreaded code was no trivial matter; it required a great deal of skill and discipline .NET tries to ease multithreaded application development by providing a rich infrastructure compared to native Windows. In particular, .NET tries to simplify component concurrency management.

COM managed concurrency through the use of apartments, which were difficult to use and understand. .NET eliminates that awkward model.

By default, all .NET components execute in a multithreaded environment, and concurrent access to them by multiple threads is allowed. As a result, the state of the object can be corrupted if it's accessed by multiple threads at the same time. .NET provides two synchronization approaches: automatic and manual. *Automatic synchronization* allows you to simply decorate their component with an attribute and have .NET synchronize concurrent access to the object. *Manual synchronization* requires using .NET synchronization objects. In fact, .NET offers a range of synchronization options in the synchronization spectrum: whether to synchronize access to a set of objects, an individual object, a particular method, or a critical code section, or just to protect an individual class member. This range lets you trade ease of use to flexibility and productivity to throughput. The next two sections first describe .NET automatic synchronization for context bound objects and then demonstrate the use of .NET locks provided for manual synchronization.

Automatic Synchronization

To understand the ways in which .NET can automatically synchronize access to components, you must first understand the relationship that .NET maintains between components, processes, application domains, and contexts. When a .NET application starts, the operating system launches an unmanaged process, which loads the .NET runtime. A .NET application can't execute in the unmanaged process directly. .NET provides a managed abstraction of the operating-system process in the form of an application domain, or app domain. Because app domains are a logical abstraction, a single unmanaged process can contain more than one app domain (see Figure 8-3). Chapter 10 discusses app domains in detail.

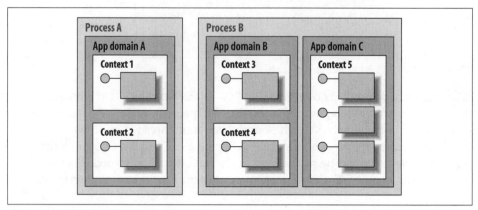

Figure 8-3. .NET app domains and contexts

That said, the app domain isn't the innermost execution scope of a .NET component. .NET provides a level of indirection between components and app domains in the form of *contexts*. Contexts enable .NET to provide *component services* such as thread synchronization to a component. In fact, one definition of a *context* is that it's a logical grouping of components, all configured to use the same set of component services. Every app domain starts with one context, called the default context, and .NET creates new contexts as required.

By default, .NET components aren't aware that contexts exist. When a client in the app domain creates an object, .NET gives the client back a direct reference to the new object. Such objects always execute in the context of the calling client. However, in order to take advantage of .NET component services, components must be context-bound, meaning they must always execute in the same context. Such components must derive directly or indirectly from the class ContextBoundObject:

```
public class MyClass : ContextBoundObject
{...}
```

Clients never have a direct reference to a context-bound object; instead, they have a reference to a proxy. .NET provides its component services by intercepting the calls clients make into the context via the proxy and performing some pre- and post-call processing. Chapter 11 discusses contexts in depth. In the context of this chapter (no pun intended), all you need to know is that you can have .NET synchronize access to any context-bound component by decorating the component class definition with the [Synchronization] attribute, defined in the System.Runtime.Remoting.Contexts namespace:

```
using System.Runtime.Remoting.Contexts;

[Synchronization]
public class MyClass : ContextBoundObject
{
  public MyClass(){}
  public void DoSomething(){}
  //other methods and data members
}
```

The [Synchronization] attribute, when applied on a ContextBoundObject based class, instructs .NET to place the object in a context and associate the object with a lock. When a client on thread T1 attempts to access the object by calling a method on it (or accessing a public member variable), the client actually interacts with a proxy. .NET intercepts the client access and tries to acquire the lock associated with the object. If the lock isn't currently owned by another thread, .NET acquires the lock and proceeds to access the object on thread T1. When the call returns from the method, .NET releases the lock and returns control to the client. If the object is accessed by another thread T2, T1 is blocked until T2 releases the lock. In fact, while the object is being accessed by one thread, all other threads are placed in a queue and are granted access to the object one at a time, in order. The result of this context-bound synchronization is that .NET provides a *macro lock*, meaning that the whole object is locked during access, even parts of the state that aren't accessed by the client.

Synchronization Domains

.NET could have allocated one lock for each context-bound object, but that would be inefficient. Often, objects can share a lock, if the components are all designed to participate in the same activity on behalf of a client and execute on the same thread. In such situations, allocating a lock per object is a waste of resources and processing time because .NET would have to perform additional locks and unlocks on every object access. Moreover, the noteworthy argument in favor of sharing locks among objects is that sharing locks reduces the likelihood for deadlocks. If two objects interact with each other, and each has its own lock, it's possible for the two objects to be used by two different clients on different threads, so they will deadlock trying to access each other. However, if the objects share a lock, only one client thread is allowed to access them.

In .NET, a set of context-bound objects that share a lock are said to be in a *synchronization domain*. Each synchronization domain has one lock, and within the same synchronization domain, concurrent calls from multiple threads aren't possible. When a thread accesses one object in a synchronization domain, that thread can access the rest of the objects in the synchronization domain. In fact, the synchronization domain locks all objects in the domain from access by other threads, even though only one object at a time is accessed by the current thread in the synchronization domain.

Synchronization Domains and Contexts

A synchronization domain is independent of contexts, and it can include objects from multiple contexts. However, the synchronization domain is limited to a single app domain, which means that objects from different app domains can't share a synchronization domain lock. A context can belong to, at most, one synchronization domain at any given time and maybe none at all. If a context belongs to a synchronization domain, all objects in that context belong to that synchronization domain. The reason is that if objects differ in the way they are configured to use synchronization domains, .NET puts them in different contexts in the first place. The relationship between app domains, synchronization domain, contexts and objects is shown in Figure 8-4.

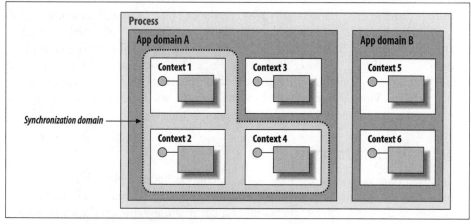

Figure 8-4. A synchronization domain

Configuring Synchronization Domains

It's up to you to decide how a component is associated with a synchronization domain lock: you need to decide whether the object needs a lock at all, it can share a lock with other objects, or it requires a new lock. The SynchronizationAttribute class provides a number of overloaded constructors:

```
public class SynchronizationAttribute :  ContextAttribute, IContextAttribute
                                         //Other interfaces
{
    public static const int NOT_SUPPORTED = 1;
    public static const int SUPPORTED     = 2;
    public static const int REQUIRED      = 4;
    public static const int REQUIRES_NEW  = 8;
```

```
    // Constructors
    public SynchronizationAttribute( );
    public SynchronizationAttribute(int flag);
    public SynchronizationAttribute(int flag, bool reentrant);
    public SynchronizationAttribute(bool reentrant);
    //Other methods and properties
}
```

The SynchronizationAttribute class defines four integer constants: NOT_SUPPORTED, SUPPORTED, REQUIRED, and REQUIRES_NEW. These constants decide in which synchronization domain the object will reside in relation to its creating client. For example:

```
[Synchronization(SynchronizationAttribute.REQUIRES_NEW)]
public class MyClass : ContextBoundObject
{}
```

The default constructor of the SynchronizationAttribute class uses REQUIRED, and so do the other constructors that don't require the constant value. As a result, these declarations are equivalent:

```
[Synchronization]
[Synchronization(SynchronizationAttribute.REQUIRED)]
[Synchronization(SynchronizationAttribute.REQUIRED,false)]
[Synchronization(false)]
```

An object can reside in any of these synchronization domains:

In its creator's synchronization domain
    The object shares a lock with its creator.

In a new synchronization domain
    The object has its own lock and starts a new synchronization domain.

In no synchronization domain at all
    There is no lock, so concurrent access is allowed.

An object's synchronization domain is determined at creation time based on the synchronization domain of its creator and the constant value provided to the Synchronization attribute. If the object is configured with synchronization support NOT_SUPPORTED, it will never be part of a synchronization domain, regardless of whether or not its creator has a synchronization domain. If the object is configured with SUPPORTED and its creator has a synchronization domain, .NET places the object in its creator's synchronization domain. If the creating object doesn't have a synchronization domain, the newly created object will not have a synchronization domain. If the object is configured with synchronization support set to REQUIRED, .NET puts it in its creator's synchronization domain if the creating object has one. If the creating object doesn't have a synchronization domain and the object is configured to require synchronization, .NET creates a new synchronization domain for the object. If the object is configured with synchronization support set to REQUIRES_NEW then .NET creates a new synchronization domain for it, regardless of whether its creator has a synchronization domain or not. The .NET synchronization domain allocation decision matrix is summarized in Table 8-1.

Table 8-1. Synchronization domain (SD) allocation decision matrix

Object SD support	Creator is in SD	The object will take part in
NOT_SUPPORTED	No	No SD
SUPPORTED	No	No SD
REQUIRED	No	New SD
REQUIRES_NEW	No	New SD
NOT_SUPPORTED	Yes	No SD
SUPPORTED	Yes	Creator's SD
REQUIRED	Yes	Creator's SD
REQUIRES_NEW	Yes	New SD

Figure 8-5 shows an example of synchronization domain flow. In the figure, a client that doesn't take part in a synchronization domain creates an object configured with REQUIRED. Because the object requires a synchronization domain, and its creator has none, .NET creates a new synchronization domain for it. The object then goes on to create four more objects. Two of them, configured with REQUIRED and SUPPORTED, are placed within the same synchronization domain. The component configured with NOT_SUPPORTED has no synchronization domain. The last component is configured with REQUIRES_NEW, so .NET creates a new synchronization domain for it. You may be asking why .NET partly bases the synchronization domain decision on the object's creating client. The heuristic .NET uses is that the calling patterns, interactions, and synchronization needs between objects usually closely match their creation relationship. The question now is, when should you use the various Synchronization attribute construction values?

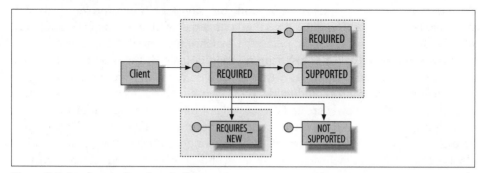

Figure 8-5. Synchronization domain flow

The designer of the `SynchronizationAttribute` class didn't follow basic type safety practices and provided the synchronization value in the form of constants instead of enumeration. As a result, this usage of the `SynchronizationAttribute`:

```
[Synchronization(1234)]
public class MyClass : ContextBoundObject
{ }
```

compiles but throws `ArgumentException` at runtime. If an enum such as:

```
public enum SynchronizationOption
{
    NotSupported,Supported,Required,RequiresNew
}
```

had been defined, the result would have been type-safe.

Synchronization NOT_SUPPORTED

An object set to `NOT_SUPPORTED` never participates in a synchronization domain. The object must provide its own synchronization mechanism. You should use this setting only if you expect concurrent access and you want to provide your own synchronization mechanisms. In general, avoid this setting. A context-bound object should take advantage of component services support as much as possible.

Synchronization SUPPORTED

An object set to `SUPPORTED` will share its creator's synchronization domain if it has one and will have no synchronization of its own if the creator doesn't have one. This is the least useful setting because the object must provide its own synchronization mechanism in case its creator doesn't have a synchronization domain, and you must make sure that the mechanism doesn't interfere with the synchronization domain when one is used. As a result, it's more difficult to develop the component. `SUPPORTED` is available for the rare case in which the component itself has no need for synchronization, yet downstream objects it creates do require it. By setting synchronization to `SUPPORTED`, the component can propagate the synchronization domain of its creating client to the downstream objects and have them all share one synchronization domain, instead of a few separate synchronization domains, and by doing so reduce the likelihood of deadlocks.

Synchronization REQUIRED

`REQUIRED` is by far the most common value for .NET context-bound objects, and this is why it's also the default of the `SynchronizationAttribute` class. When an object is set to `REQUIRED`, all calls to the object will be synchronized, and the only question is whether your object will have its own synchronization domain or share its creator's synchronization domain. If you don't care about having your own the synchronization domain, always use this setting.

Synchronization REQUIRES_NEW

When an object is set to REQUIRES NEW, the object must have a new synchronization domain, distinct from the creator's synchronization domain, and its own lock. The object will never share its context or the synchronization domain with its creator.

Choosing between REQUIRED and REQUIRES_NEW

Deciding that your object requires synchronization is usually straightforward. If you anticipate that multiple clients on multiple threads will try to access your object, and you don't want to write your own synchronization mechanism, you need synchronization. The more difficult question to answer is whether your object should require its own synchronization lock or whether you should configure it to use the lock of its creator. Try basing your decision on the calling patterns to your object. Consider the calling pattern in Figure 8-6. In this pattern, sharing the lock with the creator when the two objects don't interact causes Client B to wait until the first call is completed, even though it can safely access the object.

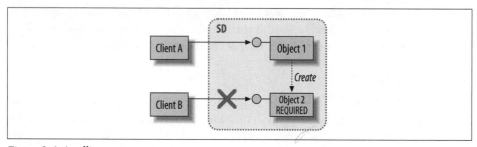

Figure 8-6. A calling pattern

Object 2 is configured with synchronization set to REQUIRED and is placed in the same synchronization domain as its creator, Object 1. In this example, except for creating Object 2, Object 1 and Object 2 don't interact with each other. While Client A is accessing Object 1, Client B on another thread comes along, wanting to call methods on Object 2. Because Client B uses a different thread, it's blocked, even though it can safely access Object 2, because it doesn't violate the synchronization requirement for the creating object, Object 1. On the other hand, if you configure Object 2 to require its own synchronization domain using REQUIRES_NEW, the object can process calls from other clients at the same time as Object 1 (See Figure 8-7). A classic example of configuring components to require a new synchronization domain is when class factories are used to create objects. Usually class factories require thread safety because they service multiple clients. However, once the factory creates an object, it hands the object back to a client and has nothing to do with it later on. You definitely don't want all the objects created by a class factory to share the same synchronization domain, and therefore you need to configure them to require a new synchronization domain.

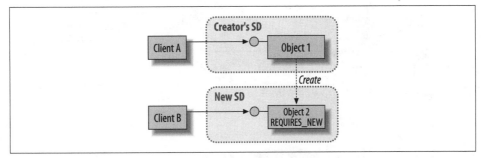

Figure 8-7. Having a separate synchronization domain enables clients to be served more efficiently

If the creator object (Object 1) does need to call Object 2, however, these calls will potentially block and be more expensive because they must cross context boundaries and pay the overhead of trying to acquire the lock.

Synchronization Domain Reentrancy

A synchronization domain allows only one thread to enter and locks all the objects in the domain. .NET releases the lock automatically when the thread winds up its way back up the call chain, leaving the synchronization domain from the same object it entered. Figure 8-8 demonstrates this point: a thread enters a synchronization domain, acquires the lock, and releases it only when it returns from Object 1, leaving the synchronization domain. However, what should .NET do if an object makes a call outside the synchronization domain while the call is still in progress inside the domain? This situation is shown in Figure 8-9.

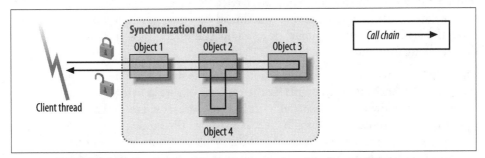

Figure 8-8. Releasing a lock when the call chain exits on the original entry object

 In the current release of .NET, synchronization domain reentrancy isn't implemented. As a result, the mechanism behaves as if you always pass in false for reentrancy.

By default, .NET doesn't release the synchronization domain lock when the thread exits the domain through a route other than the entry object, such as Object 4 in Figure 8-9. Because the thread can spend an indefinite amount of time on the

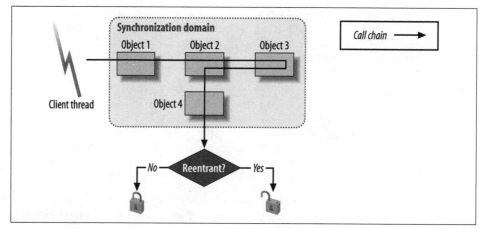

Figure 8-9. If reentrancy is set to true, NET releases the synchronization domain lock while the outgoing call is in progress

outgoing call, it can indefinitely deny other threads, access to the synchronization domain objects. If you want to allow other threads access to the synchronization domain objects while the current thread makes a call outside the synchronization domain, you need to provide true for the reentrant parameter of the SynchronizationAttribute class constructors; for example:

```
[Synchronization(true)]
public class MyClass : ContextBoundObject
{ }
```

In Figure 8-9, if Object 4 is configured to allow reentrancy, then when it makes a call outside the synchronization domain, .NET releases the lock and allows other threads to enter the domain. Note that when the thread that made the outbound call tries to enter the synchronization domain, it must reacquire the lock, just like any other thread calling from outside the domain.

Allowing for reentrancy is an optimization technique, which can increase your application performance and throughput at the expense of thread safety. In general, I recommend not allowing for reentrancy unless you are convinced the outgoing call leaves the synchronization domain in a consistent, thread-safe state. A consistent thread-safe state means the outgoing thread has no more interactions with the objects in the synchronization domain, besides returning and winding up the call chain, and it will exit via the original entry object.

 In general, it's a bad design decision to access objects outside your synchronization domain, regardless of whether you can still make things work using the reentrant parameter. If you need to access another object, then by design, that object should be part of your synchronization domain. Only clients in nonsynchronized contexts should make cross-synchronization domain calls.

Synchronization Domain Pros and Cons

Automatic synchronization for context-bound objects via synchronization domain is by far the easiest synchronization mechanism available to .NET developers. It's a modern synchronization technique that formally eliminates synchronization problems and your need to code around them and to test the handcrafted solution. The resulting productivity gain is substantial. Synchronization domains offer an additional major benefit: As explained in Chapter 1, component concurrency management is a core principle of component-oriented programming. A component vendor can't assume that his components will not be accessed by multiple concurrent client threads. As a result, unless the vendor states that its components aren't thread-safe, the vendor must provide thread-safe components. Without a way of sharing a lock with the clients, there would always be a synchronization boundary between the vendor server components and the client components. The result would impede performance because incoming calls would have to negotiate both client-side and server-side locks. More important, the result would also increase deadlock probability, in the case of different client components competing to use different server components. The ability to share a lock between components developed by different parties is an important feature of .NET as a component technology, analogous to COM's apartments but without a cumbersome model and accompanying liabilities.

Unfortunately, no technology is perfect, and synchronization domains aren't without flaws:

- You can use it only with context-bound objects. For all other .NET types, you must still use manual synchronization objects.

- There is a penalty for accessing context bound objects via proxies and interceptors. In some intense calling patterns, this can pose a problem.

- A synchronization domain doesn't protect static class members and static methods. For those, you must use manual synchronization objects.

- A synchronization domain isn't a throughput-oriented mechanism. The incoming thread locks a set of objects, even if it interacts with only one of them. That lock precludes other threads from accessing these objects, and in theory, degrades your application throughput.

That stated, I believe that in general, relying on advanced component services (such as synchronization) is a necessity in any decent size application (or whenever productivity and quality are a top priority), and it outweighs the drawbacks of context-bound objects.

Manual Synchronization

.NET manual synchronization provides a rich set of *synchronization locks*, such as monitors, events, mutexes, and interlocks, familiar to any veteran Win32

.NET Enterprise Services Activities

.NET Enterprise Services (System.EnterpriseServices namespace) offer a different automatic synchronization mechanism for serviced components (a subclass of context-bound components) called *activities*. You apply activities using what looks like an identical implementation of the Synchronization attribute. In fact, the Synchronization attribute that configures synchronization domains is based on the syntax of the Synchronization attribute in the System.EnterpriseServices namespace. Activities are similar conceptually to synchronization domains, except they lock the objects in the activity per logical thread instead of physical thread. A *logical thread* is a chain of calls that spans multiple components and threads. Some .NET Enterprise Services (such as just-in-time activation and transactions) have tight integration with activities. Synchronization domains and activities complement each other, and neither is superior to the other. In general, you should use activities for serviced components, and synchronization domains for the rest. .NET activities are beyond the scope of this book, but you can read about it in Chapters 5 and 10 of my book *COM and .NET Component Services*.

---

programmer. .NET introduces some language features that automate the use of locks and a new lock type (the reader/writer lock). Manual synchronization is at the other end of the spectrum (on a number of dimensions) from automatic synchronization. First, whereas a synchronization domain is in effect a mega-macro lock, manual synchronization offers fine-grained control over what is locked: you can control access to an object, its individual members, or even a single line of code. As a result, you can potentially improve overall application performance and throughput.

You can use manual synchronization on any .NET component, context-bound or not. Unlike the automatic synchronization domain, when you use manual synchronization (as the name implies), you explicitly manage the locking and unlocking of the lock. Finally, with manual synchronization the Pandora's box of synchronization is wide open, and unless you carefully design your manual-synchronization mechanism, you can introduce deadlock and other multithreading defects, such as object state corruption and hard-to-resolve race conditions. In this section, I will provide you (where appropriate) with design guidelines and rules of thumb to allow you to apply manual synchronization productively.

The Monitor

Monitor is a lock designed to work with .NET reference types only. Monitor associates a lock with an object. While one thread owns the lock associated with that object, no other thread can acquire the lock. Monitor provides static methods only, accepting the target object as a parameter. There is no way to instantiate a Monitor

---

object explicitly. The two most commonly used methods of Monitor are Enter( ) and Exit( ):

```
public sealed class Monitor
{
    public static void Enter(object obj);
    public static void Exit(object obj);
    //Other methods
}
```

Enter( ) acquires a lock for an object and locks it; Exit( ) unlocks it. A client that wants to access a nonthread-safe object calls Enter( ), specifying the object. The client uses the object and then calls Exit( ) to allow other threads to access the object, as shown in Example 8-3.

Example 8-3. Using Monitor to control access to an object

```
public class MyClass
{
    public void DoSomething( )
    {...}
    //Class members
}

MyClass obj;
//Some code to initialize obj;

//This section is now thread-safe:

Monitor.Enter(obj);
obj.DoSomething( );
Monitor.Exit(obj);
```

Any object, from any thread, can call Enter( ) to try to access the object. If the object is accessed by another thread (that used a monitor on the same object), Enter( ) blocks the caller until the other thread calls Exit( ). If there is more than one pending thread, they are placed in a queue called the *lock queue* and served from the queue in order. There is no harm in calling Enter( ) multiple times on the same object, provided you make a matching number of calls to Exit( ) to release the lock. Also worth mentioning is that only the thread that called Enter( ) can call Exit( ). Trying to call Exit( ) on a different thread results in an exception of type SynchronizationLockException.

Monitor provides the TryEnter( ) Boolean method that allows a client thread to try to acquire the lock without being blocked:

```
public static bool TryEnter(object obj);
```

If the lock is available, TryEnter( ) locks it and returns true. If the lock is owned by another thread, TryEnter( ) returns immediately to its caller, with a return value of false. `TryEnter( )` has two other overloaded methods that allow the client to specify a timeout to wait to acquire the lock if it's owned by another thread:

```
public static bool TryEnter(object obj,int millisecondsTimeout);
public static bool TryEnter(object obj,TimeSpan timeout);
```

In general, `TryEnter( )` is of little use because the calling client itself should be able to deal with an object that is unavailable. `TryEnter( )` is provided for the advanced and esoteric cases of high throughput threads that can't afford to block on nice-to-have operations.

 I also recommend avoiding `TryEnter( )` because of a general design guideline when dealing with locks: always postpone acquiring a lock until the last possible moment, and release it as soon as possible. This reduces the likelihood of a deadlock and improves overall through-put. If you have something to do instead of acquiring a lock, do it. As a result, `TryEnter( )` should be avoided.

Protecting static members and methods

You can also use the `Monitor` class to provide thread-safe access to static class methods or properties by giving it the type to lock instead of a particular instance, as shown in Example 8-4.

Example 8-4. Using Monitor to control access to a static method

```
public class MyClass
{
    static public void DoSomething( )
    {...}
    //Static class members
}

//This section is now thread-safe:
Monitor.Enter(typeof(MyClass));
MyClass.DoSomething( );
Monitor.Exit(typeof (MyClass));
```

Error handling

You must call `Exit( )` on the object you locked using `Enter( )`, even in the face of exceptions; otherwise, the object will not be accessible by clients on other threads. Example 8-5 shows the same code as Example 8-3, this time with proper error handling. By placing the call to `Exit( )` in the `finally` statement, `Exit( )` is called whether or not the try statement encounters an exception.

Example 8-5. Using Monitor correctly with error handling

```
public class MyClass
{
    public void DoSomething( )
```

Example 8-5. Using Monitor correctly with error handling (continued)

```
    {...}
    //Class members
}

MyClass obj;
//Some code to initialize obj;

Monitor.Enter(obj);
try
{
    obj.DoSomething( );
}
finally
{
    Monitor.Exit(obj);
}
```

To ease the task of using Monitor in conjunction with error handing, C# provides the lock statement, which causes the compiler to automatically generate calls to Enter( ) and Exit( ) in a try and finally statement. For example, when you write this code:

```
    MyClass obj;
    //Some code to initialize obj;

    lock(obj)
    {
        obj.DoSomething( );
    }
```

the compiler replaces the lock statement with the code shown in Example 8-5 instead. Visual Basic.NET has a similar compiler support via the SyncLock statement:

```
    Public Class MyVBClass
        Sub DoSomething( )
        ...
        End Sub
        'Class members
    End Class

    Dim obj As MyVBClass
    'Some code to initialize obj;

    SyncLock (obj)
        obj.DoSomething( )
    End SyncLock
```

Similar to using raw Monitor, you can use the lock statement to protect a static method or access to a static member by providing a type instead of an instance:

```
    public class MyClass
    {
        static public void DoSomething( )
        {...}
```

```
    //Static class members
}
lock(typeof(MyClass))
{
    MyClass.DoSomething();
}
```

Encapsulating Monitor

Using a Monitor object to protect an object from concurrent access as shown in Example 8-5 is asking for trouble. The reason is simple: using Monitor is done at the discretion of the client developer. Nothing prevents a client from ignoring other threads and accessing an object directly without using a lock. Of course, such an action will conflict with another thread currently accessing the object, even if that thread is disciplined enough to use a lock. The solution is simple: encapsulate the lock inside the component and use Monitor on every public method and property, passing this as the object to lock. Encapsulating the lock is the classic object-oriented solution for thread-safe objects. Example 8-6 demonstrates this point.

Example 8-6. Encapsulating Monitor to promote loose coupling and thread safety

```
public class MyClass
{
    public void DoSomething()
    {
        lock(this)
        {
            //Do Something
        }
    }
    //Class members
}
MyClass obj;
//Some code to initialize obj;
obj.DoSomething();
```

By encapsulating the lock inside the method, you promote loose coupling between the clients and the object because now the clients don't need to care about the object's synchronization needs. You also promote thread safety because the method (or property) access is safe by definition. You can also encapsulate the lock for static methods or properties:

```
public class MyClass
{
    static public void DoSomething()
    {
        lock(typeof(MyClass))
        {
            //Do Something
        }
```

```
    }
    //Static member variables
}
```

 In general, exposing public class member variables directly is inadvisable, and it's doubly so when multithreading is involved because there is no way to encapsulate the lock. At the very least, you should use properties that call lock(this) to access member variables.

Note that when you use the lock statement in a method that returns a value (such as a property), there is no need to use a temporary variable because the finally block executes after the return instruction:

```
public class MyClass
{
    int m_Number;
    public int Number
    {
        get
        {
            lock(this)
            {
                return m_Number;
            }
        }
    }
}
```

Synchronized methods

When you use Monitor, you can protect individual code sections of a method and thus have a fine level of control over when you lock the object for access. You need to lock the object only when you access its member variables. All other code that uses local stack-allocated variables is thread-safe by definition:

```
public class MyClass
{
    public void DoSomething()
    {
        //This loop doesn't need to lock the object
        for(int i=0;i<10;i++)
        {
            Trace.WriteLine(i.ToString());
        }
        // Lock the object because state is being accessed
        lock(this)
        {
            Trace.WriteLine("Num is " + m_Num.ToString());
        }
    }
    int m_Num = 0;
}
```

As a result, you can interleave locked code with unlocked code as required. This is called *fragmented locking*. However, there is a serious liability to fragmented locking because it results in error-prone code. During code maintenance someone might add access to a member variable (either directly or by using a method) in a nonlocked code section, which can result in object state corruption. Consequently, you need to avoid fragmented locking and opt for locking the object for the duration of the method:

```csharp
public class MyClass
{
    public void DoSomething()
    {
        lock(this)
        {
            for(int i=0;i<10;i++)
            {
                Trace.WriteLine(i.ToString());
            }
            Trace.WriteLine("Num is " + m_Num.ToString());
        }
    }
    int m_Num = 0;
}
```

Because this programming model is so common, .NET has built-in compiler support for it, called *synchronized methods*. The MethodImpl method attribute, defined in the System.Runtime.CompilerServices namespace, accepts an enum of type MethodImplOptions. One of the enum values is MethodImplOptions.Synchronized. When the MethodImpl method attribute is applied on a method with that enum value, the compiler instructs the .NET runtime to lock the object on method entry, and unlock it on exit. This is semantically equivalent to encasing the method code with a lock statement. For example, consider this method definition:

```csharp
using System.Runtime.CompilerServices;

public class MyClass
{
    [MethodImpl(MethodImplOptions.Synchronized)]
    public void DoSomething()
    {
        /* Method code */
    }
    //Class members
}
```

This method is semantically identical to the following:

```csharp
public class MyClass
{
    public void DoSomething()
    {
        lock(this)
```

```
        {
            /* Method code */
        }
    }
    //Class members
}
```

You can use the MethodImpl method attribute on static methods as well, and even on properties:

```
using System.Runtime.CompilerServices;

public class MyClass
{
    int Number
    {
        [MethodImpl(MethodImplOptions.Synchronized)]
        get
        {
            return m_Num;
        }
        [MethodImpl(MethodImplOptions.Synchronized)]
        set
        {
            m_Num = value;
        }
    }
    int m_Num = 0;
}
```

The difference between synchronized methods and synchronization domains is that synchronized methods can lead to deadlocks. Imagine two objects, each servicing a client on a different thread, each having a reference to each other. Say they try to access each other, as in Figure 8-2; the result is a deadlock. Had the two objects been part of a synchronization domain, the first thread to access an object would lock the other object as well and avoid a deadlock.

Waiting and signaling with Monitor

In some cases, after acquiring the lock associated with an object, you may want to release the lock and wait until another thread has accessed the object. Once the other thread is done with the object, it signals your thread, at which point you want to reacquire the lock and continue executing.

To do this, the Monitor class provides the Wait() method:

```
public static bool Wait(object obj);
```

Wait() releases the lock and waits for another thread to call Monitor. You can call Wait() on an object only after you have locked it by calling Monitor.Enter() on it and within that synchronized code section:

```
public void LockAndWait(object obj)
{
    lock(obj)
    {
        //do some work, then wait for another thread to do its work
        Monitor.Wait(obj);
        /* This code is executed only after the
        signaling thread releases the lock */
    }
}
```

While your thread is in the call to Wait( ), other threads can call Enter( ) on the object, and then Wait( ), so you can end up with multiple threads all waiting for a signal. All these pending threads are placed in a dedicated queue associated with the lock, called the *wait queue*. To unlock a waiting thread, a different thread must acquire the lock and then use the Pulse( ) or the PulseAll( ) Monitor methods:

```
public static void Pulse(object obj);
public static void PulseAll(object obj);
```

You can call Pulse() on an object only if you own its monitor:

```
public void LockAndPulse(object obj)
{
    lock(obj)
    {
        //Do some work, then pulse one other thread to continue its work
        Monitor.Pulse(obj);
        /* This code is still the owner of the lock */
    }
}
```

Pulse( ) removes the first thread from the waiting queue and adds it to the end of the lock queue, the same queue that handles multiple concurrent calls to Enter( ). Only when the pulsing thread calls Exit( ) does the next thread from the lock queue get to run, and it may not necessarily be the thread that was pulsed out of the waiting queue. If you want to pulse all the waiting threads out of the waiting queue, you can use the PulseAll( ) method. After calling PulseAll( ), all waiting threads are moved to the lock queue, where they continue to execute in order.

The Wait( ) method blocks the calling thread indefinitely. There are four other overloaded versions of the Wait( ) method that accept a timeout and return a Boolean value:

```
public static bool Wait(object obj,int millisecondsTimeout);
public static bool Wait(object obj,int millisecondsTimeout, bool exitContext);
public static bool Wait(object obj,TimeSpan timeout);
public static bool Wait(object obj,TimeSpan timeout, bool exitContext);
```

The Boolean value lets you know if Wait( ) has returned because the specified timeout has expired (false) or because the lock is reacquired (true). Note that the Wait( ) version that doesn't accept a timeout also returns a Boolean value, but that value will always be true (that version should have had a void return value).

The interesting parameter of the overloaded Wait( ) method is the bool exitContext. If Wait( ) is called from inside a synchronization domain, and if you pass in true for exitContext, .NET exits the synchronization domain before blocking and waiting. This allows other threads to enter the synchronization domain. Once the Monitor object is signaled, the thread has to enter the domain and own the Monitor lock in order to run. The default behavior in the rest of the Wait( ) versions isn't to exit the synchronization domain.

Note that you can still block indefinitely using one of the overloaded methods that accepts a TimeSpan parameter by passing the Infinite static constant of the Timeout class:

```
Monitor.Wait(obj,Timeout.Infinite);
```

 As mentioned at the beginning of the chapter, calling Thread. Interrupt( ) unblocks a thread from a Monitor call to Enter( ), TryEnter( ), or Wait( ), and throws an exception of type ThreadInter-ruptedException in it.

Waitable Handle

In Windows, you can synchronize access to data and objects using a *waitable handle* to a system-provided lock. You pass the handle to a set of Win32 API calls to block your thread or signal to other threads waiting on the handle. The class WaitHandle provides a managed code representation of a native Win32 waitable handle. The WaitHandle class is defined as:

```
public abstract class WaitHandle : MarshalByRefObject,IDisposable
{
    public WaitHandle( );
    public IntPtr Handle { virtual get; virtual set; }
    public virtual void Close( );

    public static bool WaitAll(WaitHandle[ ] waitHandles);
    public static bool WaitAll(WaitHandle[ ] waitHandles,
                            int millisecondsTimeout, bool exitContext);
    public static bool WaitAll(WaitHandle[ ] waitHandles,
                            TimeSpan timeout, bool exitContext);

    public static int WaitAny(WaitHandle[ ] waitHandles);
    public static int WaitAny(WaitHandle[ ] waitHandles,
                            int millisecondsTimeout, bool exitContext);
    public static int WaitAny(WaitHandle[ ] waitHandles,
                            TimeSpan timeout, bool exitContext);

    public virtual bool WaitOne( );
    public virtual bool WaitOne(int millisecondsTimeout, bool exitContext);
    public virtual bool WaitOne(TimeSpan timeout, bool exitContext);
}
```

WaitHandle either signals an event between one or more threads or protects a resource from concurrent access. WaitHandle is an abstract class, so you can't instantiate WaitHandle objects. Instead, you create a specific subclass of it, such as a Mutex. This design provides a common base class for the different locks, and you can wait on a lock or a set of locks in a polymorphic manner, without caring about the actual types.

A WaitHandle object has two states: signaled and nonsignaled. In the nonsignaled state, any thread that tries to wait on the handle is blocked until the state of the handle changes to signaled. The waiting methods are defined in the WaitHandle base class, while the signaling operation is defined in the subclasses.

Finally, note that WaitHandle is derived from the class MarshalByRefObject. As you will see in Chapter 10, this allows you to pass WaitHandle objects as method parameters between app domains or even machines.

 WaitHandle is used frequently in the .NET Framework, and some .NET types provide a WaitHandle object for you to wait on. For example, recall the IAsyncResult described in Chapter 7. IAsyncResult provides the AsyncWaitHandle property of type WaitHandle, which waits for one or more asynchronous method calls in progress.

Using WaitHandle

WaitHandle provides two types of waiting methods: single handle wait and multiple handles wait. The single handle wait allows you to wait on a single handle using one of the overloaded WaitOne( )methods. You have to instantiate a particular subclass of WaitHandle and then call WaitOne( ) on it. The thread calling WaitOne( ) is blocked until some other thread uses a specific method on the subclass to signal it. You will see examples for that later on. The parameter-less WaitOne( ) method blocks indefinitely, but you can use two of the overloaded versions to specify a timeout, and whether or not to exit a synchronization domain, similar to the Wait( ) method of the Monitor class.

The WaitAll( ) and WaitAny( ) methods allow you to wait on a collection of WaitHandle objects. Both are static methods, so you need to separately create an array of waitable handle objects, and then wait either for all or any one of them to become signaled, using WaitAll( ) or WaitAny( ), respectively. Similar to WaitOne( ), the WaitAll( ) and WaitAny( ) by default wait indefinitely, unless you specify a timeout. You can also specify whether you want to exit the synchronization domain. Once done with the handle, you should call Close( ) on it to close the underlying Windows handle. If you fail to do so, the handle will be closed during garbage collection.

WaitHandle has one interesting property, called Handle, defined as:

```
public IntPtr Handle { virtual get; virtual set; }
```

You can use Handle to retrieve the underlying Windows handle associated with this lock object, and you can even force a handle value yourself. Handle is provided for advanced interoperability scenarios with legacy code, in which you need to use a specific handle value that's obtained by some proprietary interoperation mechanism.

WaitHandle versus Monitor

There are two key differences between using a Monitor type to wait and signal an object and using a waitable handle. First, Monitor can be used only on a reference type; a waitable handle can synchronize access to value types as well as reference types. The second difference is the ability WaitHandle provides to wait on multiple objects as one *atomic* operation. When you are trying to wait for multiple objects, it's important to dispatch the wait request to the operating system as one atomic operation. If this is done on an individual lock basis, there's a possibility of a deadlock if a second thread tries to acquire the same set of locks but in a different order.

 It's likely the implementation of WaitOne( ) uses the Win32 API call WaitForSingleObject( ), and the implementation of WaitAny( ) and WaitAll( ) use the Win32 API call WaitForMultipleObjects( ).

Manual-Reset Event

The class ManualResetEvent derives from WaitHandle and signals an event across threads. The ManualResetEvent definition is:

```
public class ManualResetEvent : WaitHandle
{
    public ManualResetEvent(bool initialState);
    public bool Reset( );
    public bool Set( );
}
```

ManualResetEvent is very similar to the Windows manual reset event. The Set( ) method sets the state of the handle to signal; the Reset( ) method sets the handle to the nonsignaled state. The constructor of ManualResetEvent accepts the initialState flag. Constructing an event with initialState set to true creates the event in a signaled state, and false constructs it nonsignaled. Using ManualResetEvent is straightforward: you construct a new event object that multiple threads have access to. When one thread needs to block until some event takes place, it calls one of Manual-ResetEvent's base class's (WaitHandle) waiting methods. When the other thread wants to signal the event, it calls the Set( ) method. Once the state of the ManualResetEvent object is signaled, it stays signaled until some thread explicitly calls the Reset( ) method. This is why it's called a manual reset event. Note that while the event state is set to signaled, all waiting threads are unblocked. Example 8-7 demonstrates using a ManualResetEvent object.

Example 8-7. Using ManualResetEvent

```
public class EventDemo : IDisposable
{
    private ManualResetEvent m_Event;

    public EventDemo( )
    {
        m_Event = new ManualResetEvent(false);//Created unsignaled

        ThreadStart threadStart = new ThreadStart(DoWork);
        Thread thread = new Thread(threadStart);
        thread.Start( );
    }
    protected void DoWork( )
    {
        int counter = 0;
        while(true)
        {
            m_Event.WaitOne( );
            counter++;
            Trace.WriteLine("Iteration # "+ counter.ToString( ));
        }
    }
    public void GoThread( )
    {
        m_Event.Set( );
        Trace.WriteLine("Go Thread!");
    }
    public void StopThread( )
    {
        m_Event.Reset( );
        Trace.WriteLine("Stop Thread!");
    }
    public void Dispose( )
    {
        m_Event.Close( );
    }
}
```

In the example, the class EventDemo creates a new thread whose thread method DoWork( ) traces a counter value in a loop to the Output window. However, DoWork( ) doesn't start tracing right away; before every loop iteration, it waits for the m_Event member of type ManualResetEvent to be signaled first. Signaling is done by calling the GoThread( ) method, which simply calls the Set( ) method of the event. Once the event is signaled, DoWork( ) keeps tracing the counter until the StopThread( ) method is called. StopThread( ) blocks the thread by calling the Reset( ) method of the event. You can start and stop the thread execution as many times as you like using the event. A possible output of Example 8-7 might be:

```
Go Thread!
Iteration # 1
Iteration # 2
```

```
Iteration # 3
Stop Thread!
Go Thread!
Iteration # 4
Iteration # 5
Stop Thread!
```

You can clearly see the ease with which you synchronize multiple threads using .NET waitable handles. Note that the class EventDemo closes the event object in its Dispose( ) method.

 Unlike raw Windows manual reset events, there is no way to name an event so that it can be shared across app domains.

Auto-Reset Event

The AutoResetEvent is defined as:

```
public class AutoResetEvent : WaitHandle
{
    public AutoResetEvent(bool initialState);
    public bool Reset( );
    public bool Set( );
}
```

This event is identical to the ManualResetEvent, with one important difference: once the state of the event is set to signaled, it remains so until a single thread is released from its waiting call, at which point the state reverts automatically to nonsignaled. If multiple threads are waiting for the event, they are placed in a queue and are taken out of that queue in order. If no threads are waiting when Set( ) is called, the state of the event remains signaled. If the event in Example 8-7 is an auto-reset event, a possible output might be:

```
Go Thread!
Iteration # 1
Go Thread!
Iteration # 2
Go Thread!
Iteration # 3
Go Thread!
Iteration # 4
```

The worker thread traces a single iteration at a time and blocks between iterations until the next call to GoThread( ). There is no need to call StopThread( ).

 In the current release of .NET, unlike the native Windows events, both the managed manual reset and auto-reset events are unnamed. Future releases of .NET will support named events. Named events are useful in some porting or cross-process communication mechanisms.

Events Versus Monitor

Both the `WaitHandle`-derived event subclasses (`AutoResetEvent` and `ManualResetEvent`) and the `Monitor` class allow one thread to wait for an event and another thread to signal (or pulse) the event. The main difference between the two mechanisms is that after `Monitor` is pulsed, it has no recollection of action. Even if no thread is waiting for the `Monitor` when it's pulsed, the next thread to wait on the `Monitor` will be blocked. Events, on the other hand, have "memory": their state remains signaled. A manual-reset event remains signaled until it's reset explicitly, and the auto-reset event remains signaled until a thread waits on it or until it's reset explicitly.

The Mutex

A .NET `Mutex` type is a `WaitHandle`-derived class that ensures mutual exclusion of threads from a resource or code section. The `Mutex` class is defined as:

```
public sealed class Mutex : WaitHandle
{
    public Mutex( );
    public Mutex(bool initiallyOwned);
    public Mutex(bool initiallyOwned, string name);
    public Mutex(bool initiallyOwned, string name,
                 out bool createdNew);
    public void ReleaseMutex( );
}
```

An instance of `Mutex`, also known as a mutex, assigns one of two logical meanings to the handle state: owned or unowned. A mutex can be owned by exactly one thread at a time. To own a mutex, a thread must call one of the wait methods of its base class, `WaitHandle`. If the mutex instance is unowned, the thread gets ownership. If another thread owns the mutex, the thread is blocked until the mutex is released. Once the thread that owns the mutex is done with the resource, it calls the `ReleaseMutex( )` method to set the mutex state to unowned, thus allowing other threads access to the resource associated and protected by the mutex. Only the current owner of the mutex can call `ReleaseMutex( )`. If a different thread tries to release the mutex, .NET throws an exception of type `ApplicationException`, (although the exception type `SynchronizationLockException` exception would probably be a more consistent choice.) If more then than one thread tries to acquire the mutex, the pending callers are placed in a queue and served one at a time, in order. If the thread that currently already owns the mutex tries to acquire the mutex by making additional waiting calls, it isn't blocked, but it should make a matching number of calls to `ReleaseMutex( )`. If the thread that owns the mutex terminates without releasing it, .NET releases the mutex automatically. This is done regardless of how the thread was terminated, although the .NET documentation states that .NET does so only if the thread was terminated normally. Nevertheless, be sure to always call `ReleaseMutex( )` by placing the call to `ReleaseMutex( )` in a `finally` statement.

Creating a mutex

The default constructor of the Mutex class creates it in the unowned state. If the creating thread wants to own the mutex, the thread must wait for the mutex first. The three other parameterized, overloaded versions of the constructor accept the bool initiallyOwned flag, letting you explicitly set the initial state of the mutex. By setting initiallyOwned to true, the creating thread initially owns the mutex. The parameterized constructors also allow you to specify a mutex name, in the name parameter. The *mutex name* is any identifying string such as "My Mutex." By default, a mutex has no name, and you can pass in a null for an explicitly nameless mutex. However, if you do provide a name, any thread on the machine, including threads in other app domains or processes, can try to access this mutex. When you specify a name, the operating system checks whether somebody else has already created a mutex with that name, and if so, it gives the creating thread a local object representing the global mutex. A named mutex allows for cross-process and cross-app-domain communication. If you try to create a named mutex, you should pass false for initiallyOwned because even if the mutex is already owned by another thread in a different process, .NET will not block your thread. The other alternative is to call the constructor version that accepts the out bool createdNew parameter, letting you know whether you succeeded in owning the named mutex.

A named mutex has a number of liabilities. First, it couples the applications using it because they have to know the mutex name in advance. Second, it's a bad idea to have publicly exposed locks. If the mutex is supposed to protect some global resource, you should encapsulate the mutex in the resource. This decouples the client applications and is more robust because you don't depend on having the client applications disciplined to try to acquire the mutex before accessing the resource. I consider named mutexes to be a thing of the past, a relic from Windows you should use only when porting to .NET legacy code that took advantage of them.

 The same recommendation holds for named events as well, once they become available in .NET.

Using a mutex

Example 8-8 demonstrates using a mutex to provide a thread-safe string property. The mutex is created in the class constructor. The set and get methods acquire the mutex before reading or setting the actual member variable and then release the mutex. Note the use of a temporary variable in the set method, so you can release the mutex before returning. Note the call to Close( ) in the Dispose( ) method.

Example 8-8. Using a mutex

```
public class MutexDemo : IDisposable
{
   Mutex m_Mutex;
   string m_MyString;

   public MutexDemo( )
   {
      m_Mutex = new Mutex( );
   }

   public string MyString
   {
      set
      {
         m_Mutex.WaitOne( );
         m_MyString = value;
         m_Mutex.ReleaseMutex( );
      }
      get
      {
         m_Mutex.WaitOne( );
         string temp = m_MyString;
         m_Mutex.ReleaseMutex( );
         return temp;
      }
   }
   public void Dispose( )
   {
      m_Mutex.Close( );
   }
}
```

Interlocked Class

Sometimes if all you want to do is to increment or decrement a value, or exchange or compare values, there is a more efficient mechanism than using one or more mutexes. .NET provides the class Interlocked to address this need. Interlocked supports a set of static methods that access a variable in an atomic manner:

```
public sealed class Interlocked
{
   public static int  Increment(ref int location);
   public static long Increment(ref long location);
   public static int  Decrement(ref int location);
   public static long Decrement(ref long location);

   public static int   CompareExchange(ref int location1,int value,int comparand);
   public static float CompareExchange(ref float location1,float value,
                                                            float comparand);
   public static object CompareExchange(ref object location1,object value,
                                                             object comparand);
```

```
    public static float  Exchange(ref float location1, float value);
    public static object Exchange(ref object location1, object value);
    public static int    Exchange(ref int location1, int value);
}
```

Interlocked provides overloaded methods for incrementing and decrementing int and long types, returning the new value:

```
int i = 8;
int newValue = Interlocked.Increment(ref i);
Debug.Assert(i == 9);
Debug.Assert(newValue == 9);
```

Interlocked provides overloaded methods for more complex operations: Exchange() assigns a value from one variable to another. CompareExchange() compares two variables, and if they are equal, assigns a new value to one of them. Like Increment() and Decrement(), these two complex operations have overloaded methods for int and long, but also for generic object variables. Interlocked is especially useful when both a read and a write operation are needed.

 The current release of .NET doesn't provide a managed wrapper around a native Win32 semaphore lock. This oversight is likely to be rectified in future releases of .NET.

The Reader/Writer Lock

Consider a member variable or a property that is frequently read and written by multiple threads. Locking the whole object using a Monitor object is inefficient because a macro lock will lock all member variables. Using a mutex dedicated to that member variable (as in Example 8-8) is also inefficient because if no thread is writing a new value, multiple threads can concurrently read the current value. This common pattern is called *multiple readers/single writer* because you can have many threads reading a value but only one thread writing to it at a time. While a write operation is in progress, no thread should be allowed to read. .NET provides a lock designed to address the multiple readers/single writer situation called ReaderWriterLock. ReaderWriterLock is defined as:

```
public sealed class ReaderWriterLock
{
    public ReaderWriterLock();

    public bool IsReaderLockHeld{ get; }
    public bool IsWriterLockHeld{ get; }
    public int  WriterSeqNum{ get; }

    public void AcquireReaderLock(int millisecondsTimeout);
    public void AcquireReaderLock(TimeSpan timeout);
    public void AcquireWriterLock(int millisecondsTimeout);
    public void AcquireWriterLock(TimeSpan timeout);
    public bool AnyWritersSince(int seqNum);
```

```
    public void DowngradeFromWriterLock(ref LockCookie lockCookie);
    public LockCookie ReleaseLock();
    public void ReleaseReaderLock();
    public void ReleaseWriterLock();
    public void RestoreLock(ref LockCookie lockCookie);
    public LockCookie UpgradeToWriterLock(int millisecondsTimeout);
    public LockCookie UpgradeToWriterLock(TimeSpan timeout);
}
```

You use the AcquireReaderLock( ) method to acquire a lock for reading a value and
AcquireWriterLock( ) to acquire a lock for writing a value. Once you are done reading or writing, you need to call ReleaseReaderLock( ) or ReleaseWriterLock( ), respectively. ReaderWriterLock keeps track of the threads owning it and applies the multiple
readers/single writer semantics: if no thread calls AcquireWriterLock( ), every thread
that calls AcquireReaderLock( ) isn't blocked and is allowed to access the resource. If
a thread calls AcquireWriterLock( ), ReaderWriterLock blocks the caller until all the
currently reading threads call ReleaseReaderLock( ). ReaderWriterLock then blocks
any further calls to AcquireReaderLock( ) and AcquireWriterLock( ), and grants the
writing thread access.

Pending writing threads are placed in a queue and are served in order, one by one. In
effect, ReaderWriterLock serializes all writing threads, allowing access one at a time,
but it allows concurrent reading access. As you can see, ReaderWriterLock is a
throughput-oriented lock. ReaderWriterLock provides overloaded methods that
accept a timeout for acquiring the lock. ReaderWriterLock provides the
UpgradeToWriterLock( ) method to upgrade a reader's lock to a writer lock (for example, based on the information read, you may need to write something instead) and
DowngradeFromWriterLock( ) to convert a write request in progress to a read request.
ReaderWriterLock also automatically handles nested lock requests by readers and
writers. Example 8-9 demonstrates a typical case that uses ReaderWriterLock to provide multiple readers/single writer semantics to a property. The constructor creates a
new instance of ReaderWriterLock. The get method calls AcquireReaderLock( ) before
reading the member variable and ReleaseReaderLock( ) afterwards. The set method
calls AcquireWriterLock( ) before assigning a new value to the member variable and
ReleaseWriterLock( ) after updating the property with the new value.

Example 8-9. Using ReaderWriterLock

```
public class MyClass
{
   string m_MyString;
   ReaderWriterLock m_RWLock;
   public MyClass()
   {
      m_RWLock = new ReaderWriterLock();
   }

   public string MyString
   {
```

Example 8-9. Using ReaderWriterLock (continued)

```
   set
   {
      m_RWLock.AcquireWriterLock(Timeout.Infinite);
      m_MyString = value;
      m_RWLock.ReleaseWriterLock();
   }
   get
   {
      m_RWLock.AcquireReaderLock(Timeout.Infinite);
      string temp = m_MyString;
      m_RWLock.ReleaseReaderLock();
      return temp;
   }
}
}
```

 Be sure to release the ReaderWriterLock in the face of exceptions. Unfortunately, there is no built-in support via a lock-like statement. Make sure to release the ReaderWriterLock in a finally statement.

Killing a Thread

One of the most common synchronization challenges you as a developer face is the task of killing worker threads, usually upon application shutdown. As mentioned previously, you should avoid calling Thread.Abort() to terminate your thread. Instead, in each iteration, the thread method should check a flag, signaling it whether to do another iteration or return from the method. This section provides you with template code you can use for killing your threads. The template is shown in Example 8-10.

Example 8-10. A worker thread template with a Kill() method

```
public class WorkerThread : IDisposable
{
   Thread m_ThreadObj;
   bool   m_EndLoop;
   Mutex  m_EndLoopMutex;
   bool   EndLoop
   {
      set
      {
         m_EndLoopMutex.WaitOne();
         m_EndLoop = value;
         m_EndLoopMutex.ReleaseMutex();
      }
      get
      {
         bool result = false;
         m_EndLoopMutex.WaitOne();
```

Example 8-10. A worker thread template with a Kill() method (continued)

```
                result = m_EndLoop;
                m_EndLoopMutex.ReleaseMutex( );
                return result;
        }
    }
    public WorkerThread( )
    {
        m_EndLoop = false;
        m_ThreadObj = null;
        m_EndLoopMutex = new Mutex( );
    }
    ~WorkerThread( )
    {
        Kill( );
    }
    public void Dispose( )
    {
        Kill( );
    }
    public void Run( )
    {
        m_ThreadObj = Thread.CurrentThread;
        int i = 0;
        while(EndLoop == false)
        {
            Trace.WriteLine("Thread is alive, Counter is " + i);
            i++;
        }
    }
    //Kill is called on client thread—must use cached thread object
    public void Kill( )
    {
        Debug.Assert(m_ThreadObj != null);
        if(m_ThreadObj.IsAlive == false)
        {
            return;
        }
        EndLoop = true;
        //Wait for thread to die
        m_ThreadObj.Join( );
        if(m_EndLoopMutex != null)
        {
            m_EndLoopMutex.Close( );
        }
    }
}
//Using WorkerThread:
WorkerThread workerThread = new WorkerThread( );
ThreadStart  threadStart  = new ThreadStart(workerThread.Run);
Thread thread = new Thread(threadStart);
thread.Start( );
```

Example 8-10. A worker thread template with a Kill() method (continued)

```
//Sometime later:
workerThread.Kill();
```

Example 8-10 defines the class `WorkerThread`. `WorkerThread` contains the thread method `Run()`, which traces the value of a counter to the Output window in a loop:

```
while(EndLoop == false)
{
   Trace.WriteLine("Thread is alive, Counter is " + i);
   i++;
}
```

Before every loop iteration, `Run()` checks the Boolean property `EndLoop`. If `EndLoop` is set to `false`, `Run()` performs another iteration. `WorkerThread` provides the `Kill()` method, which sets the `EndLoop` to `true`, causing `Run()` to return and the thread to terminate. `EndLoop` actually gets and sets the value of the `m_EndLoop` member variable. Because `Kill()` is called on a client thread, you must provide thread-safe access to `m_EndLoop`. You can use any of the manual locks presented in this chapter: you can lock the whole `WorkerThread` object using `Monitor`; you can also use `ReaderWriterLock()`, except that it's excessive for a property that will be accessed by only one or two threads. I chose to use `Mutex`:

```
bool EndLoop
{
   set
   {
      m_EndLoopMutex.WaitOne();
      m_EndLoop = value;
      m_EndLoopMutex.ReleaseMutex();
   }
   get
   {
      bool result = false;
      m_EndLoopMutex.WaitOne();
      result = m_EndLoop;
      m_EndLoopMutex.ReleaseMutex();
      return result;
   }
}
```

`Kill()` should return only when the worker thread is dead. To that end, `Kill()` calls `Join()` on the worker thread after verifying the thread is alive. However, because `Kill()` is called on the client thread, the `WorkerThread` object must store a `Thread` object referring to the worker thread as a member variable in the `m_ThreadObj` member variable. You can only store the thread value in the thread method, not in the constructor, which executes on the creating client's thread. This is exactly what `Run()` does in this line:

```
m_ThreadObj = Thread.CurrentThread;
```

Note that calling Kill( ) multiple times is harmless. Also note that Kill( ) does the cleanup of closing the mutex. Finally, what if the client never calls Kill( )? To answer that, the WorkerThread class implements IDisposable and a destructor, both calling Kill( ):

```
public void ~WorkerThread( )
{
   Kill( );
}
public void Dispose( )
{
   Kill( );
}
```

It's important to understand that Kill( ) isn't the same as Dispose( ). Kill( ) handles execution flow such as application shutdown or timely termination of threads, whereas Dispose( ) caters to memory and resource management, and disposes of other resources the WorkerThread class might hold. The only reason why Dispose( ) is calling Kill( ) is as a contingency, in case the client developer forgets to do it. The source code accompanying this book contains the WorkerThread class, which is a high-level wrapper class around the basic .NET Thread class. It provides easy thread creation and other features, including a Kill( ) method.

Using .NET Multithreading Services

In addition to the basic .NET multithreading features described at the beginning of this chapter, .NET offers a set of advanced services. Some of these features, such as thread local storage, timers, and the thread pool, are also available in a similar format to Windows developers. Some other features, such as thread-relative static variables, are .NET innovations or are specific aspects of .NET application frameworks. This section briefly describes these .NET multithreading services.

Thread-Relative Static Variables

By default, static variables are visible to all threads in an app domain. This is similar to classic C++ (or Windows), in which static variables are accessible to all threads in the same process. The problem with having all the threads in the app domain able to access the same static variables is the potential for corruption and the need to synchronize access to those variables. As a result, you increase the likelihood of deadlock. The need to synchronize access may be a necessary evil if indeed the static variables need to be shared between multiple threads. However, for cases in which you have no need to share the static variables between threads, .NET supports thread-relative static variables: each thread in the app domain gets its own copy of the static variable. You use the ThreadStaticAttribute to mark a static variable as thread-relative:

```
public class MyClass
{
    [ThreadStatic]
    static string m_MyString;
    public static string MyString
    {
        set{m_MyString = value;}
        get{return m_MyString;}
    }
}
```

You can apply the ThreadStaticAttribute only to static member variables, not to static properties or static methods, but you can still wrap the static member with a static property. Thread-relative static variables enforce thread safety and the need to protect the variables because they can be accessed only by a single thread and because each thread gets its own copy of the static variables. Thread-relative static variables usually also imply thread affinity between objects and threads because the objects will expect to always run on the same thread, and so they will have their version of the variable. You should be aware of the following pitfall when using thread-relative static variables: each thread must perform initialization of the thread-relative static variables in case the values provided by the static constructor aren't good enough. I find thread-relative static to be an interesting feature of the .NET runtime, but I also find it of little practical use. First, you are more likely to want to share the static variables with other threads than to make it thread-relative. Second because exposing a member variable directly is a bad idea in general, you are likely to use the static property to access the variable. As you have seen in the manual synchronization section, encapsulating the locking in the property is easy enough, and it seems to be worth the trouble to be able to share the variable between threads.

Thread Local Storage

Objects allocated off the global managed heap are all visible and accessible to all threads in that app domain. NET provides a thread-specific heap called the *thread local storage*, or TLS. The TLS is actually part of the thread's stack, and therefore only that thread can access it. You can use the TLS for anything you'd use the global heap for, except there is no need to synchronize access to objects allocated off the TLS because only one thread can access them. The downside to using the TLS is that components that wish to take advantage of it must have thread affinity because they must execute on the same thread to access the same TLS. The TLS provides *slots* in which you can store objects. The slot is an object of type LocalDataStoreSlot. LocalDataStoreSlot is nothing more than a type-safe key object, defined as:

```
public sealed class LocalDataStoreSlot
{}
```

You use the LocalDataStoreSlot object to identify the slot itself. There are two kinds of slots: named and unnamed. An *unnamed slot* is freed automatically by the garbage collector; you must free a *named slot* explicitly. You allocate and use slots via static methods of the Thread class:

```
public sealed class Thread
{
    public static LocalDataStoreSlot AllocateDataSlot();
    public static LocalDataStoreSlot AllocateNamedDataSlot(string name);

    public static void FreeNamedDataSlot(string name);
    public static LocalDataStoreSlot GetNamedDataSlot(string name);

    public static void SetData(LocalDataStoreSlot slot, object data);
    public static object GetData(LocalDataStoreSlot slot);
}
```

Using a named slot

You can use the AllocateNamedDataSlot() method to allocate a named slot and get back a LocalDataStoreSlot object. You then use the SetData() method to store data in the slot:

```
int num = 8;
LocalDataStoreSlot dataSlot;
dataSlot = Thread.AllocateNamedDataSlot("My TLS Slot");

Thread.SetData(dataSlot,num);
```

Any object on the thread can use the GetNamedDataSlot() to get back a LocalDataStoreSlot object and then call GetData() to retrieve the data stored:

```
object obj;

LocalDataStoreSlot dataSlot;
dataSlot = Thread.GetNamedDataSlot("My TLS Slot");

obj = Thread.GetData(dataSlot);
Thread.FreeNamedDataSlot("My TLS Slot");

int num = (int)obj;
Debug.Assert(num == 8);
```

Once you are done with the named slot, you must call FreeNamedDataSlot() to deallocate it.

Using an unnamed slot

The method AllocateDataSlot() allocates a LocalDataStoreSlot object similar to the AllocateNamedDataSlot() method. The two main differences are that all clients accessing the slot must share the LocalDataStoreSlot object because there is no way to reference it by name. In addition, there is no need to free the slot object manually:

```
//Storing:

int num = 8;
LocalDataStoreSlot dataSlot;
dataSlot = Thread.AllocateDataSlot();

Thread.SetData(dataSlot,num);

//Retrieving:
object obj;

obj = Thread.GetData(dataSlot);
int num = (int)obj;

Debug.Assert(num == 8);
```

The Thread Pool

Creating a worker thread and managing its lifecycle yourself gives you ultimate control over that thread. It also increases the overall complexity of your application. If all you need is to dispatch a unit of work to a worker thread, then instead of creating a thread, you can take advantage of a .NET-provided thread. .NET provides in each process a pool of worker threads called the *thread pool*. The thread pool is managed by .NET, and it has a set of threads ready to serve application requests. .NET makes extensive use of the thread pool itself. For example, it uses the thread pool for asynchronous calls (discussed in Chapter 7), remote calls (discussed in Chapter 10), and for timers (discussed later on in this chapter). You access the .NET thread pool via the public static methods of the ThreadPool class. Using the thread pool is straightforward: first you create a delegate of type WaitCallback, targeting a method with a matching signature:

```
public delegate void WaitCallback(object state);
```

You then provide the delegate to one of the ThreadPool class static methods, typically QueueUserWorkItem():

```
public sealed class ThreadPool
{
    public static bool QueueUserWorkItem(WaitCallback callBack);
    /* Other methods */
}
```

As the method name implies, dispatching a work unit to the thread pool is subject to pool limitations, meaning if there are no available threads in the pool, the work unit is queued and is served only when a worker thread returns to the pool. Pending requests are served in order.

Example 8-11 demonstrates using the thread pool. For diagnostic purposes, you can find out whether the thread your code runs on originated from the thread pool using the IsThreadPoolThread property of the Thread class (as shown in Example 8-11).

Example 8-11. Posting a work unit to the thread pool

```
void ThreadPoolCallback(object state)
{
   Thread currentThread = Thread.CurrentThread;
   Debug.Assert(currentThread.IsThreadPoolThread);
   int threadID = currentThread.GetHashCode( );
   Trace.WriteLine("Called on thread with ID :" + threadID.ToString( ));
}

WaitCallback callBack = new WaitCallback(ThreadPoolCallback);
ThreadPool.QueueUserWorkItem(callBack);
```

A second overloaded version of QueueUserWorkItem( ) allows you to pass in an identifier to the callback method, in the form of a generic object:

```
public static bool QueueUserWorkItem(WaitCallback callBack,object state);
```

The identifier is passed in as a single parameter to the callback method. If you don't provide such a parameter, (as in Example 8-11), .NET passes in null. The identifier enables the same callback method to handle multiple posted requests, while at the same time, it's able to distinguish between them. The ThreadPool class supports a number of other useful ways to queue a work unit. The RegisterWait-ForSingleObject( ) method allows you to provide a waitable handle as a parameter. The thread from the thread pool waits for the handle and only calls the callback once the handle is signaled. You can also specify a timeout to wait for. The GetAvailableThreads( ) method allows you to find out how many threads are available in the pool, and the GetMaxThreads( ) returns the maximum size of the pool.

> In the current release of .NET, the thread pool isn't boundless. Avoid lengthy operations in the callback so that the thread returns to the pool as soon as possible, to service other clients. If you require lengthy operations, create dedicated threads.

ISynchronizeInvoke

When a client on thread T1 calls a method on an object, that method is executed on the client's thread, T1. However, what should be done in cases when the object must always run on the same thread, say T2? Such situations are common when thread affinity is required. For example, .NET Windows Forms windows and controls must always process messages on the same thread that created them. To address such situations, .NET provides the ISynchronizeInvoke interface, in the System. ComponentModel namespace:

```
public interface ISynchronizeInvoke
{
   object Invoke(Delegate method,object[ ] args);
   IAsyncResult BeginInvoke(Delegate method,object[ ] args);
```

```
    object EndInvoke(IAsyncResult result);
    bool InvokeRequired {get;}
}
```

Using ISynchronizeInvoke

ISynchronizeInvoke provides a generic and standard mechanism to invoke methods
on objects residing on other threads. For example, if the object implements
ISynchronizeInvoke, the client on thread T1 could call ISynchronizeInvoke's Invoke( )
on an object. The implementation of Invoke( ) blocks the calling thread, marshals the
call to T2, executes the call on T2, marshals the returned values to T1, and returns
control to the calling client on T1. Invoke( ) accepts a delegate targeting the method
to invoke on T2, and a generic array of objects as parameters. Example 8-12 demonstrates the use of ISynchronizeInvoke. In the example, a Calculator class implements
ISynchronizeInvoke and provides the Add( ) method for adding two numbers.

Example 8-12. Using ISynchronizeInvoke

```
public class Calculator : ISynchronizeInvoke
{
    public int Add(int arg1,int arg2)
    {
        int threadID = Thread.CurrentThread.GetHashCode( );
        Trace.WriteLine("Calculator thread ID is " + threadID.ToString( ));
        return arg1 + arg2;
    }
    //ISynchronizeInvoke implementation
    public object Invoke(Delegate method,object[ ] args)
    {...}
    public IAsyncResult BeginInvoke(Delegate method,object[ ] args)
    {...}
    public object EndInvoke(IAsyncResult result)
    {...}
    public bool InvokeRequired
    {...}
}
}
//Client-side code
public delegate int AddDelegate(int arg1,int arg2);

int threadID = Thread.CurrentThread.GetHashCode( );
Trace.WriteLine("Client thread ID is " + threadID.ToString( ));

Calculator  calc;
/* Some code to initialize calc */

AddDelegate addDelegate = new AddDelegate(calc.Add);

object[ ] args = {3,4};
int sum = 0;
sum = (int)calc.Invoke(addDelegate,args);
Debug.Assert(sum ==7);
```

Example 8-12. Using ISynchronizeInvoke (continued)

```
/* Possible output:
Calculator thread ID is 29
Client thread ID is 30
*/
```

Because the call is marshaled to a different thread from that of the caller, you might want to invoke it asynchronously, which is exactly what the BeginInvoke( ) and EndInvoke( ) methods provide. These methods are used in accordance with the general asynchronous programming model described in Chapter 7. In addition, because ISynchronizeInvoke can be called on the same thread as the thread the caller tries to redirect the call to, the caller can check the InvokeRequired property. If it returns false, the caller can call the object methods directly.

ISynchronizeInvoke methods aren't type-safe. In case of a mismatch, an exception is thrown at runtime instead of a compilation error. Pay extra attention when using ISynchronizeInvoke because the compiler won't be there for you.

Windows Forms and ISynchronizeInvoke

Windows Forms base classes make extensive use of ISynchronizeInvoke. The Control class and every class derived from Control relies on the underlying Windows messages and a message-processing loop (the *message pump*) to process them. The message loop must have thread affinity because messages to a window are delivered only to the thread that created it. In general, you must use ISynchronizeInvoke to access a Windows Forms window from another thread.

Implementing ISynchronizeInvoke

Implementing ISynchronizeInvoke requires a delegate to dynamically invoke the method with late binding. As presented in Chapter 6, the delegate type provides the DynamicInvoke( ) method, defined as:

```
public object DynamicInvoke(object[ ] args);
```

In the abstract, when you implement ISynchronizeInvoke, you need to post the method delegate to the actual thread the object needs to run on and to have it call DynamicInvoke( ) on the delegate in Invoke( ) and BeginInvoke( ). In particular, implementing ISynchronizeInvoke is a nontrivial programming feat. The source files accompanying this book contain a helper class called Synchronizer. Synchronizer is a generic implementation of ISynchronizeInvoke. You can use Synchronizer as-is by either deriving from it or containing it as a member object and then delegating your implementation of ISynchronizeInvoke to it.

Here are the key elements of implementing Synchronizer:

- Synchronizer uses a nested class called WorkerThread.
- WorkerThread has a queue of work items. WorkItem is a class containing the method delegate and the parameters.
- Both Invoke( ) and BeginInvoke( ) add to the work item queue.
- WorkerThread creates a worker thread, which monitors the work item queue. When the queue has items, the worker thread retrieves them and calls DynamicInvoke( ) on the method.

Timers

Applications often need a certain task to occur at regular time intervals. Such service is implemented by timers. A *timer* is an object that repeatedly calls back into the application at set intervals. For example, you can use a timer to update the user interface with anything from stock quotes to available disk space. You can also use a timer to implement a *watchdog*, which periodically checks the status of various components or devices in your application. With timers, you can also poll communication ports or check the status of job queues. In short, many decent-sized applications use timers. In the past, developers were left to their own devices when implementing timers. They usually created a worker thread, whose thread method executed the following logic in pseudocode:

```
public class Timer
{
   public void ThreadMethod( )
   {
      while(true)
      {
         Tick( );
         Thread.Sleep(Interval);
      }
   }
   public int Interval
   {get;set;}
   void Tick( )
   {
      /* Call back into the application */
   }
}
```

However, such solutions had disadvantages: you had to write code to start and stop the timer, manage the worker thread, change the interval, and hook the timer to the callback function into the application. Furthermore, even if you took advantage of timers made available by the operating system, such as the CreateWaitableTimer( ) function of the Win32 API, you coupled your application to that mechanism, and switching to a different implementation wasn't trivial.

.NET comes out of the box with not one, but three complementary timer mechanisms you can use in your application. All three mechanisms comply with the same set of generic requirements, allowing the application using the timer to:

- Start and stop the timer repeatedly
- Change the timer interval
- Use the same callback method to service multiple timers and be able to distinguish among the different timers

This section discusses and contrasts .NET timers support and recommends where and when to use each of them.

System.Timers.Timer

The System.Timers namespace contains the definition of the Timer class:

```
public class System.Timers.Timer : Component,ISupportInitialize
{
    public Timer();
    public Timer(double interval);

    // Properties
    public bool AutoReset{get; set; }
    public bool Enabled{get; set; }
    public double Interval{get; set;}
    public ISynchronizeInvoke SynchronizingObject { get; set; }

    //Events
    public event ElapsedEventHandler Elapsed;

    // Methods
    public void Close();
    public void Start();
    public void Stop();

    /* Other members  */
}
```

The System.Timers.Timer class has an event member called Elapsed, which is a delegate of type ElapsedEventHandler, defined as:

```
public delegate void ElapsedEventHandler(object sender,ElapsedEventArgs e);
```

You provide Elapsed with timer handling methods with a matching signature:

```
void OnTick(object sender,ElapsedEventArgs e){...}
```

System.Timers.Timer class calls into these methods at specified timer intervals, using a thread from the thread pool. You then specify an interval using the Interval property. The sender argument to the timer handling method identifies the timer object. As a result, you can have the same timer method called by multiple timers and use the sender argument to distinguish among them. You can hook up the timer to more than one timer handling method by simply adding more targets to the Elapsed event. The ElapsedEventArgs class provides the time the method was called and is defined as:

```
public class ElapsedEventArgs : EventArgs
{
    public DateTime SignalTime{get;}
}
```

To start or stop the timer notifications, simply call the Start( ) or Stop( ) methods. The Enabled property allows you to silence the timer by not raising the event. As a result, Enabled and Start( ) and Stop( ) methods are equivalent. Finally, when the application shuts down, call the Close( ) method of the timer, to dispose of the system resources it used. Example 8-13 demonstrates using System.Timers.Timer.

Example 8-13. Using System.Timers.Timer

```
using System.Timers;

class SystemTimerClient
{
    System.Timers.Timer m_Timer;
    int m_Counter;
    public SystemTimerClient( )
    {
        m_Counter = 0;
        m_Timer = new System.Timers.Timer( );
        m_Timer.Interval = 1000;//One second
        m_Timer.Elapsed += new ElapsedEventHandler(OnTick);
        m_Timer.Start( );
        //Can block this thread because the Timer uses thread from thread pool
        Thread.Sleep(4000);
        m_Timer.Stop( );
        m_Timer.Close( );
    }
    void OnTick(object source,ElapsedEventArgs e)
    {
        string tickTime = e.SignalTime.ToLongTimeString( );
        m_Counter++;
        Trace.WriteLine(m_Counter.ToString( ) + " " + tickTime);
    }
}

SystemTimerClient obj = new SystemTimerClient( );

//Output:
1 4:20:48 PM
2 4:20:49 PM
3 4:20:50 PM
```

Because the timer handling method is called on a different thread, make sure you synchronize access to the object members; this prevents state corruption.

Of particular interest is the SynchronizingObject property of System.Timers.Timer. It allows you to specify an object implementing ISynchronizeInvoke to be used by the timer to call back into the application instead of directly calling using the thread pool. For example, here is the code required to use System.Timers.Timer in a Windows Forms Form-derived class:

```
public class SystemTimerClient : Form
{
    System.Timers.Timer m_Timer;
    int m_Counter;

    public SystemTimerClient( )
    {
        m_Counter = 0;
        m_Timer = new System.Timers.Timer( );
        m_Timer.Interval = 1000;//One second
        m_Timer.Elapsed += new ElapsedEventHandler(OnTick);
        m_Timer.SynchronizingObject = this;//Form implements ISynchronizeInvoke
        m_Timer.Start( );
    }
    void OnTick(object source,ElapsedEventArgs e)
    {
        //Called on the main UI thread, not on a thread from the pool.
    }
}
```

By default, SynchronizingObject is set to null, so the timer uses the threads from the pool directly.

 Visual Studio.NET has built-in Designer support for System.Timers. Timer. Simply drag and drop a timer from the Components toolbox control to the form, be it Windows Forms, an ASP.NET form, or a web service. The Designer then displays the timer icon underneath the form and allows you to set its properties. In the case of a Windows Forms application, the Designer also sets the SynchronizingObject property to the form itself.

System.Threading.Timer

The System.Threading namespace contains another timer class, defined as:

```
public sealed class System.Threading.Timer : MarshalByRefObject,IDisposable
{
    public Timer(TimerCallback callback,object state,long dueTime,long period);
    /* More overloaded constructors */

    public bool Change(int dueTime, int period);
    /* More overloaded Change( ) */

    public virtual void Dispose( );
}
```

System.Threading.Timer is similar to the System.Timers.Timer: it too uses the thread pool. The main differences are that it provides fine-grained and advanced control; you can set its due time (when should it start ticking), and you can pass any generic information to the callback tick method. To use System.Threading.Timer, you need to provide its constructor with a delegate of type TimerCallback, defined as:

```
public delegate void TimerCallback(object state);
```

The delegate targets a timer callback method, invoked on each timer tick. The state object is typically the object that created the timer, so you can use the same callback method to handle ticks from multiple senders, but you can of course pass in any other argument you like. The other parameter the timer constructor accepts is the timer period (the timer interval). To change the timer period, simply call the Change( ) method, which accepts the new due time and period. System.Threading. Timer doesn't provide an easy way to start or stop it. It starts ticking immediately after the constructor (actually, after the due time has elapsed), and to stop it, you must call its Dispose( ) method. If you want to restart it, you need to create a new timer object. Example 8-14 demonstrates the use of System.Threading.Timer.

Example 8-14. Using System.Threading.Timer

```
using System.Threading;

class ThreadingTimerClient
{
    System.Threading.Timer m_Timer;
    int m_Counter;
    public ThreadingTimerClient( )
    {
        m_Counter = 0;
        Start( );
        //Can block this thread because the Timer uses thread from thread pool
        Thread.Sleep(4000);
        Stop( );
    }
    void Start( )
    {
        TimerCallback callBack = new TimerCallback(OnTick);
        m_Timer = new System.Threading.Timer(callBack,null,0,1000);
    }
    void Stop( )
    {
        m_Timer.Dispose( );
        m_Timer = null;
    }
    void OnTick(object state)
    {
        m_Counter++;
        Trace.WriteLine(m_Counter.ToString( ));
    }
}
```

Example 8-14. Using System.Threading.Timer (continued)

```
ThreadingTimerClient obj = new ThreadingTimerClient();

//Output:
1
2
3
```

System.Windows.Forms.Timer

The System.Windows.Forms namespace contains the Timer class, defined as:

```
public class System.Windows.Forms.Timer : Component
{
    public Timer();
    public Timer(IContainer container);
    public bool Enabled {virtual get; virtual set; }
    public int Interval {get; set; }
    public event EventHandler Tick;
    public void Start();
    public void Stop();
}
```

Even though System.Windows.Forms.Timer methods look like those of System.Timers. Timer, System.Windows.Forms.Timer doesn't use the thread pool to call back into the Windows Forms application. Instead, it's based on the good old WM_TIMER Windows message. Instead of using a thread, the timer posts a WM_TIMER message to the message queue of its current thread at the specified interval. Using System.Windows. Forms.Timer is like using System.Timers.Timer, except the timer-handling method is of the canonical signature defined by the EventHandler delegate. The fact that virtually the same set of methods can use drastically different underlying mechanisms is a testimony to the degree of decoupling from the ticking mechanisms that timers provide to the application using them.

 Visual Studio.NET has built-in Designer support for Windows Forms Timer. Simply drag and drop a timer from the Windows Forms toolbox control to the form. The Designer then displays the timer icon underneath the form and allows you to set its properties.

Because all the callbacks are dispatched on the main UI thread, there is no need to manage concurrency when using Windows Forms timers. On the other hand, that may be a problem if the processing is long because during the processing, the user interface will not be responsive.

Choosing a timer

If you are developing a Windows Forms application, you should use the System. Windows.Forms.Timer. In all other cases, I recommend using System.Timers.Timer. Its

---

methods are easy to use, while `System.Threading.Timer`'s methods are cumbersome and offer no substantial advantage.

Volatile Fields

The compiler tries to optimize access to object fields by caching recently read values. When a member variable is read repeatedly without an attempted write, the compiler can cache the value after the first read in a local temporary variable. Subsequent reads access the temporary variable instead of the actual object:

```
class MyClass
{
    public int Num;
}
MyClass obj = new MyClass();
int num1 = obj.Num;
int num2 = obj.Num;//Compiler may use cached value here
```

This may yield better performance, especially in tight loops:

```
while(<some condition>)
{
    int num = obj.Num;
    /* Using num */
}
```

The problem is that if a thread context switch takes place after the assignment to num1 but before the assignment to num2, and another thread changes the value of the field, num2 will have the old cached value. Of course, it's a bad idea to expose member variables directly in public, and you should always access them via properties. However, in the rare case that you do want to expose public fields without synchronizing access to them, the C# compiler supports volatile fields. A *volatile* field is a field defined using the `volatile` reserved word:

```
class MyClass
{
    public volatile int Num;
}
```

When a field is marked as `volatile`, the compiler doesn't cache its value and always reads the field value. Similarly, the compiler writes assigned values to volatile fields immediately, even if no read operation takes place in between. Visual Basic.NET has no equivalent to the C# volatile word.

 Avoid volatile fields; lock your object or fields instead to guarantee deterministic and thread-safe access.

.NET and COM's Apartments

.NET doesn't have an equivalent to COM's apartments. As you have seen throughout this chapter, every .NET component resides in a multithreaded environment, and it's up to you to provide proper synchronization. The question is, what threading model should .NET components present to COM when interoperating with COM components as clients? The Thread class has a property called ApartmentState of the enum type ApartmentState, defined as:

```
public enum ApartmentState
{
    STA,
    MTA,
    Unknown
}
```

STA stands for single-threaded apartment; MTA stands for multithreaded apartment. The semantic of ApartmentState.Unknown is the same as that of ApartmentState.MTA.

By default, the Thread class's ApartmentState property is set to ApartmentState.Unknown, resulting in the MTA apartment state.

 Threads from the thread pool use the MTA apartment state.

You can programmatically instruct .NET as to what apartment to present to COM by setting the value of the thread's ApartmentState property to either ApartmentState.STA or ApartmentState.MTA (but not ApartmentState.Unknown):

```
Thread currentThread = Thread.CurrentThread;
currentThread.ApartmentState = ApartmentState.STA;
```

If the apartment state of the managed thread matches that of the COM object on which it tries to invoke a method, COM will run the object on that thread. If the threading model is incompatible, COM will marshal the call to the COM object's apartment, according to the COM rules. Obviously, a match in apartment model will result in better performance.

You can set the threading model even before the thread starts to run:

```
ThreadStart threadStart = new ThreadStart(ThreadMethod);
Thread workerThread = new Thread(threadStart);
currentThread.ApartmentState = ApartmentState.STA;
workerThread.Start();
```

You can also use either the STAThread or the MTAThread method attribute to declaratively set the apartment state. Although the compiler doesn't enforce that, you should apply these attributes only to the Main() method and use programmatic settings for your worker threads:

```
[STAThread]
static void Main( )
{...}
```

Note that you can set the apartment model only once, regardless of whether you do it declaratively or programmatically. Future attempts are ignored.

 The Windows Forms application wizard automatically applies the [STAThread] attribute to the Main( ) method of a Windows Forms application. This in done for two reasons. The first is in case the application hosts ActiveX controls, which are STA objects by definition. The second is in case the Windows Forms application interacts with the Clipboard, which still uses COM interop. With the [STAThread] attribute, the underlying physical thread uses OleInitialize( ) instead of CoInitializeEx( ) to set up the apartment model. OleInitialize( ) automatically does additional initialization required for enabling drag and drop.

There is, however, one side effect to selecting an apartment threading model: you can't call WaitHandle.WaitAll( ) from a thread whose apartment state is set to ApartmentState.STA. If you do, .NET throws an exception of type NotSupportedException. This is probably because the underlying implementation of WaitHandle.WaitAll( ) uses the Win32 call WaitForMultipleObjects( ), and that call blocks the STA thread from pumping COM calls in the form of messages to the COM objects. Note that when a managed thread makes a call outside managed code for the first time, .NET calls CoInitializeEX( ) with the appropriate apartment state, even if the thread doesn't intend to interact with COM objects directly.

CHAPTER 9
Serialization and Persistence

In a component-oriented application, the component instances (the objects) maintain their *state* (the object's member variables) in memory and apply business logic on that state. The question is, how is this state initially generated, and what happens to it when the application shuts down or when the user selects Save? In almost every application, object states aren't created out of thin air when the application starts. An application typically loads some file containing data and converts the information in the file into live objects. Similarly, when the application shuts down, the object state is saved to a file or, to use a currently popular term, *persisted* to a file. Traditionally, this sequence is referred to as *serialization* and *deserialization*. The terms were originally coined to describe a simple binary dump of an object's state to a file and its later recovery. In such cases, the application wrote the state of the object serially, one bit at a time. When the application later read the information, it processed the information serially in exactly the same order into a memory location and associated that location with an object.

Classic object-oriented programming offered very little when it came to implementing serialization. The result was that not only did developers spend much of their valuable time on mundane serialization code instead of adding business value, but the resulting solution was proprietary and singular. There was no generic way for two applications to share serialization files because each used its own format, even if both applications ran on the same platform and used the same language, the same memory layout, word size, and so on.

With component-oriented applications, serialization becomes a critical issue. If an application contains several components from various vendors, how will it persist its objects into a single file without having the individual components overwrite and destroy the information persisted there by other components?

.NET provides a standard, straightforward way to serialize and deserialize objects. Even though the .NET solution is trivial to use (in most cases, you aren't required to provide any explicit serialization code), it's also extensible, and you can provide your own serialization format and implementation. .NET serialization is used not only to implement object persistence but also to facilitate the marshaling of objects and object references to remote clients.

This chapter describes the .NET types and tools for implementing serialization on the server and the client side, shows how to provide custom serialization and suggests solutions for dealing with special cases such as the serialization of class hierarchies.

Automatic Serialization

.NET implements the automatic serialization of objects by means of reflection, a simple and elegant technique that uses metadata exposed by every .NET component. Reflection is discussed in detail in Appendix C. .NET can capture the value of every field of an object, and serialize it to memory, a file, or a network connection. .NET also supports automatic deserialization: .NET can create a new object; read its persisted field values; and using reflection, set the value of its fields. Because reflection can access private fields including base-class fields, .NET can take a complete snapshot of the state of an object during serialization and perfectly reconstruct that state during deserialization. Another advantage of reflection-based serialization is that the code used by .NET is completely generic because .NET can serialize any type. There is nothing you need to do to support it. The state of every .NET type can be read or set using reflection.

.NET serializes the object state into a stream. A *stream* is a logical sequence of bytes, independent of a particular medium such as a file, memory, a communication port, or other resource. This extra level of indirection lets you use the same serialization infrastructure with any medium, simply by selecting an appropriate stream type. The various stream types provided by .NET all derive from the abstract class Stream, defined in the System.IO namespace. Although you need a Stream instance to serialize and deserialize an object, there is usually no need to interact explicitly with the methods and properties of the Stream itself.

.NET serialization is object-based. As a result, only instance fields are serialized. Static fields are excluded from serialization.

The Serialization Attribute

By default, user-defined types (classes and structs) aren't serializable. The reason is that .NET has no way to know whether a reflection-based serial dump of the object state to a stream makes sense. Perhaps the object members have some transient value or state (such as an open database connection or communication port). If .NET simply serialized the state of such an object, then after constructing a new object by deserializing it from the stream, you'd end up with a defective object. Consequently, serialization has to be performed by consent of the class's developer.

Enumerations and delegates are always serializable.

To indicate to .NET that instances of your class are serializable, you can add the SerializableAttribute to your class definition. For example:

```
[Serializable]
public class MyClass
{
    public string SomeString;
    public int SomePublicNum;
    int m_SomePrivateNum;
    /* Methods and properties */
}
```

In most cases, decorating a user-defined type definition with the Serializable attribute is all you need to do. If the class has member variables that are complex types themselves, .NET automatically serializes and deserializes these members as well:

```
[Serializable]
public class MyOtherClass
{...}

[Serializable]
public class MyClass
{
    MyOtherClass m_Obj;
    /* Methods and properties */
}
```

The result is recursive iteration over an object and all its contained objects. The object can be the root of a huge graph of interconnected objects, as shown in Figure 9-1.

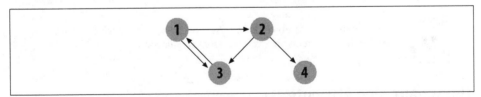

Figure 9-1. NET serialization traverses the entire object graph

Regardless of its depth, .NET captures the entire state of any graph and serializes it. The recursive traversal algorithm used by .NET is smart enough to detect cyclic references in the graph, tagging objects it has already visited and thereby avoiding processing the same object twice. This approach allows .NET to serialize complex data structures such as doubly linked lists.

Nonserializable Members

When a class is serializable, .NET insists that all its member variables be serializable as well, and if it discovers a nonserializable member, it throws an exception of type SerializationException during serialization . However, what if the class has a member that can't be serialized? That type will not have the Serializable attribute and will preclude the containing type from being serialized. Commonly, that nonserializable member is a reference type that requires some special initialization. The solution to this problem requires marking such a member as nonserializable and taking a custom step to initialize it during deserialization.

To allow a serializable type to contain a non-serializable type as a member variable, you need to mark the member with the NonSerialized field attribute; for example:

```
public class MyOtherClass
{..}

[Serializable]
public class MyClass
{
    [NonSerialized]
    MyOtherClass m_Obj;
    /* Methods and properties */
}
```

When NET serializes a member variable, it first reflects it to see whether it has the NonSerialized attribute. If so, .NET ignores that variable and simply skips over it. However, when .NET deserializes the object, it initializes the nonserializable member variable to the default value for that type (a null for all reference types). It's then up to you to provide code to initialize the variable to its correct value. To that end, the object needs to know when it's being deserialized. The notification takes place by implementing the interface IDeserializationCallback, defined in the System.Runtime.Serialization namespace:

```
public interface IDeserializationCallback
{
    void OnDeserialization(object sender);
}
```

IDeserializationCallback's single method OnDeserialization( ) is called after .NET has finished deserializing the object, allowing it to perform the required custom initialization steps. The sender parameter is ignored and is always set to null by .NET. Example 9-1 demonstrates how you can implement IDeserializationCallback. In the example, the class MyClass has a database connection as a member variable. The connection object (SqlConnection) isn't a serializable type and so is marked using the NonSerialized attribute. In its implementation of OnDeserialization( ), MyClass creates a new connection object because after deserialization, the connection member is set to its default value of null. MyClass then initializes the connection object by providing it with a connection string and opens it.

Example 9-1. Custom deserialization using IDeserializationCallback

```
using System.Runtime.Serialization;

[Serializable]
public class MyClass : IDeserializationCallback
{
    [NonSerialized]
    IDbConnection m_Connection;

    public void OnDeserialization(object sender)
    {
        Debug.Assert(m_Connection == null);
        m_Connection = new SqlConnection();
        m_Connection.ConnectionString = "data source= ... ";
        m_Connection.Open();
    }
    /* Other members  */
}
```

> You can't initialize in OnDeserialization() class members marked with the readonly directive because such members can only be initialized in a constructor. If you need to initialize read-only members, you have to use custom serialization, described later on.

Serialization Formatters

It's up to the client to decide which stream type to use for serialization and in which format that data should be represented. A formatter is an object that implements the IFormatter interface, defined in the System.Runtime.Serialization namespace:

```
public interface IFormatter
{
    object Deserialize(Stream serializationStream);
    void Serialize(Stream serializationStream, object graph);
    /* Other methods */
}
```

IFormatter's significant methods are Serialize() and Deserialize(), which perform the actual serialization and deserialization. .NET ships with two formatters: a binary formatter and a Simple Object Access Protocol (SOAP) formatter. The binary formatter generates a compact binary representation of the object's state. It's relatively fast to serialize an object into binary format, and likewise, it's relatively fast to deserialize an object from binary format. The SOAP formatter, as the name implies, persists the object's state, using a text-based XML format. Naturally, the SOAP formatter is considerably slower than the binary formatter because serialization requires composing a SOAP envelope, and deserialization requires SOAP parsing. In addition, the resulting serialization data (the file size or memory footprint) is bigger. The only advantage of using SOAP format is that it's platform-neutral. You can provide the serialization information (via network stream or file access) to applications running on non-

Windows based platforms, and they can deserialize an equivalent object on their side or serialize back to the .NET side their objects. In general, unless cross-platform interoperability is required, you should always use the binary formatter.

Using a binary formatter

The binary formatter is the class `BinaryFormatter` defined in the `System.Runtime.Serialization.Formatters.Binary` namespace. To serialize an object, you need to create a stream object (such as a file stream) and simply call the `Serialize()` method of the formatter, providing the formatter with the object to serialize and the stream to serialize it to. When you are done with the stream, remember to close it. Example 9-2 shows how to serialize an object of type `MyClass` to a file stream.

Example 9-2. Binary serialization using a file stream

```
using System.Runtime.Serialization.Formatters.Binary;

MyClass obj = new MyClass();

//Creating a stream
Stream stream;
stream = new FileStream(@"C:\temp\obj.bin",FileMode.Create,FileAccess.Write);

IFormatter formatter = new BinaryFormatter();

formatter.Serialize(stream,obj);
stream.Close();
```

To deserialize an object, you need to open the appropriate stream (matching the type of stream used for serialization) and call the `Deserialize()` method of the formatter, receiving back an object reference, as shown in Example 9-3.

Example 9-3. Binary deserialization using a file stream

```
using System.Runtime.Serialization.Formatters.Binary;

MyClass obj; //No new!

//Opening a stream

Stream stream;
stream = new FileStream(@"C:\temp\obj.bin",FileMode.Open,FileAccess.Read);
IFormatter formatter = new BinaryFormatter();

obj = (MyClass)formatter.Deserialize(stream);
stream.Close();
```

There are a few things worth mentioning regarding deserialization. First, make sure to open a stream on an existing media, instead of creating a new one and destroying the existing serialized information. Second, note that there is no need to create an object explicitly using new. The Deserialize( ) method creates a new object and returns a reference to it. Third, Deserialize( ) returns a generic object reference, so you need to downcast it to the correct object type being deserialized. If the downcast type is different from the type serialized, an exception is thrown. Finally, be sure to close the stream when you are finished.

Using a SOAP formatter

The class SoapFormatter defined in the System.Runtime.Serialization.Formatters. Soap namespace is used exactly like the BinaryFormatter class. The only difference is that it serializes using SOAP format instead of binary format. Example 9-4 demonstrates serialization into a file stream using the SOAP formatter, and Example 9-5 shows the resulting file content. The deserialization using a SOAP formatter is exactly like Example 9-3, except you should use the SOAP formatter instead of the binary one.

Example 9-4. SOAP serialization using a file stream

```
using System.Runtime.Serialization.Formatters.Soap;

//In the MyClassLibrary assembly:
namespace MyNamespace
{
    [Serializable]
    public class MyClass
    {
        public int Num1;
        public int Num2;
    }
}

//In the client's assembly:
MyClass obj = new MyClass( );
obj.Num1 = 123;
obj.Num2 = 456;

//Creating a stream
Stream stream;
stream = new FileStream(@"C:\temp\obj.xml",FileMode.Create,FileAccess.Write);

IFormatter formatter = new SoapFormatter ( );

formatter.Serialize(stream,obj);
stream.Close( );
```

Example 9-5. The SOAP format serialization output of Example 9-4

```
<SOAP-ENV:Envelope
    xmlns:xsi="http://www.w3.org/2001/XMLSchema-instance"
    xmlns:xsd="http://www.w3.org/2001/XMLSchema"
    xmlns:SOAP-ENC="http://schemas.xmlsoap.org/soap/encoding/"
```

Example 9-5. The SOAP format serialization output of Example 9-4

```
xmlns:SOAP-ENV="http://schemas.xmlsoap.org/soap/envelope/"
xmlns:clr="http://schemas.microsoft.com/soap/encoding/clr/1.0"
SOAP-ENV:encodingStyle="http://schemas.xmlsoap.org/soap/encoding/">
<SOAP-ENV:Body>
    <a1:MyClass
        id="ref-1"
        xmlns:a1="http://schemas.microsoft.com/clr/nsassem/
                    MyNamespace/MyClassLibrary%2C%20
                    Version%3D1.0.898.27976%2C%20
                    Culture%3Dneutral%2C%20
                    PublicKeyToken%3Dnull">
        <Num1>123</Num1>
        <Num2>456</Num2>
    </a1:MyClass>
/SOAP-ENV:Body>
</SOAP-ENV:Envelope>
```

.NET XML Serialization

.NET provides an alternate serialization infrastructure, available in the System.Xml. Serialization namespace. XML serialization is similar in concept to the text-based SOAP formatter. The main difference is that with XML serialization, you have granular control over the layout and structure of the serialized information. Such control is often needed when interoperating with other platforms, or when you need to comply with a predefined data schema. Although XML-based serialization and deserialization is used much the same as the serialization support described so far, it doesn't persist private object fields. XML-based serialization is oriented towards exchanging data across the Internet with other platforms, while .NET serialization is component-based and oriented toward applications and interacting objects.

Serialization and streams

Besides a file stream, you can use any other type of a stream, such as a network or memory stream. Example 9-6 demonstrates how to serialize and deserialize an object to and from a memory stream using the same definitions as in Example 9-4.

Example 9-6. Serialization and deserialization using a memory stream

```
MyClass obj = new MyClass();
obj.Num1 = 123;

//Creating a memory stream
Stream stream = new MemoryStream();

IFormatter formatter = new BinaryFormatter(); //Can be any formatter
formatter.Serialize(stream,obj);
```

Example 9-6. Serialization and deserialization using a memory stream (continued)

```
obj = null;
stream.Position = 0; //Seek to start of the memory stream

obj = (MyClass)formatter.Deserialize(stream);
stream.Close();//Can only close stream after finishing using it

Debug.Assert(obj.Num1 == 123);
```

 .NET remoting uses a memory stream when marshaling an object by value across app domains. Marshaling by value is covered in Chapter 10.

The noteworthy aspect of using streams in serialization is that there are no limits to the number of objects or types you can serialize into a stream. It all depends on the way you manage the stream and the sequence in which you write and read the information. For example, in order to serialize additional objects into the same stream, all you need to do is continue to write to the stream with the formatter. Of course, you have to deserialize in exactly the same order, as shown in Example 9-7. You can use the same formatter object or create a new one.

Example 9-7. Serializing multiple objects to the same stream.

```
MyClass obj1 = new MyClass();
MyClass obj2 = new MyClass();
MyOtherClass obj3 = new MyOtherClass();

//Creating a stream

Stream stream;
stream = new FileStream(@"C:\temp\obj.bin",FileMode.Create,FileAccess.Write);

IFormatter formatter = new BinaryFormatter();

formatter.Serialize(stream,obj1);
formatter.Serialize(stream,obj2);
formatter.Serialize(stream,obj3);
stream.Close();

obj1 = obj2 = obj3 = null;

//Later on:
stream = new FileStream(@"C:\temp\obj.bin",FileMode.Open,FileAccess.Read);

obj1 = (MyClass)formatter.Deserialize(stream);
obj2 = (MyClass)formatter.Deserialize(stream);
obj3 = (MyOtherClass)formatter.Deserialize(stream);
stream.Close();
```

You can achieve a similar effect with memory streams as well (as long as the memory stream automatically allocates additional memory).

Another option is to append the state of additional objects to an existing storage. In the case of a file stream, open the file in append mode:

```
MyClass obj1 = new MyClass();
MyClass obj2 = new MyClass();

IFormatter formatter = new BinaryFormatter();

//Creating a new file
Stream stream;
stream = new FileStream(@"C:\temp\obj.bin",FileMode.Create,FileAccess.Write);

formatter.Serialize(stream,obj1);
stream.Close();

//Append another object:
stream = new FileStream(@"C:\temp\obj.bin",FileMode.Append,FileAccess.Write);

formatter.Serialize(stream,obj2);
stream.Close();
```

Serialization, Types, and Versioning

An application may wish to serialize the state of multiple objects of multiple types to the same stream. For that reason, a simple dump of object state isn't sufficient. The formatter must also capture the objects' type information. During deserialization, the formatter needs to read the type's metadata and initialize a new object according to the information serialized, populating the corresponding field. The easiest way to capture the type information is to record the type's name and reference its assembly. For each object serialized, the formatter persists the state of the object (the value of the various fields) and the version and full name of its assembly, including a token of the assembly's public key (if a strong name is used). This can be seen in Example 9-5. When the formatter deserializes the object, it loads its assembly and reflects the type's metadata.

The formatters comply with the general version binding and resolving policy of .NET described in Chapter 5. If the serialized type's assembly doesn't have a strong name, the formatters try to load a private assembly and completely ignore any version incompatibility between the version captured during serialization and the version of the assembly found. If the serialized type's assembly has a strong name, .NET insists on using a compatible assembly. If such an assembly isn't found, .NET raises an exception of type FileLoadException.

Both the binary and SOAP formatters provide a way to record only the friendly name of the assembly without any version or public key token, even if the assembly has a strong name. The formatters provide a public property, called AssemblyFormat, of the

enum type `FormatterAssemblyStyle`, defined in the `System.Runtime.Serialization.`
`Formatters` namespace:

```
public enum FormatterAssemblyStyle
{
    Full,
    Simple
}
public sealed class BinaryFormatter : IFormatter,...
{
    public FormatterAssemblyStyle AssemblyFormat{get; set;}
    //Other members, including implementation of IFormatter
}
public sealed class SaopFormatter : IFormatter,...
{
    public FormatterAssemblyStyle AssemblyFormat{get; set;}
    //Other members, including implementation of IFormatter
}
```

Note that the `AssemblyFormat` property isn't part of the `IFormatter` interface. The
default value of `AssemblyFormat` is `FormatterAssemblyStyle.Full`. If you set it to
`FormatterAssemblyStyle.Simple`, no version-compatibility checks will take place during deserialization. For example, consider this SOAP serialization code:

```
MyClass obj = new MyClass();
obj.Num1 = 123;
obj.Num2 = 456;

SoapFormatter formatter = new SoapFormatter();
formatter.AssemblyFormat = FormatterAssemblyStyle.Simple;

Stream stream;
stream = new FileStream(@"C:\temp\obj.xml",FileMode.Create,FileAccess.Write);
formatter.Serialize(stream,obj);
stream.Close();
```

This code results in the following SOAP envelope body:

```
<SOAP-ENV:Body>
    <a1:MyClass id="ref-1"
        xmlns:a1="http://schemas.microsoft.com/clr/nsassem/
        MyNamespace/MyClassLibrary">
        <Num1>123</Num1>
        <Num2>456</Num2>
    </a1:MyClass>
</SOAP-ENV:Body>
```

However, I strongly discourage you from circumventing serialization version and
type verification. At best, a potential incompatibility (such as fields being removed)
will result with an exception of type `SerializationException`. At worst, your application may later crash unexpectedly because the incompatible type required some custom initialization steps.

Custom Serialization

Sometimes, the default automatic serialization provided by the Serializable attributed is insufficient. Perhaps the object state contains sensitive information such as a credit card number. In that case, you may want to encrypt the state instead of using a plain by-value serialization, or perhaps which members get serialized depends on the state of the object. Yet another case is when you want to perform additional proprietary initialization steps during deserialization.

The ISerializable Interface

.NET provides an easy-to-use mechanism for custom serialization that extends the serialization infrastructure. To provide custom serialization and deserialization behavior, you need to implement the ISerializable interface defined in the System. Runtime.Serialization namespace:

```
public interface ISerializable
{
    void GetObjectData(SerializationInfo info,StreamingContext context);
}
```

Every time a client serializes an object, .NET reflects the object's metadata to see whether the serializable object implements ISerializable. If it does, .NET calls GetObjectData( ) to retrieve the object's state. At this point, it's up to the object to provide the state information in whichever way it wants. You will see an example for implementing ISerializable shortly.

To support the matching custom deserialization, the object must provide a special parameterized deserialization constructor with this signature:

```
<Class Name>(SerializationInfo info,StreamingContext context);
```

.NET calls this constructor during deserialization. The constructor can (and should) be defined as protected to prevent normal clients from calling it.

 When you define a protected or private constructor, the type must have at least one other public constructor, which you define. The compiler doesn't provide a default public constructor.

.NET uses reflection to invoke the deserialization constructor and thus isn't impeded by the constructor being protected. If the class implements the ISerializable interface but doesn't provide the deserialization constructor, the compiler doesn't warn you. Instead, during deserialization, .NET throws an exception of type SerializationException.

In .NET, interfaces aren't allowed to have any shred of implementation detail and therefore can't define a constructor. The design decision the architects of .NET serialization took was to force a runtime check for the deserialization constructor instead of a compile-time check. However, I believe a better design decision would have been to provide a SetObjectData( ) method on ISerializable and, during deserialization, use reflection to set the fields of a new object.

Note that the client isn't required to treat an object that implements ISerializable any differently from an object that uses automatic serialization. Custom serialization is purely a server-side facility. The client uses the formatters and streams as with any other type.

Implementing ISerializable

Both GetObjectData( ) and the deserialization constructor accept a parameter of type SerializationInfo called info. SerializationInfo provides methods for getting or adding field values. Each field is identified by a string. SerializationInfo has type-safe methods for most of the CLR-defined types, such as int and string. For each such type, SerializationInfo provides two methods in this form:

```
<Type> Get<Type>(string name);
void AddValue(string name, <Type> value);
```

Here's an example:

```
public sealed class SerializationInfo
{
    public void AddValue(string name, short value);
    public void AddValue(string name, int value);
    //Other AddValue( ) methods

    public int    GetInt32(string name);
    public string GetString(string name);
    //Other Get<Type>( ) methods

    //Other methods and properties
}
```

For all other field types, SerializationInfo provides methods to add or get a generic object:

```
public void AddValue(string name, object value);
public object GetValue(string name, Type type);
```

The second parameter that both GetObjectData( ) and the deserialization constructor accept is the context parameter, of type StreamingContext. StreamingContext is a structure letting the object know why it's being serialized. StreamingContext provides the State property of the enum type StreamingContextStates. Possible reasons for serialization are remoting (across context or app domain), persisting to a file, and so on. The context parameter is largely ignored and used only in advanced esoteric scenarios, in which the serialization and deserialization action is context-sensitive.

Example 9-8 demonstrates both ISerializable and the deserialization constructor. The way the class in Example 9-8 implements custom serialization has no advantage over automatic serialization; it shows only how to provide custom serialization. It's up to you to provide the required custom steps.

Example 9-8. Implementing ISerializable

```
[Serializable]
public class MyClass : ISerializable
{
    int m_Num;
    string m_SomeString;
    public virtual void GetObjectData(SerializationInfo info,
                                                StreamingContext context)
    {
        info.AddValue("m_Num",m_Num);
        info.AddValue("m_SomeString",m_SomeString);
    }
    protected MyClass(SerializationInfo info,StreamingContext context)
    {
        m_Num = info.GetInt32("m_Num");
        m_SomeString = info.GetString("m_SomeString");
    }
    public MyClass(){ }//Must have at least one public constructor
}
```

> When you implement ISerializable, the type must still be decorated with the [Serializable] attribute. Otherwise, .NET considers the type as nonserializable and ignores ISerializable.

Custom serialization and IDeserializationCallback

Implementing IDeserializationCallback allows a type to be notified after deserialization takes place and to perform additional, custom deserialization steps. You can implement both IDeserializationCallback and ISerializable, but in reality, when you implement ISerializable, there is no need for IDeserializationCallback because you can place the custom steps in the deserialization constructor.

Custom serialization and versioning

One reason why you may need to use custom serialization is to deal with version issues between the serialized information and the current class definition. Imagine a class library vendor that provides a serializable component. The various client applications are responsible for managing the serialization media (typically a file). Suppose the vendor changes the component definition in a backward-compatible way, such as by adding a member variable. Such a change doesn't necessitate a version change because binary compatibility is maintained. New client applications can serialize the new component properly. However, the serialization information captured by the old applications is now incompatible and will result in SerializationException if used. The vendor has two options: either mark the new field as nonserializable or increment the version number. Changing the version number prevents the old clients from taking advantage of the new functionality. As it turns out, there is a third option that uses custom serialization. If the new field has a good-enough default value, such as application default directory or user preferences, the vendor can use values provided by the new clients and synthesize a value for the old clients. The component needs to be able to tell with which version of its assembly the serialized information was saved and act accordingly.

The SerializationInfo class provides the AssemblyName property, and you can extract from it the version of the assembly used to serialize the information. For example, suppose Version 1.0.0.0 of the serializable class MyClass is distributed to clients:

```
//Version 1.0.0.0
[Serializable]
public class MyClass
{
    public int Num;
}
```

The clients persisted this version in the serialized state information. With Version 1.0.1.0 of the assembly, the vendor adds the new field NewField to the class definition. Using version checks, the component can decide during deserialization whether to use the serialized value or assign a default value. Example 9-9 demonstrates this technique; it uses the helper class SerializationUtil to extract the version information from the assembly's full name. Note that the version extracted is the version of the assembly in which the original serialized type resided.

Example 9-9. Deserializing old serialization information with a new class definition

```
//Version 1.0.1.0
[Serializable]
public class MyClass : ISerializable
{
    public int Num;
    public int NewField;

    public void GetObjectData(SerializationInfo info,StreamingContext context)
    {
        info.AddValue("Num",Num);
        info.AddValue("NewField",NewField);
    }
    protected MyClass(SerializationInfo info,StreamingContext context)
    {
        Num = info.GetInt32("Num");
        Version storedVersion = SerializationUtil.GetVersion(info);
```

Example 9-9. Deserializing old serialization information with a new class definition (continued)

```
        if(storedVersion.ToString( ) == "1.0.1.0")
        {
            NewField = info.GetInt32("NewField");
        }
        else
        {
            NewField = 123;//Some default value
        }
    }
    public MyClass( ){ }
}
//The SerializationUtil helper class:
public class SerializationUtil
{
    static public Version GetVersion(SerializationInfo info)
    {
        string assemblyName = info.AssemblyName;
        /* assemblyName is in the form of "MyAssembly, Version=1.2.3.4,
                                    Culture=neutral,PublicKeyToken=null" */
        char[ ] separators = {',',' ','='};
        string[ ] nameParts = assemblyName.Split(separators);
        return new Version(nameParts[2]);
    }
}
```

Serialization and Class Hierarchies

When you apply the Serialization attribute to a class, it affects that class only and doesn't make any derived class serializable because the Inherited property of the AttributeUsage attribute applied on the SerializableAttribute is set to false. For example, if you derive MyClass from MyBaseClass, MyClass isn't serializable:

```
[Serializable]
public class MyBaseClass
{ }
public class MyClass : MyBase
{ }
```

At first glance this may appear awkward, but it does make design sense: MyBaseClass has no way to know whether its subclasses will have nonserializable members, so it would be wrong to inherit the serializable status. The conclusion is simple: if you design a class hierarchy and you want to support serialization of any type in the hierarchy, be sure to mark each level with the Serializable attribute:

```
[Serializable]
public class MyBaseClass
{ }
[Serializable]
public class MyClass : MyBaseClass
{ }
```

```
[Serializable]
public class MyOtherClass : MyClass
{}
```

Custom Serialization and Base Classes

If any of the classes in the hierarchy implements ISerializable, there are a few design guidelines you have to follow to allow subclasses to provide their own custom serialization and to correctly manage the custom serialization of the base classes:

- Only the topmost base class that uses custom serialization needs to derive from ISerializable.

- A base class must define its GetObjectData( ) as virtual to allow subclasses to override it.

- In a subclass implementation of GetObjectData( ), after serializing its own state, the subclass must call its base class implementation of GetObjectData( ).

- In its implementation of the deserializing constructor, the subclass must call its base class's deserializing constructor.

- The deserializing constructor shouldn't be private, to allow a subclass to call its base class's deserializing constructor.

Example 9-10 demonstrates how to implement these points; you can use it as a template for combining custom serialization and class hierarchies.

Example 9-10. Combining custom serialization with a class hierarchy

```
[Serializable]
public class MyBaseClass : ISerializable
{
    public MyBaseClass(){}
    int m_BaseNum;
    public virtual void GetObjectData(SerializationInfo info,
                                      StreamingContext context)
    {
        //Add to info MyBase class members
        info.AddValue("m_BaseNum",m_BaseNum);
    }
    protected MyBaseClass(SerializationInfo info,StreamingContext context)
    {
        //Read from info MyBase class members and initialize them
        m_BaseNum = info.GetInt32("m_BaseNum");
    }
}

[Serializable]
public class MySubClass : MyBaseClass
{
    public MySubClass(){}
    int m_SubNum;
```

Example 9-10. Combining custom serialization with a class hierarchy (continued)

```
   public override void GetObjectData(SerializationInfo info,
                                      StreamingContext context)
   {
      //Add to info MySubClass class members
      info.AddValue("m_SubNum",m_SubNum);
      base.GetObjectData(info,context);
   }
   protected MySubClass(SerializationInfo info,StreamingContext context):
                                                 base(info,context)
   {
      //Read from info MySubClass class members and initialize them
      m_SubNum = info.GetInt32("m_SubNum");
   }
}
```

If a base class provides custom serialization, all subclasses derived from it can use only custom serialization.

Manual Base Class Serialization

Combining class hierarchies and serialization, whether fully automatic or custom, is straightforward: all classes use only the Serializable attribute or they all implement ISerializable. The picture isn't so clear when it comes to deriving a serializable class from a class not marked with the Serializable attribute, as in this case:

```
public class MyBaseClass
{}
[Serializable]
public class MySubClass : MyBaseClass
{}
```

In fact, in such a case, .NET can't serialize objects of type MySubClass at all because it can't serialize its base classes. Trying to serialize an object of type MySubClass results in an exception of type SerializationException. Such a situation may happen when deriving from a class in a third-party assembly if the vendor neglected to mark its classes as serializable.

The good news is that you can provide a solution even for such a case. The solution presented next isn't a sure cure: it assumes that none of the base classes require custom serialization steps. The solution merely compensates for the oversight of not marking the base class as serializable.

The workaround is simple: the subclass can implement ISerializable, use reflection to read and serialize the base classes' fields, and use reflection again to set these fields during deserialization. The source code accompanying this book contains the

SerializationUtil helper class (introduced already), which provides the two static methods SerializeBaseType( ) and DeserializeBaseType( ), defined as:

```
public class SerializationUtil
{
    public static void SerializeBaseType(object obj,
                                         SerializationInfo info,
                                         StreamingContext context);
    public static void DeserializeBaseType(object obj,
                                           SerializationInfo info,
                                           StreamingContext context);
}
```

All the subclass needs to do is implement ISerializable, and use SerializationUtil to serialize and deserialize its base classes:

```
public class MyBaseClass
{}
[Serializable]
public class MySubClass : MyBaseClass,ISerializable
{
    public MySubClass(){}
    public void GetObjectData(SerializationInfo info,StreamingContext context)
    {
        SerializationUtil.SerializeBaseType(this,info,context);
    }
    protected MySubClass(SerializationInfo info,StreamingContext context)
    {
        SerializationUtil.DeserializeBaseType(this,info,context);
    }
}
```

If the subclass has no need for custom serialization, and the only reason it implements ISerializable is to serialize its base class, you can use SerializationUtil to serialize the subclass as well. SerializationUtil provides these overloaded versions of SerializeBaseType( ) and DeserializeBaseType( ):

```
public static void SerializeBaseType(object obj,bool serializeSelf,
                                     SerializationInfo info,
                                     StreamingContext context);
public static void DeserializeBaseType(object obj,bool deserializeSelf,
                                       SerializationInfo info,
                                       StreamingContext context);
```

These versions accept a flag instructing them whether to start serialization with the type itself instead of its base class:

```
public void GetObjectData(SerializationInfo info,StreamingContext context)
{
    //Serializing this type and its base classes
    SerializationUtil.SerializeBaseType(this,true,info,context);
}
protected MyClass(SerializationInfo info,StreamingContext context)
{
```

```
        //Deserializing this type and its base classes
        SerializationUtil.DeserializeBaseType(this,true,info,context);
    }
```

Example 9-11 presents the implementation of SerializationUtil.

Example 9-11. SerializationUtil implementation

```
public class SerializationUtil
{
   public static void SerializeBaseType(object obj,
                                   SerializationInfo info,StreamingContext context)
   {
      Type baseType = obj.GetType( ).BaseType;
      SerializeBaseType(obj,baseType,info,context);
   }
   static void SerializeBaseType(object obj,Type type,SerializationInfo info,
                                                   StreamingContext context)
   {
      if(type == typeof(object))
      {
         return;
      }
      BindingFlags flags = BindingFlags.Instance|BindingFlags.DeclaredOnly|
                        BindingFlags.NonPublic|BindingFlags.Public;
      FieldInfo[ ] fields = type.GetFields(flags);
      foreach(FieldInfo field in fields)
      {
         if(field.IsNotSerialized)
         {
            continue;
         }
         string fieldName = type.Name + "+" + field.Name;
         info.AddValue(fieldName,field.GetValue(obj));
      }
      SerializeBaseType(obj,type.BaseType,info,context);
   }
   public static void DeserializeBaseType(object obj,SerializationInfo info,
                                                   StreamingContext context)
   {
      Type baseType = obj.GetType( ).BaseType;
      DeserializeBaseType(obj,baseType,info,context);
   }
   static void DeserializeBaseType(object obj,Type type,SerializationInfo info,
                                                   StreamingContext context)
   {
      if(type == typeof(object))
      {
         return;
      }
      BindingFlags flags = BindingFlags.Instance|BindingFlags.DeclaredOnly|
                        BindingFlags.NonPublic|BindingFlags.Public;
      FieldInfo[ ] fields = type.GetFields(flags);
```

Example 9-11. SerializationUtil implementation (continued)

```
    foreach(FieldInfo field in fields)
    {
       if(field.IsNotSerialized)
       {
          continue;
       }
       string fieldName = type.Name + "+" + field.Name;
       object fieldValue = info.GetValue(fieldName,field.FieldType);
       field.SetValue(obj,fieldValue);
    }
    DeserializeBaseType(obj,type.BaseType,info,context);
  }
}
```

When SerializationUtil serializes an object's base class, it needs to serialize all the base classes leading to that base class as well. You can access the base class type using the BaseType property of Type. Accessing an object's base type is straightforward:

```
    Type baseType = obj.GetType().BaseType;
```

With the GetFields() method of Type, you can get all the fields (private and public) declared by the type as well as any public or protected fields available via its own base classes. This isn't good enough for serialization because you need to capture all the private fields available from all levels of the class hierarchy. The solution is to serialize each level of the class hierarchy separately and thus access that level's private fields. SerializeBaseType() calls a private helper method also called SerializeBaseType(), providing it with the level of the class hierarchy to serialize:

```
    SerializeBaseType(obj,baseType,info,context);
```

The private SerializeBaseType() serializes that level and then calls itself recursively, serializing the next level up the hierarchy:

```
    SerializeBaseType(obj,type.BaseType,info,context);
```

The recursion stops once it reaches the System.Object level:

```
    static void SerializeBaseType(object obj,Type type,SerializationInfo info,
                                  StreamingContext context)
    {
       if(type == typeof(object))
       {
          return;
       }
       /* Rest of the implementation  */
    }
```

To serialize a particular level, the private SerializeBaseType() calls GetFields() with a binding flags mask, which instructs it to return all fields defined by this type only and not its base types (BindingFlags.DeclaredOnly), so that as it visits the next level up, it doesn't serialize fields more than once. It also binds to instance and not static fields because static fields are never serialized anyway:

```
BindingFlags flags = BindingFlags.Instance|BindingFlags.DeclaredOnly|
                     BindingFlags.NonPublic|BindingFlags.Public;
```

The private SerializeBaseType( ) then calls GetFields( ) and stores the result in an array of FieldInfo objects:

```
FieldInfo[] fields = type.GetFields(flags);
```

The solution needs to deal with a class hierarchy in which some levels actually use the Serializable attribute, such as class A in this example:

```
[Serializable]
class A
{}
class B : A
{}
[Serializable]
class C : B,ISerializable
{}
```

Because class A may have some fields marked with the NonSerialized attribute, the solution needs to check that a field is serializable. This is easy to do via the IsNotSerialized Boolean property of FieldInfo:

```
foreach(FieldInfo field in fields)
{
    if(field.IsNotSerialized)
    {
        continue;
    }
    //Rest of the iteration loop
}
```

Because different levels can declare private fields with the same name on the same class hierarchy, the private SerializeBaseType( ) prefixes a field name with its declaring type separated by a +:

```
string fieldName = type.Name + "+" + field.Name;
```

The value of a field is obtained via the GetValue( ) method of FieldInfo and is then added to the info parameter:

```
info.AddValue(fieldName,field.GetValue(obj));
```

Deserialization of the base class (or classes) is similar to serialization and is done recursively as well, until it reaches the System.Object level. The public DeserializeBaseType( ) method accesses the base type and calls the private helper method DeserializeBaseType( ) method. At each level in the class hierarchy, the private DeserializeBaseType( ) retrieves the collection of the fields for that type. For each field, it creates a name by appending the name of the current level to the name of the field, gets the value from info, and sets the value of the corresponding field, using the SetValue( ) method of the FieldInfo class:

```
string fieldName = type.Name + "+" + field.Name;
object fieldValue = info.GetValue(fieldName,field.FieldType);
field.SetValue(obj,fieldValue);
```

CHAPTER 10

Remoting

Modern applications are no longer isolated, standalone entities limited to a single process or machine. Distributed applications allow you to put components in close proximity to the resources they use, let multiple users access the application, improve scalability and throughput, and increase overall availability and fault isolation. It's difficult to imagine a modern distributed application without components. Component-oriented programming is especially geared towards distribution because it's all about breaking the application into a set of interacting components you can then distribute to different locations.

This chapter shows how to access remote .NET components using a technology called *.NET remoting*. Remoting is related to .NET as DCOM is to COM in its ability to connect to components on remote machines, and like DCOM, .NET remoting can also access components in other processes, similar to COM's local servers. .NET remoting is a vast topic, and it's no wonder that this chapter is the longest in this book. Although each facet of remoting is simple enough, there is a multitude of terms and details to master before you can build even a simple distributed application, but nevertheless, the richness offers a flexible programming model.

This chapter begins by explaining the fundamental concepts of remoting and the key elements of the .NET remoting architecture. You will then see how to apply .NET remoting in a set of comprehensive code samples. Like most things in .NET, there are many ways to achieve the same result. The emphasis in this chapter is on understanding the basic concepts, the tradeoffs you face in using them, and the practical aspects of using remoting; we won't go into every nook and cranny. Armed with an understanding of the basics of remoting, you can go after the more esoteric features if the need ever arises.

Application Domains

All .NET components and applications require a managed environment to run in. However, the underlying operating system knows nothing about managed code; it provides processes only. Processes are also unaware that .NET exists; they provide raw elements such as memory, handle tables, etc. Managed code therefore can't execute directly in the native operating system process. There is a need for a bridge between managed code and unmanaged code. The bridging link is a concept called *application domain* or *app domain*. You can think of the app domain as the .NET equivalent of a process, with one important difference: an app domain is built on top of the unmanaged process, and there is no requirement for one-to-one mapping between app domains and operating system processes. As a result, a single physical process can actually host multiple app domains (see Figure 10-1).

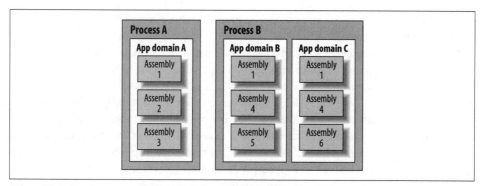

Figure 10-1. Processes, app domains, and assemblies

App Domains Versus Physical Processes

App domains are better perceived as *logical* processes, instead of real processes. The fact that a single physical process can host multiple app domains yields important benefits. The main reason why developers resorted to multiple processes in the past was to provide fault isolation. If all the components of an application and their clients are in the same process and a component has a fatal error that crashes the process, it brings down the entire application, including the client. Similarly, if the client has a fatal error, the components go down with it. By distributing the clients and servers of an application to separate processes, an application achieves fault isolation because in the event of a fault, only the culprit process goes down, allowing you to handle the error or perform a graceful exit.

Another reason for distributing the components of an application across processes is security. Server objects are often called on to authenticate incoming client calls or to perform access control and authorization before allowing a given call to access the component. Having separate processes allows for separate security identifiers per process and the enforcement of authentication on cross process calls. Unfortunately, there are significant penalties for using multiple processes, including:

- Creating a new process is time consuming, as is the disposal of an existing process.

- Keeping a process running is expensive, both in terms of memory and of the resources the operating system allocates per process. Having too many processes can significantly degrade system performance.

- Making a cross-process call involves a call penalty because crossing a process boundary is very expensive compared to making a direct call. Cross-process calls rely on special mechanisms such as named pipes, sockets, and LPC/RPC.

- Unless DCOM is used, the client's code for making a direct local call on an object is very different from that of making the same call on the object in a different process.

Compared with traditional unmanaged processes, .NET app domains can provide single process performance and lower overhead, together with the isolation and benefits of multiple processes, even if they share the same physical process. You can start and shut down app domains independently of their hosting process, and you can even debug them separately. For example, all ASP.NET web applications share the same physical worker process (*aspnet_wp.exe*) by default, but each web application is put in its own dedicated app domain. The time it takes to create or destroy an app domain is a fraction of that required for a physical process, and keeping an app domain alive is considerably cheaper as well. Furthermore, cross-app domain calls in the same process are faster than cross-process calls. In addition, .NET maintains a strict security boundary between app domains, and objects in one app domain can't interfere with the objects (or data) in another, unless the objects agree to cooperate using .NET remoting.

 In unmanaged C++, static variables are visible to all clients in the same process. In .NET, each app domain gets its own separate set of static variables.

In the interest of fault isolation and security, each app domain loads and maintains its own set of assemblies. Consider, for example, the app domains in Figure 10-1. Because App domain B and App domain C require the class library Assembly 1, .NET loads Assembly 1 twice and gives each app domain its own copy. This allows clients in each app domain to interact with Assembly 1 independently of other clients in other app domains.

App Domains and the .NET Platform

The .NET runtime itself is a set of Windows DLLs, implemented in unmanaged C++. These DLLs provide the managed heap, garbage collector, JIT compiler, assembly resolver and loader, and all the other elements that make managed code possible. The app domain merely makes it possible for the assemblies it loads to access these services (see Figure 10-2). In effect, this is how the app domain bridges the unmanaged world and the managed world. However, it's important to note that all app domains in the same process share the same managed heap.

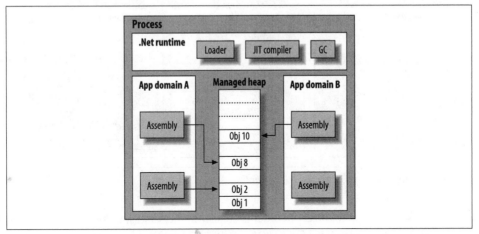

Figure 10-2. App domains provide their assemblies with access to the .NET runtime services

 Sharing the same heap has security implications, which are addressed in Chapter 12.

App domains and threads

.NET managed threads have no app domain affinity, meaning that a thread can enter and exit any app domain that runs in the same underlying process. Typically, when you create a thread in your app domain, that thread executes a thread method and accesses only local objects. However, nothing prevents you from having threads created in one app domain access objects in another app domain in the same process. There is one detail you need to be aware of, though: when an app domain shuts down (when AppDomain.Unload( ) is called), it terminates all the threads that happen to be calling objects in it by calling Thread.Abort( ) on each of them.

App Domains and Remoting

Much like a traditional cross-process call, you make cross-app domain calls using *remoting*, a programmatic act that accesses an object outside its hosting app domain. .NET uses exactly the same remote call architecture for all cases, whether the cross-app domain call is between two app domains in the same process, between app domains in two different processes on the same machine, or between app domains on two separate machines (see Figure 10-3).

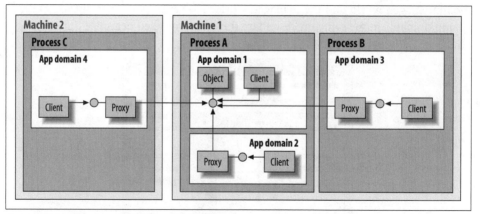

Figure 10-3. All cross app domain call use remoting

 Accessing an object outside its context in the same app domain is a special case of remoting and is discussed in Chapter 11.

Clients in the same app domain as the called object can each have a direct reference to the object (see Figure 10-3). Clients in a different app domain access the object using a proxy to connect to the object. A *proxy* is an object that provides exactly the same interfaces, public methods, properties, and members as the real object. .NET generates a proxy on the fly, based on the object's metadata. Even though the proxy has the same public entry points as the object, it can't serve the clients because the object's actual code and state reside only where the object is. All the proxy knows is how to bind to the object and forward the calls made on the proxy to the object. Forwarding a call to an object is called *marshaling*. Marshaling is a nontrivial feat: its end goal is to provide the client with the illusion that it's calling a local object and to provide the server with the illusion that it's servicing a local client. Neither the server nor the client explicitly use remote mechanisms such as pipes, RPC, or sockets because these details are encapsulated in the proxy. .NET does require, however, that if an object is accessed by remote clients, the object's class must derive directly or indirectly from the abstract class `MarshalByRefObject`. You will learn more about marshaling and how it relates to the .NET remoting architecture later in this chapter.

The AppDomain Class

.NET represents app domains with the `AppDomain` class, which provides numerous methods for loading assemblies, creating objects from these assemblies, and configuring app domain security. You can get hold of an object representing the current app domain within which your component code runs by accessing the static property `CurrentDomain` of the `AppDomain` class:

```
AppDomain currentAppDomain;
currentAppDomain = AppDomain.CurrentDomain;
```

Alternatively, you can call the GetDomain( ) static method of the thread class, which also returns an AppDomain object representing the current domain:

```
AppDomain currentAppDomain;
currentAppDomain = Thread.GetDomain( );
```

The AppDomain class offers a few permutations of a CreateInstance method that allows you to explicitly create a new instance of any type in the app domain. For example, one of the versions of CreateInstance( ) is called CreateInstanceAndUnwrap( ), (the origin of the term is discussed shortly.) defined as:

```
public object CreateInstanceAndUnwrap(string assemblyName, string typeName);
```

CreateInstanceAndUnwrap( ) accepts an assembly filename and a fully qualified type name. CreateInstanceAndUnwrap( ) then creates an instance of the type and returns an object representing it. Example 10-1 demonstrates CreateInstanceAndUnwrap( ).

> When you specify an assembly name to any of the methods of AppDomain, the calling assembly must reference the assembly being specified.

Example 10-1. Explicitly creating an object in the current app domain

```
//In the MyClassLibrary.dll assembly:
using System.Diagnostics;

namespace MyNamespace
{
   public class MyClass
   {
      public void TraceAppDomain( )
      {
         AppDomain currentAppDomain;
         currentAppDomain = AppDomain.CurrentDomain;

         Trace.WriteLine(currentAppDomain.FriendlyName);
      }
   }
}

//In the MyApp.exe assembly:
using System.Diagnostics;
using MyNamespace;

public class MyClient
{
   static void Main( )
   {
      AppDomain currentAppDomain;
```

```
        currentAppDomain = AppDomain.CurrentDomain;
        Trace.WriteLine(currentAppDomain.FriendlyName);

        MyClass obj;
        obj = (MyClass)currentAppDomain.CreateInstanceAndUnwrap("MyClassLibrary",
                                                    "MyNamespace.MyClass");
        obj.TraceAppDomain();
    }
}
//Output:
MyApp.exe
MyApp.exe
```

In the preceding example, a class called MyClass is defined in the MyNamespace namespace in the *MyClassLibrary.dll* class library assembly. MyClass provides the TraceAppDomain() method, which traces the name of its current app domain to the Output window using the FriendlyName read-only property of the AppDomain class. The client is in a separate EXE assembly called *MyApp.exe*. The client obtains its current AppDomain object and traces its name using the AppDomain class's FriendlyName property. The trace yields MyApp.exe—the name of the application. Next, instead of creating an instance of MyClass directly using new, the client then calls CreateInstanceAndUnwrap(), providing the assembly name and the fully qualified type name. When the client calls the TraceAppDomain() method on the new MyClass object, the object traces MyApp.exe to the Output window because it shares the app domain of the client.

The client can use CreateInstanceAndUnwrap() to create types defined in its own assembly as well by providing its own assembly name. Note that CreateInstanceAndUnwrap() uses the default constructor of the object. If you need to provide construction parameters, you need to use another version of CreateInstanceAndUnwrap(), which accepts an array of construction parameters:

```
public object CreateInstanceAndUnwrap(string assemblyName, string typeName,
                                      object[] activationAttributes);
```

The client can also specify explicitly how to bind to the server assembly, using yet another overloaded version of CreateInstanceAndUnwrap().

> Interacting with app domains is usually required by framework vendors who want to explicitly create new app domains and load assemblies and types into them. I find that during conventional development I need to interact with app domains only to configure security policies or for advanced security purposes. For example, Chapter 12 uses the current AppDomain object to set an authorization policy to take advantage of .NET role-based security, and Appendix B uses the AppDomain object to change the default security principal.

The default app domain

Every unmanaged process hosting .NET components is created by launching a .NET EXE assembly, such as a console application, a Windows Forms application, or a Windows Service application. Each such EXE has a Main( ) method, which is the entry point to the new app domain in the process. When the EXE is launched, .NET creates a new app domain and gives it the same name as the EXE assembly; it's called the *default app domain*. The default app domain can't be unloaded, and it remains running throughout the life of the hosting process.

Creating a new app domain

You typically create new app domains for the same reason you create processes in traditional Windows development: to provide for fault and security isolation. The AppDomain class provides the static CreateDomain( ) method, which allows you to create new app domains:

```
public static AppDomain CreateDomain(string friendlyName);
```

CreateDomain( ) creates a new app domain in the same process and returns an AppDomain object representing the new app domain. The new app domain must be given a new name when you call CreateDomain( ).

The AppDomain type is derived from MarshalByRefObject. Deriving from MarshalByRefObject allows .NET to pass a reference to the app domain object outside its app domain boundaries. When you create a new app domain using the CreateDomain( ) method, .NET creates a new app domain, retrieves a local copy of the AppDomain object, and marshals it back to your current domain.

Example 10-2 demonstrates how to create a new app domain and then instantiate a new object in the new app domain.

Example 10-2. Creating a new app domain and a new object in it

```
//In the MyClassLibrary.dll assembly:
using System.Diagnostics;

namespace MyNamespace
{
   public class MyClass : MarshalByRefObject
   {
      public void TraceAppDomain( )
      {
         AppDomain currentAppDomain;
         currentAppDomain = AppDomain.CurrentDomain;

         Trace.WriteLine(currentAppDomain.FriendlyName);
```

Example 10-2. Creating a new app domain and a new object in it (continued)

```
      }
   }
}

//In the MyApp.exe assembly:
using System.Diagnostics;
using MyNamespace;

public class MyClient
{
   static void Main( )
   {
      AppDomain currentAppDomain;
      currentAppDomain = AppDomain.CurrentDomain;
      Trace.WriteLine(currentAppDomain.FriendlyName);

      AppDomain newAppDomain;
      newAppDomain = AppDomain.CreateDomain("My new AppDomain");
      MyClass obj;
      obj = (MyClass)newAppDomain.CreateInstanceAndUnwrap("MyClassLibrary",
                                                "MyNamespace.MyClass");

      obj.TraceAppDomain( );
   }
}
//Output:
MyApp.exe
My new AppDomain
```

Example 10-2 is similar to Example 10-1, with the following noticeable exceptions: The class MyClass is derived from MarshalByRefObject so that you can access it across app domains. The client traces its own app domain name (MyApp.exe) and then creates a new app domain using the CreateDomain( ) static method. As in Example 10-1, the client creates a new object of type MyClass in the new app domain and asks it to trace its app domain. When the program is executed, the name My new AppDomain is displayed at the console, confirming that the object is in the newly created app domain.

Unwrapping remote objects

You were probably wondering why the word Unwrap is appended to the CreateInstanceAndUnwrap( ) method. As already mentioned, accessing a remote object is done through a proxy. For optimization purposes, .NET separates the act of creating an object from the act of setting up a proxy on the client's side. This allows you to create a remote object and set up the proxy later. The AppDomain class provides a set of CreateInstance( ) methods that create a new object but return a handle to the remote object in the form of ObjectHandle:

```
    ObjectHandle public virtual CreateInstance(string assemblyName, string typeName);
```

ObjectHandle is defined in the System.Runtime.Remoting namespace. ObjectHandle implements the IObjectHandle interface:

```
public interface IObjectHandle
{
    object Unwrap( );
}
public class ObjectHandle : MarshalByRefObject,IObjectHandle
{
    public ObjectHandle(object obj);
    public virtual object Unwrap( );
}
```

The Unwrap( ) method sets up the proxy on the client side. You can actually unwrap a handle multiple times by the same client or by different clients. Using the same objects definitions as Example 10-2, here is how to unwrap an object handle:

```
AppDomain newAppDomain;
IObjectHandle  handle;
MyClass obj;

newAppDomain = AppDomain.CreateDomain("My new AppDomain");
handle = newAppDomain.CreateInstance("MyClassLibrary","MyNamespace.MyClass");

//Only now a proxy is set up:
obj = (MyClass)handle.Unwrap( );
obj.TraceAppDomain( );
```

Typically, there is no need to manually unwrap object handles. .NET provides the option for the advanced case in which you want to pass the handle between clients in different app domains, instead of the object itself. As a result, the client can defer loading the assembly containing the object metadata (a required step when setting up a proxy) until the client actually needs to use the object.

The Host App Domain

.NET calls the app domain that contains the server object the *host* app domain. The host app domain can be in the same process as the client app domain, in a different process on the same machine or on a different machine altogether. To qualify as a host, the app domain must register itself as such with .NET, letting .NET know which objects the host is willing to accept remote calls on, and in what manner. Because .NET is aware of the host only after registration, the host must be running before remote calls are issued. We'll discuss the available hosting options later in this chapter.

 Requiring the host to be running before the clients access it is unlike COM, where if the hosting process was not running, COM would launch it and let it host objects. New COM activation requests would be redirected to the already running process. COM could do that because the Registry held the registration information regarding which process to launch and because once the process was running, it registered the objects it was hosting programmatically. .NET doesn't use the registry and hence the limitation.

Both the client and the host app domains require access to the server assembly. The client app domain needs the server metadata to compile against, and at runtime, .NET requires it on the client side so it can reflect its metadata and build a proxy. The IL code in the assembly isn't required at compile- or at runtime on the client's side. The host app domain requires the server assembly at runtime to create the hosted components and for call-marshaling purposes. If the host is doing programmatic registration (discussed later on), that host must have access to the server assembly at compile-time as well. Unless you explicitly create a new app domain in your own process (as in Example 10-2), the host app domain will be in a different process in the form of an EXE assembly. You could put the server code in the same EXE as the host, but that presents a problem to the client: how to access the metadata of the host, both at runtime and at compile-time? In fact, Visual Studio.NET doesn't allow client applications to add a reference to an EXE assembly at all. But even if you could do that at compile-time, how would the client application access the server metadata if it were part of a remote EXE? The common solution to this problem is to separate the client, the host, and the server to different assemblies. The host resides in an EXE assembly, the server in a class library assembly, and the client application can be in a class library or an EXE assembly. That way, the client can use the metadata in the server class library at compile-time. At runtime, the client loads the class library only to use its metadata, but has no need for the code in it. The host assembly can use the server assembly's metadata at compile-time if it uses programmatic object registration; at runtime the host uses both the metadata and the code in the server assembly to host the class library objects. Figure 10-4 depicts what the client and the host require of the class library at compile time and at runtime.

 Making a class library DLL available to remote clients by hosting it in an EXE host is analogous to providing a surrogate process to a COM in-process DLL. In fact, the canonical COM surrogate process is called *dllhost.exe*.

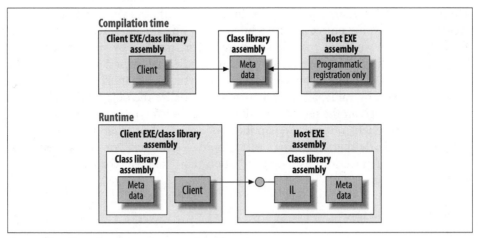

Figure 10-4. Keep the server objects in class libraries

Remote Object Types

If the object is in the same app domain as the client, usually no proxies are involved, and the client will hold a direct reference to the object. The question is what happens when you try to call methods on a remote object in another app domain? It turns out that by default, objects aren't accessible from outside their app domain, even if the call is made between two app domains in the same process. The rationale behind this decision is that .NET must first enforce app domain isolation and security. If you intend your objects to be accessed from outside their app domains, you must allow it explicitly in your design and class definition. .NET provides two options for accessing an object across an app domain boundary: by value or by reference. *By value* means when a client in App Domain 2 calls a method on an object in App Domain 1, the object is first copied to App Domain 2, so the client gets its own cloned copy of the object. Once a copy is transferred to the remote client, the two objects are distinct and can change state independently. Any change made to the object's state in App Domain 2 applies only to that local copy, completely separate from the original object. This is similar to COM's marshal by value and is often referred to as *marshaling by value*. The second way to access a remote object is *by reference*, meaning the remote clients hold only a reference to the object, in the form of a proxy. Access by reference is often referred to as *marshaling by reference*. Marshaling by reference was, incidentally, the standard behavior provided by COM.

Marshaling by Value

When an object is marshaled by value, .NET must make a copy of the object's state, transfer the state to the other app domain, and build up a new object based on that state. There are some difficulties, however. .NET needs to know which parts of the object's state can be marshaled by value and which parts can't. .NET has to obtain the state of an existing object and then build a new object based on that state. What if the object also wants to provide some custom marshaling by value mechanism? Luckily, .NET already has the infrastructure to handle such issues: serialization. The requirements for marshaling by value and for generic serialization are identical. To marshal an object by value, all .NET has to do is serialize the object to a stream and deserialize the object in the remote app domain. As a result, to enable marshaling by value, the component must be serializable. As explained in Chapter 9, serializable components can either use the Serializable attributes or implement the ISerializable interface for custom serialization. For example, consider the following class definition:

```
[Serializable]
public class MyClass
{
    public int Num;
}
```

Suppose an instance of this class has 3 as the value of the Num member and is accessed across an app domain boundary by a remote client. .NET marshals the object by value and gives the remote client a copy of the object. Immediately after marshaling, the cloned object has 3 as the value of the Num member (see Figure 10-5). When the remote client in App Domain 3 assigns 4 to Num, this assignment affects only its own new distinct copy. Marshaling by value works across any app domain boundary, be it in the same process or across machines.

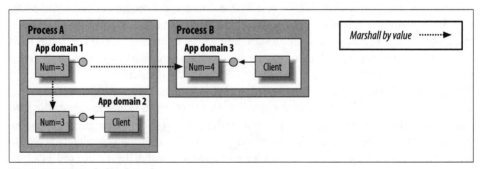

Figure 10-5. Marshaling by value

The primary use for marshaling by value is when you want to pass a structure as a method parameter. Typically, structures are used as data containers and have no logic associated with them. Structures are very useful as method parameters, but unless a struct is serializable, you can't use it as a parameter to a remote call.

 Marshaling by value is considerably easier in .NET than it was with DCOM. The only way to marshal by value in DCOM was to provide custom marshaling—a daunting task, even for proficient DCOM experts.

When you marshal a struct by value to a remote object, you actually get the same semantics as with a local object because value types are, by default, passed in by value:

```
[Serializable]
public struct MyPoint
{
    public int X;
    public int Y;
}

public class RemoteClass : MarshalByRefObject
{
    public void MyMethod(MyPoint point)
    {
        point.X++;
    }
}
```

Changes made to the structure on the server side don't affect the structure on the client side:

```
//Remote client:
MyPoint point;
point.X = 1;

RemoteClass obj = new RemoteClass();
obj.MyMethod(point);
Debug.Assert(point.X == 1);
```

However, if you pass the structure by reference using the out or ref parameter modifiers, changes made on the remote server side will affect the client's copy of the structure:

```
public class RemoteClass : MarshalByRefObject
{
    public void MyMethod(ref MyPoint point)
    {
        point.X++;
    }
}
```

```
//Remote client:
MyPoint point;
point.X = 1;

RemoteClass obj = new RemoteClass();
obj.MyMethod(ref point);
Debug.Assert(point.X == 2);
```

This is the same as when you pass a structure by reference in the local case.

The usefulness of marshaling a class instance by value is marginal because the classic client-server model doesn't fit well with marshaling by value. Marshaling by value for reference types is provided when the client needs to make frequent calls of short duration to the object and paying the penalty for marshaling the object state to the client is better then paying the penalty multiple times for marshaling the call to the object and back. Imagine, for example, a distributed image capturing and processing system. You want the machine capturing the images to do so as fast as it can and have the processing done on a separate machine. The capturing machine can create an image object, have the processing client access it (that would make it copy the image), and process it locally. That said, there is usually a better design solution, such as transferring the image data explicitly as a method parameter. In general, it's often a lot easier to simply marshal to the client a reference to the object and have the client invoke calls on the object.

Marshaling by Reference

The second remoting option is marshal by reference, and it's by far a more common way to access objects across app domains. As explained previously, when marshaling by reference is employed, the client accesses the remote object using a proxy (see Figure 10-3). Calls on the proxy are forwarded by the proxy to the actual object. To designate a component for marshaling by reference, the class must derive directly (or have one of its base classes derive) from the class MarshalByRefObject, defined in the System namespace. Objects derived from MarshalByRefObject are bound for life to the app domain in which they were created and can never leave it. Examine Example 10-2 again. The client has a reference to a proxy, which forwards the call to TraceAppDomain() to the new app domain, and this is why it traces the remote app domain's name. If the remote object is serializable in addition to being derived from MarshalByRefObject, the object is still accessed by reference. You can still, of course, use serialization to persist the object's state. Finally, any static method or member variable on a marshaled by reference class is always accessed directly, and no proxy is involved because statics aren't associated with any particular object.

.NET does allow the client app domain and the host app domain to be the same app domain. In that case, the client interacts with the marshal by reference object using a proxy, even though both share the same app domain. Clients may want to do that in order to activate the object in different ways. However, short-circuiting remoting this way is an esoteric case. In the vast majority of cases, deriving from MarshalByRefObject has no bearing on intra-app domain calls, and clients in the same app domains get a direct reference to the object.

Marshaling by Reference Activation Modes

.NET supports two kinds of marshal by reference objects: *client-activated* and *server-activated*. The two kinds map to three activation modes: *client-activated object*, *server-activated single call*, and *server-activated singleton*. The different activation modes control object state management, object sharing, object life cycle, and the way in which the client binds to an object. The client decides whether to use client-activated or server-activated objects. If the client chooses client-activated object, then the client has just one activation mode available. If the client chooses server-activated object, it's up to the hosting app domain to decide whether the client will get a server-activated single call object or a server-activated singleton object. It's called server-activated because it's up to the host to activate an object on behalf of the client and bind it to the client. The hosting app domain indicates to .NET which activation modes it supports, using server registration. The host can support both client and server activated objects, or either one. It's completely at the discretion of the host. If the host decides to support server-activated mode, the host needs to register it either as single-call or as singleton, but not both. This will all become clearer later in the chapter, when you see the actual registration code. The next sections explain the different activation modes.

Client-Activated Object

Client-activated object mode is the classic client-server activation mode: when a client creates a new object, the client gets a new object. That object is dedicated to the client, and it's independent of all other instances of the same class. Different clients in different app domains get different objects when they create new objects on the host (see Figure 10-6). There are no limitations on constructing client-activated objects, and you can use either parameterized constructors or the default constructor. The constructor is called exactly once, when the client creates the new remote object, and .NET marshals the construction parameters to the new object, if parameterized constructors are used. Clients can choose to share their objects with other clients, either in their own app domains or in other app domains. Like local objects, client-activated objects can maintain state in memory. To make sure the remote object isn't disconnected from the remoting infrastructure and collected by its local garbage collector, client-activated objects require leasing when they make cross-process calls, to keep the objects alive as long as the clients use them. Leasing provides a timestamp extending the life of the object and is discussed later in this chapter. Client-activated object mode is similar to the default DCOM activation model, with one important difference: the host app domain must register itself as a host willing to accept client-activated calls before remote calls are issued. As mentioned earlier, this means the process containing the host app domain must be running before such calls are made.

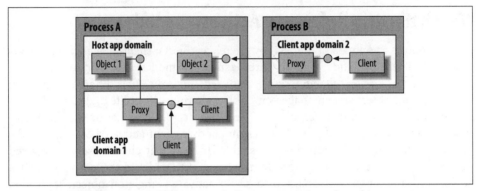

Figure 10-6. With client-activated objects, each client gets an independent object to use

Server-Activated Single Call

The fundamental problem with the client-activated object mode is that it doesn't scale well. The server object may hold expensive or scarce resources such as database connections, communication ports, or files. Imagine an application that has to serve many clients. Typically, these clients create the remote objects they need when the client application starts and dispose of them when the client application shuts down. What impedes scalability with client-activated objects is that the client applications can hold onto objects for long periods of time, while actually using the object for only a fraction of that time. If your design calls for allocating an object for each client, you will tie up such crucial limited resources for long periods and will eventually run out of resources. A better object model is to allocate an object for a client only while a call is in progress from the client to the object. That way, you have to create and maintain in memory only as many objects as there are concurrent calls, not as many objects as there are clients. This is exactly what the single call activation mode is about: when the client uses a server-activated single-call object, for each method call .NET creates a new object, lets it service the call, and then discards it. Between calls, the client holds a reference on a proxy that doesn't have an actual object at the end of the wire. The following list shows how single call activation works; its steps are illustrated in Figure 10-7.

1. The object executes a method call on behalf of a remote client.

2. When the method call returns, if the object implements IDisposable, .NET calls IDisposable.Dispose() on it. .NET then releases all references it has on the object, making it a candidate for garbage collection. Meanwhile, the client continues to hold a reference to a proxy and doesn't know that its object is gone.

3. The client makes another call on the proxy.

4. The proxy forwards the call to the remote domain.

5. .NET creates an object and calls the method on it.

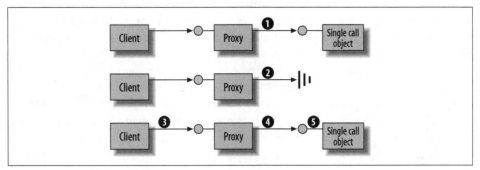

Figure 10-7. Single-call activation mode

Benefits of single-call objects

The obvious benefit of using single-call object is the fact that you can now dispose of the expensive resources the object occupies long before the client disposes of the object. By that same token, acquiring the resources is postponed until they are actually needed by a client. Keep in mind that creating and destroying the object repeatedly on the object side without tearing down the connection to the client (with its client-side proxy) is a lot cheaper than creating and disposing of the object. Another benefit is that even if the client isn't disciplined enough to explicitly discard the object; it has no effect on scalability because the object is discarded automatically.

> If the client does call IDisposable.Dispose() on the object, it has the detrimental effect of recreating the object just so the client can call Dispose() on it. This is followed by a second call to Dispose() by the proxy.

Designing a single-call object

Although in theory you can use single-call activation on any component type, in practice, you need to design the component and its interfaces to support single-call activation mode from the ground up. The main problem is that the client doesn't know it's getting a new object each time. Single-call components must be state-aware; that is, they must proactively manage their state, giving the client the illusion of a continuous session. A state-aware object isn't the same as a stateless object. In fact, if the single-call object were truly stateless, there would be no need for single-call activation in the first place. A single-call object is created just before every method call and deactivated immediately after each call. Therefore, at the beginning of each call, the object should initialize its state from values saved in some storage and at the end of the call, it should return its state to the storage. Such storage is typically either a database or the filesystem. However, not all an object's state can be saved as-is. For example, if the state contains a·database connection, the object must reacquire the connection at the beginning of every call and dispose of the connection at the end of the call or in its implementation of IDisposable.Dispose( ). Using single-call activation mode has one important implication for method design: every method call must include a parameter to identify the object whose state needs to be retrieved. The object uses that parameter to get its state from the storage and not the state of another instance of the same type. Examples for such parameters are the account number for bank account objects, the order number for objects processing orders, and so on. Example 10-3 shows a template for implementing a single-call class. The class provides the MyMethod( ) method, which accepts a parameter of type Param (a pseudotype invented for this example) that identifies the object:

```
public void MyMethod(Param objectIdentifier)
```

The object then uses the identifier to retrieve its state and to save the state back at the end of the method call.

Another design constraint of dealing with single-call objects is constructors. Because .NET re-creates the object automatically for each method call, it doesn't know how to use parameterized constructors or which parameters to provide to them. As a result, a single call object can't have parameterized constructors. In addition, because the object is constructed only when a method calls takes place, the actual construction call on the client side is never forwarded to the objects:

```
MySingleCallComponent obj;
obj = new MySingleCallComponent( ); //No constructor call is made

obj.MyMethod( );//Constructor executes
obj.MyMethod( );//Constructor executes
```

 Single-call activation clearly offers a tradeoff in performance (the overhead of reconstructing the object's state on each method call) with scalability (holding on to the state and the resources it ties in). There are no hard-and-fast rules as to when and to what extent you should trade performance for scalability. You may need to profile your system and ultimately redesign some objects to use single-call activation and some not to use it.

Applying the single-call mode

The single call activation mode (see Example 10-3) works only when the amount of work to be done in each method call is finite, and there are no more activities to complete in the background once a method returns. For this reason, you should not spin off background threads or dispatch asynchronous calls back into the object because the object will be disposed of once the method returns. Because the single-call object retrieves its state from some storage in every method call, single-call objects work very well in conjunction with a load-balancing machine, as long as the state repository is some global resource accessible to all machines. The load balancer can redirect calls to different machines at will, knowing that each single-call object can service the call after retrieving its state.

Example 10-3. Implementing a single-call component

```
public class Param
{...}

public class MySingleCallComponent : MarshalByRefObject,IDisposable
{
public MySingleCallComponent( ){ }
public void MyMethod(Param objectIdentifier)
{
   GetState(objectIdentifier);
   DoWork( );
   SaveState(objectIdentifier);
}
protected void GetState(Param objectIdentifier){...}
protected void DoWork( ){...}
protected void SaveState(Param objectIdentifier){...}

public void Dispose( ){...}

/* Class members/state */
}
```

Enterprise Services JITA

.NET Enterprise Services offer a set of smart instance management techniques for .NET-serviced components. One of those services is just-in-time activation (JITA), which works much like single-call objects. JITA has a few advantages over single-call objects, mainly the ability to combine it with other Enterprise Services instance management techniques such as object pooling. Other advantages are JITA's integration with distributed transaction and its ability to manage local, as well as remote objects. JITA is described in my book *COM and .NET Component Services* in Chapters 3 and 10.

Server-Activated Singleton

Server-activated singleton activation mode provides a single, well-known object to all clients. Because the clients connect to a single, well-known object, .NET ignores the client calls to new, even if the singleton object isn't created yet (the .NET runtime in the client app domain has no way of knowing what goes on in the host app domain anyway). The singleton is created when the first client tries to access it. Subsequent client calls to create new objects and access attempts are all channeled to the same singleton object (see Figure 10-8). Example 10-4 demonstrates these points: you can see from the trace output that the constructor is called only once on the first access attempt, and that obj2 is wired to the same object as obj1.

Example 10-4. A singleton object is created when first accessed, then used by all clients

```
public class MySingleton : MarshalByRefObject
{
   public MySingleton( )
   {
      m_Counter = 0;
      Trace.WriteLine("MySingleton.MySingleton( )");
   }
   public void TraceCounter( )
   {
      m_Counter++;
      Trace.WriteLine(Counter.ToString( ));
   }
   int m_Counter;
}
//Client-side code:
MySingleton obj1;
MySingleton obj2;

Trace.WriteLine("Before calling obj1 constructor");
obj1 = new MySingleton( );
Trace.WriteLine("After  calling obj1 constructor");

obj1.TraceCounter( ); //Constructor will be called here
obj1.TraceCounter( );

Trace.WriteLine("Before calling obj2 constructor");
obj2 = new MySingleton( );
Trace.WriteLine("After  calling obj2 constructor");

obj2.TraceCounter( );
obj2.TraceCounter( );

//Output:
Before calling obj1 constructor
After  calling obj1 constructor
MySingleton.MySingleton( )
1
2
```

Example 10-4. A singleton object is created when first accessed, then used by all clients (continued)

```
Before calling obj2 constructor
After  calling obj2 constructor
3
4
```

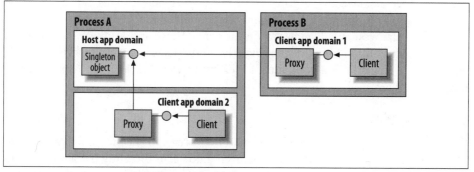

Figure 10-8. With a server-activated singleton object, all clients share the same well-known object

Because the singleton constructor is only called implicitly by .NET under the covers, a singleton object can't have parameterized constructors. Parameterized constructors are banned also because of an important semantic characteristic of the singleton activation mode: at any given point in time, all clients share the same state of the singleton object (see Figure 10-8). If parameterized constructors were allowed, different clients could call them with different parameters, which would result in a different state for each client. If you try to create a singleton object using a parameterized constructor, .NET throws an exception of type RemotingException.

> COM also supported singletons by allowing you to provide a special class factory, which always returned the same object. The COM singleton behaved much like a .NET singleton. Using ATL, designating a class as a singleton was done by replacing the default class factory macro with the singleton macro. The main difference between a COM singleton and a .NET singleton is that with .NET, the object becomes a singleton because the host registers it as such. Other hosts can register the same component type as single-call or client-activated object. With COM, the singleton was always a singleton.

Using singleton objects

Singleton objects are the sworn enemy of scalability; there are only so many concurrent client calls a single object can sustain. Take care before deciding to use a singleton object. Make sure that the singleton will not be a hot spot for scalability and that your design will benefit from sharing the singleton's object state. In general, use a singleton object if it maps well to a true singleton in the application logic, such as a logbook that all components should log their activities to. Other examples are a single communication port or a single mechanical motor. Avoid using a singleton if there is even the slightest chance that the business logic will allow more than one such object in the future, such as adding another motor or a second communication port, etc. The reason is clear: if your clients all depend on implicitly being connected to the well-known object, and more than one object is available, the clients would suddenly need to have a way to bind to the correct object. This can have severe implications on the application's programming model. Because of these limitations, I recommend that you avoid singletons in the general case and find ways to share the state of the singleton, instead of the singleton object itself. That said, there are cases when using a singleton is a good idea; for example, class factories are usually implemented as singletons.

Singleton object lifecycle

Once a singleton object is created, it should live forever. That presents a problem to the .NET garbage collection mechanism; even if no client presently has a reference to the singleton object, the semantics of the singleton activation mode stipulate that the singleton be kept alive so that future clients can connect to it and its state. .NET uses leasing to keep an object in a different process alive, but once the lease expires, .NET disconnects the singleton object from the remoting infrastructure and eventually garbage-collects it. You need to explicitly provide the singleton with a long enough (or even infinite) lease. The leasing section in this chapter demonstrates a few ways of providing a lease.

A singleton object shouldn't provide a deterministic mechanism to finalize its state, such as implementing IDisposable. If it's possible to deterministically dispose of a singleton object, it will present you with a problem: once disposed of, the singleton object becomes useless. Furthermore, subsequent client attempts to access or create a new singleton will be channeled to the disposed object. A singleton by its very nature implies that it's acceptable to keep the object alive in memory for a long period of time, and therefore there is no need for deterministic finalization. A singleton object should use only a Finalize( ) method (the C# destructor).

Activation Modes and Synchronization

In a distributed application, the hosting domain registers the objects it's willing to expose, and their activation modes, with .NET. Each incoming client call into the host is serviced on a separate thread from the thread pool. That allows the host to serve remote client calls concurrently and maximize throughput. The question is, what effect does this have on the object synchronization requirements?

You can use synchronization domains to synchronize access to remote objects, but bear in mind that synchronization domains can't flow across app domains. If a client creates a remote object, and the remote object requires synchronization, the object will have a new synchronization domain, even if the remote client was part of a synchronization domain.

Client-activated objects and synchronization

Client-activated objects are no different from classic client-server objects with respect to synchronization. If multiple clients share a reference to an object, and the clients can issue calls on multiple threads at the same time, you must provide for synchronization to avoid corrupting the state of the object. As explained in Chapter 8, it would be best if the locking were encapsulated in the component itself, either by using synchronization domains or manual synchronization. The reason is clear: any client-side locking (such as the lock statement) locks only the proxy, not the object itself. Another noteworthy point is thread affinity: because each incoming call can be on a different thread, the client-activated object should not make any assumptions about the thread it's running on and avoid mechanisms such as thread-relative static or thread local storage. This is true even if the object is always accessed by the same client, and that client runs always on the same thread.

Single-call objects and synchronization

In the case of a single-call object, object-state synchronization isn't a problem because the object's state in memory exists only for the duration of that call and can't be corrupted by other clients. However, synchronization is required when the objects store state between method calls. If you use a database, you have to explicitly lock the tables, or you can use transactions with the appropriate isolation level to lock the data. If you use the filesystem, you need to prevent sharing the files you access while a call is in progress.

Singleton objects and synchronization

Unlike client-activated objects, the clients of a singleton object may not even be aware they are actually sharing the same object and thus not take the necessary precautions to lock the object before access. As a result, synchronization of a singleton object should be enforced on the object side. You can use either a synchronization domain or manual synchronization, as explained in Chapter 8. Similar to a client-activated object, a singleton object must avoid thread-affinity.

It's important to emphasize again that, in principle, you don't need to cross app domains when using the different activation modes. As long as a proxy is present between the client and the marshal-by-reference object, the client can activate the object as single call or singleton, even in the same app domain. In practice, you're likely to use server-activated single call or server-activated singleton call only on remote objects.

.NET Remoting Architecture

The .NET remoting architecture is a modular and extensible architecture. The basic building blocks on the client side are proxies, formatters, and transport channels, and on the host side, the building blocks are transport channels, formatters, and call dispatchers. These building blocks are shown in Figure 10-9.

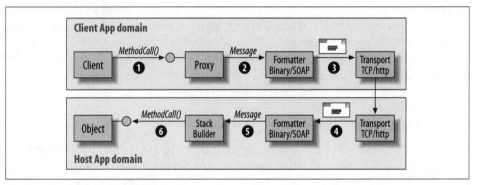

Figure 10-9. .NET remoting architecture

In addition, .NET provides a way to uniquely locate and identify a remote object. This section provides an overview of the architecture building blocks and how they interact with each other.

Client-Side Processing

The client never interacts with a remote object directly. The client interacts instead with a *proxy*, which provides the exact same public entry points as the remote object. It's the proxy's job to allow the client to make a method call or access a property on it, and then marshal that call to the actual object. Every proxy is bound to at most one object, although a single object can be accessed by multiple proxies. The proxy also knows where the object is. When the client makes a call on the proxy (Step 1 in Figure 10-9), the proxy the takes the parameters to the call (the stack frame), creates a message object, and asks a formatter object to process the message (Step 2 in Figure 10-9). The formatter serializes the message object and passes it to a channel object, to transport to the remote object (Step 3 in Figure 10-9). While all this is happening, the proxy blocks the client, waiting for the call to return. Once the call returns from the channel, the formatter deserializes the returned message and returns it to the proxy. The proxy places the output parameters and the returned value on the client's call stack (just like the real object does for a direct call), and finally returns control to the client.

The proxy has actually two parts to it (see Figure 10-10). The first is called a *transparent proxy*. The transparent proxy exposes the same entry points (as well as base type and interfaces) as the actual object. The transparent proxy is implemented by the sealed private class TransparentProxy. The transparent proxy converts the stack frame to a message and then passes the message to the real proxy. The *real proxy* knows how to connect to the remote object and forward the message to it. The real proxy is a class derived from the RealProxy abstract class; it has nothing to do with the actual remote object type. .NET provides by default a concrete subclass (the internal class RemotingProxy). The advantage of breaking the proxy into two parts is that it allows you to use the .NET provided transparent proxy while providing your own custom real proxy.

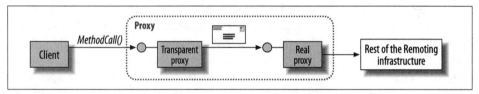

Figure 10-10. The proxy has two parts: a transparent and a real proxy

Server-Side Processing

Once the method is received by the server-side channel, it forwards the message to a formatter (Step 4 in Figure 10-9). The formatter deserializes the message and passes it to the *stack-builder* (Step 5 in Figure 10-9). The stack-builder reads the message and calls the object based on the method and its parameters in the message (Step 6 in Figure 10-9). The object itself is never aware that it's being accessed by a remote client because as far as it's concerned, the client is the stack-builder. Once the call returns to the stack-builder, it returns a reply message to the server-side formatter. The formatter serializes the message and returns it to the channel to transport to the client.

Formatters

Because the proxy and the stack-builder serialize and deserialize messages, all they need to do is take advantage of the serialization mechanism described in Chapter 9. Out of the box, .NET provides a SOAP formatter and a binary formatter. The binary formatter requires much less processing time to serialize and deserialize than the SOAP formatter, and as a result, in intense calling patterns, the binary formatter gets better performance. This is because it takes more time to compose and parse a SOAP message, as opposed to the binary format, which is practically used as-is. In addition, the message in a binary format has a smaller payload and reduces overall network latency. The main advantage of the SOAP format is that it can interoperate with other platforms. In addition, SOAP is the format of choice when going through a firewall in which HTTP is used for the transport protocol. (You can also go through firewalls over HTTP with a binary format.) If there is no interoperability need, or a firewall isn't present between the host and the client, you should use binary format for performance reasons.

Transport Channels

Once the message (either from the proxy to the stack-builder or back) is serialized, what protocol transports the message to the other side? Out of the box, .NET provides two transport protocols for remote calls: TCP and HTTP. These are called *transport channels*. It's important to state that the question of what transport protocol to use is independent of the question of what format is used to serialize the message. You can use either SOAP or binary over either TCP or HTTP. However, if you select the default transport channel configuration, when you select TCP, .NET uses binary format; when you select HTTP, .NET uses the SOAP format. This policy makes sense because if there is no firewall between the client and the host, a binary protocol (TCP) with a binary format yields the best performance. If a firewall is present, a text-based protocol (HTTP) with SOAP format is required to go through the firewall. Both the client and the host app domains need to indicate to .NET which channels they intend to use. This is called *channel registration*. The client needs to register the channels it wishes to make outgoing remote calls on. The client can register either TCP and HTTP or both. The host app domain needs to register the channels through which it's willing to accept calls from remote clients. The host app domain can register either channel or both. In fact, if you have access to other custom channels, you can use them on both sides.

 Binary formatting over TCP channel is very close in spirit and performance to classic DCOM.

In the case of a remote call across two app domains in the same physical process, .NET uses the same architecture as with a call across processes or across machines. However, .NET doesn't use the network-oriented channels because it would be a waste of resources and a performance penalty. Instead, .NET automatically (as in Example 10-2) uses a dedicated channel for this case called CrossAppDomainChannel. This channel is an internal channel to the remoting infrastructure assembly and isn't available to you. Because both client and server share the same physical process, the

`CrossAppDomainChannel` uses the client's thread to invoke the call on the object, and the thread pool isn't involved.

Object Locations and Identity

Every remote object is associated with a Uniform Resource Locator (URL). The URL provides the location of the remote object, and it must be mapped to an actual location in which a host app domain is listening for remote activation requests. The URL has the following structure:

```
<protocol>://<machine name>:<port number>
```

The URL provides .NET with where and how to connect with a remote object: what protocol to use to transport the call, to what machine, and on which port of the host machine to try to connect. For example, here is a possible URL:

```
tcp://localhost:8005
```

This URL instructs .NET to connect to a host on the local machine on port 8005, and to use TCP for the transport protocol. It also instructs .NET to use *http* for transport protocol and to try to connect to port 8006 on the local machine:

```
http://localhost:8006
```

A URL can optionally contain an application name section:

```
<protocol>://<machine name>:<port number>[/<application name>]
```

For example:

```
http://localhost:8006/MyApp
```

If a client wants to use a client-activated remote object, the information in the URL is sufficient for .NET to connect to the remote host, create an object on the remote machine, and marshal a reference back to the client. As a result, a URL is all that is required to identify a remote client-activated object.

The situation is different for server-activated objects. When the client tries to connect to a server-activated object, it must provide the server with additional information identifying which well-known object it wants to activate. For example, the host could have a number of singleton objects of the same type, servicing different clients. That additional identification information is in the form of a Uniform Resource Identifier (URI). The URI is appended to the activation URL:

```
<URL>/<URI>
```

Here are two examples:

```
tcp://localhost:8005/RemoteServer
http://localhost:8006/RemoteServer
```

The URI can be any string, as long as it's unique in the scope of the host app domain. The host is responsible for registering with .NET the well-known objects it's willing to export, and the URIs have to match to those supplied by the clients. Note that the URI is supplied by the client, but the host is the one deciding whether the client gets a well-known singleton object identified by the URI or a single-call object, which is actually not a well-known instance at all. Nonetheless, both server-activation types are called *well-known objects*.

Error Handling

When a client has a direct reference to an object, exceptions thrown by the object wind their way up the call stack. The client can then catch the exception and handle it or let it propagate up the call chain. With remote objects, the client has a direct reference to a proxy only, and the object is called on a different stack frame. If a remote object throws an exception, .NET catches that exception, serializes it, and sends it back to the proxy. The proxy then rethrows the exception on the client's side. The resulting programming model as far as the client is concerned is very similar to that of handling errors with local objects in the same app domain as the client.

Building a Distributed Application

Finally, after so many definitions and abstractions, its time to put it all to use and see how to build a server, a host app domain to host the server object, and a client application to consume the remote object. Both the host and the client application need to indicate to .NET how they intend to use remoting. The host needs to register with .NET the channels and formats on which it's willing to accept remote calls, the remote types it's willing to export and their activation modes, and their URIs, if applicable. The client application needs to register with .NET the channels and formats in which it wants to make outgoing calls, and depending on the way the client creates the objects, the client may need to register the types it wants to access remotely. There are two ways to achieve all this: programmatically and administratively. If you use programmatic configuration, you gain maximum flexibility because you can change runtime activation modes, object location, and channels used. Both the client and the host can use programmatic configuration. If you use administrative configuration, you save your remoting settings in the application's configuration file. Both the client and the server can use administrative configuration. You can also mix and match: have some settings in the configuration files and programmatically configure others, although normally you use either one or the other, but not both at the same time. Administrative settings let you change the settings and affect the way your distributed application behaves, even after deployment; it's the preferred way to handle remoting in most cases. This section demonstrates both techniques using the same sample application. I will explain programmatic configuration first and, armed with the understanding of the basic steps, will then examine the administrative configuration settings.

Programmatic Channel Registration

A remoting channel is any component that implements the IChannel interface, defined in the System.Runtime.Remoting.Channels namespace. You rarely need to interact with a channel object directly. All you have to do is register a channel, without caring what the channel actually does. Out of the box, .NET provides two implementations of the IChannel interface: the TcpChannel and HttpChannel classes, defined in the System.Runtime.Remoting.Channels.Tcp and System.Runtime.Remoting.Channels.Http namespaces, respectively. Both the client and the host application need to register which channels they wish to use, using the static method RegisterChannel() of the ChannelServices class:

```
public sealed class ChannelServices
{
```

```
        public static void RegisterChannel(IChannel channel);
        //Other methods
    }
```

Typically, both the host and the client will put the channel registration code in their
Main() method, but they can put it anywhere else, as long as it takes place before
remote calls are issued. Note that you can register the same channel type only once
per app domain, unless you explicitly assign it a different name, as described later.

Host channels registration

The host must register at least one channel if it wants to export objects. To register a
channel, the host first creates a new channel object, providing as a construction
parameter the port number associated with this channel. Next, the host registers the
new channel. For example:

```
using System.Runtime.Remoting.Channels;
using System.Runtime.Remoting.Channels.Tcp;

//Registering TCP channel
IChannel channel = new TcpChannel(8005);
ChannelServices.RegisterChannel(channel);
```

When a new remote call is accepted, the channel grabs a thread from the thread pool
and lets it execute the call, while the channel continues to monitor the port. This
way, .NET can serve incoming calls as soon as they come off the channel. Note that
the number of concurrent calls .NET remoting can service is subject to the threadpool limitation. Once the pool is exhausted, new requests are queued until requests
in progress are complete.

The host can choose to register multiple channels:

```
using System.Runtime.Remoting.Channels;
using System.Runtime.Remoting.Channels.Tcp;
using System.Runtime.Remoting.Channels.Http;

//Registering TCP channel
IChannel tcpChannel = new TcpChannel(8005);
ChannelServices.RegisterChannel(tcpChannel);

//Registering http channel
IChannel httpChannel = new HttpChannel(8006);
ChannelServices.RegisterChannel (httpChannel);
```

When the host instantiates a channel, .NET creates a background thread to open a
socket and listen to activation requests on the port. As a result, you can run blocking
operations after creating and registering a channel because you won't affect the
thread monitoring the channel. For example, this is valid host-side registration code:

```
static void Main()
{
```

```
        //Registering TCP channel
        IChannel channel = new TcpChannel(8005);
        ChannelServices.RegisterChannel(channel);

        Thread.Sleep(Timeout.Infinite);
    }
```

An inherent limitation of network programming is that a given port can be opened only once to listen on. Consequently, you can't open multiple channels on the same port on a given machine. For example, you can't register channels this way:

```
//You can't register multiple channels on the same port
IChannel tcpChannel = new TcpChannel(8005);
ChannelServices.RegisterChannel(tcpChannel);

//Registering http channel
IChannel httpChannel = new HttpChannel(8005);
ChannelServices.RegisterChannel(httpChannel);
```

Registering multiple channels targeting the same port number throws an exception of type SocketException at runtime. In addition, you can register a channel type only once, even if you use different ports:

```
//You can only register a channel once, so this will not work:

IChannel tcpChannel1 = new TcpChannel(8005);
ChannelServices.RegisterChannel(tcpChannel1);

IChannel tcpChannel2 = new TcpChannel(8007);
ChannelServices.RegisterChannel(tcpChannel2);//Throws RemotingException
```

When the host application shuts down, .NET automatically frees the port so it may be used by other hosts on the machine. However, it's customary that as soon as you no longer need the channels, you unregister them explicitly using the static method UnregisterChannel( ) of the ChannelServices:

```
IChannel channel = new TcpChannel(8005);
ChannelServices.RegisterChannel(channel);

/* Accept remote calls here */

//When done—unregister channel(s):
ChannelServices.UnregisterChannel(channel);
```

Client channels registration

The client must register the channels it would like to issue remote calls on. The channel's type must match what the host is willing to accept remote calls on, so if the host has registered only the TCP channel, the client must register and use the TCP channel. However, if the host has registered other channels, the client can register them as well and use any one of them to issue the call.

The client doesn't need to indicate the port number on the host machine because that information will be part of the URL that points at the remote object:

```
//Client channels registration:
//No port number as parameter. Input it in activation URL
IChannel tcpChannel  = new TcpChannel();
IChannel httpChannel = new HttpChannel();

ChannelServices.RegisterChannel(tcpChannel);
ChannelServices.RegisterChannel(httpChannel);
```

Channels and formats

The channel classes provide three overloaded constructors. Both versions shown so far (host and client registration) automatically select the appropriate default formatter. The TcpChannel class uses the binary formatter to format messages between the client and the host applications by default. The HttpChannel class uses the SOAP formatter by default. However, as stated previously, you can combine any channel with any format. Both the TcpChannel class and the HttpChannel class provide the following constructor:

```
public class TcpChannel : <base types>
{
    public TcpChannel(IDictionary properties,
                  IClientChannelSinkProvider clientSinkProvider,
                  IServerChannelSinkProvider serverSinkProvider);
     /* Other constructors and methods  */
}

public class HttpChannel : <base types>
{
    public HttpChannel(IDictionary properties,
                  IClientChannelSinkProvider clientSinkProvider,
                  IServerChannelSinkProvider serverSinkProvider);
     /* Other constructors and methods  */
}
```

These constructors accept a collection of key/value pairs and two sink interfaces. The collection is a dictionary of predetermined channel configuration properties, such as the new channel's name and the port number. The two sink interfaces are where you can provide a formatter instead of accepting the default. The client-SinkProvider parameter registers a channel on the client's side; the serverSinkProvider registers a channel on the host's side. The available formatters for the host include SoapServerFormatterSinkProvider and BinaryServerFormatterSinkProvider, implementing the IServerChannelSinkProvider interface. On the client side, the available formatters are SoapClientFormatterSinkProvider and BinaryClientFormatterSinkProvider, implementing the IClientChannelSinkProvider interface. The details of these interfaces and format providing classes are immaterial. The important thing is that you can simply use one to explicitly force a message format.

Please refer to the MSDN library for more information on the configuration parameters and the way they affect the channel.

Here is how to register a SOAP formatter using a TCP channel on the host side:

```
IServerChannelSinkProvider formatter;
formatter = new SoapServerFormatterSinkProvider();

IDictionary channelProperties = new Hashtable();
channelProperties["name"] = "MyServerTCPChannel";
channelProperties["port"] = 8005;

IChannel channel = new TcpChannel(channelProperties,null,formatter);
ChannelServices.RegisterChannel(channel);
```

Note that the second construction parameter is ignored. When doing the same on the client side, you need not provide a port number, and you provide the formatter as the second, instead of the third parameter:

```
IClientChannelSinkProvider formatter;
formatter = new SoapClientFormatterSinkProvider();

IDictionary channelProperties = new Hashtable();
channelProperties["name"] = "MyClientTCPChannel";

IChannel channel = new TcpChannel(channelProperties,formatter,null);
ChannelServices.RegisterChannel(channel);
```

Programmatic Type Registration

The host must indicate to .NET which objects it's willing to expose as client-activated objects, and which to activate as server-activated objects and in what mode. The client can indicate to .NET which objects it wants to access remotely. Both host and client register these types using the static methods of the RemotingConfiguration class. Configuration can be done only once per app domain, for both the host and the client.

Host type registration

To register the instances of the MyClass type as a well-known server activated object, the host uses the static method RegisterWellKnownServiceType() of the Remoting-Configuration class:

```
public static void RegisterWellKnownServiceType(Type type,
                                                string objectUri,
                                                WellKnownObjectMode mode);
```

More on Registering Channels

The classes TcpChannel and HttpChannel are bidirectional, meaning that both the client and the server can use them. The client uses them to issue calls to the server, and the host uses them to listen for client requests. However, .NET provides a set of directional channels; TcpClientChannel and HttpClientChannel transport a client call to the server using TCP or HTTP, respectively. Similarly, TcpServerChannel and HttpServerChannel are used on the host side. All the directional channels are polymorphic with IChannel. The bidirectional channels encapsulate the directional channels and use the directional channels automatically as required. That said, you can explicitly specify to use a directional channel:

```
//Explicit registration of a server channel:
IChannel channel = new TcpServerChannel(8005);
ChannelServices.RegisterChannel(channel);
```

or:

```
//Explicit registration of a client channel:
IChannel channel = new TcpClientChannel();
ChannelServices.RegisterChannel(channel);
```

However, usually there is no need to do that. In fact, doing so precludes remote callbacks, discussed later in the chapter.

The host needs to provide the server type, a URI, and the desired server-activation mode: singleton or single-call. The mode parameter is of the enum type WellKnownObjectMode, defined as:

```
public enum WellKnownObjectMode {SingleCall,Singleton}
```

For example, to register the type MyClass defined as:

```
public class MyClass : MarshalByRefObject
{...}
```

as a single-call object, the host writes:

```
Type serverType = typeof(MyClass);

RemotingConfiguration.RegisterWellKnownServiceType(serverType,
                                        "MyRemoteServer",
                                        WellKnownObjectMode.SingleCall);
```

If the object URL contains an application name section, the host can prefix the URI with the application name:

```
RemotingConfiguration.RegisterWellKnownServiceType(serverType,
                                        "MyApp/MyRemoteServer",
                                        WellKnownObjectMode.SingleCall);
```

The host can't associate multiple URIs with the same type, even it uses different activation modes for each URI, because the more recent registration overrides the previous one:

```
RemotingConfiguration.RegisterWellKnownServiceType(serverType,
                                        "MyRemoteServer1",
                                        WellKnownObjectMode.SingleCall);

//Last registration wins
RemotingConfiguration.RegisterWellKnownServiceType(serverType,
                                        "MyRemoteServer2",
                                        WellKnownObjectMode.Singleton);
```

The host can use the same URI with multiple types:

```
Type serverType1 = typeof(MyClass);
Type serverType2 = typeof(MyOtherClass);

RemotingConfiguration.RegisterWellKnownServiceType(serverType1,
                                        "MyRemoteServer",
                                        WellKnownObjectMode.SingleCall);

RemotingConfiguration.RegisterWellKnownServiceType(serverType2,
                                        "MyRemoteServer",
                                        WellKnownObjectMode.SingleCall);
```

When registering a type on the host's side as a client-activated object, there is no need to provide a URI. Registering a type as client-activated object is done using the static method RegisterActivatedServiceType( ):

```
Type serverType = typeof(MyClass);

RemotingConfiguration.RegisterActivatedServiceType(serverType);
```

If the client-activated object's URL contains an application name part, the host must register an application name via the ApplicationName static property:

```
RemotingConfiguration.ApplicationName = "MyApp";
```

If the object URL doesn't contain an application name, setting the ApplicationName property has no effect on client-activated objects. Setting the ApplicationName property always affects server-activated objects, making it mandatory to use the application name as part of the URL.

Client-side type registration

.NET provides clients with a number of ways to activate remote objects. One of them is the same as for local objects—using new. Another is by using the static methods of the Activator class, GetObject( ) and CreateInstance( ). The Activator class provides quite a few overloaded versions for each method. This chapter discusses the Activator class later on. If you use new or some version of the CreateInstance( ) method, you need to register the object on the client side as a remote object. In essence, client-side registration associates a type with a URL and URI, so that when the client tries to create an instance of the type, .NET knows it should create the object at the location specified, rather than as a local object. If you use the GetObject( ) method, you need not register the type on the client side because the parameters to GetObject( ) contains the object URI and URL. However, you can use only GetObject( ) for server-activated objects, so in general, type registration is a required step on the client side as well.

To register a type as a client-activated object, the client uses the RegisterActivatedClientType( ) method, providing the type and the URL:

```
Type serverType = typeof(MyClass);
string url = "tcp://localhost:8005";

RemotingConfiguration.RegisterActivatedClientType(serverType,url);
```

To register a type as a server-activated object, the client uses the RegisterWellKnownClientType( ) method, providing the type, the URL, and the well-known object's URI:

```
Type serverType = typeof(MyClass);
string url = "tcp://localhost:8005/MyRemoteServer";

RemotingConfiguration.RegisterWellKnownClientType(serverType,url);
```

Remember that the client decides whether it wants a client- or a server-activated object, and the host decides which kind of server-activated object to serve the client. This is why the client doesn't need to specify the activation mode in the call to RegisterWellKnownClientType( ).

Once registration is done on the client side, any new activation requests in the client app domain are redirected to the remote host:

```
using RemoteServer;

MyClass obj = new MyClass ();
obj.SomeMethod( );
```

Programmatic Configuration Example

Instead of fragmented code samples, it's time for a more comprehensive example, showing how the different steps required for programmatic configuration fit together, on both the client and the host side. As mentioned previously, since the host and the client require the server's metadata, it's best if the server is in a class library. This section walks you through Example 10-5—a fully functional distributed application. The source code accompanying this book contains the Remoting-Demo (Programmatic) solution, with three projects: the ServerAssembly class library, the RemoteServerHost EXE assembly, and the Client EXE assembly. Both EXE assemblies are Windows Forms applications that allow you to select channels and activation modes. The class MyClass provides a parameter-less constructor to be used in all activation modes. The constructor brings up a message box so that you can tell when a new object is created, especially when experimenting with single call or singleton objects. The single public method of MyClass is Count( ), which pops up a message box, showing the incremented value of a counter. The counter will indicate the state lifecycle in the different activation modes. The message boxes have as their caption the name of the current app domain. The RemoteServerHost application is a dialog-based application. Its Main( ) method registers both HTTP and TCP channels and then displays the dialog shown in Figure 10-11.

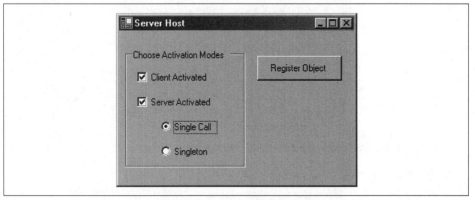

Figure 10-11. Server Host lets you programmatically decide which activation modes to register

Displaying a form by calling Application.Run( ) is a blocking operation, and control returns to the Main( ) method only when the dialog is closed. This, of course, has no effect on the channels registered because they use worker threads to monitor the channels. When the dialog is closed, the Main( ) method unregisters the channels and exits. The Server Host dialog lets you check how the host registers the MyClass type it exports: as client-activated, server-activated, or both. If you select Server Activated, you need to choose between Single Call and Singleton using the radio buttons. When you click Register Object, The OnRegister( ) method is called (see Example 10-5). OnRegister( ) simply registers the object based on the user-interface selections. Note that you can register the object both as client- and server-activated.

The Client application registers both the TCP and HTTP channels in its Main( ) method and then displays the dialog shown in Figure 10-12. You can select either Client Activated or Server Activated (but not both), and then register the type in the OnRegister( ) method. The interesting part of the client application is the way it constructs the activation URL for the object registration. The helper method GetActivationURL( ) constructs a URL based on the channel selected (starts with tcp: // or http://) and appends the URI only if Server Activated mode is selected. OnRegister( ) calls GetActivationURL( ) and then registers the type accordingly. When you click new in the Client dialog, it simply uses new to create a new instance of MyClass and calls Count( ) twice, either remotely (if you registered) or locally (if no registration took place).

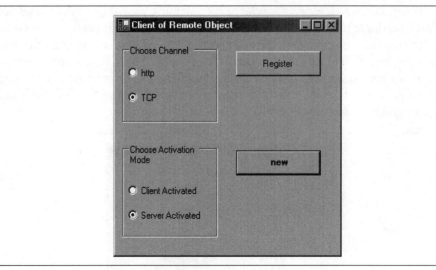

Figure 10-12. Client lets you choose a channel and an activation mode

Example 10-5. Programmatic remoting configuration

```
///////////////////////  ServerAssembly class library  ///////////////////////////
namespace RemoteServer
{
    public class MyClass : MarshalByRefObject
    {
        public MyClass( )
        {
            string appName = AppDomain.CurrentDomain.FriendlyName;
            MessageBox.Show("Constructor",appName);
            Counter = 0;
        }
        protected int Counter;
        public void Count( )
        {
            Counter++;
            string appName = AppDomain.CurrentDomain.FriendlyName;
            MessageBox.Show("Counter value is " + Counter.ToString( ),appName);
        }
    }
}
///////////////////////  RemoteServerHost EXE assembly  ///////////////////////////
using RemoteServer;

public class ServerHostDialog : Form
{
    private Button RegisterButton;
    private RadioButton m_SingletonRadio;
    private RadioButton m_SingleCallRadio;
    private CheckBox m_ClientActivatedCheckBox;
    private CheckBox m_ServerActivatedCheckBox;
```

Example 10-5. Programmatic remoting configuration (continued)

```csharp
private GroupBox m_GroupActivationMode;

public ServerHostDialog( )
{
   InitializeComponent( );
}
private void InitializeComponent( )
{...}

static void Main( )
{
   //Registering TCP channel
   IChannel tcpChannel = new TcpChannel(8005);
   ChannelServices.RegisterChannel(tcpChannel);

   //Registering http channel
   IChannel httpChannel = new HttpChannel(8006);
   ChannelServices.RegisterChannel(httpChannel);

   Application.Run(new ServerHostDialog( ));

   //Do not have to, but cleaner:
   ChannelServices.UnregisterChannel(tcpChannel);
   ChannelServices.UnregisterChannel(httpChannel);
}
private void OnRegister(object sender,EventArgs e)
{
   Type serverType = typeof(MyClass);

   //if the client activated checkbox is checked:
   if(m_ClientActivatedCheckBox.Checked)
   {
      RemotingConfiguration.RegisterActivatedServiceType(serverType);
   }

   //if the server activated checkbox is checked:
   if(m_ServerActivatedCheckBox.Checked)
   {
      if(m_SingleCallRadio.Checked)
      {
         //Allow Server activation, single call mode:
         RemotingConfiguration.RegisterWellKnownServiceType(serverType,
                                                "MyRemoteServer",
                                       WellKnownObjectMode.SingleCall);
      }
      else
      {
         //Allow Server activation, singleton mode:
         RemotingConfiguration.RegisterWellKnownServiceType(serverType,
                                                "MyRemoteServer",
                                       WellKnownObjectMode.Singleton);
      }
```

Example 10-5. Programmatic remoting configuration (continued)

```
            }
        }
    }
}
/////////////////////////// Client EXE assembly /////////////////////////////////
using RemoteServer;

public class ClientForm : Form
{
    private RadioButton m_HttpRadio;
    private RadioButton m_TCPRadio;
    private RadioButton m_ServerRadio;
    private RadioButton m_ClientRadio;
    private GroupBox m_ChannelGroup;
    private GroupBox m_ActivationGroup;
    private Button m_NewButton;
    private Button m_RegisterButton;

    public ClientForm()
    {
        InitializeComponent();
    }
    private void InitializeComponent()
    {...}
    static void Main()
    {
        //No port number as parameter. Input it in activation URI
        IChannel  tcpChannel = new TcpChannel();
        ChannelServices.RegisterChannel(tcpChannel);

        IChannel  httpChannel = new HttpChannel();
        ChannelServices.RegisterChannel(httpChannel);

        Application.Run(new ClientForm());
    }
    private string GetActivationURL()
    {
        if(m_TCPRadio.Checked)
        {
            if(m_ServerRadio.Checked)
            {
                //Server activation over TCP. Note object URI
                return "tcp://localhost:8005/MyRemoteServer";
            }
            else
            {
                //Client activation over TCP
                return "tcp://localhost:8005";
            }
        }
        else//http channel
        {
```

Example 10-5. Programmatic remoting configuration (continued)

```
        if(m_ServerRadio.Checked)
        {
            //Server activation over http. Note object URI
            return "http://localhost:8006/MyRemoteServer";
        }
        else
        {
            //Client activation over http
            return "http://localhost:8006";
        }
    }
}
private void OnRegister(object sender,EventArgs e)
{
    Type serverType = typeof(MyClass);
    string url = GetActivationURL( );

    if(m_ServerRadio.Checked)
    {
        RemotingConfiguration.RegisterWellKnownClientType(serverType,url);
    }
    else //Client activation mode
    {
        //Register just once:
        RemotingConfiguration.RegisterActivatedClientType(serverType,url);
    }
}
private void OnNew(object sender,EventArgs e)
{
    MyClass obj;
    obj = new MyClass( );
    obj.Count( );
    obj.Count( );
}
}
```

Administrative Configuration

Both client and host applications can take advantage of a configuration file to specify their remoting settings instead of making programmatic calls. The configuration file must be in the same directory as the application assembly. Although you can use whatever name you want for the configuration file, the convention is to give it the same name as the application but suffixed with *.config*, this way: *<app name>.config*. For example, if the host assembly is called *RemoteServerHost.exe*, the configuration file is called *RemoteServerHost.exe.config*. The configuration file is an XML file and is the same configuration file that captures custom version binding policies, as discussed in Chapter 5. You'll find the remoting configuration section under the <system.runtime.remoting> tag, in the <application> tag.

```
<?xml version="1.0"?>
<configuration>
   <system.runtime.remoting>
      <application>
         <!--Remoting configuration setting goes here -->
      </application>
   </system.runtime.remoting>
</configuration>
```

Both the client and the host load the configuration file using the static Configure( ) method of the RemotingConfiguration class, providing the name of the configuration file:

```
public static void Configure(string filename);
```

Based on the instructions in the configuration file, .NET programmatically registers the channels and the objects, so that you don't need to write appropriate code. If at runtime .NET can't locate the specified file, an exception of type RemotingException is thrown. Typically, both the client and the host application call the Configure( ) method in their Main( ) method, but you can call it anywhere else, as long as you call it before making any interaction with .NET remoting.

 All the design directives and limitations described in the context of programmatic configuration also apply to administrative configuration.

Administrative Channel Registration

The machine-wide configuration file *Machine.Config* contains global channel definitions and configurations, under the <system.runtime.remoting> tag. In particular, it contains a definition for the HTTP and TCP channels and points to where the types implementing them reside. You can take advantage of these definitions and reference them in your configuration file.

Host channels registration

To register a channel, the host needs to add a <channel> tag for each channel it wishes to register, providing the port number and the channel type. The channels are added under the <channels> tag. For example, to register a TCP channel on port 8005, write:

```
<?xml version="1.0"?>
<configuration>
   <system.runtime.remoting>
      <application>
         <channels>
            <channel ref="tcp"  port="8005"/>
         </channels>
```

```
            </application>
        </system.runtime.remoting>
    </configuration>
```

The host uses the `ref` element to refer to the predefined `tcp` channel. You can register different channels this way, as long as they use different ports:

```
<channels>
    <channel ref="tcp"  port="8005"/>
    <channel ref="http" port="8006"/>
</channels>
```

Client channels registration

The client uses the `<channel>` as well to register a channel, except the client doesn't have to provide a port number. The client too can register different channels:

```
<channels>
    <channel ref="tcp"/>
    <channel ref="http"/>
</channels>
```

 If you want to register custom channels, you can either add their definitions to the *Machine.Config* file and simply reference them, or include the type name and the assembly identity (including strong name) in the `<channel>` tag. Please see the MSDN library for more information on using custom channels.

Channels and formats

When the client or the host configures a channel as just shown, .NET uses the default formatters associated with each transport protocol. However, you can configure it to use a different formatter, using the `<clientProviders>` tag. For example, here are the settings required to configure a client-side HTTP channel to use the binary formatter:

```
<configuration>
    <system.runtime.remoting>
        <application>
            <channels>
                <channel ref="http">
                    <clientProviders>
                        <formatter ref="binary"/>
                    </clientProviders>
                </channel>
            <channels>
        </application>
    </system.runtime.remoting>
</configuration>
```

You can do the same on the host side.

Administrative Type Registration

Similar to the programmatic type registration, the host configuration file must contain a list of the objects it's willing to expose, either as client-activated objects or as server-activated objects, and in what mode. The client configuration file can have a list of the remote types and their URLs and URIs, if required. When the client or host references a type, it must specify a fully qualified name (type name and its namespace) as well as the type's assembly. Any misspelling or versioning incompatibility will be discovered only at runtime.

Host type registration

The host uses the `<service>` tag to contain a list of the types it exposes. Each type has an entry indicating its activation mode and URI, if required. For example, here is how the host registers the type `MyClass` from the `RemoteServer` namespace in the `ServerAssembly` assembly as a client-activated object:

```
<application>
   <service>
      <activated  type="RemoteServer.MyClass,ServerAssembly"/>
   </service>
</application>
```

The host can also expose the type `MyClass` as a server-activated object and specify the activation mode and the URI:

```
<application>
   <service>
      <activated  type="RemoteServer.MyClass,ServerAssembly"/>
      <wellknown  type="RemoteServer.MyClass,ServerAssembly"
                  mode="SingleCall" objectUri="MyRemoteServer"/>
   </service>
</application>
```

With administrative configuration, the host is subjected to the same URI constraints as with programmatic configuration. The host can also specify an application name with the same semantics as assigning a name programmatically:

```
<application name="MyApp">
   ...
</application>
```

Client-side type registration

The host uses the `<client>` tag to contain a list of the types it wants to consume remotely. The client needs to provide the object URL and URI, if required. The client can register a given type only once, just as when registering programmatically.

To register a type as a client-activated object, the client uses the `<activated>` tag, providing the type's name, assembly, and URL:

```
<application>
  <client url="tcp://localhost:8005">
    <activated  type="RemoteServer.MyClass,ServerAssembly"/>
  </client>
</application>
```

To register a type as a server-activated object, the client uses the `<wellknown>` tag:

```
<application>
  <client>
    <wellknown type="RemoteServer.MyClass, ServerAssembly"
               url="tcp://localhost:8005/MyRemoteServer"/>
  </client>
</application>
```

Note that when you use the `<wellknown>` tag, the URL and the URI are specified as attributes of the `<wellknown>` tag, rather than as attributes of the `<client>` tag. If you need to register multiple remote types on the client's side, you need to use multiple `<client>` tags:

```
<application>
  <client url="tcp://localhost:8005">
    <activated  type="RemoteServer.MyClass,ServerAssembly"/>
  </client>
  <client>
    <wellknown  type="RemoteServer.MyOtherClass,ServerAssembly"
    url="tcp://localhost:8005/MyRemoteServer"/>
  </client>
</application>
```

 The .NET Configuration tool has what looks like visual administrative support for managing the remoting part of an application configuration file. Unfortunately, with the current release of .NET, it appears that support leaves much to be desired: the tool doesn't generate a blank configuration file and its ability to edit existing files with existing remoting attributes is partial at best. I expect this to be rectified in future versions of .NET.

Administrative Configuration Example

Example 10-6 demonstrates a host and client using a configuration file to provide remote access to the same object as in Example 10-5. The source code accompanying this book contains the RemotingDemo (Administrative) solution, with three projects: The ServerAssembly class library, the RemoteServerHost EXE assembly, and the Client EXE assembly. Both EXE assemblies are Windows Forms applications, except this time, there are no settings to select because they are all defined in the configuration file. The ServerAssembly class library is the same class library from Example 10-5, providing the class MyClass. The host configuration file exposes the MyClass type both as a client-activated object and as a single-call object. The host registers both TCP and HTTP as transport channels. The host calls RemotingConfiguration.Configure( ) in its Main( ) method and then displays a blank dialog. The client's configuration file registers the type MyClass as a client-activated object (the client can only have the type associated with a single activation mode). The client configuration file provides the type's URL using TCP as transport channel. The client registers both TCP and HTTP channels, but in this case, only the TCP channel is used. The client application calls RemotingConfiguration.Configure( ) in its Main( ) method and then displays the client dialog. The client dialog has a single button on it, allowing you to create new remote objects.

Example 10-6. Administrative remoting configuration using configuration files

```
/////////////// RemoteServerHost.exe.config : the host configuration file ////////
<?xml version="1.0"?>
<configuration>
    <system.runtime.remoting>
        <application>
            <service>
                <activated  type="RemoteServer.MyClass,ServerAssembly"/>
                <wellknown  type="RemoteServer.MyClass,ServerAssembly"
                            mode="SingleCall" objectUri="MyRemoteServer"/>
            </service>
            <channels>
                <channel ref="tcp"  port="8005"/>
                <channel ref="http" port="8006"/>
            </channels>
        </application>
    </system.runtime.remoting>
</configuration>
//////////////////////// RemoteServerHost EXE assembly ///////////////////////////
public class ServerHostDialog : Form
{
    public ServerHostDialog( )
    {
        InitializeComponent( );
    }
    private void InitializeComponent( )
    {...}

    static void Main( )
    {
        RemotingConfiguration.Configure("RemoteServerHost.exe.config");
        Application.Run(new ServerHostDialog( ));
    }
}
//////////////// Client.exe.config: the client configuration file ///////////////
<?xml version="1.0"?>
<configuration>
    <system.runtime.remoting>
        <application>
            <client url="tcp://localhost:8005">
                <activated  type="RemoteServer.MyClass,ServerAssembly"/>
            </client>
```

```
        <channels>
            <channel ref="tcp"/>
            <channel ref="http"/>
        </channels>
    </application>
 </system.runtime.remoting>
</configuration>
///////////////////////////  Client EXE assembly  ///////////////////////////////
using RemoteServer;

public class ClientForm : Form
{
    private Button m_NewButton;

    public ClientForm( )
    {
        InitializeComponent( );
    }

    private void InitializeComponent( )
    {...}

    static void Main( )
    {
        RemotingConfiguration.Configure("Client.exe.config");
        Application.Run(new ClientForm( ));
    }
    private void OnNew(object sender,EventArgs e)
    {
        MyClass obj;
        obj = new MyClass( );
        obj.Count( );
        obj.Count( );
    }
}
```

Creating Remote Objects

If the client has registered a type as a remote type (either programmatically or administratively), the client can use the plain new operator to create any kind of remote type, be it client- or server-activated. However, as mentioned already, .NET provides clients with several ways to connect to remote objects. These options differ in the need for preregistration of the type and in the ability to create client-activated objects.

RemotingServices.Connect( )

The client can choose to connect explicitly to a remote object using the static method Connect( ) of RemotingServices:

```
    public static object Connect(Type classToProxy, string url);
```

Calling Connect( ) explicitly creates a proxy on the client side to the remote object. You can use Connect( ) only to connect to server-activated objects, and you can use only the default constructor. Using the same definitions as in Example 10-5, here is how to create a remote server-activated object using Connect( ):

```
using RemoteServer;

Type serverType = typeof(MyClass);
string url = "tcp://localhost:8005/MyRemoteServer";

MyClass obj;

obj = (MyClass)RemotingServices.Connect(serverType,url);
obj.Count();
```

Connect( ) doesn't affect other attempts of the client to create instances of the type, meaning that if no type registration takes place and then, after a class to Connect( ), calls to new create the type locally in the client's app domain. In fact, you can even register the type, associate it with one location, and have Connect( ) activate an instance at another location.

Activator.GetObject( )

The Activator class provides the static method GetObject( ):

```
public static object GetObject(Type type,string url);
```

GetObject( ) works like RemotingServices.Connect does, allowing the client to connect to a server-activated object:

```
using RemoteServer;

Type serverType = typeof(MyClass);
string url = "tcp://localhost:8005/MyRemoteServer";

MyClass obj;

obj = (MyClass)Activator.GetObject(serverType,url);
obj.Count();
```

GetObject( ) doesn't require type registration on the client side, and it doesn't affect registration of the type.

Activator.CreateInstance( )

The Activator class provides many overloaded versions of the static method CreateInstance( ). CreateInstance( ) lets you create any object type (client- or server-activated) and lets you have fine-grained control over the creation process. Some of the versions require type registration before invocation. This version:

```
public static object CreateInstance(Type type);
```

is no different from new and creates the instance at the remote location registered:

```
using RemoteServer;

Type serverType = typeof(MyClass);
MyClass obj;

obj = (MyClass)Activator.CreateInstance(serverType);
obj.Count();
```

The following version allows you to pass in construction parameters for client-activated objects in the form of an array of objects:

```
public static object CreateInstance(Type type, object[ ] args);
```

CreateInstance( ) chooses the best fitting constructor, similar to how the compiler chooses a constructor. If you want to create a remote instance without type registration beforehand, use one version that accepts an array of activation attributes:

```
public static object CreateInstance(Type type,object[ ] args,
                                    object[ ] activationAttributes);
```

You can pass in as an activation attribute an instance of the UrlAttribute, defined in the System.Runtime.Remoting.Activation namespace:

```
using System.Runtime.Remoting.Activation;
using RemoteServer;

object[ ] attArray = {new UrlAttribute("tcp://localhost:8005")};
Type serverType = typeof(MyClass);

//No registration is required:
MyClass obj = (MyClass)Activator.CreateInstance(serverType,null,attArray);
obj.Count();
```

In essence, CreateInstance( ) is available for advanced creation scenarios. For example, this version:

```
public static ObjectHandle CreateInstance(string assemblyName,string typeName);
```

creates an instance of the specified type and delays setting up a proxy and loading the server assembly until the object handle is unwrapped:

```
using RemoteServer;

ObjectHandle handle;
handle = Activator.CreateInstance("ServerAssembly","RemoteServer.MyClass");

//Proxy is only set up here, and assembly is loaded locally
MyClass obj = (MyServer)handle.Unwrap();
obj.Count();
```

Note that you have to specify the fully qualified type name. Other versions of CreateInstance( ) allow you to specify locale and security information.

Table 10-1 compares the various options available when creating or activating remote objects.

Table 10-1. Creating and activating remote object options

Creating option	Requires registration	Client-activated objects	Server-activated objects
new	Yes	Yes	Yes
RemotingServices.Connect( )	No	No	Yes
Activator.GetObject( )	No	No	Yes
Activator.CreateInstance( )	Depends	Yes	Yes

Remote Callbacks

In a distributed application, callbacks are just as useful as they are for local applications. A client can pass in as a method parameter a reference to a client-side marshal-by reference object to be used by a remote object. A client can provide a remote server with a delegate targeting a client-side method, so that the remote server can raise an event or simply call the client-side method. The difference in the case of remote callbacks is that the roles are reversed: the remote server object becomes the client, and the client (or a client-side object) becomes the server. In fact, as far as the server is concerned, the client (or the target object) is essentially a client-activated object because the server has no URI associated with the target object, nor can it treat it as a well-known object. To receive a remote callback, the client needs to register a port and a channel, and have .NET listen on that port for remote callbacks. The problem is, how would the remote server know about that port, or for that matter, how will the remote server object know what URL to use to connect to the client? The answer is built into the remoting architecture. Whenever a reference to an object is marshaled across an app domain boundary, the object reference contains information about the location of the remote object and the channels the host has registered. The object reference is part of the proxy. When the server calls the proxy, the proxy knows where to marshal the call and which channel and port to use. Things are a bit more complex when it comes to delegates. The client can create a delegate targeting a method on an object on the clients' side and then add that delegate to a public delegate or an event maintained by the server object. The delegate has a public read-only property of type object called Target, which references the target object, stored in the _Target private field. All delegates are marshaled by value (using the Serializable attribute), so the delegate is cloned to the server's side. When the delegate crosses the client's app domain boundary, the _Target field will have only a proxy to the target object, and the proxy will have the target object reference (location and information on the client-side channels).

As a result, to support remote callbacks, all the client needs to do is provide a port number to the channel constructor just like the host application does:

```
//Registering a channel with a specific port number on the client side,
//to enable callbacks:
IChannel channel = new TcpChannel(9005);
ChannelServices.RegisterChannel(channel);
```

When the client invokes a call on the server, the client needs to know in advance which ports the host listens on. This isn't the case when the server makes a callback to the client because the proxy on the server side already knows the client-side port number. Consequently, the client doesn't really have to use any predesignated port for the callback; any available port will do. To instruct .NET to select an available port automatically and listen on that port for callbacks, the client simply needs to register the channels with port 0:

```
//Instructing .NET to select any available port on the client's side
IChannel channel = new TcpChannel();
ChannelServices.RegisterChannel(channel);
```

Or if you're using a configuration file:

```
<channels>
    <channel ref="tcp"  port="0"/>
</channels>
```

An interesting scenario is when the client registers multiple channels for callbacks. The client can assign a priority to the channel, using a channel-named property called priority as part of a collection of named properties provided to the channel constructor (similar to explicitly specifying a formatter). The client can also assign priority to channels in the configuration file:

```
<application>
    <channels>
        <channel ref="tcp"   port="0" priority="1"/>
        <channel ref="http"  port="0" priority="2"/>
    </channels>
</application>
```

The channels' priority information is captured by the object reference. The remote server tries to use the channels according to their priority (that is, if the host has registered matching channels). If the client registers multiple channels but doesn't assign a priority, the host selects one for the call.

Remote callbacks and metadata

Another side effect of reversing the roles of the client and server when dealing with remote callbacks is the client's metadata. At runtime, the host must be able to build a proxy to the client-side object, and therefore the host needs to have access to the object's metadata. As a result, you need to package the client-side callback object (or event subscribers) in class libraries and have the host reference these assemblies. You can use the technique shown in Chapter 6 for sinking interfaces with remote event subscribers. The host needs to have access only to the metadata describing the interface, not the actual subscribers.

Remote callbacks and error handling

On top of the usual things that can go wrong when invoking a callback, with remote callbacks there is also the potential for network problems and other wire-related issues. This is a particular concern in the case of remote event publishers because they have to try to reach every subscriber and wait a considerable amount of time for each because of network latency. Because a publisher-subscriber relationship is by its very nature a looser relationship than that of a client and server, often the publisher doesn't need to concern itself with whether the subscriber managed to process the event successfully or even if the event was delivered at all. If that is the case with your application, it's better if you don't publish events simply by calling the delegate. Instead, publish the event using the asynchronous event publishing technique that uses the EventsHelper class, as shown in Chapter 7.

There is something you can do on the subscriber's side, however, to make the life of the remote publisher easier. Chapter 7 introduced the OneWay attribute, defined in the System.Runtime.Remoting.Messaging namespace. The OneWay attribute makes any remote method call a fire-and-forget asynchronous call. If you designate a subscriber's event handling method as a OneWay method, the remoting infrastructure only dispatches the callback and doesn't wait for a reply or for completion. As a result, even if you publish an event by calling a delegate directly, the event publishing will be asynchronous and concurrent. It's asynchronous because the publisher doesn't wait for the subscribers to process the event. It's concurrent because every remote subscriber is served on an impendent worker thread, since remote calls use threads from the thread pool. In addition, any errors on the subscriber's side don't propagate to the publisher's side, so the publisher doesn't need to program to catch and handle exceptions raised by the event subscriber.

 Because static members and methods aren't remotable (no object reference is possible), you can't subscribe to a remote static event, and you can't provide a static method as a target for a remote publisher. You can only pass to a remote object a delegate targeting an instance method on the client side. If you pass a remote publisher a delegate targeting a static method, the event is delivered to a static method on the remote host side.

Remote callback example

Example 10-7 shows a publisher firing events on a remote subscriber. The source code accompanying this book contains the Remote Events solution, with three projects: The ServerAssembly class library, the RemoteServerHost EXE assembly, and the Client EXE assembly. These projects are a variation of the projects presented in Example 10-6. The host is identical to Example 10-6, and the changes are in the host's configuration file. The host exposes the type RemoteServer.MyPublisher as a client-activated object and as a server-activated object. The ServerAssembly class library contains both the subscriber and the publisher classes. Recall that this is required so that both the client and the host can gain access to these types' metadata. Note that both the publisher and the subscriber are derived from MarshalByRefObject. The publisher provides a public event of type NewNumberEvent:

```
public delegate void NewNumberEvent(int num);
```

The publisher publishes to the subscribers in the FireEvent( ) method by simply calling the delegate. The subscriber is the MySubscriber class. The subscriber's event handling method is OnNewNumber( ), which pops a message box with the value of the event's argument:

```
[OneWay]
public void OnNewNumber(int num)
{
    MessageBox.Show("New Value: " + num.ToString( ));
}
```

The interesting part of OnNewNumber( ) is that it's decorated with the [OneWay] attribute. As a result, the publisher's FireEvent( ) method actually fires the event asynchronously and concurrently to the various subscribers. The client's configuration file is the same as in Example 10-6, except this time the client registers the port 0 with the channel, which allows the client to receive remote callbacks. The client configuration file registers the publisher as a remote object. The client creates local instances of the subscriber and a remote instance of the publisher, and saves them as class members. The client is a Windows Forms dialog. The dialog allows the user to subscribe to or unsubscribe from the publisher, and to fire the event. The dialog reflects the event's argument in a text box. Subscribing and unsubscribing to the event is done using the conventional += and -= operators, as in the local case.

Example 10-7. Remote events

```
////////////// RemoteServerHost.exe.config : the host configuration file  ////////
<?xml version="1.0"?>
<configuration>
  <system.runtime.remoting>
    <application>
      <service>
        <activated  type="RemoteServer.MyPublisher,ServerAssembly"/>
        <wellknown  type="RemoteServer.MyPublisher,ServerAssembly"
                    mode="SingleCall" objectUri="MyRemotePublisher"/>
      </service>
      <channels>
        <channel ref="tcp"  port="8005"/>
        <channel ref="http" port="8006"/>
      </channels>
    </application>
  </system.runtime.remoting>
</configuration>
```

Example 10-7. Remote events (continued)

```
////////////////////    ServerAssembly class library  //////////////////////////
namespace RemoteServer
{
    public delegate void NewNumberDelegate(int num);
    public class MyPublisher : MarshalByRefObject
    {
        public event NewNumberDelegate NewNumberEvent;
        public void FireEvent(int num)
        {
            if(NewNumberEvent != null)
            {
                NewNumberEvent(num);
            }
        }
    }
    public class MySubscriber : MarshalByRefObject
    {
        [OneWay]
        public void OnNewNumber(int num)
        {
            MessageBox.Show("New Value: " + num.ToString( ));
        }
    }
}
///////////////// Client.exe.config: the client configuration file  //////////////
<?xml version="1.0"?>
<configuration>
    <system.runtime.remoting>
        <application>
            <client url="tcp://localhost:8005">
                <activated  type="RemoteServer.MyPublisher,ServerAssembly"/>
            </client>
            <channels>
                <channel ref="tcp"  port="0"/>
            </channels>
        </application>
    </system.runtime.remoting>
</configuration>
///////////////////////// Client EXE assembly  /////////////////////////////////
using RemoteServer;

public class SubscriberForm : Form
{
    private Button m_FireButton;
    private Button m_SubscribeButton;
    private Button m_UnsubscribeButton;
    private TextBox m_NumberValue;

    MyPublisher  m_Publisher;
    MySubscriber m_Subscriber;
```

Example 10-7. Remote events (continued)

```
public SubscriberForm( )
{
    InitializeComponent( );

    m_Publisher  = new MyPublisher( );
    m_Subscriber = new MySubscriber( );
}
private void InitializeComponent( )
{...}

static void Main( )
{
    RemotingConfiguration.Configure("Client.exe.config");

    Application.Run(new SubscriberForm( ));
}
private void OnFire(object sender,EventArgs e)
{
    int num = Convert.ToInt32(m_NumberValue.Text);
    m_Publisher.FireEvent(num);
}
private void OnUnsubscribe(object sender,EventArgs e)
{
    m_Publisher.NewNumberEvent -= new
                        NewNumberDeleagte(m_Subscriber.OnNewNumber);
}
private void OnSubscribe(object sender,EventArgs e)
{
    m_Publisher.NewNumberEvent += new
                        NewNumberDelegate(m_Subscriber.OnNewNumber);
}
}
```

Separating the Server Code from its Metadata

As explained previously, both the client and the host require the server assembly. The client requires the server's metadata to compile against and to build a proxy at runtime. At runtime, the host requires the server's IL to host the components and the metadata for call marshaling purposes. If the host is doing programmatic registration, the host requires the metadata at compile-time as well.

You can reduce the client's application dependency on the server class library by allowing access to the server objects via interfaces only and splitting the server into two class libraries: one with the interface definitions only and one with the actual interface implementation. You can then deploy on the client's side only the interfaces assembly, not the assembly with the actual code, which remains on the server. The only issue now is how will the client instantiate the types that support the interfaces? In fact, there are a number of options.

- Name the interfaces and the implementation assemblies the same, including the strong name. Make sure both have the same version number. Add to the interfaces assembly the definitions of the classes implementing them, with stubbed-out implementation; this allows the client to compile. Using type registration, redirect the types to the host.

- Use a class factory to instantiate the objects and have the factory return interfaces only. The class factory will be in a separate class library assembly altogether. The factory assembly will require access to the assembly implementing the interfaces, but no other clients will need that assembly.

- If the remote object is server-activated, use `Activator.GetObject( )` or `RemotingServices.Connect( )` to create an instance of the interface. This works because the host instantiates the type behind the interface and returns only the interface. This technique doesn't work with new because it won't compile, and `Activator.CreateInstance( )` will fail at runtime.

To avoid deploying assemblies with code on the client's side you can use the *SoapSuds.exe* command-line utility. *SoapSuds.exe* extracts the metadata of the types in a server assembly and generates wrapper classes that point to the server assembly remote location. For each public class that derives from `MarshalByRefObject`, *SoapSuds.exe* generates a class with a matching name that derives from the abstract class `RemotingClientProxy`.

Use command-line switches to provide the input assembly and the remote host URL:

```
soapsuds -inputassemblyfile:ServerAssembly
         -outputassemblyfile:ClientProxy.dll
         -serviceendpoint:http://localhost:8006/MyRemoteServer
```

Next, add a reference in the client's assembly to the wrapper classes assembly instead of the actual server assembly. In that respect, the wrapper classes act as a proxy to the real proxy. *SoapSuds.exe* has a number of limitations:

- It hardcodes the channel into the wrapper classes, formatter, and host location. If you want the client to use them to connect to other hosts, you have to programmatically set the `Url` property of the wrapper class.

- The wrapper classes work only if the host is listening on HTTP channels and using SOAP format.

- You can use only the wrapper classes to connect to server-activated object.

- It's cumbersome to create wrapper classes if the host uses multiple URIs associated with the types in the input assembly.

The main advantage of *SoapSuds.exe* has is that you can use it to generate wrapper classes even if the server assembly is an EXE assembly (i.e., the host and the server are the same assembly).

Host as a System Service

Implementing a host requires only a few lines of code, as shown in Example 10-6. The downside isn't the amount of work required to provide a host; it's that the host has to be running before remote calls are issued. As a result, you are likely to provide your host in the form of a system service. .NET makes implementing a service straightforward, as shown in Example 10-8. Add to an EXE assembly a class derived from ServiceBase, which is found in the System.ServiceProcess namespace. In the Main() method of the assembly, run the service. Override the OnStart() method of ServiceBase, and either register channels and objects or load a configuration file. You will also need to include in the assembly a class derived from Installer (defined in the System.Configuration.Install namespace) to install the EXE as a system service. The Installer-derived class captures various service parameters, such as the start-up mode and the account under which to run the service. Next, you need to install the service using the *InstallUtil.exe* command-line utility. Visual Studio.NET can automate many of these phases, including the installer class, and it can even generate a service setup project to install the service. Please refer to the MSDN documentation for additional information on developing system services.

Example 10-8. Providing a host as a system service

```
using System.ServiceProcess;
using System.Configuration.Install;

public class MyHostService : ServiceBase
{
   static void Main( )
   {
      ServiceBase.Run(new MyHostService( ));
   }
   protected override void OnStart(string[ ] args)
   {
      RemotingConfiguration.Configure("HostService.exe.config");
   }
}

[RunInstaller(true)]
public class HostInstaller : Installer
{
   private ServiceProcessInstaller m_ServiceProcessInstaller;
   private ServiceInstaller m_ServiceInstaller;

   public HostInstaller( )
   {
      InitializeComponent( );
   }
   private void InitializeComponent( )
   {
```

Example 10-8. Providing a host as a system service (continued)

```
        m_ServiceProcessInstaller = new ServiceProcessInstaller( );
        m_ServiceInstaller = new ServiceInstaller( );

        m_ServiceProcessInstaller.Account = ServiceAccount.LocalSystem;
        m_ServiceProcessInstaller.Password = null;
        m_ServiceProcessInstaller.Username = null;

        m_ServiceInstaller.DisplayName = "MyHostService";
        m_ServiceInstaller.ServiceName = "MyHostService";
        m_ServiceInstaller.StartType   = ServiceStartMode.Automatic;

        Installer[ ]installers = {m_ServiceProcessInstaller,m_ServiceInstaller};
        Installers.AddRange(installers);
   }
}
```

Hosting with IIS

Instead of providing your own service, you can host your remote components in the worker process IIS uses to host web applications. There are a few reasons why you would want to host your components with IIS. The first is that the worker process is a service, so it will always be running when client requests are sent. The second reason is security: you can take advantage of IIS built-in security to provide call authentication. The third is that your remote objects will also be available as web services. In order to host with IIS, follow these steps:

1. Create a new virtual root under IIS.
2. The server assembly must be in a known location. You can put it either in the GAC, or in a *\bin* folder under the root.
3. Server-activated objects URIs must end with either `.rem` or `.soap`, such as `MyServer.rem`.
4. Avoid registering channels. IIS requires you to use HTTP, over port 80 by default. If you need a different port, configure it using the IIS snap-in. The only reason to register a channel would be to use the binary format instead of the default SOAP.
5. Don't register an application name. IIS will use the virtual root as the app name.
6. If you use a configuration file:
   - Place it in the root.
   - The configuration filename must be *web.config*.

You can host in IIS both client- and server-activated objects.

Leasing and Sponsorship

.NET manages the lifecycle of objects using garbage collection. .NET keeps track of memory allocation and objects accessed by all the clients in the app domain. When an object becomes unreachable by its clients, it's eventually collected by the garbage collector. If the objects are in the same app domain, garbage collection functions fine. In fact, even in the case of a client in one app domain accessing an object in a different app domain, but in the same process, garbage collection still works. This is because in the same process, all app domains share the same managed heap. In the case of remote objects across processes and machines, the strategy breaks: the object may not have local clients at all. If garbage collection were to take place, the garbage collector may not find any reference to the object and will deem it garbage, even though there are remote clients (on other machines on even in a separate app domain in the same process) who wish to use the object. The rest of this section addresses this challenge.

In the following discussion, a remote object is an object in a different process. The core piece of the .NET remoting architecture designed to address this problem is called leasing and sponsorship. The idea behind *leasing* is simple: each server object accessed by remote clients is associated with a lease object. The *lease object* literally gives the server object a lease on life. When a client creates a remote server object (that is, actually creates, rather than connects to, an existing instance), .NET creates a lease object and associates it with the server object. A special entity in .NET remoting called the *lease manager* keeps track of the server objects and their lease objects. Each lease object has an initial lease time. The clock starts ticking as soon as the first reference to the server object is marshaled across the app domain boundary, and the lease time is decremented as time goes by. As long as the lease time doesn't expire, .NET considers the server object as being used by its clients. The lease manager keeps a reference on the server object, which prevents the server object from being collected in case garbage collection is triggered. When the lease expires, .NET assumes that the server object has no remote clients. .NET then disconnects the server object from the remoting infrastructure. The server object becomes a candidate for garbage collection and is eventually destroyed. After disconnecting the object, any client attempt to access it results in an exception of type RemotingException, letting the client know the object was disconnected. This may appear strange at first because the object may very well be still alive. .NET behaves this way because otherwise, the client's interaction with the remote object will be nondeterministic. If .NET allowed remote clients to access objects past their lease time, it would work some of the time but fail in those cases in which garbage collection took place already.

 If the remote object is disconnected because the lease has expired, the client can't call any method on it, especially IDisposable.Dispose( ). This may have serious consequences on scalability. Make sure you use single-call objects if that is the case in your application because single-call objects don't require leasing, and .NET calls IDisposable. Dispose( ) on them automatically.

It would be incorrect to disconnect the object every time a lease expires: what if there are still some remote clients who would like to keep the server object alive? The smart thing to do is to contact such clients and ask them to extend the lease, or in .NET terminology, to *sponsor* the lease. Clients that wish .NET to contact them when the lease expires need to provide .NET with a special *sponsor* object. .NET will contact the sponsor object, giving it a chance to extend the lease. The sponsor can extend the lease or refuse to do so. A given server object can have multiple sponsors associated with its lease. The lease manager keeps a list of all the sponsors associated with each lease. When the lease expires, the lease manager starts traversing the sponsor list, looking for a sponsor willing to extend the lease. If such a sponsor is found, the lease manager extends the lease. Otherwise, the lease manager disconnects the server object.

Lease Properties

Every lease has a number of properties associated with it. These properties control the manner in which the lease manager interacts with the remote object's lease. .NET assigns some global default values to these properties, but you can instruct .NET to use other default values. You can even override the default lease properties for individual objects. The *expired time* is the time that has expired since the beginning of the lease. A lease has an *lease time* property. By default, if you don't configure it differently, the lease time is initially set to five minutes. .NET could have simply disconnected the object when the expired time is equal to the lease time, but what to do if the clients continue to call the object? This clearly indicates that the object is useful. Every lease has a *renew on call time* property; if the lease is about to expire, .NET automatically extends the lease on every call by the value set in the call time renewal property. The default call time renewal is two minutes. The value of the *current lease time* (the time the object has to live unless the lease is extended) is a product of the lease time and renew-on-call time, according to this formula:

```
current lease time = MAX(lease time—expired time,renew on call time)
```

If the renew-on-call time value is less than the lease time minus the expired time, it will have no affect. The renew-on-call time has an effect only if the renew on call time is greater than the lease time minus the expired time. In that case, the expired-time property is reset, and the lease time is set to the renew-on-call time. The result is that even if an object is very busy, its lease time doesn't grow in proportion to the amount of traffic it has. Even if the object has a spike in load, after some quiet time, its lease will expire.

Lease manager properties

There are two properties pertaining to the lease manager itself. Obviously, the lease manager needs to monitor the leases of all remote server objects in its app domain. The question is, how often should the lease manager examine the leases? The lease manager's *poll time* governs the rate at which the lease manager polls the leases. The default poll time is set to 10 seconds. The other lease-manager property has to do with sponsors. The lease sponsors can reside on remote machines, or it may take them a long time to reach a decision on the lease's fate. The lease manager's *sponsorship timeout* property controls how long the lease manager should wait for a reply from a sponsor. The sponsorship timeout is required to handle network failures or even the case of the sponsor machine being down. If the lease manager tries to reach a sponsor, and the sponsor doesn't reply within the sponsorship timeout, the lease manager removes that sponsor from the sponsor list associated with the lease.

Configuring global default properties

If you don't like the default values of the various lease and lease manager properties, you can provide your own. You can do so both programmatically and administratively, using the application configuration file. To configure global defaults programmatically, use the static properties of the LifetimeServices class, defined in the System.Runtime.Remoting.Lifetime namespace:

```
public sealed class LifetimeServices
{
    public static TimeSpan LeaseManagerPollTime { get; set; }
    public static TimeSpan LeaseTime           { get; set; }
    public static TimeSpan RenewOnCallTime      { get; set; }
    public static TimeSpan SponsorshipTimeout   { get; set; }
}
```

You typically use these properties in the `Main()` method of your host:

```
static void Main()
{
    LifetimeServices.LeaseTime       = TimeSpan.FromMinutes(10);
    LifetimeServices.RenewOnCallTime = TimeSpan.FromMinutes(15);

    /* Register objects or load configuration file */
}
```

Note that you must set the global leasing defaults before you register objects (programmatically or using the configuration file). The reason is that immediately after registration, the host may start servicing remote calls, and these calls will not be using the new defaults.

You can also provide new global default values in the host configuration file using the `<lifetime>` element:

```
<configuration>
    <system.runtime.remoting>
        <application>
            <lifetime
                leaseTime = "10M"
                sponsorshipTimeOut = "1M"
                renewOnCallTime = "15M"
                LeaseManagePollTime = "8s"
            />
        </application>
    </system.runtime.remoting>
</configuration>
```

Configuring Instance's Lease

Every lease object implements the `ILease` interface, defined in the `System.Runtime.Remoting.Lifetime` namespace:

```
public interface ILease
{
    TimeSpan CurrentLeaseTime    {get;}
    LeaseState CurrentState      {get;}
    TimeSpan InitialLeaseTime    {get;set;}
    TimeSpan RenewOnCallTime     {get;set;}
    TimeSpan SponsorshipTimeout  {get;set;}

    void Register(ISponsor obj);
    void Register(ISponsor obj,TimeSpan renewalTime);
    TimeSpan Renew(TimeSpan renewalTime);
    void Unregister(ISponsor obj);
}
```

The `ILease` interface allows you to control and configure the lease properties for an individual object, as well as to manage sponsors for that lease. Both the object and its clients can obtain the `ILease` interface. An individual lease can be in one of a number of states; the most important are initial, active, or expired. You can obtain the state of the lease by accessing the CurrentState read-only property of the ILease interface. CurrentState is of the enum type LeaseState:

```
public enum LeaseState
{
    Active,
    Expired,
    Initial,
    Null,
    Renewing
}
```

A remote class can provide its own values to the lease's properties, giving the object control over its lifetime. To do so, override the InitializeLifetimeService() method defined in MarshalByRefObject and return a lease object. InitializeLifetimeService() is called by .NET immediately after the remote object's constructor, but before a reference to the object is marshaled back to the client. InitializeLifetimeService() is never called if the object is created by a local client. Although you can return from InitializeLifetimeService() any object that implements the ILease interface, in practice you need to obtain the lease already associated with your object and modify its properties. You do that by calling your base class's InitializeLifetimeService() and modifying the lease properties, as shown in Example 10-9. You can set the lease properties only if the lease is in the LeaseState.Initial state, and this is asserted in the example.

Example 10-9. Providing new lease properties for an object

```
public class MyServer : MarshalByRefObject
{
    public override object InitializeLifetimeService()
    {
        ILease lease = (ILease)base.InitializeLifetimeService();
        Debug.Assert(lease.CurrentState == LeaseState.Initial);

        //Set lease properties
        lease.InitialLeaseTime     = TimeSpan.FromMinutes(30);
        lease.RenewOnCallTime      = TimeSpan.FromMinutes(10);
        lease.SponsorshipTimeout   = TimeSpan.FromMinutes(2);
        return lease;
    }
}
```

Renewing Instance's Lease

Both the object and its clients can extend the lease explicitly by obtaining the object's lease and calling the ILease.Renew() method, providing a new lease time. Renewing a lease explicitly affects the current lease time according to this formula:

```
current lease time = MAX(lease time–expired time, renewal time)
```

This means that the renewal time will have an effect only if the renewal time is greater then the lease time minus the expired time. In that case, the expired time is reset, and the lease time becomes the renewal time. Consequently, if different clients all try to explicitly renew a lease, the lease will not grow to the value of their combined renewal sum; this makes sure that the object remains connected only when clients require it. Both the client and the object obtain the lease associated with the object using the static method GetLifetimeService( ) of the RemotingServices class:

```
public static object GetLifetimeService(MarshalByRefObject obj);
```

You can renew a lease only if it's in the LeaseState.Active state. For example, here is how a client renews a lease:

```
MyClass obj;
obj = new MyClass( );

ILease lease = (ILease)RemotingServices.GetLifetimeService(obj);
Debug.Assert(lease.CurrentState == LeaseState.Active);
lease.Renew(TimeSpan.FromMinutes(30));
```

If the object wants to renew its own lease, it simply calls GetLifetimeService( ), providing itself as the parameter:

```
public class MyServer : MarshalByRefObject
{
    public void SomeMethod( )
    {
        ILease lease = (ILease)RemotingServices.GetLifetimeService(this);
        Debug.Assert(lease.CurrentState == LeaseState.Active);

        lease.Renew(TimeSpan.FromMinutes(30));
        //Do some work
    }
}
```

Proving a Sponsor

As mentioned already, a sponsor is a third party .NET consults when a lease expires, giving that party an opportunity to renew the lease. The sponsor must implement the ISponsor interface, defined as:

```
public interface ISponsor
{
    TimeSpan Renewal(ILease lease);
}
```

The lease manager calls ISponsor's single method Renewal( ) when the lease expires, asking for new lease time. To add a sponsor to a lease object, simply obtain the lease object by using GetLifetimeService( ) and call the ISponsor.Register( ) method:

```
public class MySponsor : MarshalByRefObject,ISponsor
{
```

```
   public TimeSpan Renewal(ILease lease)
   {
      Debug.Assert(lease.CurrentState == LeaseState.Active);
      //Renew lease by 5 minutes
      return TimeSpan.FromMinutes(5);
   }
}
ISponsor sponsor = new MySponsor();
MyClass obj = new MyClass();

/Register the sponsor
ILease lease = (ILease)RemotingServices.GetLifetimeService(obj);
lease.Register(sponsor);
```

If the sponsor doesn't want to renew the lease, it can return TimeSpan.Zero:

```
public TimeSpan Renewal(ILease lease)
{
   Debug.Assert(lease.CurrentState == LeaseState.Active);
   //Refuse to renew lease:
   return TimeSpan.Zero;
}
```

It probably makes more sense to unregister the sponsor instead, however. Because the sponsor is called across an app domain boundary, the sponsor must be a remotable object, meaning it must be marshaled either by value or by reference. If you derive the sponsor from MarshalByRefObject, the sponsor will reside on the client's side, and it can base its decision of the renewal time on client-side events or properties that it's monitoring. That raises an interesting question: if the lease keeps the remote server object alive, and if the sponsor keeps the lease alive, who keeps the sponsor alive? The answer is that somebody on the client side must keep a reference on the sponsor, typically as a class member variable. Doing so also allows the client to remove the sponsor from the lease when the client shuts down, by calling the ILease.Unregister() method (the client can also unregister the sponsor in its implementation of IDisposable.Dispose()). Unregistering a sponsor improves overall performance because the lease manager doesn't spend time trying to reach a sponsor that isn't available.

If you mark only the sponsor as serializable, then when you register the sponsor, it's marshaled by value to the host's side, and the sponsor will reside there. This eliminates the marshaling overhead of contacting the sponsor, but it will also disconnect it from the client. A marshaled by value sponsor can base its decision on information available on the host's side.

Sponsors and remoting

When the sponsor is a marshaled by reference object, the client application must register a port with its channels to allow the remote lease manager to call back to the sponsor. Because the client generally doesn't care which port is used, by registering port number 0, the client can instruct .NET to automatically select an available port.

The channel, port number, and sponsor object location is captured when the reference to the sponsor object is marshaled to the remote host.

Client and leases

A single lease can have multiple sponsors, and multiple clients can all share the same sponsor. In addition, a single sponsor can be registered with multiple remote leases. Typically, a client application will have one sponsor for all its remote objects. As a result, a remote object will typically have as many sponsors to its lease as the number of its distinct clients. When the client application shuts down, it unregisters the sponsor from all the remote leases it sponsors.

Leasing and Remote Activation Modes

Server-activated single-call objects don't need leasing because such objects are disconnected immediately after each call. This isn't the case for client-activated and server-activated singleton objects.

Leasing a singleton object

The singleton design pattern semantics mandate that once it's created, the singleton object lives forever. This doesn't coincide with the default lease time of five minutes. If no client accesses a singleton object for more than five minutes after it's created (or just two minutes after the first five minutes), .NET deactivates the singleton. Future calls from the clients are silently routed to a new singleton object. Fortunately, .NET supports infinite lease time: when you design a singleton object, override `InitializeLifetimeService()` and return a `null` object as the new lease, indicating to .NET that this lease never expires:

```
public class MySingleton : MarshalByRefObject
{
    public override object InitializeLifetimeService()
    {
        return null;
    }
}
```

Returning an infinite lease relieves you of managing global lease defaults or dealing with sponsors. In fact, you can have any object activation mode use an infinite lease, but it makes sense only in the case of a singleton.

Leasing a client-activated object

The case of the client-activated object is the one affected the most by the leasing mechanism. The only safe way to manage client-activated objects is to use sponsors. All other options, such as setting global lease properties or configuring individual objects' leases, are guesses or heuristics at best. Ultimately, only the client knows when it no longer requires the object. The sponsor should renew the lease with an amount of time that balances on one hand network traffic and load on the lease manager, and on the other hand is granular enough to manage the resources the object may hold. If the sponsor provides too short a renewed lease, it creates too many queries from the lease manager to renew the lease, which may result in unnecessary traffic. If the sponsored lease is too long, the client may have no need for the remote object, but the lease manager still keeps it alive. Every case is unique, and throughput and performance are a concern, so you will have to investigate and profile the system with various sponsorship renewal times. I can, however, offer the following rule of thumb: the sponsorship time in general should be the same as the initial lease time. The reason is that if the initial lease time is good enough for your case, and it doesn't generate too much traffic and isn't too coarse, it's likely to be just as fine for the sponsors as well on subsequent lease extensions requests. Example 10-10 demonstrates a client by using a client-activated object whose lifetime is controlled by a sponsor. You can use Example 10-10 as a template or a starting point for your remote client-activated objects.

The source code accompanying this book contains Example 10-10 in the Leasing solution. The solution has three projects: The ServerAssembly class library, the RemoteServerHost EXE assembly, and the Client EXE assembly. These projects are very similar to those presented in Example 10-6. The host is identical to the one in Example 10-6; the only difference is that it registers the MyCAO type as a client-activated object. The rest of the host is omitted from Example 10-10. The ServerAssembly class library contains the MyCAO definition, so that both the client and the host could access its metadata. The client assembly contains the MySponsor class because there is no need to put the sponsor in a class library; all the host needs is the metadata for the ISponsor interface, which is already part of the .NET class libraries. The MySponsor implementation of Renewal( ) simply extends the lease by the initial lease time. The client configuration file designates the MyCAO type as a remote client-activated object, and it registers the port 0 with the channel to allow calls back to the sponsor. The client's class (ClientForm) has as member variables both the remote client-activated object and the sponsor. In its constructor, the client creates new instances of the server and the sponsor, and registers the sponsor with the lease of the client-activated object. The client is a Windows Forms dialog, with a single button. When clicked, the button simply calls the client-activated object. When the user closes the dialog, the client unregisters the sponsors.

Example 10-10. Sponsoring a client-activated object

```
/////////////// RemoteServerHost.exe.config : the host configuration file ////////
<?xml version="1.0"?>
<configuration>
  <system.runtime.remoting>
    <application>
      <service>
        <activated  type="RemoteServer.MyCAO,ServerAssembly"/>
```

Example 10-10. Sponsoring a client-activated object (continued)

```
      </service>
      <channels>
        <channel ref="tcp"  port="8005"/>
        <channel ref="http" port="8006"/>
      </channels>
    </application>
  </system.runtime.remoting>
</configuration>
//////////////////////  ServerAssembly class library  /////////////////////////
namespace RemoteServer
{
   public class MyCAO : MarshalByRefObject
   {
      public void Count( )
      {
         Counter++;
         string appName = AppDomain.CurrentDomain.FriendlyName;
         MessageBox.Show("Counter value is " + Counter.ToString( ),appName);
      }
      protected int Counter = 0;
   }
}
//////////////////  Client.exe.config: the client configuration file  //////////////
<?xml version="1.0"?>
<configuration>
   <system.runtime.remoting>
      <application>
         <client url="tcp://localhost:8005">
            <activated  type="RemoteServer.MyCAO,ServerAssembly"/>
         </client>
         <channels>
            <channel ref="tcp" port="0"/>
         </channels>
      </application>
   </system.runtime.remoting>
</configuration>
//////////////////////////  Client EXE assembly  ///////////////////////////////
using System.Runtime.Remoting.Lifetime;

public class MySponsor : MarshalByRefObject,ISponsor
{
   public TimeSpan Renewal(ILease lease)
   {
      Debug.Assert(lease.CurrentState == LeaseState.Active);

      return lease.InitialLeaseTime;
   }
}

using RemoteServer;
```

Example 10-10. Sponsoring a client-activated object (continued)

```csharp
public class ClientForm : Form
{
   private Button m_CallButton;

   private ISponsor m_Sponsor;
   private MyCAO m_Obj;

   public ClientForm( )
   {
      InitializeComponent( );

      m_Sponsor = new MySponsor( );
      m_Obj = new MyCAO( );

      //Register the sponsor
      ILease lease = (ILease)RemotingServices.GetLifetimeService(m_Obj);
      lease.Register(m_Sponsor);
   }
   private void InitializeComponent( )
   {...}

   static void Main( )
   {
      RemotingConfiguration.Configure("Client.exe.config");

      Application.Run(new ClientForm( ));
   }
   private void OnCall(object sender,EventArgs e)
{
      m_Obj.Count( );
   }
   private void OnClosed(object sender,EventArgs e)
   {
      //Unegister the sponsor
      ILease lease = (ILease)RemotingServices.GetLifetimeService(m_Obj);
      lease.Unregister(m_Sponsor);
   }
}
```

.NET and Location Transparency

As explained in Chapter 1, a core principal of component-oriented programming is location transparency. Location transparency means that the same client-side code can interact both with local objects and with remote objects, and ideally, the same component can be used either locally or remotely (see Figure 10-3). Put differently, if a component works locally, it should work remotely, and if a client can use a component locally, it should be able to use the component remotely. There should be nothing in the client code pertaining to location. DCOM supported location transparency; as long as the registry contained the right settings, location transparency was a reality in DCOM. Thus, after dozens of pages analyzing .NET remoting, it's time to ask: does .NET support location transparency, and if so, to what degree?

This section examines location transparency with regard to marshal-by-reference objects only. Both DCOM and .NET allow marshal-by-value objects (although not with the same ease), but marshal-by-value objects clearly don't comply with location transparency in DCOM or in .NET. I also don't think that the location transparency principle on the component side is relevant to singleton or single-call objects. These server-activated components are different by design. A single-call object must manage its state, and a singleton object is bound to a particular single resource. However, the client of a server-activated object can still benefit from location transparency.

As you've seen, there are many ways to achieve the same result in .NET remoting, and the differences are usually a tradeoff between flexibility and ease of use. To maximize compliance with location transparency, the host and the client should use configuration files and always load them, even if they don't contain a remoting section. This allows you to modify component location and make changes only in the configuration files, similar to making changes in the registry to modify the location of DCOM components. The client and the host should avoid explicit channel and object registration, and the client should use new to create remote objects. The result on both the client and the host side is a single line of code (loading the configuration file):

```
RemotingConfiguration.Configure("<app name>.config");
```

However, even if the host and the client use configuration files, there are still unavoidable deviations from full compliance with location transparency:

- The remote component must derive from MarshalByRefObject. In .NET, you can't take any component the client uses and access it remotely (unlike DCOM).

- The remote host must be running before the clients try to connect to it, unlike DCOM, which can launch the remote process automatically.

- The client has to provide a sponsor for client-activated objects. DCOM used reference counting instead.

With these constraints in mind, if I were to grade it, I'd give .NET a C in absolute terms on compliance with location transparency but a B in comparison with DCOM.

CHAPTER 11

Context and Interception

One of the most important aspects of .NET as a component technology is its use of contexts to facilitate component services. The core design pattern is *interception*: intercepting a call from a client to an object, performing some pre-call processing, forwarding the call to the object, and doing some post-call processing before returning control back to the client. Objects indicate to .NET which component services they need, and using interception, .NET makes sure the objects get the required runtime environment. .NET component services are mostly the result of integrating COM+ into .NET. In addition, .NET allows you to provide your own custom component services. This chapter starts by providing a brief introduction to interception-based component services. You will then learn how .NET components can use such services and what the underlying architecture is that enables them. The chapter concludes by demonstrating how you can extend .NET by providing your own custom component services.

.NET Component Services

.NET provides component services via call interception. To intercept the call, .NET must insert a proxy between the client and the object and do some pre- and post-call processing. Call interception is the key to valuable, productivity-oriented component services. For example, interception can provide thread safety by trying to acquire a lock before accessing the object and then proceeding to call the object. While the call is in progress, calls coming in from other clients are intercepted as well, and those calls will be blocked when they try to access the lock. When the call returns from the object to the proxy, it unlocks the lock to allow other clients to use the object. Another example for an interception-based component service is *call authorization*: the proxy can verify that the caller has appropriate credentials (such as being a member of a specified role) to call the object, and deny access otherwise. The problem is that an app domain is too coarse an execution scope; even though cross-app domain calls always go through a proxy, some app domain calls use direct reference. To address this, app domains are actually subdivided further into contexts, and objects execute in contexts rather than app domains (see Figure 11-1).

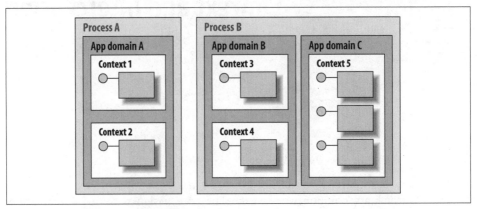

Figure 11-1. App domains and contexts

In .NET, the *context* is the innermost execution scope of an object. All objects in the same context are compatible with their component services requirements, and .NET doesn't need to perform pre- and post-call processing when these objects access one another. You can therefore define a context as a logical grouping of objects that rely on the same set of services. Calls into the context are intercepted to ensure the objects always get the appropriate runtime environment they require to operate. Components indicate to .NET which services they require using special context attributes.

Context and Object Types

What if a component doesn't require any service? Why should it pay the interception penalty for cross-context access? To address this point, .NET objects are classified into two categories: those that care about component services and want to use them, and those that don't. By default, objects are context-agnostic and have no context affinity, which means they always execute in the context of their calling clients. Because such context-agnostic objects "jump" from one context to the next, they are referred to as *context-agile objects*. The clients of a context-agile object have a direct reference to it, and no proxies are involved when making intra-app domain calls. Note that objects that derive from MarshalByRefObject are accessed via a proxy across app domains but are agile inside an app domain. Marshal-by-value objects are also context-agile.

The other object type is called *context-bound object*. Context-bound objects always execute in the same context. The designation and affinity of a context-bound object to a context is decided when the object is created and is fixed for the life of the object. To qualify as a context-bound object, the object must derive directly (or have one of its base classes derive) from the abstract class ContextBoundObject:

```
public class MyClass : ContextBoundObject
{...}
```

The client of a context-bound object never has a direct reference to it. Instead, the client always interacts with a context-bound object via a proxy. Because ContextBoundObject is derived from MarshalByRefObject, every context-bound object is also marshaled by reference across an app domain boundary. This makes perfect sense because the context-bound object can't leave its context, let alone its app domain.

Component Services Types

.NET provides two kinds of component services: context-bound services and Enterprise Services. The *context-bound services* are available to any context-bound object. Presently (with the release of .NET 1.0), there is only one such service: the synchronization domain, described in Chapter 8. Using the Synchronization context attribute, a context-bound component gains automatic synchronization and lock sharing:

```
[Synchronization]
public class MyClass : ContextBoundObject
{
    public MyClass(){ }
    public void DoSomething(){ }
}
```

By adding the Synchronization attribute, .NET makes sure only one thread at a time is allowed to access the object, without requiring you to spend the effort implementing this functionality or worry about deadlocks. Clients of such objects don't need to worry about synchronization either. However, the .NET context is an extensible mechanism, and you can define their own custom context attributes for custom services and extensions. The rest of this chapter examines the .NET context and context-bound objects in detail, and demonstrates how to develop custom context-bound services and attributes.

The second kind of component services is *.NET Enterprise Services* (see the sidebar ".NET Enterprise Services"). Enterprise Services offer more than 20 component services, covering an impressive array of domains, from transactions to loosely coupled events to web services. Enterprise Services are available only to classes derived from the class ServicedComponent. ServicedComponent is in turn derived from ContextBoundObject, so you can say that Enterprise Services are a specialization of context-bound services. If you develop a serviced component, you normally indicate which services the component relies on by using dedicated attributes. Future releases of .NET may allow you to add a custom service to Enterprise Services.

As of this writing, the Enterprise Services attributes aren't .NET context attributes but rather COM+ context attributes. This may change in future versions of .NET.

.NET Enterprise Services

.NET Enterprise Services are a set of component services designed to ease the development of Enterprise applications. .NET Enterprise Services are the result of integrating COM+ into .NET, and they offer the same range of services essential to any Enterprise application. The semantics of the services, the algorithms behind them, the benefits, and the implied programming models remain for the most part exactly the same as they were for COM components. .NET components that take advantage of Enterprise Services are called *Serviced Components* because they derive from the class ServicedComponent, defined in the System.EnterpriseServices namespace. You can configure the services using context-attributes in your code or after deployment, using the COM+ Component Services Explorer. For example, if you want .NET to maintain a pool of your objects, and have at least three objects in the pool, but no more than ten, use the ObjectPooling attribute:

```
using System.EnterpriseServices;

[ObjectPooling(MinPoolSize = 3,MaxPoolSize = 10)]
public class MyComponent : ServicedComponent
{...}
```

You can also configure the pool parameters during deployment by using the Component Services Explorer. If you also want transaction support, use the Transaction attribute:

```
using System.EnterpriseServices;

[Transaction]
[ObjectPooling(MinPoolSize = 3,MaxPoolSize = 10)]
public class MyComponent : ServicedComponent
{...}
```

Due to .NET's ability to persist the attributes in the assembly metadata, there is often no need to use the Component Services Explorer for services configuration. You can read about .NET Enterprise Services in my book *COM and .NET Component Services*.

The .NET Context

Every new app domain starts with a single context, called the *default context*. The default context provides no component services at all. The main reason why the default context exists is for a consistent programming model; the first object created in the new app domain is placed in the default context, even if it isn't a context-bound object. This maintains the design principle that all objects execute in a context, even if they don't care about component services. An app domain can contain multiple contexts, and .NET creates new contexts as needed. There is no limit to the number of contexts an app domain can contain. A given context belongs to exactly one app domain. A single context can host multiple context-bound objects (see Figure 11-1). Every context has a unique ID (an integer) called the *context ID*. The context ID is guaranteed to be unique in the scope of an app domain. Every .NET context has a *context object* associated with it. The context object is an instance of the class Context, defined in the System.Runtime.Remoting.Contexts namespace. You typically don't need to interact with the context object. However, for diagnostics and tracing purposes, it's sometimes useful to retrieve the context ID, using the ContextID read-only property of the context object:

```
public class Context
{
    public int ContextID{ virtual get; }
    //Other members
}
```

Every object can access the context object of the context it's executing by using the CurrentContext static read-only property of the Thread class:

```
public sealed class Thread
{
    public static Context CurrentContext{ get; }
    /* Other members  */
}
```

For example, here is how an object can trace its context ID:

```
int contextID = Thread.CurrentContext.ContextID;
Trace.WriteLine("Context ID is " + contextID.ToString( ));
```

Note that threads can enter and exit contexts, and in general have no affinity to any particular context.

Assigning Objects to Contexts

As presented earlier, there are two kinds of .NET types: context-agile and context-bound. Both always execute in a context, and the main difference is in their affinity to that context. The context-agile behavior is the .NET default. Any class that doesn't derive from ContextBoundObject is context-agile. Context-agile objects have no interest in component services and as such, can execute in the context of their calling clients because .NET doesn't need to intercept incoming calls to them. When a client creates a context-agile object, the object executes in the context of its creating client. The client gets a direct reference to the object, and no proxies are involved. The client can pass the object reference to a different client in the same context or in a different context. When the other client uses the object, the object executes in the context of that client. The context-agile model is shown in Figure 11-2. Note that it's incorrect to state that a context-agile object has no context. It does have one—the context of the client making the call. If the context-agile object retrieves its context object and queries the value of the context ID, it gets the same context ID as its calling client.

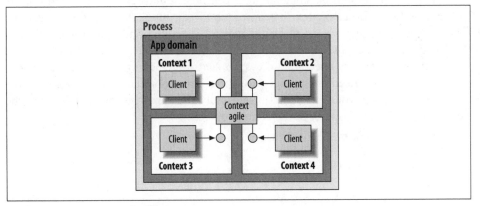

Figure 11-2. A context-agile object

 COM+ also had the notion of context-agile objects, in the form of objects that aggregated the free-threaded marshaler (FTM). The problem with the FTM was that it introduced some nasty side effects in cases in which the object had other COM+ objects as members, and was therefore a technique to avoid.

The picture is drastically different when it comes to context-bound objects. A context-bound object is bound to a particular context for life. The decision regarding which context the object resides in takes place when the object is created and is based on the services the object requires and the context of its creating client. If the creating client's context is "good enough" for the object's needs; i.e., the context has adequate properties, and the client and the object use a compatible set of component services, the object is placed in its creating client's context. If, on the other hand, the object requires some other service the creating client context doesn't support, .NET creates a new context and places the new object in it. Note that .NET doesn't try to find out if there is already another appropriate context for the object in that app domain. The algorithm is simple: the object either shares its creator's context or gets a new context. This algorithm intentionally trades memory and context management overhead for speed in allocating the new object to a context. The other alternative would be to search a potentially long list of existing contexts and examine each one, but that might take a long time to complete and impede performance. If the object is placed in a different context from that of its creating client, the client gets back from .NET a reference to a proxy instead of a direct reference (see Figure 11-3). The proxy intercepts the calls the client make on the object and performs some pre- and post-call processing to provide the object with the services it requires.

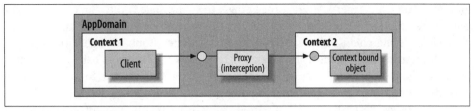

Figure 11-3. Clients of a context-bound object access it via a proxy

 The .NET policy for context-bound object allocation to context is very similar to the COM+ context activation policy.

Call Interception Architecture

The cross-context interception architecture is similar to the one used across app domain boundaries. Recall from Chapter 10 that in .NET, the proxy has two parts: a transparent proxy and a real proxy. The transparent proxy exposes the same public entry points as the object. When the client calls the transparent proxy, it converts the stack frame to a message and passes the message to the real proxy. The message is an object implementing the IMessage interface:

```
public interface IMessage
{
    IDictionary Properties{ get; }
}
```

The message is a collection of properties, such as the method's name and its arguments. The real proxy knows where the actual object resides. In the case of a call across app domains, the real proxy needs to serialize the message using a formatter and pass it to the channel. In the case of a cross-context call, the real proxy needs to apply interception steps before forwarding the call to the object. It turns out that an elegant design solution allows .NET to use the same real proxy in both cases. The real proxy doesn't know about formatters, channels, or context interceptors. The real proxy passes the message to a message sink. A message sink is an object that implements the IMessageSink interface, defined in the System.Runtime.Remoting. Messaging namespace:

```
public interface IMessageSink
{
    IMessageSink NextSink{ get; }
    IMessageCtrl AsyncProcessMessage(IMessage msg,IMessageSink replySink);
    IMessage SyncProcessMessage(IMessage msg);
}
```

.NET strings together message sinks in a linked list. Each message sink knows about the next sink in the list (you can also get the next sink via the NextSink property). The real proxy calls the SyncProcessMessage( ) method of the first sink, allowing it to process the message. After processing the message, the first sink calls `SyncProcessMessage()` on the next sink. In the case of cross app-domain calls, the first sink on the client's side is the message formatter (look at Figure 10-9 again). After formatting the message, the formatter sink passes it to the next sink—the transport channel. When the `SyncProcessMessage()` method returns to the proxy, it returns the returned message from the object. The `IMessageSink` interface also provides the `AsyncProcessMessage()` method, which intercepts asynchronous calls (a topic that's beyond the scope of this book).

Cross-context sinks

In the case of a cross-context call, there is no need for a formatter; .NET uses an internal channel called `CrossContextChannel`, which is also a message sink. However, there is a difference in component services configuration between the client and the object. It's up to the sinks to compensate for these differences. .NET installs as many message sinks as required between the client's context and the object (see Figure 11-4).

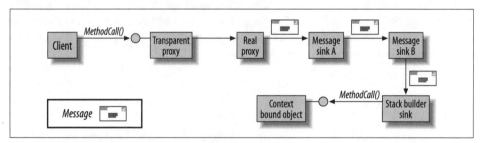

Figure 11-4. A cross-context call to a context-bound object

The .NET context interception architecture is similar to the Decorator design pattern[*] and is a private case of aspect-oriented programming.[†] A typical message sink does both pre- and post-call processing. The canonical example is again thread synchronization. The sink needs to acquire a lock before proceeding to call the object, and release the lock after the method returns. The next sink down the call chain may enforce security, and so on.

It's best to use an example to demystify the way sinks work. Example 11-1 shows a generic sink implementation. The sink constructor accepts the next sink in the chain. When the `SyncProcessMessage()` method is called, the sink performs some pre-call processing and then calls `SyncProcessMessage()` on the next sink. The call will advance down the sink chain, until it reaches a *stack-builder sink*, the last sink. The

---

[*] See *Design Patterns* by Gamma, Helm, Johnson, and Vlissides.

[†] "See AOP: Aspect-Oriented Programming Enables Better Code Encapsulation and Reuse," *MSDN Magazine*, March 2002.

---

stack builder converts the message to a stack frame and calls the object. When the call returns to the stack builder, it constructs a return message with the method results and returns that message to the sink that called it. That sink can do its post-call processing and return control to the sink that called it, and so on. Eventually, the call returns to the generic sink. The generic sink now has a chance to examine the returned message and do some post-call processing before returning control to the sink that called it. The first sink in the chain returns control to the real proxy, providing it with the returned message from the object. The real proxy returns the message to the transparent proxy, which places it back on the calling client's stack.

Example 11-1. Generic implementation of a message sink

```
public class GenericSink : IMessageSink
{
    IMessageSink m_NextSink;

    public GenericSink(IMessageSink nextSink)
    {
        m_NextSink = nextSink;
    }

    public IMessageSink NextSink
    {
        get
        {
            return m_NextSink;
        }
    }
    public IMessage SyncProcessMessage(IMessage msg)
    {
        PreCallProcessing(msg);

        //This calls the object:
        IMessage returnedMessage = m_NextSink.SyncProcessMessage(msg);

        PostCallProcessing(returnedMessage);

        return returnedMessage;
    }
    void PreCallProcessing(IMessage msg)
    {
        /* Do some pre-call processing */
    }
    void PostCallProcessing(IMessage msg)
    {
        /* Do some post-call processing */
    }
    public IMessageCtrl AsyncProcessMessage(IMessage msg,IMessageSink replySink)
    {
```

Example 11-1. Generic implementation of a message sink (continued)

```
    /* Handle the asynchronous call, then: */
    return m_NextSink.AsyncProcessMessage(msg,replySink);
  }
}
```

Message sink types

Call interception can take place in two places: the sinks can intercept calls coming into the context and do some pre- and post-call processing, such as locking and unlocking a thread lock. Such sinks are called *server-side sinks*. The sinks can also intercept calls going out of the context and do some pre- and post-call processing. Such sinks are called *client-side sinks*. For example, the Synchronization attribute can optionally track calls outside the synchronization domain and unlock the lock to allow other threads access. This is done using a client-side sink. You will see later how to install sinks. Server-side sinks intercepting all calls into the context are called *server context sinks*. Server-side sinks intercepting calls to a particular object are called *server object sinks*. The server is responsible for installing server-side sinks. Client-side sinks installed by the client are called *client context sinks*, and they affect all calls going out of the context. Client-side sinks installed by the object are called *envoy sinks*. An envoy sink intercepts calls only to the particular object it's associated with. The last sink on the client's side and the first sink on the server's side is an instance of type CrossContextChannel. The resulting sink chain is comprised of segments, each segment made of a different type of sinks, as shown in Figure 11-5. Because there is a need for a stack builder at the end of the sink chain to convert messages, .NET installs a terminator at the end of each segment. A *terminator* is a sink of the segment's type; it does the final processing for that segment and forwards the message to the next segment. For example, the last message sink in the server context sink segment is called the ServerContextTerminatorSink. The terminators behave like a true dead end: if you call IMessageSink.NextSink on a terminator, you get back a null reference. The real next sink (the first sink in the next segment) is a private member of the terminator. As a result, there is no way to iterate using IMessageSink.NextSink on the entire length of the interception chain.

> There is another type of a sink called *dynamic sink*, which lets you add a sink programmatically at runtime without using attributes. Dynamic sinks are beyond the scope of this book.

Same-Context Calls

A context-bound object must always be accessed via a proxy across a context boundary, so that the various sinks can be in place to intercept the calls. The question now is what happens if a client in the same context as the object passes a reference to the object to a client in a different context by setting the value of some static variable, for

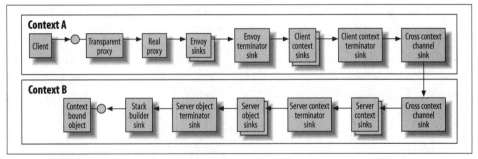

Figure 11-5. Client-side and server-side sink chains

example? If the same-context client has a direct reference to the object, how can .NET detect that and introduce a proxy between the object and the new client? .NET solves the problem by always having the object accessed via a proxy, even by clients in the same context (see Figure 11-6). Because the client and the object share the same context, there is no need for message sinks to perform any pre- or post-call processing. The interception layer consists of the transparent and real proxy, and a single message sink—the stack builder. When the same-context client passes its reference to the transparent proxy to clients in other contexts, .NET detects that and sets up the correct interception chain between the new clients and the object.

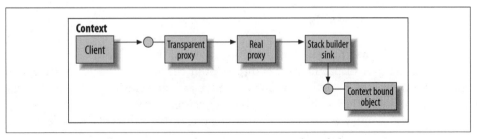

Figure 11-6. Even in the same context, clients access a context-bound object using a proxy

 In the COM+ world, same-context clients had direct reference to the object. As a result, developers had to manually marshal that reference, i.e., they had to manually set up the proxy, and the two clients had to coordinate on the marshaling protocol. This was often done using the Global Interface Table (GIT).

Context-Bound Objects and Remoting

Context-bound objects are a special case of .NET remoting in particular, that of client-activated objects. It many respects, .NET treats them just like remote objects. However, .NET does optimize some elements of its remoting architecture for context-bound objects. For example, as mentioned already, the channel used is an optimized channel for cross context calls, called CrossContextChannel. For real remote client-activated objects, .NET creates a lease and manages the life of the object via the lease and its sponsors. However because the client of a context-bound object shares with it the same app domain, .NET can still use garbage collection. In fact, when .NET creates a context-bound object, it creates a lease for it, and the object can even override `MarshalByRefObject.InitializeLifetimeService()` and provide its own lease. However, the lease doesn't control the lifetime of the object.

 With real remote objects, when the TCP or HTTP channels marshal a reference across a process boundary, these channels set up the lease. With cross context or cross app-domain objects, the `CrossContextChannel` and `CrossAppDomainChannel` simply ignore the lease and let the remote object be managed via garbage collection.

Another interesting aspect of context-bound objects being remote objects is the use of the `OneWay` attribute. As explained in Chapter 10, when a method on a remote object is decorated with that attribute, the method becomes an asynchronous fire-and-forget method. This is also the case with context-bound objects:

```
using System.Runtime.Remoting.Messaging;

public class MyClass : ContextBoundObject
{
    [OneWay]
    public void MyMethod(){ }
}
```

The `OneWay` attribute makes a method on a context-bound object asynchronous because the call is dispatched on a thread from the thread pool. Any exception thrown in the one-way method or any outgoing parameters isn't propagated to the client. In fact, .NET uses the `IMessageSink.AsyncProcessMessage()` on the message sinks to invoke a one-way method, as if the client used `BeginInvoke()` on a delegate.

Custom Component Services

In .NET, the ability to install custom component services is a major advancement for software engineering and component-oriented programming. Custom component services allow you to fine-tune and optimize the way .NET services your particular application and business logic. Custom component services decouple clients from objects because they don't need to coordinate the execution of the custom service. You can instead focus on implementing the business logic, rather than the service. Examples for custom services include application logging and tracing, performance counters, custom thread management, method calls filtering, parameter checks, event subscriptions, and so on. Custom component services are provided in the form of *custom context attributes*. Generic custom attributes (such as ones discussed in Appendix C) have no use unless you provide the reflection code to look for these attributes, interpret their values, and act upon them. .NET is indifferent to such custom attributes. Unlike generic custom attributes, .NET is very much aware of custom context attributes when used on context-bound objects. Context attributes must derive from the class `ContextAttribute,` defined in the `System.Runtime.Remoting.Contexts` namespace. When creating a new context-bound object, .NET reflects the object's metadata and places it in the appropriate context based on the behavior of the attributes. Custom context attributes can affect the context in which the object is activated, as well as install all four types of message sink interceptors. The next two sections demonstrate how to build custom context attributes and component services. First, you will see how to develop a custom context attribute and how it affects the activation context; then you'll walk though the development of a real-life, useful custom component service.

 Custom context attributes and custom message sinks are undocumented features of .NET. In future releases of .NET, Microsoft intends to fully document and support custom component services. It's unlikely that Microsoft will change much of the following discussion, but the possibility does exist. I believe that it's a risk worth taking, in order to unleash the power of custom component services. In any case, because of CLR version management and side-by-side execution, such changes will not affect existing applications.

Custom Context Attribute

Each context has a set of *properties* associated with it. The properties are the component services this context supports. A context-bound object shares a context with its client only if the client's context has the services the component requires, or put differently, if the context has the required properties. If the client's context doesn't have at least one property the object requires, .NET creates a new context and puts the object in it. In addition, a context property may require a new context regardless of the client's context. You use context attributes to specify the required services. The context attributes are those that decide whetheror not the client's context is sufficient.

To understand how context attributes affect context activation, consider a custom context attribute that adds a color property to a context. The color is an enum of type `ColorOption`:

```
public enum ColorOption{Red,Green,Blue};
```

You use `ColorAttribute` as a class attribute on a class derived from `ContextBoundObject`:

```
[Color(ColorOption.Blue)]
public class MyClass: ContextBoundObject
{...}
```

Obviously, a color property isn't much of a service, but it's a good example. .NET creates objects of the class `MyClass` in the client's context only if the creating client's context has a color property and if its value is set to `ColorOption.Blue`. Otherwise, .NET creates a new context, lets the attribute set its color property to ColorOption.Blue, and places the new object in the new context. The ColorAttribute also has a default constructor, setting the context color to ColorOption.Red:

```
[Color]//Default is ColorOption.Red
public class MyClass: ContextBoundObject
{...}
```

Example 11-2 shows the implementation of the ColorAttribute custom context attribute.

Example 11-2. The Color custom context attribute

```
using System.Runtime.Remoting.Contexts;
using System.Runtime.Remoting.Activation;

public enum ColorOption {Red,Green,Blue};

[AttributeUsage(AttributeTargets.Class)]
public class ColorAttribute : ContextAttribute
{
   ColorOption m_Color;

   public ColorAttribute():this(ColorOption.Red)//Default color is red
   {}

   public ColorAttribute(ColorOption color):base("ColorAttribute")
   {
      m_Color = color;
   }
   //Add a new color property to the new context
   public override void GetPropertiesForNewContext(IConstructionCallMessage ctor)
   {
      IContextProperty colorProperty = new ColorProperty(m_Color);
      ctor.ContextProperties.Add(colorProperty);
   }
   //ctx is the creating client's context
   public override bool IsContextOK(Context ctx,IConstructionCallMessage ctorMsg)
   {
      ColorProperty contextColorProperty = null;
      //Find out if the creating context has a color property. If not, reject it
      contextColorProperty = ctx.GetProperty("Color") as ColorProperty;
      if(contextColorProperty == null)
      {
         return false;
      }
      //It does have a color property. Verify color match
      return (m_Color == contextColorProperty.Color);
   }
}
```

Example 11-2. The Color custom context attribute (continued)

```
//The ColorProperty is added to the context properties collection by the
//ColorAttribute class
public class ColorProperty : IContextProperty
{
   ColorOption m_Color;

   public ColorProperty(ColorOption ContextColor)
   {
      Color = ContextColor;
   }
   public string Name
   {
      get
      {
         return "Color";
      }
   }
   //IsNewContextOK called by the runtime in the new context
   public bool IsNewContextOK(Context ctx)
   {
      ColorProperty newContextColorProperty = null;
      //Find out if the new context has a color property. If not, reject it
      newContextColorProperty = ctx.GetProperty("Color") as ColorProperty;
      if(newContextColorProperty == null)
      {
         return false;
      }
      //It does have color property. Verify color match
      return (this.Color == newContextColorProperty.Color);
   }

   public void Freeze(Context ctx)
   {}
   //Color needs to be public so that the attribute class can access it
   public ColorOption Color
   {
      get
      {
         return m_Color;
      }
      set
      {
         m_Color = value;
      }
   }
}
```

ColorAttribute has a member called m_Color that contains the required context color. The color is specified during the attribute construction, either explicitly or by using the default constructor. As a custom context attribute, it derives from ContextAttribute. The single constructor of ContextAttribute requires a string naming the new context attribute. This is provided by a call to the `ContextAttribute` constructor in the `ColorAttribute` constructor:

```
public ColorAttribute(ColorOption color):base("ColorAttribute")
{...}
```

`ContextAttribute` derives and provides virtual implementation of the `IContextAttribute` interface, defined as:

```
public interface IContextAttribute
{
    void GetPropertiesForNewContext(IConstructionCallMessage msg);
    bool IsContextOK(Context ctx,IConstructionCallMessage msg);
}
```

The `IsContextOK()` method lets the context attribute examine the creating client's context, which is provided in the `ctx` parameter. If the client's context is adequate, no further action is required, and .NET activates the new object in the creating client's context. If the context attribute returns `false` from `IsContextOK()`, .NET creates a new context and calls `GetPropertiesForNewContext()`, letting the context attribute add new properties to the new context. Because there can be more than one context attribute on a single object, .NET can optimize its queries of the attributes. .NET starts iterating over the attribute list, asking each one `IsContextOK()`. As a soon as it finds one attribute in the list that returns `false`, .NET aborts the iteration and creates a new context. It then calls `GetPropertiesForNewContext()` on each context attribute, letting it add its properties to the new context. `ColorAttribute` needs to override both methods of `IContextAttribute` and manage its single context property. Context properties are objects that implement the `IContextProperty` interface:

```
public interface IContextProperty
{
    string Name{ get; }
    void Freeze(Context newContext);
    bool IsNewContextOK(Context newCtx);
}
```

Each context property is identified by name via the `Name` property of `IContextProperty`. `ColorAttribute` uses a helper class called `ColorProperty` to implement `IContextProperty`. `ColorProperty` names itself as "Color." `ColorProperty` also provides the `Color` public property of type `ColorOption`. This allows for type-safe checking of the color value.

In its implementation of `IsContextOK()`, `ColorAttribute` checks whether the client's context has a property called "Color." If it doesn't, `IsContextOK()` returns `false`. If the client's context has a color property, `ColorAttribute` verifies that there is a color match by comparing the value of the `Color` property with its own color.

The implementation of `GetPropertiesForNewContext()` is straightforward as well: the single parameter is an object of type `IConstructionCallMessage`, providing a collection of properties for the new context via the `ContextProperties` property. ColorAttribute creates an object of type ColorProperty, initializes it with the required color, and adds it to the collection of properties for the new context.

Because a single context-bound object can have multiple context attributes, it's possible that some will conflict with others. To handle such an eventuality, after adding all the properties to the new context, .NET calls IsNewContextOK( ) on each property. If a property returns false, .NET aborts creating the new object and throws an exception of type RemotingException. In IsNewContextOK( ), ColorAttribute simply verifies that the new context has the correct color. The Freeze( ) method lets a context property know that the final location of the context is established and available for advanced use only.

Figure 11-7 is a UML activity diagram summarizing the process flow when using a custom context attribute and a context property. The diagram shows the order in which the various methods take place and the resulting activation logic.

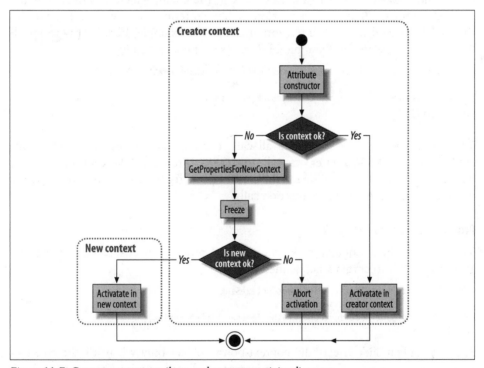

Figure 11-7. Custom context attribute and property activity diagram

Custom Message Sink

To provide a useful component service, the custom context attribute must install at least one custom message sink. The message sink can be either a server context sink, a server object sink, a client context sink, or an envoy sink. Commonly, a custom context attribute installs only a server context sink. The other sinks are intended for advanced cases, but you can install one if the need arises. For each type of custom sink you wish to contribute to the interception chain, the custom context property must implement a matching interface.

Providing a server context sink

To contribute a server context sink, the custom context property needs to implement the IContributeServerContextSink interface, defined as:

```
public interface IContributeServerContextSink
{
    IMessageSink GetServerContextSink(IMessageSink nextSink);
}
```

In its implementation of GetServerContextSink( ), the context property creates a sink object and concatenates it to the next sink in the chain, which is provided as the method parameter. GetServerContextSink( ) should return the new sink it created so that .NET can add it to the interception chain. For example, here is how to install GenericSink (presented in Example 11-2) as a server context sink:

```
public IMessageSink GetServerContextSink(IMessageSink nextSink)
{
    IMessageSink sink = new GenericSink(nextSink);
    return sink;
}
```

The server context sink intercepts all calls coming into the context. .NET calls GetServerContextSink( ) after its call to IContextProperty.IsNewContextOK( ) and before creating the object, allowing the context property to provide the sink. A server context sink can intercept construction calls.

Providing a client context sink

To install a client context sink, the context property needs to implement the IContributeClientContextSink, defined as:

```
public interface IContributeClientContextSink
{
    IMessageSink GetClientContextSink(IMessageSink nextSink);
}
```

A client context sink affects the context-bound object only when it's the client of another object outside the context; it intercepts all calls exiting the context. .NET calls GetClientContextSink( ) only when the object makes its first call outside the context. The information in the message object passed to the sink pertains to the target object, not the client.

Providing an envoy sink

If the context property implements the `IContributeEnvoySink` interface, defined as:

```
public interface IContributeEnvoySink
{
    IMessageSink GetEnvoySink(MarshalByRefObject obj,IMessageSink nextSink);
}
```

then when a proxy is set up to the object on the client's side, the proxy has the envoy sink as part of the interception chain leading to the particular object. The envoy sink intercepts all calls going from the client to the object. Other objects accessed by the client aren't affected. Every time a new client in a different context connects to the object, .NET installs an envoy sink in the client's context. .NET calls `GetEnvoySink()` after creating the new object but before returning control to the client. You can't intercept construction calls with an envoy sink.

Providing an object sink

To install an object sink, the context property needs to implement the `IContributeObjectSink` interface, defined as:

```
public interface IContributeObjectSink
{
    IMessageSink GetObjectSink(MarshalByRefObject obj,IMessageSink nextSink);
}
```

The object sink is installed on an object-by-object basis, which means it intercepts calls only to the object whose reference is provided in the `GetObjectSink()` call. Other calls into the context aren't affected. .NET calls `GetObjectSink()` before the first method call is forwarded to the object. As a result, you can't intercept construction calls with an object sink.

Processing messages

The `IMessage` interface presented previously is a collection of information about the method being intercepted. Although you can retrieve that information from the dictionary, there is a better way. When you intercept an incoming call, the different message objects (used for synchronous methods, asynchronous methods, and constructor calls) all support the `IMethodMessage` interface, defined as:

```
public interface IMethodMessage : IMessage
{
    int ArgCount{ get; }
    object[ ] Args{ get; }
    bool HasVarArgs{ get; }
    LogicalCallContext LogicalCallContext { get; }
    MethodBase MethodBase { get; }
    string MethodName{ get; }
    object MethodSignature{ get; }
    string TypeName{ get; }
    string Uri{ get; }
```

```
    object GetArg(int argNum);
    string GetArgName(int index);
}
```

IMethodMessage provides information about the method name, its arguments, the type on which the method is called, and the object's location. You can use that information in your pre-call message processing logic. After the last sink—the stack builder—invokes the call on the object, it returns a different message object. Again, there are several types of returned method objects, but they are all polymorphic with the IMethodReturnMessage interface, defined as:

```
public interface IMethodReturnMessage : IMethodMessage
{
    Exception Exception { get; }
    int OutArgCount { get; }
    object[ ] OutArgs { get; }
    object ReturnValue { get; }
    object GetOutArg(int argNum);
    string GetOutArgName(int index);
}
```

IMethodReturnMessage derives from IMethodMessage and provides additional information about the method returned value, the value of outgoing parameters, and exception information. The fact that exception information is captured is of particular interest. If the object throws an exception, the stack builder sink silently catches it and saves it in the returned message object. This allows all the sinks up the call chain to examine the exception object. When control returns to the proxy, if exception information is present, the proxy re-throws it on the calling client's side.

The Logbook Service

It's time to put all the knowledge and intricacies described so far to a good use with a comprehensive and useful real-life example. One of the most beneficial steps you can take to achieve a robust application and faster time to market is to add a logging capability to your application. This section presents you with the logbook—a simple custom component service that allows you to automatically log method calls and exceptions. The logbook is your product's flight recorder, and in a distributed environment, it's worth its weight in gold; with it, you can analyze why something didn't work the way it was supposed to. By examining the logbook entries, you can analyze what took place across machines and applications, and the source of the problem is almost immediately evident. The logbook is also useful for troubleshooting customer problems in post-deployment scenarios. The logbook intercepts incoming calls to your context-bound objects and logs most of the information in the message. As you will see shortly, you can use the same logbook to record method invocation from multiple machines and have the various entries interleaved in order. Each logbook entry contains the following information, captured automatically by the logbook:

- The location where was the method was invoked: machine name, app domain name, on what thread (ID and name), and the context ID
- The caller's identity (username)
- Information about the target object: its assembly, its type, and the member being accessed (constructor, method, property, indexer, or event)
- Invocation date and time
- Error information if an exception was thrown: the type of the exception and the exception message

Using the logbook

A key requirement in designing the logbook was that it should require no explicit participation on behalf of the object. The object should focus on implementing its business logic, and the logbook should do the logging. To add logging support for a context-bound object, add the LogbookAttribute custom context attribute, defined in the ContextLogger namespace:

```
using ContextLogger;

[Logbook]
public class MyClass : ContextBoundObject
{...}
```

The logbook service allows you to choose what information to log. Sometimes, it's necessary to record everything that takes place: method calls and errors. In other situations, it's sufficient to log only errors and exceptions. To that end, the logbook provides the enum LogOption, defined as:

```
public enum LogOption
{
   MethodCalls,
   Errors
}
```

You can provide the constructor of LogbookAttribute with the appropriate enum value. For example, to log only errors, write:

```
[Logbook(LogOption.Errors)]
public class MyClass : ContextBoundObject
{...}
```

The parameterless constructor of LogbookAttribute defaults to LogOption. MethodCalls, so these two declarations are equivalent and can log both method calls and errors:

```
[Logbook]
[Logbook(LogOption.MethodCalls)]
```

The logbook service architecture

When you apply LogbookAttribute to a context-bound class, it requires private contexts for each instance to support logging all calls coming into the object. If it were possible for two objects using the LogbookAttribute to share a context, cross-context calls would be logged, but intracontext calls made on one another wouldn't. The LogbookAttribute adds to the new context a property called LogContextProperty, which contributes a server-context sink called LogSink. LogSink intercepts all calls to the object but doesn't log them itself; instead, it uses the Logbook component, which encapsulates the actual logging mechanism. The implementation provided here logs to a SQL Server database, but you can replace that with any other repository. The Logbook is a remote singleton residing in an EXE host. As a result, all objects using the logbook service actually log to the same repository, in order. This is a key feature that allows you to trace the execution of a distributed application because the host can be on a dedicated machine, used by all other machines. Figure 11-8 depicts the logbook architecture. In addition, a logbook viewer application is provided; it displays in a grid control the content of the logbook database entries table. The logbook viewer allows you to filter the grid to display methods and errors or just errors. The application has another feature: you can export the logbook entries to a log file, as well as display the content of an existing log file. The logbook viewer doesn't connect to the database directly. Instead, it too connects to the singleton Logbook. The viewer doesn't directly connect to the database for two reasons. The first is that if it did, you would couple the viewer to the repository used and have to modify the viewer each time you switched repositories. The Logbook provides the necessary indirection. Second, to avoid database synchronization issues, the Logbook is the single data access component, and it provides the synchronization.

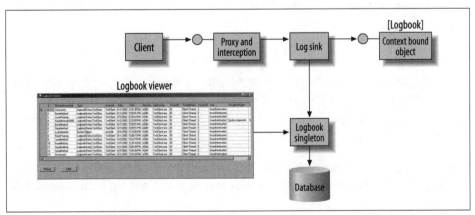

Figure 11-8. The logbook service architecture supports logging in a distributed environment

The source files accompanying this book provide the Logbook solution. The solution has the following projects: the ContextLogger class library contains the LogbookAttribute, the LogContextProperty, the LogSink, and the Logbook component itself. Logbook is an ADO.NET component that can access a SQL Server database. (You will need to create a database called Logbook with the Entries table by running the included *Logbook.sql* script file.) The LogbookHost project is a simple Windows Forms EXE, which hosts Logbook. The LogbookHost configuration file exposes the Logbook type as a server-activated singleton object. The TestClient project is Windows Forms application, which has a test class and the test client. The test class is a context-bound class that uses the LogbookAttribute. The test client is a form, which is able to exercise various calls on the test object. The configuration file of the TestClient application registers the Logbook component as a remote server activated object, whose URL connects to the LogbookHost application. The LogbookViewer project contains the logbook viewer, which lets you browse the logbook entries or clear the table (see Figure 11-9). The LogbookViewer application registers the Logbook component as a remote server as well.

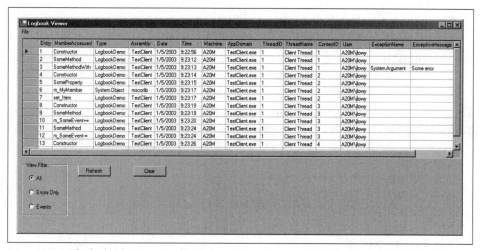

Figure 11-9. The logbook viewer application

You can extend and modify the logbook to your particular need: you can log parameter types and values, and you can use other repositories besides SQL Server.

Implementing the logbook

The LogbookAttribute class isn't that much different from the ColorAttribute class presented in Example 11-2. It refuses the client's context in its IsContextOK( ) and installs the LogContextProperty in its GetPropertiesForNewContext( ) method. Example 11-3 shows the implementation of LogbookAttribute.

Example 11-3. Implementation the LogbookAttribute class

```
[AttributeUsage(AttributeTargets.Class)]
public class LogbookAttribute : ContextAttribute
{
```

Example 11-3. Implementation the LogbookAttribute class (continued)

```
    LogOption m_LogOption;

    public LogbookAttribute( ): this(LogOption.MethodCalls)
    {}

    public LogbookAttribute(LogOption logOption):base("LogbookAttribute")
    {
        m_LogOption = logOption;
    }
    /// Add a new logbook property to the new context
    public override void GetPropertiesForNewContext(IConstructionCallMessage ctor)
    {
        IContextProperty logProperty = new LogContextProperty(m_LogOption);
        ctor.ContextProperties.Add(logProperty);
    }

    //Called by the runtime in the creating client's context
    public override bool IsContextOK(Context ctx,IConstructionCallMessage ctorMsg)
    {
        return false;
    }
}
```

The `LogContextProperty` implements the `IContributeServerContextSink` interface, installing the `LogSink` server context sink:

```
    public class LogContextProperty : IContextProperty,IContributeServerContextSink
    {
        LogOption m_LogOption;

        public IMessageSink GetServerContextSink(IMessageSink nextSink)
        {
            IMessageSink logSink = new LogSink(nextSink,m_LogOption);
            return logSink;
        }
        /* Rest of the implementation  */
    }
```

The interesting part of the logbook service is the `LogSink` class. The `LogSink` implements the `IMessageSink` interface. In its implementation of `IMessageSink`, `LogSink` processes the message object and constructs an instance of the `LogbookEntry` structure, providing it with the information extracted from the message. `LogbookEntry` stores the information provided as construction parameters and captures additional information such as object location and execution scope. Example 11-4 contains the code for `LogbookEntry`. `LogSink` then passes the `LogbookEntry` object to the `Logbook` component. Because the logbook is accessed as a remote component, `LogbookEntry` is marshaled by value using the `Serializable` attribute.

Example 11-4. The LogbookEntry structure

```csharp
[Serializable]
public struct LogbookEntry
{
    public LogbookEntry(string assemblyName,string typeName,string methodName,
            string eventDescription): this(assemblyName,methodName,typeName,"","")
    {
        Event = eventDescription;
    }
    public LogbookEntry(string assemblyName,string typeName,string methodName):
                              this(assemblyName,methodName,typeName,"","")
    {}
    public LogbookEntry(string assemblyName,string typeName,string methodName,
                            string exceptionName,string exceptionMessage)
    {
        AssemblyName      = assemblyName;
        TypeName          = typeName;
        MemberAccessed    = methodName;
        ExceptionName     = exceptionName;
        ExceptionMessage  = exceptionMessage;
        Event = "";

        MachineName   = Environment.MachineName;
        AppDomainName = AppDomain.CurrentDomain.FriendlyName;
        ThreadID      = Thread.CurrentThread.GetHashCode();
        ThreadName    = Thread.CurrentThread.Name;
        ContextID     = Thread.CurrentContext.ContextID;
        Date = DateTime.Now.ToShortDateString();
        Time = DateTime.Now.ToLongTimeString();
        if(Thread.CurrentPrincipal.Identity.IsAuthenticated)
        {
            UserName = Thread.CurrentPrincipal.Identity.Name;
        }
        else
        {
            UserName = "Unauthenticated";
        }
    }
    //Location
    public readonly string MachineName;
    public readonly string AppDomainName;
    public readonly int    ThreadID;
    public readonly string ThreadName;
    public readonly int    ContextID;
    //Identity
    public readonly string UserName;
    //Object info
    public readonly string AssemblyName;
    public readonly string TypeName;
    public readonly string MemberAccessed;
    public readonly string Date;
    public readonly string Time;
```

Example 11-4. The LogbookEntry structure (continued)

```
   //Exception
   public readonly string ExceptionName;
   public readonly string ExceptionMessage;
   //Event
   public readonly string Event;
}
```

Example 11-5 contains most of the implementation of LogSink. The constructor saves the logging filer (methods or errors), as well as the next message sink in the chain, and creates a new Logbook object (a proxy to the remote singleton). In SyncProcessMessage( ), LogSink downcasts the message object to IMethodMessage and passes it to a few helper-parsing methods. LogSink then forwards the call to the next sink down the chain, to eventually call the object. When the call returns, LogSink downcasts the returned message to IMethodReturnMessage and uses other helper methods to get the exception information (if an exception took place). When the processing is done, LogSink constructs a LogbookEntry object and adds it to the log-book using the Logbook object.

Example 11-5. The LogSink class

```
public class LogSink : IMessageSink
{
   IMessageSink m_NextSink;
   LogOption m_LogOption;
   Logbook m_Logbook;

   public LogSink(IMessageSink nextSink,LogOption logOption)
   {
      m_LogOption = logOption;
      m_NextSink = nextSink;
      m_Logbook = new Logbook( );
   }
   public IMessageSink NextSink
   {
      get {return m_NextSink;}
   }
   public IMessage SyncProcessMessage(IMessage msg)
   {
      IMethodMessage methodMessage = (IMethodMessage)msg;
      string assemblyName = GetAssemblyName(methodMessage);
      string typeName      = GetTypeName(methodMessage);
      string methodName    = GetMethodName(methodMessage);

      IMethodReturnMessage returnedMessage;
      returnedMessage = (IMethodReturnMessage)m_NextSink.SyncProcessMessage(msg);

      string exceptionName     = GetExceptionName(returnedMessage);
      string exceptionMessage  = GetExceptionMessage(returnedMessage);
```

Example 11-5. The LogSink class (continued)

```
    LogbookEntry logbookEntry = new LogbookEntry(assemblyName,
                                          typeName,methodName,
                                          exceptionName,exceptionMessage);

    DoLogging(logbookEntry);

    return returnedMessage;
}
public IMessageCtrl AsyncProcessMessage(IMessage msg,IMessageSink replySink)
{
    /* Processing of the message, similar to SyncProcessMessage( )  */
}

void DoLogging(LogbookEntry logbookEntry)
{
    if(m_LogOption == LogOption.MethodCalls)
    {
        LogCall(logbookEntry);
    }
    if(m_LogOption == LogOption.Errors)
    {
        if(logbookEntry.ExceptionName != "")
        {
            LogCall(logbookEntry);
        }
    }
}
void LogCall(LogbookEntry logbookEntry)
{
    m_Logbook.AddEntry(logbookEntry);
}
static string GetMethodName(IMethodMessage methodMessage)
{
    /* Processes methodMessage.MethodName  */
}
static string GetTypeName(IMethodMessage methodMessage)
{
    /* Processes methodMessage.TypeName  */
}
static string GetAssemblyName(IMethodMessage methodMessage)
{
    /* Processes methodMessage.TypeName  */
}
static string GetExceptionName(IMethodReturnMessage returnedMessage)
{
    /* Processes returnedMessage.Exception */
}

static string GetExceptionMessage(IMethodReturnMessage returnedMessage)
{
```

Example 11-5. The LogSink class (continued)

```
     /* Processes returnedMessage.Exception.Message */
   }
}
```

The Logbook component derives from the Component class, defined in the System. ComponentModel namespace. Deriving from Component allows you to use Visual Studio. NET to generate much of the ADO.NET data connectivity classes and code. However, the Logbook must be available for remoting. Fortunately, Component derives from MarshalByRefObject. The Logbook component overrides InitializeLifetimeService( ) and provides a null lease. This is required to maintain the singleton semantics:

```
public class Logbook : Component
{
   //Logbook should be used as a singleton
   public override object InitializeLifetimeService( )
   {
      return null;
   }
   /* Rest of the implementation */
}
```

The Logbook component uses ADO.NET to connect to the Logbook database and store or retrieve the entries using a DataSet. Logbook is a thread-safe component that locks itself in every method call to synchronize concurrent access.

Although unrelated to context and interception, I thought it would be handy if any object (even not a context-bound object using the service) could explicitly log information to the logbook. This is done using the static method AddEvent( ) of Logbook:

```
public class MyClass
{
   public void SomeMethod( )
   {
      Logbook.AddEvent("Some event took place");
   }
}
```

The AddEvent( ) implementation captures the same information as the LogSink, and it uses the same LogbookEntry struct. The big difference is that AddEvent( ) doesn't use interception. Instead, it uses the StackFrame class, defined in the System.Diagnostics namespace:

```
public static void AddEvent(string description)
{
   StackFrame frame = new StackFrame(1);//Get the frame of the caller

   string typeName     = frame.GetMethod( ).DeclaringType.ToString( );
   string methodName   = frame.GetMethod( ).Name;
   string assemblyName = Assembly.GetCallingAssembly( ).GetName( ).Name;
```

```
        LogbookEntry logbookEntry = new LogbookEntry(assemblyName,
                                         typeName,methodName,description);

        Logbook logbook = new Logbook();
        logbook.AddEntry(logbookEntry);
    }
```

The StackFrame provides access to information on every caller up the call chain. In this case, AddEvent( ) simply extracts the information on the method that called it.

CHAPTER 12
Security

In traditional operating systems such as Windows or Unix, the security model is user-oriented: processes execute under a certain security identity, usually that of the launching user. The operating system grants access to resources or permission to perform certain operations based on that identity. Typically, the user is either omnipotent (an administrator or root account), or the user is restricted and can perform only a narrow set of operations. The user-oriented security model has a number of shortcomings: even powerful users can make mistakes such as installing harmful applications from dubious sources or simply launching an email virus. In general, all users are vulnerable to attacks and only through experience do users learn how to prevent them. Even if no foul play is involved, the user is often required to be involved in making runtime decisions about the nature of components, such as whether or not to trust content coming from a particular source. The restricted users often don't get to work in an environment that is tailored to their needs and preferences, and the overall quality of their session suffers. New breeds of threats such as worms, lurking attacks, or Trojan horses target such weaknesses and can wait for an administrator to log on before striking—long after the initial security breach.

In today's component-oriented environment, there is a need for a component-oriented security model. A component-oriented operating system (such as the CLR) needs to examine not only what the user is allowed to do, but also what operations a given piece of code is allowed to do and what evidence that code provides to establish its identity and authenticity. This is exactly what the .NET security model is all about. .NET component-oriented security complements Windows user-based security, providing system administrators and developers granular control and flexibility without compromising overall security. The result is a productivity gain because for the most part, you don't need to bother with programmatic security, and it's an improvement in the trustworthiness .NET can bring to applications. This chapter describes the component- and the user-oriented security facilities available to .NET developers.

.NET application frameworks such as ASP.NET and Web Services provide their own security infrastructure to authenticate and authorize callers. Such application-specific security is built on top of the security concepts described in this chapter.

.NET Security Architecture

.NET component-oriented security is based on an elegant concept: using an administration tool, the system administrator grants assemblies certain permissions to perform operations with external entities such as the filesystem, the registry, the user interface, and so on. .NET provides the system administrator with multiple ways to identify which assembly gets granted what permission and what evidence the assembly needs to provide in order to establish its identity. At runtime, whenever an assembly tries to perform a privileged operation or access a resource, .NET verifies that the assembly and its calling assemblies have permission to perform that operation. Although the idea is intuitive enough, there is a substantial amount of new terms and concepts to understand before configuring .NET security. The rest of this section describes the elements of the .NET security architecture. The next sections describe how to administratively configure security and take programmatic control over security.

Permissions

A *permission* is a grant to perform a specific operation. Permissions have both a type and a scope. A file I/O permission is different from a user-interface permission in type because they control access to different types of resources. Similarly, reflection permission is different from unmanaged code-access permission because they control the execution of different type of operations. In scope, a permission can be very narrow, wide, or unrestricted. For example, a file I/O permission can allow reading from a particular file. Writing to the same file may be represented by a different file I/O permission. A file I/O permission can grant access to an entire directory (or a drive), or it can grant unrestricted access to the filesystem. .NET defines 19 types of permissions that govern all operations and recourses an application is likely to use (see Table 12-1).

Of particular interest is the security permission, which controls both sensitive operations and security configuration. The list of privileged operations includes the right to execute self, invoking unmanaged code, creating and controlling app domains, serialization, thread manipulation, and remoting configuration. The security configuration aspect includes permission to assert granted permissions, skip assembly verification, control policy, evidence, and principal, as well as permission to extend the security infrastructure. These facets are described later on.

.NET permissions are subject to the underlying Windows or resource security permissions. For example, if the filesystem is NTFS, the filesystem can still deny the application access to a file if the identity it's running under isn't granted access to the file. Other examples are accessing user-specific environment variables or accessing a SQL server that may have its own security policy.

Table 12-1. Security permission types

Permission type	Grants permission to	Example
Directory Services	Access to Active Directory. Allows browsing a path or writing to it.	Browse all content under *LDAP://*.
DNS	Domain-name servers. Permission is required to resolve URLs at runtime.	Either no access or unrestricted access to DNS.
Environment Variables	Read or write the value of specific environment variables.	Write the PATH environment variable.
Event Log	Write, browse, or audit an event log on a specified machine. Can also deny access to event log.	Browse the event log on *localhost*.
File Dialog	Display the common dialogs used to open or save files or deny permission to display the dialogs	Display the File Save dialog.
File IO	Read, write, append data to a file, or all files in a directory. Grants path discovery permission as well.	Write to *c:\temp\Myfile.txt*
Isolated Storage	Allow or disallow administration, configure isolation policy, and disk quotas.	Allow administration of isolated storage by the user of the assembly and allocate at most 10K bytes of disk quota.
Message Queue	Browse, peek, send, or receive messages from a specified message queue. Allow queue administration as well.	Grant unrestricted access to all message queues.
OLE DB	Access specified OLE DB providers. Can specify whether blank password is permitted for all providers.	Grant access to the Microsoft OLE DB provider for SQL Server.
Performance Counter	Browse or instrument[a] specified performance counters on designated machines.	Instrument the threads performance counter on the current machine.
Printing	Print (either in safe mode, default mode, or all modes).	Allow all printing operations to all accessible printers.
Reflection	Discover member and type information about other assemblies using reflection. Emit code at runtime.	Reflects both type and member information on other assemblies but can't emit new code at runtime.
Registry	Read, write, or create registry keys.	Read the values stored under *HKEY_LOCAL_MACHINE\SOFTWARE*.
Security	Control various security aspects.	Allow unmanaged code access.
Service Controller	Control or browse services on specified machines.	Control (start and stop) the fax service on the local machine.

Table 12-1. Security permission types (continued)

Permission type	Grants permission to	Example
Socket access	Accept connections on or connect to specific ports on specified machines using either TCP or UDP (or both).	Allow connecting and accepting calls on port 8005 using TCP on the local machine.
SQL Client	Access SQL servers using ADO.NET, and specify whether a blank password is permitted.	Allow unrestricted access to all SQL servers available on the Intranet.
User Interface	Interact with the user using all top-level windows and events, safe top-level windows, safe subwindows, or no windows at all. Control access to the clipboard.	Allow displaying all windows but disallow clipboard access.
Web Access	Allow connecting or accepting requests from specified web hosts.	Allow both to connect and accepts requests from *www.oreilly.com*

a "The term *instrumentation* refers to an ability to monitor or measure the level of a product's performance and to diagnose errors. In programming, this means the ability of an application to incorporate." (MSDN)

Permission Sets

Individual permissions are just that—individual. To function properly, a given assembly often requires a set of permissions of particular scope and type. .NET allows system administrators to use *permission sets*—a collection of individual permissions. A permission set can contain as many individual permissions as required. Administrators can construct custom permission sets, or they can use a preexisting, well-known permission set. .NET provides seven predefined permission sets, also known as *named permission sets*; they include Nothing, Execution, Internet, LocalIntranet, Everything, FullTrust, and SkipVerification. Table 12-2 presents the individual permissions granted by each named permission set.

The named permission sets offer a spectrum of trust:

- The Nothing permission set grants nothing. Code that has only the Nothing permission set can't execute, and .NET will refuse to load it. The Nothing permission set is used when there is a need to prevent assemblies from running, typically because the code origin is known to be not trustworthy and dangerous. For example, the default .NET security policy associates any code coming from the list of untrusted sites (maintained by Internet Explorer) with the Nothing permission set, effectively preventing such code from causing any harm.

- The Execution permission set allows code to load and run, but it doesn't permit interaction with any kind of external resource and it doesn't perform any privileged operation. When an assembly is assigned the Execution permission (but nothing else), the assembly can perform only operations such as numerical calculations, but it can't save the results. By default, .NET doesn't use the Execution permission set.

Table 12-2. The named permission sets

Named permission set	Nothing	Execution	Internet	Local-Intranet	Everything	Full-Trust	Skip Verification
Directory Services					Unrestricted	Unrestricted	
DNS				Unrest.	Unrestricted	Unrestricted	
Environment Variables				Read USERNAME	Unrestricted	Unrestricted	
Event Log				Instrument on local machine	Unrestricted	Unrestricted	
File Dialog			File Open	Unrest.	Unrestricted	Unrestricted	
File IO					Unrestricted	Unrestricted	
Isolated Storage			Domain isolation by user with 10K disk quota	Assembly isolation by user, unrestricted disk quota	Unrestricted	Unrestricted	
Message Queue					Unrestricted	Unrestricted	
OLE DB					Unrestricted	Unrestricted	
Performance Counter					Unrestricted	Unrestricted	
Printing			Safe printing	Default	Unrestricted	Unrestricted	
Reflection				Member and type	Unrestricted	Unrestricted	
Registry					Unrestricted	Unrestricted	
Security		Execution	Execution	Execution and assert	All, except skip verification	Unrestricted	Skip code safety verification
Service Controller					Unrestricted	Unrestricted	
Socket access					Unrestricted	Unrestricted	
SQL Client					Unrestricted	Unrestricted	
User Interface			Safe top-level windows, clipboard ownership	Unrestricted	Unrestricted	Unrestricted	
Web Access					Unrestricted	Unrestricted	

- The Internet permission set should be used carefully because it gives code some ability to execute and display a user interface. Generally, you shouldn't trust code coming from the Internet unless the site of origin is explicitly trusted. Note that the default .NET security policy grants the Internet permission set to all code coming from the Internet. Administrators can change that and explicitly assign the Internet permission set to selected trusted sites.

- Code coming from the local intranet is, of course, more trustworthy than code coming from the Internet. As a result, the LocalIntranet permission set grants code wide permissions. .NET's default associates the LocalIntranet permission set with code originating from the local intranet.

- The Everything permission set grants code every permission, and the only requirement is that the code be verifiable. *Verifiable code* is code that can be verified in a formal manner as type-safe. CLR-compliant compilers can emit unverifiable code, such as unsafe code in C#. You can use the Everything permission set to make sure the managed code invoked has all the permissions required for normal operation and at the same time ensures that it doesn't use techniques such as pointer arithmetic to access restricted memory areas or areas owned by other app domains (more on that at the end of the chapter). By default, .NET doesn't use the Everything permission set.

- The FullTrust permission set is just that: .NET trusts such code implicitly and allows it unimpeded access to all resources; it also allows it to perform all operations. Only the most trustworthy code should be granted this permission because there are no safeguards. Because it's likely that on a given machine only trustworthy applications are installed, all code executing from the local machine is granted full trust by default.

- The SkipVerification set is the inverse of the Everything permission set. This set skips code-safety verification but grants nothing else. You can use the SkipVerification permission set to explicitly allow unverifiable code, without risking it touching any external resource or performing sensitive operations. For example, imagine porting legacy C or C++ code to C#, when the legacy code uses complex pointer arithmetic. In that case, it may be easier to keep that pointer arithmetic in place using unsafe code instead of fully rewriting safer C#. It's overkill to grant that code FullTrust; instead, grant it the SkipVerification permission set and any other specific permissions it may require. Granting assemblies only the minimum permissions they require is a good guideline because it reduces the chances of damage caused by a malicious party luring the benign assembly to do dirty work on its behalf.

Security Evidence

System administrators grant permissions to assemblies based on the assembly's identity. The question is what sort of evidence should an assembly present to .NET in order to establish its identity? A *security evidence* is some form of proof that an assembly can provide to substantiate its identity. Evidences are vital for .NET security because without them, rogue assemblies can pretend to be something they aren't and gain unauthorized access to resources or operations. There are two types of evidences: origin-based and content-based evidences. An *origin-based evidence* simply examines where the assembly is coming from and is independent of the actual content of the assembly. The standard origin-based evidences are Application Directory, Site, URL, and Zone. A *content-based evidence* examines the content of the assembly, looking for a specific match with specified criteria. The standard content-based evidences are Strong Name, Publisher, and Hash. There is no relationship between permission sets and evidences. A single assembly can be granted multiple permissions sets and have a different evidence for each permission set, or it can use the same evidence for multiple sets. .NET also defines a wild card—the All Code evidence.

The All Code evidence

The All Code evidence is blank evidence, which simply means that all assemblies meet its criteria. When the administrator uses the All Code evidence to bind a permission set to assemblies, it means that all assemblies are granted that set.

The Application Directory evidence

The Application Directory evidence grants the permission set associated with it to all assemblies coming from the same directory or from a child directory of the running application. Typically, this evidence allows an application to trust code deployed together with it but distrust other code on the same machine or anywhere else.

The Site evidence

The Site evidence grants the permission set associated with it to all assemblies coming from a specified site, such as:

http://www.somesite.com or ftp://www.somesite.com

The protocol (and port number if specified) is ignored, and only the top-level domain portion is used. .NET also ignores any subsite specification, such as:

http://www.somesite.com/myfolder

and extracts the domain name only. Sites can also point to a specific machine:

tcp://somemachine:8005

The URL evidence

The URL evidence grants the permission set associated with it to all assemblies coming from a specified URL. A URL evidence is more specific than a Site evidence because .NET takes into account protocol, port number, and subfolders. For example, the following are considered different URL evidences but identical Site evidences:

http://www.somesite.com
ftp://www.somesite.com
http://www.somesite.com/myfolder
tcp://somesite.com

You can use an asterisk at the end of a URL to indicate that the URL evidence applies to all code coming from a sub-URL as well:

http://www.somesite.com/*

The Zone evidence

The Zone evidence grants the permission set associated with it to all assemblies coming from the specified zone. .NET defines five zones: My Computer, Local Intranet, Internet, Trusted Sites, and Untrusted Sites.

The My Computer zone
Identifies code coming from the local machine.

The Local Intranet zone

Identifies code coming from machines on the same LAN. The local intranet is any location identified by a universal name convention (UNC), usually in the form of \\<*machinename*>\<*further scope*>, for example:

\\Somemachine\SomeSharedFolder

You can also identify a location as part of the Local Intranet zone using a URL, as long as the URL doesn't contain dots, such as:

http://Somemachine\SomeSharedFolder
tcp://Somemachine\SomeSharedFolder

Note that even if you specify your own local machine name, such as:

\\MyMachine or http://localhost

it will be considered part of the Local Intranet zone, not the My Computer zone. Network-mapped drives are also considered part of the Local Intranet zone.

The Internet zone

Identifies code coming from the Internet. The Internet is considered as any location identified by a dotted or numeric IP address, such as:

http://www.somesite.com
http://66.129.71.238

Note that by default, even if the IP (or site) points to a location on the LAN (including the local machine), such as:

http://127.0.0.1

it's still considered part of the Internet zone.

 If you wish to include local intranet sites as part of the local intranet, but refer to them using a generic Internet dotted or numeric URL, you need to add those sites explicitly to the intranet site list. To do so, open Internet Explorer and display the Security tab on the Internet Options dialog. Select the Local Intranet icon, and click the Sites button (see Figure 12-1). In the Local Intranet dialog, click Advanced, and add web sites to this zone. You can add even non-intranet web sites to the Local Intranet zone.

The Trusted Sites zone

Identifies code coming from a list of trusted Internet sites. You can add and remove sites to the Trusted Sites list using Internet Explorer. Select the Trusted Sites icon, and click Sites (see Figure 12-1). In the Trusted Sites dialog, you can add sites to the list of trusted sites.

The Untrusted Sites zone

Identifies code coming from a list of untrusted Internet sites. You can add sites to and remove them from the Untrusted Sites list using Internet Explorer, similarly to adding sites to the Trusted sites list.

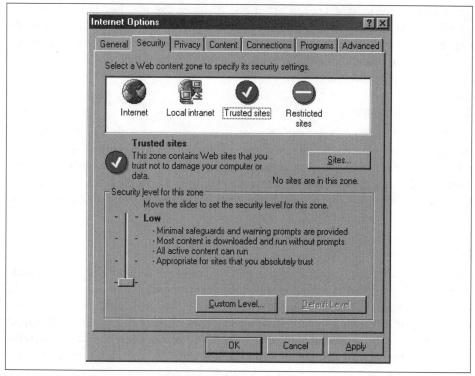

Figure 12-1. Managing zones using Internet Explorer

 When you add sites to the list of trusted or untrusted sites using Internet Explorer, the lists are maintained per user and not per machine. There is no documented, easy way to add sites to a machine-wide list.

The Strong Name evidence

The Strong Name evidence grants the permission set associated with it to all assemblies whose public key matches a specified key value. The Strong Name evidence is an excellent way to trust all code coming from a particular vendor, assuming the vendor uses the same public key to sign all its assemblies. The Strong Name evidence can optionally contain the name and version of assemblies (both or either). As a result, the system administrator can trust only a particular version of a specific assembly coming from a particular vendor identified by a public key.

The Hash evidence

The Hash evidence grants the permission set associated with it to an assembly only if a computational hash of that assembly matches a predetermined specified hash. The assembly in question need not have a strong name. As a result, the Hash evidence is useful only when uniquely identifying an assembly with a friendly name and granting permissions only to that trusted assembly. Another use for the Hash evidence is when a vendor provides you with a new assembly, but you want to keep using the old one, even if the new assembly has the same strong name and version number. System administrators can configure which cryptographic hashing algorithm to use, either SHA1 (the default) or MD5.

The Publisher evidence

The Publisher evidence grants the permission set associated with it to all assemblies that are digitally signed with a specified certificate, such as AuthentiCode. To digitally sign an assembly with a certificate, first build it, and then use the *signcode.exe* command-line utility, specifying the assembly to sign and the file containing the digital certificate. *signcode.exe* can optionally launch a wizard to guide you thorough the signing process.

Selecting a security evidence

The security level applied is always a tradeoff between taking risks and usability. There are no hard and fast rules as to which security evidence to use and when. In general, you should prefer content- to origin-based evidence because content-based is more accurate. For example, Strong Name evidence safely and consistently identifies an assembly. With origin-based evidence such as Site evidence, the same assembly may not be trusted if it comes from one site but trusted if it comes from a different site. In addition, origin-based evidence is more susceptible to subversion than content-based evidence. It's next to impossible to fake a strong name, but it's possible to fool your machine into thinking that a certain IP address maps to a trusted site by subverting the DNS server. Another breach of origin-based evidence is compromising the proxy server on the local network so that instead of returning the assembly from a trusted site, it returns a different assembly but makes it look like it came from a trusted site. You should do a careful threat analysis, and trust origin-based evidences only as far as the DNS and other network facilities can be trusted. However, origin-based evidences let you interact with much wider sets of assemblies, as opposed to the content-based evidences, which require individual configuration.

Code Groups and Security Policies

.NET uses code groups to classify assemblies when it decides on the security permissions granted for each assembly. A *code group* is a binding of a single permission set with a particular evidence (see Figure 12-2).

To be granted the permissions in the permission set associated with the code group, an assembly must first satisfy the evidence of that code group. However, a meaningful security policy needs to be much more granular than what a single code group with a single evidence and permission set can express. A .NET *security policy* is a collection of code groups. Code groups in a policy are independent of one another in

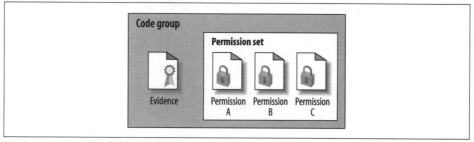

Figure 12-2. A code group is a binding of a single permission set and a single evidence

every respect. They can all use the same evidence, different evidences, or a mix. Similarly, different code groups can use different or identical permission sets. The permissions granted by a policy to a given assembly is the union of all the individual permissions granted by the code groups in that policy, whose evidence the assembly satisfies. For example, consider the security policy in Figure 12-3. In the figure, an assembly satisfies the evidences of code groups A, B, and C, but not the evidences required by code groups D and E. As a result, that assembly will be granted only the union of permissions A, B, and C.

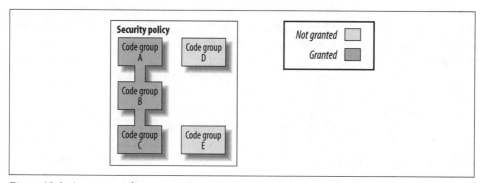

Figure 12-3. A security policy

Combining policies

.NET allows administrators to provide multiple security policies. The benefit of multiple security policies is that it enables policies to have different scopes. Some policies can be restrictive and should be applied only in specific cases, such as with individual users or machines with limited privileges. Some policies can be more permissive and apply to all machines and users in an organization. Therefore it's quite possible that an assembly is granted some permissions by one policy but is denied the same permissions by another policy. Because all policies must concur on the allowed permissions, the actual permissions granted to an assembly is the intersection of all the permissions granted by all the security policies (see Figure 12-4).

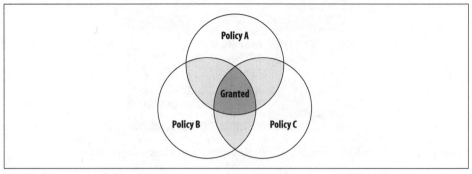

Figure 12-4. An assembly is allowed the intersection of permissions granted by the various polices

Policy levels

In actuality, there are only four types (or levels) of security policies, and .NET is aware of these four levels. Although technically, administrators can configure these levels in any way, the convention is to use these levels according to their intent. The *Enterprise policy* should define a policy that affects all machines in the Enterprise. Each machine should have a *Machine policy* defining a policy specific to that machine, and the *User policy* should define a policy per individual user. These three policy levels are configured by the system administrator. The last policy level is the *Application Domain* policy, which applies only to code running in a specific application domain. You can only configure the Application Domain policy programmatically, by calling the `SetAppDomainPolicy()` method of the `AppDomain` class. Customizing the Application Domain policy is available primarily for advanced cases only, for example, for creating an app domain with deliberately low permissions, and loading untrusted code into that domain. As a result, the new app domain is isolated from other trusted app domains. The default Application Domain policy grants all code full trust. App domain security policy is beyond the scope of this chapter.

System administrators typically take advantage of the hierarchical nature of the policy levels, placing policies that are more restrictive downstream and the more liberal policies upstream. This allows overall flexibility with granular security policy, tight in some places and looser in others. For example, the Enterprise policy is likely to contain only the known, must-be-blocked web sites or vendors. Other than that, the Enterprise policy can be very liberal, permitting all other operations and zones. Individual machines can be restricted if necessary. For instance, a development machine can have more permissions that a public machine in a reception area. Similarly, some users such as system administrators can have a liberal if not unrestricted User policy, while nontechnical staff can have a very restricted User policy, even if they all share the same machine.

How It All Works Together

When .NET loads an assembly, it computes the permissions that assembly is granted: for each security policy, .NET aggregates the permissions from the code groups satisfied in that policy, and then .NET intersects the policies to find the combined overall collection of permission the assembly is granted. That set of permissions is calculated only once (per app domain), and it persists in memory for as long as the assembly remains loaded. Whenever an assembly invokes calls on one of the .NET framework classes (or any other class, including your own, as explained later), that class may demand from .NET that the assembly calling it have the required security permission to access it. For example, when using the file I/O classes, they demand appropriate file I/O permission for that access, and when displaying Windows Forms, they demand User Interface permissions. If the assembly doesn't have the appropriate security permission, a security exception is thrown. However, it isn't sufficient that the assembly that called the demanding class has the requested permissions. The reason is, if .NET were to check for permissions only on the assembly immediately up the call chain, that could constitute a security breach. Imagine a malicious assembly that doesn't have permissions to access a class such as FileStream. That assembly could work around the lack of permissions by calling instead a benign assembly, which has the permissions, to do its dirty work for it. As a result, whenever a class demands security permission checks, .NET traverses the entire call stack, making sure that every assembly up the call chain has the required permissions. This is known as the security permission *stack walk*. When the first assembly without permissions is found during the stack walk, .NET aborts the stack walk and throws an exception at the point where the original security demand took place.

 If an exception is raised because of lack of security permission, you can find which permission was missing by examining the PermissionType property of the SecurityException object.

Configuring Permissions

Now it's time to learn how to configure the various policies, code groups, permissions, and evidences. .NET provides two ways system administrators can configure code access security policy. The first is to use a command-line utility called *caspol. exe*; the second is to use the .NET Configuration tool. Both methods are comparable in features and capabilities. You typically use the .NET Configuration tool to configure security and export the security policies to deploy on other machines. You can use *caspol.exe* during installation to make dynamic changes. This chapter demonstrates the .NET Configuration tool. Please refer to the MSDN library to learn about the equivalent command-line switches for *caspol.exe*.

The .NET Configuration tool has a folder called Runtime Security Policy. Once expanded, the folder contains an item for each policy: Enterprise, Machine, and

User. System administrators use these three policies to manage code-access security. Each policy item has subfolders, containing its code groups, permissions sets and custom Policy Assemblies (see Figure 12-5).

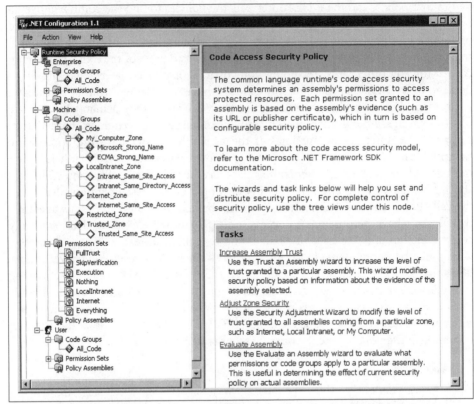

Figure 12-5. Runtime Security Policy configuration using the .NET Configuration tool

The .NET Configuration tool lets system administrators nest code groups. In the Property page on the General tab of each parent code group, an administrator can specify what to do when the evidence associated with this code group is satisfied. By default, .NET continues to examine child code groups and aggregate their permissions (if their evidence requirement is met), but administrators can instruct .NET to stop evaluating child code groups if the parent membership condition (the evidence) is met. This instruction is called *Level Final*. The other instruction, called *Exclusive*, instructs .NET to include only permissions from this code group in the policy. Multiple code groups can claim to be exclusive. However, if a policy has at least a single exclusive code group, all code groups must be mutually exclusive, meaning that the evaluated assembly can, at most, meet the membership condition of a single code group. It's considered an error if the assembly meets more than one code group membership condition. The added degree of code group coupling and restriction when using exclusive code groups makes it a setting to avoid.

Each security policy is stored in a dedicated XML-formatted security configuration file, and the .NET Configuration tool is merely a visual editor of those files. The Enterprise policy file resides at:

> *<Windows Directory>\Microsoft.NET\Framework\<Version>\config*
> *enterprisesec.config*

The Machine policy file resides at:

> *<Windows Directory>\Microsoft.NET\Framework\<Version>\config*
> *security.config*

The User policy file resides at:

> *<Documents and Settings>\<User Name>\Application Data\Microsoft\CLR*
> *Security Config\<Version>\security.config*

In principle, only a system administrator should modify the security policy configuration files. On an NTFS system, be sure to allow only administrators the right to modify these files. A non-NTFS system has a potential security breach because any user can modify these files using a text editor. A truly secure .NET system must rely on a properly configured NTFS filesystem.

.NET Default Configuration

All three policies contain in their Permission Sets folder the same set of named permission sets, although none of the policies uses all its permission sets. The reason why the policies are deployed with all the named sets is so that system administrators can use these predefined sets in their own custom code groups. In addition, system administrators can change the default code groups to use other permission sets (you will see how shortly). Each policy contains code groups named after the evidence they use, by default. Note that this is only a convention, intended to clarify the purpose of the code groups at a glance. You can name (or rename) code groups arbitrarily.

The Enterprise and User policies

Both the Enterprise and the User policies contain by default a single code group called All_Code. The All_Code code group (as its name implies) uses the All Code evidence with the FullTrust permission set, which means that by default, as far as the Enterprise and User policies are concerned, all assemblies are unrestricted. As a result, by default, neither the Enterprise nor the User policies have any effect on restricting code access because their intersection with the third policy—the Machine policy—yields the Machine policy intact. Administrators can add custom child code groups to both the Enterprise and User All_Code code groups, thus customizing these policies. In that case, make sure to change the default because it will mask out any child code group.

The Machine policy

The Machine policy is where the default .NET code access security takes place. The Machine policy has a single root code group called All_Code. All_Code uses the All Code evidence with the Nothing permission set. As a result, by itself, it grants nothing, and instead it relies on the following nested code groups to grant permissions:

- The My_Computer_Zone code group uses the Zone evidence, with the zone set to My Computer (see Figure 12-6).

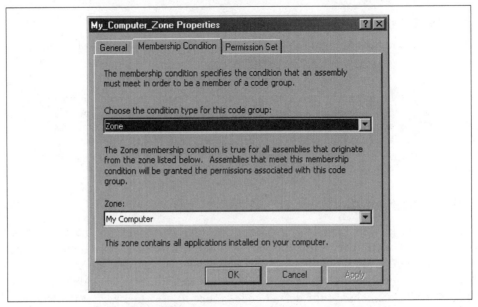

Figure 12-6. The Membership Condition tab on a code group's Properties page

This code group grants the FullTrust permission set. Consequently, by default, all code coming from the local computer gets full trust. The My_Computer_ Zone code group has two nested child code groups, called Microsoft_Strong_ Name and ECMA_Strong_Name (see Figure 12-5). These nested code groups use the Strong Name evidence, in which the value is set to the Microsoft public key and ECMA public key, respectively. The permission set granted by both these nested code groups is FullTrust. As a result, by default, any assembly originating from Microsoft or ECMA is granted unrestricted access regardless of its zone, even if other code groups restrict that zone. This is because when calculating a policy, .NET unites all permissions under that policy.

- The LocalIntranet_Zone code group uses the zone evidence with a value set to the Local Intranet zone. The permission set is LocalIntranet. The problem is that the LocalIntranet permission set doesn't grant any file I/O permission, nor does it grant any web access (see Figure 12-7).

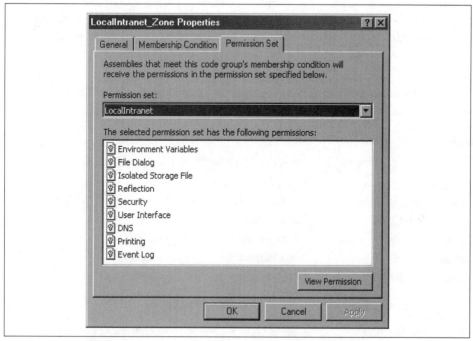

Figure 12-7. The Permission Set tab of a code group Property page

This may prevent an assembly originating in the intranet from functioning properly because it requires access to its original install directory or access to its original site. There is really no harm in allowing these two because the originators of the assembly, by definition, trust their own product. To compensate for these two limitations, the LocalIntranet_Zone code group contains two nested code groups (see Figure 12-5). The Intranet_Same_Site_Access code group allows code to access its site of origin, and the Intranet_Same_Directory_Access code group allows code to access its original install directory. These custom code groups can't be edited using the .NET Configuration tool; they use special custom permissions. See the MSDN Library for information about custom permissions.

- The Internet_Zone code group uses the zone evidence with a zone set to Internet. The permission set used is Internet. This code group has a child code group called Internet_Same_Site_Access (see Figure 12-5). Because the Internet permission doesn't grant Web access, the Internet_Same_Site_Access uses a custom permission, which allows code coming from a site to connect to its site of origin.

- The Restricted_Zone code group uses the zone evidence, with a zone set to Untrusted Sites. Not surprising, the permission set used is Nothing.

- The Trusted_Zone code group uses the zone evidence, with a zone set to Trusted Sites. The permission set used is the Internet permission set. This code group has a child code group called Trusted_Same_Site_Access (see Figure 12-5). Because the Internet permission doesn't grant web access, the Trusted_Same_Site_Access uses a custom permission, which allows code coming from a trusted site to connect to its site of origin. This is the same custom permission used by the Internet_Same_Site_Access code group.

Table 12-3 summarizes the default permissions granted by the Machine policy (same as the overall default policy).

Table 12-3. The default Machine policy

Code group	Evidence	Permission set granted
All_Code	Any code	Nothing
My_Computer_Zone	My Computer zone	FullTrust
Microsoft_Strong_Name	Microsoft public key	FullTrust
ECMA_Strong_Name	ECMA public key	FullTrust
LocalIntranet_Zone	Local Intranet zone	LocalIntranet
Intranet_Same_Site_Access	Local Intranet zone	Access site of origin
Intranet_Same_Directory_Access	Local Intranet zone	Access directory of origin
Internet_Zone	Internet zone	Internet
Internet_Same_Site_Access	Internet site	Access site of origin
Restricted_Zone	Untrusted site	Nothing
Trusted_Zone	Trusted site	Internet
Trusted_Same_Site_Access	Trusted site	Access site of origin

 The first version of .NET (Version 1.0) granted the Internet zone the Internet permission set. Because of some security concerns and potential security breaches with code coming from the Internet, Microsoft changed this policy in Service Pack 1 for Version 1.0. In the service pack, the Internet zone was associated with the Nothing permission set. After addressing the issue, Microsoft reassigned the Internet zone the Internet permission set in Version 1.1 of .NET.

Custom Permission Sets

System administrators typically apply the predefined named permission sets in the context indicated by their name. However, you can't modify a named permission set. Instead, you can duplicate a named set and modify the copy. System administrators can define custom permission sets and compose very granular permissions, suitable for their particular needs. The only requirement is that a custom permission will not have the same name as one of the existing permission sets because permission sets must be given unique names.

 You can modify the Everything permission set because it isn't considered part of the standard .NET predefined named permission sets. The Everything named permission set is likely just a nice addition done by the developers of the .NET Configuration tool.

To duplicate a named permission set (or any other custom permission set), right-click it and select Duplicate from the pop-up context menu. The .NET Configuration tool then creates a new permission set in the policy named Copy of *<original name>*.

To create a new permission set from scratch, right-click the Permissions Sets folder and select New from the context menu. This brings up the Create Permission set wizard. The first screen lets you name the new permission set, such as "My Permission Set," and provide a description (see Figure 12-8).

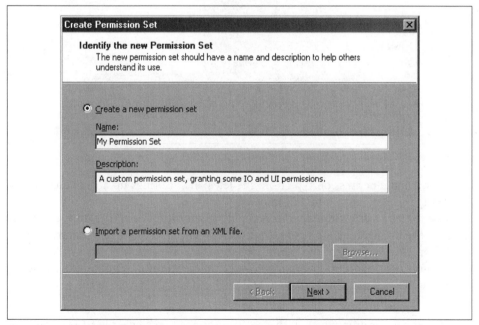

Figure 12-8. Identifying a new permission set

Once created, the description is displayed in the right pane of the .NET Configuration tool when the permission set is selected. The first screen also lets you provide an XML file with definitions of a custom permission (such as the permission to access site of origin for assemblies coming from the Intranet zone). In most cases, you are likely to simply select permissions from the existing permission types. Click Next to move to the next dialog, which allows you to assign individual permissions to the new permission set (see Figure 12-9).

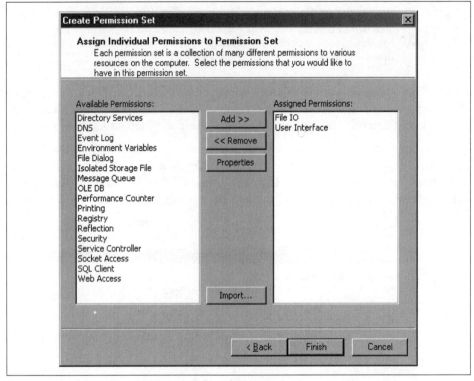

Figure 12-9. Selecting individual permissions in the permission set

When you add a permission type from the left pane, it brings up a dedicated dialog for that type, allowing you to add individual permissions of that type. For example, suppose the new permission set is required to grant file I/O and UI permissions: for file I/O, the permissions are read permission for the C drive, and full access to C:\ *temp*. For UI permissions, the permissions granted are access to all windows and events but no access to the clipboard. To configure the file I/O permissions, select File IO on the left pane of the dialog, and click Add. This brings up the File IO Permission Setting dialog, shown in Figure 12-10.

The dialog has a grid in which each line corresponds to a single file I/O permission. You can also grant unrestricted access to the filesystem. Configure the required setting, and click OK to return to the previous dialog. To configure UI permission, select User Interface in the left pane, and click Add. This brings up a the UI Permission Setting dialog (see Figure 12-11). Grant access to all windows and events, and deny access to the clipboard. Click OK to return to the previous dialog, and Finish to

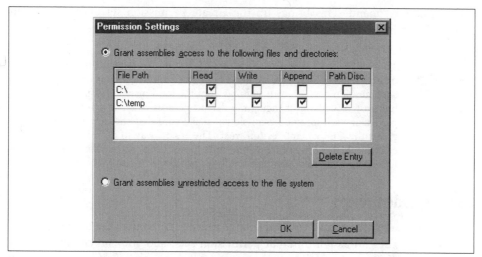

Figure 12-10. Configuring file I/O permissions

complete configuring the new permission set. You can now use this permission set with any code group in the policy.

 You can't share permission sets between policies. If you want the same custom permission set in a different policy, copy the custom policy by dragging and dropping it to the other policy.

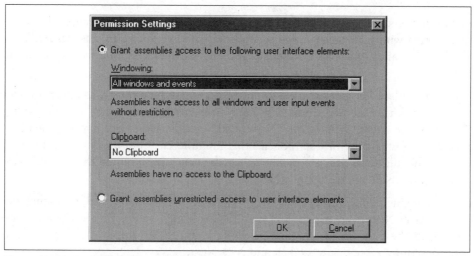

Figure 12-11. Configuring UI permissions

Once you have created a custom permission set (either from scratch or by duplicating an existing permission set), you can change it by selecting Change Permissions...

from its context menu. This brings up the Create Permission set dialog shown in Figure 12-9, which lets you change the permission set.

 To operate, the Microsoft-provided CLR assemblies demand the full trust permission set. This demand is satisfied by the default policies configuration because code coming from the local machine is granted full trust. Whenever changing the default policies (such as granting a particular user specific permissions), make sure that the new policy grants the CLR assemblies full trust. The easiest way to do that is to copy the Microsoft_Strong_Name code group from the Machine policy and add it to the Enterprise and User policies.

Custom Code Groups

With predefined code groups, you can change every detail, unlike the predefined permission sets. You can assign different permission sets, and you can change the evidence required. To make such changes, simply bring up the code group Property page and change the evidence condition or the permission set used. You can even delete any existing code group. You can also duplicate an existing code group (with all its nested code groups), rename it, and modify its composition. With the .NET Configuration tool, you can even drag and drop code groups across policies. In addition, the .NET Configuration tool allows you to create new code groups, but only as a child code group of an existing code group. Once created, you can move the new code group anywhere under the policy code group tree by dragging and dropping it to a new location.

For example, suppose you want to create a new code group that grants all assemblies signed with your organization's public key the Everything permission set. This can be very handy when different teams use each other's assemblies across the local Intranet.

The logical place for the new code group is in the Machine policy, as another child code group under the My_Computer_Zone code group, a sibling to the Microsoft_Strong_Name and ECMA_Strong_Name code groups. Note that if your organization is using Enterprise or User policies that are different from the default (of granting all code full trust), you will have to place the new code group in those policies as well because .NET intersects policies.

In the Machine policy, highlight the My_Computer_Zone code group, right-click on it, and select New from the context menu. This brings up the Create Code Group wizard. In the first screen, name the new code group My Applications, provide a short description (see Figure 12-12), and click Next.

In the "Choose a condition type" dialog, you need to select the evidence type used by this code group and its value. In the condition type textbox, select Strong Name from the drop-down combo box (see Figure 12-13). This changes the lower part of

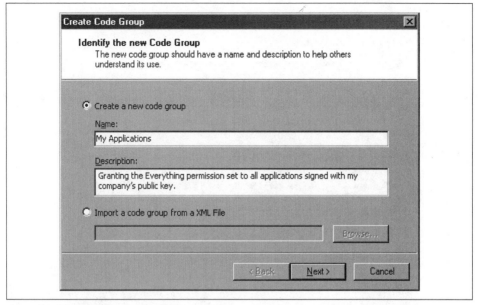

Figure 12-12. Creating a new code group

the dialog to reflect the value of the requested strong key. The easiest way to provide the public key value is to import it from an already signed assembly. Click the Import button to bring up a file-browsing dialog. Browse to a signed assembly (either an EXE or a DLL), and select it. The wizard then reads the public key from the assembly's manifest and populates the Public Key textbox.

Click Next to proceed to the next dialog, where you need to assign a permission set to the new code group. You can use any existing permission set in the policy (see Figure 12-14) by selecting it from the drop-down combo box. Select Everything, click Next, and click Finish in the next dialog. The new code group is now part of the policy.

> .NET provides the class `SecurityManager`, which lets you programmatically configure the security policy. `SecurityManager` offers no advantage over using *caspol.exe* or the .NET Configuration tool. It's likely these two administration tools actually use `SecurityManager` under the covers.

Security Administration Utilities

The .NET Configuration tool provides a number of utilities and services to manage security at a level above code groups and policies. It addition, the tool provides ways to examine or trust an individual assembly, reset policies, and deploy security policies.

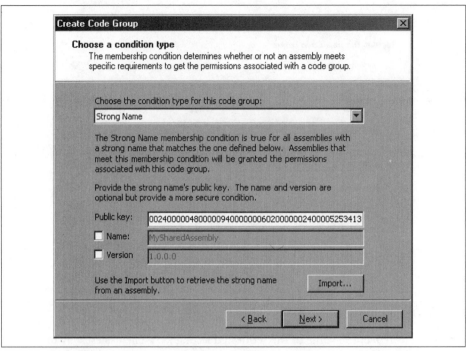

Figure 12-13. Choosing an evidence type and value for a code group

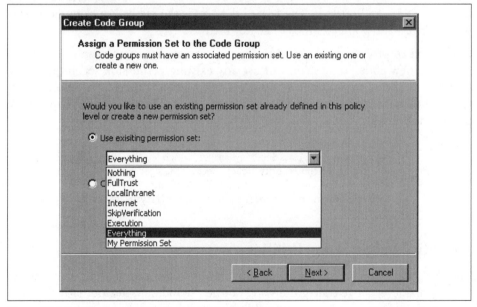

Figure 12-14. Assigning a permission set to a code group

Resetting policies

One essential feature of the .NET configuration tool is the ability to reset a policy (or all of them) to the default value. This is instrumental when experimenting with security configuration. To reset an individual policy, simply select Reset from its context menu. You can also undo the last change made by selecting Undo from the policy context menu. There is a Redo option as well. To reset all policies at once to their default configuration, select Reset All from the context menu of the Runtime Security Policy folder.

Managing policy files

You can create new security policy files by selecting New from the context menu of the Runtime Security Policy folder. The New Security Policy dialog lets you specify the level of policy file to create—Enterprise, Machine, or User—and a name for the new file. The new file will have as a starting point the default for that policy level. You can then assign this new file on the same machine or anywhere else. First, select Open from the context menu of the Runtime Security Policy folder. This brings up the Open Security Policy dialog, which lets you specify which policy level to apply to the configuration file. You can open the default configuration file for that level or assign a specific configuration file (see Figure 12-15).

Figure 12-15. Opening and assigning a new security policy file

Adjusting security

The .NET Configuration tool provides a simple, coarse way for system administrators to manage code groups, without bothering with permission sets, evidences, and the like. Selecting Adjust Security from the context menu of the Runtime Security Policy folder brings up the Security Adjustment Wizard. The first screen lets you decide whether the adjustments should apply to the machine or the current user level only; there is no Enterprise level. The next screen presents the five zones (My Computer, Local Intranet, Internet, Trusted Sites, and Untrusted Sites) and a track bar (see Figure 12-16).

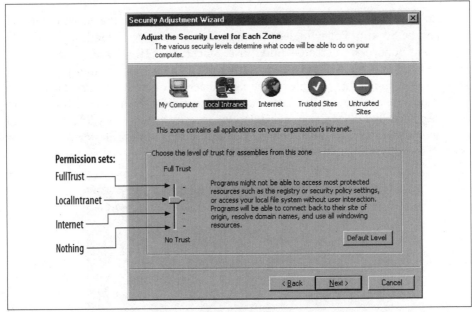

Figure 12-16. Adjusting zone security using the adjustment wizard

Adjusting the track-bar position assigns a different permission set to the selected zone. Even though the description of the positions of the track bar to the right don't state so, the positions map to the FullTrust, LocalIntranet, Internet, and Nothing permission sets, as shown in Figure 12-16. After you click Next, the last dialog of the adjustment wizard presents a summary of the new security setting for the five zones.

Evaluating an assembly

Sometimes it isn't easy to find out why a particular assembly isn't granted the expected security permissions. The .NET Configuration tool lets you evaluate an assembly and find which code group grants permissions to that assembly and which permissions. Selecting Evaluate Assembly from the context menu of the Runtime Security Policy folder brings up the Evaluate an Assembly dialog. You need to specify the filename and location of the assembly to evaluate and what to evaluate (see Figure 12-17).

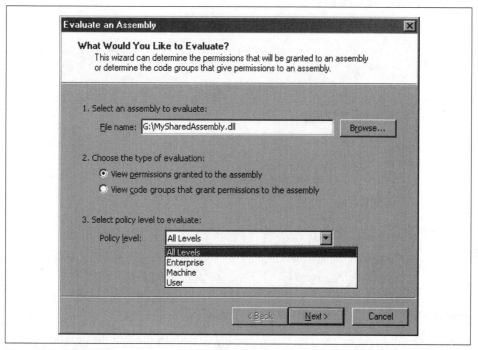

Figure 12-17. Selecting an assembly to evaluate and the evaluation information

If you need to verify which evidences the assembly meets, you can have the wizard list all the code groups that grant permissions to the assembly. Alternatively, you can have the wizard list the actual permissions granted to see what the assembly ends up with. You also need to select the evaluation level; you can select a specific policy or all levels. Once you select that information, click Next to see the evaluation report. Depending on your selections in the previous dialog, you are either presented with a hierarchical list of code groups (as in Figure 12-18) or a list of permission sets. If you select permission sets, you can examine each permission set type to see the value of individual permissions it grants.

Trusting an assembly

Sometimes, the system administrator may have explicit knowledge that a particular assembly is trustworthy even though it doesn't satisfy enough code groups to operate. In that case, the administrator can simply add a new code group, identifying that assembly with a hash evidence (or a strong name and version), and grant it the desired permission sets. The .NET Configuration tool supports an automated way to reach the same end result. Select Trust Assembly from the context menu of the Runtime Security

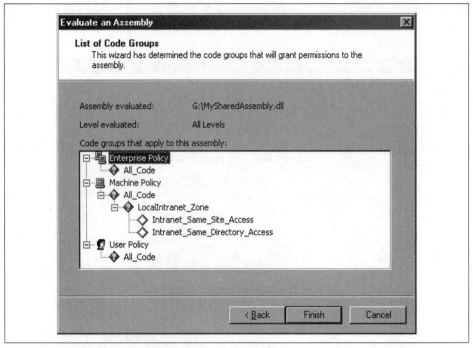

Figure 12-18. Code group membership evaluation report

Policy folder to bring up the Trust an Assembly wizard. In the first dialog, you need to decide whether to make the changes apply machine-wide or just to the current user. The next dialog lets you browse to where the assembly in question resides. After providing a path or URL to the assembly, the wizard presents a track bar, which lets you select the minimum level of security permission for the assembly (see Figure 12-19). The different positions of the track bar assign the FullTrust, LocalIntranet, Internet, and Nothing permission sets, as shown in Figure 12-16. The next wizard dialog presents a summary of changes made. After quitting the wizard, it adds a new code group to the policy specified in the first dialog, called Wizard_<N>, in which N stands for the number of times the wizard was asked to trust a different assembly. If you run the wizard on the same assembly multiple times, it modifies the existing wizard-added code group. If you don't like the permission set assigned by the wizard, you can change it to another permission set defined in the policy. In such a case, you should rename the code group to prevent future invocations of the wizard from reverting your changes.

Exporting security policies

Once the system administrator has finished configuring security on a master machine, you need to replicate that configuration. This chapter has already hinted at a number of manual ways to deploy security configuration by manipulating the actual configuration files. The .NET Configuration tool provides an automated way.

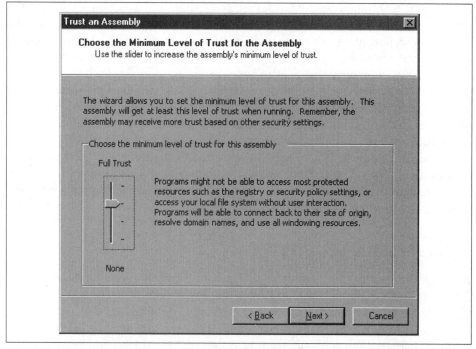

Figure 12-19. Trusting a particular assembly and assigning it an explicit permission set

Select Create Deployment Package from the context menu of the Runtime Security Policy folder to bring up the Deployment Package Wizard dialog. In the dialog, you need to select which policy level you wish to export into an MSI file, and specify the MSI filename. You can now incorporate the MSI file into your application's installation files or send it to other machines. When activated, the exported MSI file overrides the existing policy and installs the exported policy instead.

It's easy to modify permission sets and code groups (by restricting them) to a point at which .NET is completely paralyzed (when the CLR assemblies aren't granted full trust) and even the .NET Configuration tool can't function. As a result, you can't undo your changes. When experimenting with .NET Security, I recommend making a copy of the default policy configuration files so that you can manually restore security and functionality to a known state. You can either copy the files directly or use the .NET Configuration tool to replicate the default configuration files. Another recovery strategy is to generate deployment packages of the policies and use them to restore the old policies.

Security Infrastructure Benefits

The .NET component-oriented security model provides important benefits to both component vendors and consumers. Component vendors can rely on not being lured to carry out malicious operations because every caller up the chain must have the required security permissions. Component consumers can rely on the fact that the malicious components won't cause harm because the evidence-based security mechanism grants permissions only to known, trusted components. This is all achieved in a loosely coupled manner: the security policy is managed outside both the client and server code, and they aren't coupled to each other by the details of the security infrastructure. Changes in security policies don't cascade to components, and system administrators have both a great deal of granular control and the freedom to exercise it because there is nothing in the client or component code pertaining to security. The end user gets a consistent experience, regardless of the operation performed, and no real-time involvement is required to decide whether to trust content coming from a vendor or site. Finally, .NET provides administrators with a centralized place to administer security and deployment.

Programmatic Security

Although for the most part, administrative security configuration is sufficient, .NET provides various programmatic ways you can use to control and enforce security. These powerful techniques can tighten security, optimize performance, handle unknown security policies, and deal with questionable components. In addition, programmatic security can configure security at the component level, unlike administrative security configuration, which is only as granular as a single assembly. All the permission types available administratively have corresponding classes available to you. In fact, the administrative configuration uses these classes indirectly; the security configuration files are just a list of classes to use when providing the configurable permissions.

Although system administrators can grant assemblies permissions by using administrative configuration, there is no programmatic way to grant permission. The reason is clear: if that were possible, a rogue assembly could grant itself permissions and go about causing harm.

Programmatic security can deny security permissions or demand that some permission be granted. You can use the permission classes dynamically during runtime or apply them as class or assembly attributes, indicating which security action to take and when.

The Permission Classes

The permission types listed in Table 12-1 all have corresponding permission classes, such as the FileIOPermission class or the UIPermission class. Most permission classes are defined in the System.Security.Permissions namespace. All permission classes implement a set of interfaces, including IPermission, which is defined as:

```
public interface IPermission : ISecurityEncodable
```

```
{
    IPermission Copy();
    void Demand();
    IPermission Intersect(IPermission target);
    bool IsSubsetOf(IPermission target);
    IPermission Union(IPermission target);
}
```

IPermission is defined in the System.Security namespace. The base interface ISecurityEncodable provides methods to convert the permission to and from XML security elements, used mostly when constructing and persisting custom permissions.

Permission demand

The predominantly useful method of IPermission is Demand(), which triggers a stack walk demanding the permission of all the callers up the stack. For example, here is the code required to trigger a stack walk; it verifies that all the callers up the stack have permission to write to the *C:\Temp* directory:

```
IPermission permission;
string path = @"C:\Temp\";
permission = new FileIOPermission(FileIOPermissionAccess.Write,path);
permission.Demand(); //Trigger stack walk
```

If during the stack walk .NET discovers a caller coming from an assembly without the demanded permission, it aborts the stack walk, and the call to Demand() throws an exception of type SecurityException.

Using Demand() is how the various .NET application frameworks classes require whoever calls them have the required security permissions. For example, the file I/O class FileStream demands permission to perform the appropriate operations (such as opening or creating files) in its constructors. You can take advantage of Demand() as well to tighten security and optimize performance.

For example, demanding permissions is recommended when a component uses a resource on behalf of a client. Consider the StreamWriter class. It demands file I/O permission when it's constructed with a path parameter, but subsequent calls on its methods cause no demands. That may be fine if a component creates a StreamWriter object and never uses it on behalf of external clients, not even indirectly. But in reality, the reason why a component creates a resource is to use it when servicing clients. A malicious untrusted client could wait for another trusted client to successfully create the component and its resources, and then call the component resource-accessing methods. The component can compensate by explicitly demanding the appropriate permissions, as shown in Example 12-1.

Example 12-1. Protecting a resource by demanding access permission

```
using System.IO;
using System.Security;
using System.Security.Permissions;
```

Example 12-1. Protecting a resource by demanding access permission (continued)

```
public class MyClass
{
   public MyClass( )
   {
      //The StreamWriter demands permissions here only:
      m_Stream = new StreamWriter(m_FileName);
   }
   public void Save(string str)
   {
      //Must demand permission here:
      IPermission permission;
      permission = new FileIOPermission(FileIOPermissionAccess.Write,m_FileName);
      permission.Demand( );
      m_Stream.WriteLine(str);
   }
   StreamWriter m_Stream;
   string m_FileName = @"C:\Temp\MyFile.txt";
}
```

Another example is an object that is about to perform a lengthy, intensive calculation and then save it to the disk. Ultimately, if the callers up the stack don't have the required permission, the file I/O classes throw an exception when trying to open the file. Instead of wasting time and resources performing a calculation that can't eventually be saved, the object can first demand the permission and then proceed with the calculation only if it's certain it can persist the results. Example 12-2 demonstrates this technique.

Example 12-2. Optimizing by demanding permission before performing operation

```
class MyClass
{
   public void Calclulate(string resultsFileName)
   {
      IPermission permission;
      permission = new FileIOPermission(FileIOPermissionAccess.Write,
                                                     resultsFileName);
      try
      {
         permission.Demand( );
      }
      catch(SecurityException exception)
      {
         string message = exception.Message;
         message += ": Caller does not have permission to save results";
         MessageBox.Show(message);
         return;
      }
      // Perform calculation here and save results
      DoWork( );
      SaveResults(resultsFileName);
```

Example 12-2. Optimizing by demanding permission before performing operation (continued)

```
   }
   //Helper methods:
   void DoWork( ){...}
   void SaveResults(string resultsFileName){...}
}
```

Note that calling Demand( ) verifies only that the callers up the call chain have the requested security permission. If the object calling Demand( ) itself doesn't have permission, then when it tries to access the resource or perform the operation, the resource (or operation) may still throw a security exception.

Permissions interaction

Some permissions imply other permissions. For example, file I/O access permission to a folder implies access permission to individual files in the same folder. The IPermission interface provides a number of methods that examine how two different permissions relate to each other. The IsSubsetOf( ) method returns true if a specified permission is a subset of the current permission object:

```
   IPermission  permission1;
   IPermission  permission2;
   string path1 = @"C:\temp\";
   string path2 = @"C:\temp\MyFile.txt";

   permission1 = new FileIOPermission(FileIOPermissionAccess.AllAccess,path1);
   permission2 = new FileIOPermission(FileIOPermissionAccess.Write,path2);

   Debug.Assert(permission2.IsSubsetOf(permission1));
```

The Intersect( ) method of IPermission returns a new permission object that is the intersection of the original permission object and the specified permission object, and the Union( ) method returns a new permission object, equivalent to the union of the two. .NET uses these methods when calculating the union of permissions granted by the code groups in a policy and when calculating the interception of the policies.

Stack Walk Modifiers

An object can modify the behavior on the stack walk as it passes though it. Each permission class implements the IStackWalk interface, defined as:

```
   public interface IStackWalk
   {
      void Assert( );
      void Demand( );
      void Deny( );
      void PermitOnly( );
   }
```

Custom Permission

In the rare case of components using a resource type (such as a hardware item) not protected by any of the built-in permissions, you can provide custom permission classes. The custom permission typically grants access to the resource only, instead of the communication mechanism (such as a communication port or the filesystem) that can access other resources. All .NET permission classes derive from the abstract class CodeAccessPermission, which provides the implementation of the stack walk. You can start creating a custom permission by deriving from CodeAccessPermission. Custom permission classes can be used both programmatically and administratively (via custom XML representation). The assembly containing the custom permissions must be strongly named and deployed in the GAC. In addition, it must be granted full trust, and .NET must be aware of it. To register the assembly with .NET, use the .NET Configuration tool. Each policy has a folder called Policy Assemblies (see Figure 12-5). From the folder context menu select Add..., and select the custom permission assembly from the list of assemblies in the GAC. Note that you must deploy the custom permission assembly and register it on every machine that has applications using it.

The Demand( ) method of IStackWalk triggers a stack walk, and the permission classes channel the implementation to that of IPermission.Demand( ). The other three methods, Assert( ), Deny( ), and PermitOnly( ), install a *stack walk modifier*—an instruction modifying the behavior of the walk. At any given stack frame (i.e., the scope of a method), there can be only a single stack walk modifier. Trying to install a second modifier results in an exception of type SecurityException. The stack modifier removes itself automatically once the method returns or when a call to a static reversion method of CodeAccessPermission is called, such as RevertDeny( ), RevertAssert( ), RevertPermitOnly( ), or RevertAll( ). Stack walk modifiers are very useful for optimizing and tightening the current security policy, serving as a programmatic override to the configuration set by the administrator.

Denying and permitting permissions

In general, a component vendor can't assume that her components will always be deployed in a properly configured and secure environment. Sometimes you should be able to override the administrative security policy and programmatically enforce stricter policies. Imagine a case in which global security policy is turned off, too liberal for your sensitive needs, or simply unknown. Other cases may involve dealing with components from questionable origin. Calling IStackWalk.Deny( ) denies the permission represented by the underlying permission class and aborts the stack walk, even if the global security policy configuration grants the calling assembly that permission. Example 12-3 demonstrates denying write permission to all the drives on the machine before invoking a method on a questionable component.

Example 12-3. Explicitly denying permissions

```
public void SomeMethod( )
{
    string[ ] drives = Environment.GetLogicalDrives( );

    IStackWalk stackWalker;
    stackWalker = new FileIOPermission(FileIOPermissionAccess.Write,drives);

    stackWalker.Deny( );

    QuestionableComponent obj = new QuestionableComponent( );
    obj.DoSomething( );

    CodeAccessPermission.RevertDeny( );

    /* Do more work */
}
```

In Example 12-3, SomeMethod( ) constructs a new FileIOPermission object, targeting all the drives on the machine. Using the IStackWalk interface, SomeMethod( ) denies all write access to these drives. Any attempt by the questionable component to write to these drives results in an exception of type SecurityException. The permission denial remains in effect until the method that called Deny( ) returns. If you want to revert the denial in the scope of the calling method (for example, to do some file I/O yourself), you need to call the static method RevertDeny( ) of the CodeAccessPermission class, as shown in Example 12-3.

Sometimes it's simpler to just list what you permit, using the PermitOnly( ) method of IStackWalk. When a stack walk reaches a method that called PermitOnly( ), only that permission is presented, even if other permissions are granted administratively. Example 12-4 demonstrates permitting access only to the *C:\temp* directory, but nothing else:

Example 12-4. Permitting a particular permission only

```
public void SomeMethod( )
{
    string path = @"C:\temp";
    IStackWalk stackWalker;
    stackWalker = new FileIOPermission(FileIOPermissionAccess.AllAccess,path);

    stackWalker.PermitOnly( );

    QuestionableComponent obj = new QuestionableComponent( );
    obj.DoSomething( );

    CodeAccessPermission.RevertPermitOnly( );

    /* Do more work */
}
```

Similar to Deny( ), PermitOnly( ) remains in effect until the calling method returns or until the method calls the static method RevertPermitOnly( ) of CodeAccessPermission.

 Another example that calls a questionable component is when using a delegate to fire an event at unknown subscribers. You can explicitly deny or permit only some permissions, which limits the risk of calling a delegate that may have lured a more trusted component into calling it on a different call chain.

Asserting permissions

A stack walk to verify security permissions is a powerful and elegant idea, but it doesn't come without a cost. A stack walk is expensive, and in intense calling patterns or when the call stack is long, it results in a performance and throughput penalty. Consider the following code:

```
void SaveString(string str,string fileName)
{
    StreamWriter stream = new StreamWriter(fileName,true);//append text
    stream.WriteLine(str);
    stream.Close( );
}

string[ ] array = new string[9];

array[0] = "Every";
array[1] = "string";
array[2] = "in";
array[3] = "this";
array[4] = "array";
array[5] = "causes";
array[6] = "a";
array[7] = "stack";
array[8] = "walk";

string fileName = @"C:\Temp\MyStrings.txt";

foreach(string str in array)
{
    SaveString(str,fileName);
}
```

Every time the code writes to the file, it triggers a walk all the way up the stack. Except for the first stack walk, all the subsequent stack walks are redundant because the call chain doesn't change between loop iterations. To efficiently handle such cases, use the Assert( ) method of IStackWalk. When asserting security permission, stack walks stop in the current stack frame and don't proceed up:

```
string fileName = @"C:\Temp\MyStrings.txt";
```

```
IStackWalk stackWalker;
stackWalker = new FileIOPermission(FileIOPermissionAccess.Write,fileName);
stackWalker.Assert( );

foreach(string str in array)
{
    SaveString(str,fileName);
}
CodeAccessPermission.RevertAssert( );
```

The assertion remains in effect until the method returns or until the static method RevertAssert( ) is called. Note that you can assert a single permission only in the same method scope (unless RevertAssert( ) or RevertAll( ) is called).

Because the stack walk stops at the level that asserts the permission, it's quite possible callers up the call chain that initiated the call don't have the permission to do the operations carried out by the downstream objects. It looks as if the ability to assert permission is a technique that circumvents enforcing .NET code access security policy; a malicious assembly can assert whatever security permission it wants and start roaming on the machine. Fortunately, there are two safeguards. If the asserting assembly isn't granted the permission it tries to assert, the assertion has no effect. When code down the call chain demands the asserted permission, it triggers a stack walk. When the stack walk reaches the assertion stack walk modifier, it also verifies that the asserting assembly has that permission. If it doesn't, the stack walk is aborted, and the call demanding permission throws a security exception. The second safeguard is that not all code can assert permissions. Only code granted the security permission, with the right to assert permissions, can call Assert( ). If the permission to assert isn't granted, a security exception is thrown on the assertion attempt. .NET doesn't use a stack walk to verify that assert permission is granted. Instead, it verifies that the asserting assembly has that permission at link time, as described later on in this chapter.

 Only the most trustworthy code should be granted the right to assert because of the level of risk involved in not completing stack walks.

Another imported point regarding permission assertion is that it doesn't always guarantee stopping the stack walk because the asserted permission can be only a subset of the permission demand that triggered the stack walk. In that case, the assert instruction only stops the stack walk for its particular type and value. The stack walk may proceed up the call stack looking for other permission grants.

Asserting unmanaged code permission

A potential security loophole opens when you call outside the managed code environment using the interoperation (*interop*) layer. The interop layer allows managed code to invoke calls on COM components or simply call DLL entry points using the platform-specific invocation mechanism (*P-Invoke*). Unmanaged code is completely exempt from .NET code access policies because it executes directly against the operating system. Using interop, a malicious managed component can have the unmanaged code do its dirty deed on its behalf. Naturally, only the most trustworthy assemblies should be granted unmanaged code permission. Accordingly, the managed side of the interop layer demands that all code accessing it have the Security permission with the right to access unmanaged code.

The problem is, all .NET framework classes that rely on the underlying services of the operating system require the interop layer. Consider the case of the FileStream class. To call it, code requires only file I/O permission, which is a more liberal and less powerful permission than the unmanaged code access permission. However because the FileStream class uses P-Invoke to call the Win32 API on behalf of the caller, any attempt to use the FileStream class triggers a demand for unmanaged code permission by the interop layer. To shield the caller, the FileStream class asserts the unmanaged code access permission, so it doesn't propagate the demand for unmanaged code access permission to its clients. Instead, it demands only file I/O permission. Because it's on the local machine zone and is signed with the Microsoft public key, the FileStream class is granted (by default) the FullTrust permission set, and the assertion for unmanaged code succeeds.

The next question is how should you handle your own interop calls to the unmanaged world? For example, consider the following code that uses P-Invoke to import the definition of the MessageBoxA Win32 API call, which displays a message box to the user:

```
using System.Runtime.InteropServices;

public class MsgBox
{
    [DllImport("user32",EntryPoint="MessageBoxA")]
    public static extern int Show(IntPtr handle,string text,string caption,
                                                               int msgType);
}
//Client side:
MsgBox.Show(IntPtr.Zero,"Called using P-Invoke","Some Caption",0);
```

Every time the Show( ) method is called, it triggers a demand for unmanaged code access. This has the detrimental effect of both a performance penalty and functionality impasse if the caller doesn't have generic unmanaged code permission but is trusted to call the specific imported unmanaged call. There are a few solutions. The first is to mimic the behavior of the .NET framework classes and assert the unmanaged code permission, using a managed wrapping method around the imported unmanaged call. Example 12-5 demonstrates this technique.

Example 12-5. Asserting unmanaged code access permission around an interop method

```
using System.Runtime.InteropServices;
using System.Security;
using System.Security.Permissions;

public class MsgBox
{
   [DllImport("user32",EntryPoint="MessageBoxA")]
   private static extern int Show(int hWnd,string text,string caption,
                                                      uint msgType);
   public static void Show(string text,string caption)
   {
      IStackWalk stackWalker;
      stackWalker = new SecurityPermission(SecurityPermissionFlag.UnmanagedCode);
      stackWalker.Assert();

      Show(0,text,caption,0);
   }
}
//Client side:
MsgBox.Show("Called using P-Invoke","Some Caption");
```

To assert the unmanaged code access permission, you assert the SecurityPermission constructed with the SecurityPermissionFlag.UnmanagedCode enum value. You can even take it one step further and demand instead UI permission, as shown in Example 12-6.

Example 12-6. Asserting unmanaged code permission and demanding UI permission

```
public static void Show(string text,string caption)
{
   IStackWalk stackWalker;
   stackWalker = new SecurityPermission(SecurityPermissionFlag.UnmanagedCode);
   stackWalker.Assert();

   IPermission permission;
   permission = new UIPermission(UIPermissionWindow.SafeSubWindows);
   permission.Demand();
   Show(0,text,caption,0);
}
```

The second solution is to suppress the demand for unmanaged code by the interop layer altogether. .NET provides a special attribute called the SuppressUnmanaged-CodeSecurityAttribute, defined in the System.Security namespace:

```
[AttributeUsage(AttributeTargets.Class | AttributeTargets.Method |
                                 AttributeTargets.Interface)]
public sealed class SuppressUnmanagedCodeSecurityAttribute : Attribute
{
    public SuppressUnmanagedCodeSecurityAttribute();
}
```

You can apply this attribute only to an interop method, to a class that contains interop methods, or to an interface that the class implements. The attribute is ignored in all other cases. You can apply the attribute SuppressUnmanaged-CodeSecurityAttribute to an interop method, like this:

```
[SuppressUnmanagedCodeSecurity]
[DllImport("user32",EntryPoint="MessageBoxA")]
public static extern int Show(int hWnd,string text,string caption,uint msgType);
```

The interop layer doesn't demand the unmanaged code permission when the method is invoked. When the attribute is applied at the scope of a class, it suppresses the unmanaged code demand for all interop methods defined in that class. The only safeguard is that at runtime, during the link phase to the interop method, .NET will demand unmanaged code permission from the immediate caller up the stack (you will see how to demand permission at link time later on). This allows callers up the chain call without unmanaged code permission to call other clients with that permission and actually invoke the interop method. Needless to say, you should use SuppressUnmanagedCodeSecurityAttribute with extreme caution and only when you know the call chain to the interop method is secure.

The third solution is to use security permission attributes, discussed next.

 In general, never assert permission without demanding a different permission instead. Using assertion, your code should convert a generic demand to a more specific demand, as shown in Example 12-6.

Permission Attributes

All security permission classes have equivalent attribute classes. You can apply the security attributes instead of programmatically creating a permission class and demanding a stack walk or installing a stack walk modifier. Using the permission attributes is called *declarative security*. All the attributes are used in a similar manner: their constructor accepts an enum of type SecurityAction, indicating what security action to take:

```
public enum SecurityAction
{
    Assert,
    Demand,
    Deny,
    InheritanceDemand,
    LinkDemand,
    PermitOnly,
    RequestMinimum,
    RequestOptional,
    RequestRefuse
}
```

In addition, you need to set public properties of the attribute, instructing .NET what permission value to take upon the security action. Example 12-7 is similar to Example 12-2, except it uses declarative security to demand file I/O permission to a specific predetermined file before proceeding to perform the calculation.

Example 12-7. Declaratively demanding permission before performing operation

```
class MyClass
{
   [FileIOPermission(SecurityAction.Demand,Write = @"C:\Results.txt")]
   public void Calclulate( )
   {
      // Perform calculation here and save results
      DoWork( );
      SaveResults( );
   }
   //Helper methods:
   void DoWork( ){...}
   void SaveResults( ){...}
}
```

In Example 12-7, .NET demands file I/O permission in every call to the method. If you need to repeat the same security actions in all the methods of a class, you can apply the security attribute on the class itself, instead of on every method:

```
[FileIOPermission(SecurityAction.Demand,Write = @"C:\Results.txt")]
class MyClass
{...}
```

The main difference between declarative security and programmatic security is evident when you compare Example 12-7 to Example 12-2. With programmatic security, the value of the permission (such as a filename, call time, parameter values, etc.) can be decided at runtime. With declarative security, the value is static and has to be known at compile-time. In general, whenever the permission value is known at compile-time, you should use declarative instead of programmatic security. Example 12-8 is functionally identical to Example 12-6 except it's much simpler because it uses declarative instead of programmatic security.

Example 12-8. Declaratively asserting unmanaged code permission and demanding UI permission

```
[SecurityPermission(SecurityAction.Assert,UnmanagedCode = true)]
[UIPermission(SecurityAction.Demand,
                              Window = UIPermissionWindow. SafeSubWindows)]
public static void Show(string text,string caption)
{
   Show(0,text,caption,0);
}
```

You can also apply declarative security directly on the interop method, instead of the wrapper method.

When you apply a security attribute at the scope of a class, it affects all members of the class.

Link-time demand

Declarative security offers capabilities not available with programmatic security demands. You can request that the permission be demanded at link time during JIT compilation, instead of at call time. Link-time demand is specified using the SecurityAction.LinkDemand value for the security action, for example:

```
[UIPermission(SecurityAction.LinkDemand,
              Window = UIPermissionWindow.SafeTopLevelWindows)]
public void DisplaySomeUI( )
{ }
```

When the security action is set to the SecurityAction.LinkDemand value, .NET demands permission only of the caller immediately up the call chain linking to the method. Subsequent calls to the method aren't verified to have the permission. If the client doesn't have the demanded permission, a security exception is raised as early as possible, usually when the client first tries to link to the method instead of at a later point in time. You can still demand the security permission on every call using programmatic security. If you don't demand permission on every call, you eliminate the stack walk penalty. The downside is that malicious clients can use a middleman component with permissions to link against the demanding component and then call the middleman, without being subjected to stack walk. Use SecurityAction. LinkDemand without per-call demand only if you know that the call chain leading to the object will remain static and is secure.

Link-time demand is especially useful in conjunction with the attribute StrongNameIdentityPermissionAttribute, defined as:

```
[AttributeUsage(AttributeTargets.Assembly | AttributeTargets.Class
                | AttributeTargets.Struct | AttributeTargets.Constructor |
                                           AttributeTargets.Method)]
public sealed class StrongNameIdentityPermissionAttribute :
                                           CodeAccessSecurityAttribute
{
   public StrongNameIdentityPermissionAttribute(SecurityAction action);
   public string Name{get;set;}
   public string PublicKey{get;set;}
   public string Version { get; set; }
}
```

The attribute lets you insist that the assembly linking into your code is signed with a specified public key:

```
[StrongNameIdentityPermission(SecurityAction.LinkDemand,PublicKey = "0024480...090")]
public void MyMethod( )
{...}
```

You can apply the attribute `StrongNameIdentityPermissionAttribute` at any scope from assembly down to methods. You can even insist on a particular version number and assembly name. The canonical use of the `StrongNameIdentityPermission-Attribute` is when you are forced to use a public class or a public method because of design considerations, so that you can call it from other assemblies you provide. Logically, however, these public types or methods are for your application's internal private use. In that case, all you need to do is demand your own public key so that no other party can use these public types or methods.

To use `StrongNameIdentityPermissionAttribute`, you need a string representing a public key. You can use the .NET Configuration tool to extract the public key out of an assembly by constructing a code group that uses a strong name evidence (see Figure 12-13), and simply copying and pasting the value from the "Public Key:" text box. Another solution is to use the *sn.exe* command-line utility. The *-e* switch extracts the public key from an assembly, and the *-tp* switch converts the key to a string representation.

Identity Permissions

The `StrongNameIdentityPermission` is a special type of permission called identity permissions. *Identity permissions* allow code to demand that its callers have a particular identity. The `PublisherIdentityPermission` demands that the caller is signed with a particular certificate. The `UrlIdentityPermission`, `SiteIdentityPermission`, and `Zone-IdentityPermission` provide for demanding that the calling assemblies originate from a specific URL, site, or zone, respectively. You can demand (or assert) identity permissions programmatically just like any other permission, or you can apply them declaratively using a matching set of attribute classes. However, you can't use administrative configuration to grant or manage identity permissions.

Inheritance demand

A malicious party can derive from a class, override demanding methods, or use protected members and helper methods for its own purposes. Component library vendors can use declarative security to prevent a malicious party from abusing their components via inheritance. The component vendor can apply the required security permissions using the `SecurityAction.InheritanceDemand` value, indicating to .NET to demand the permission of the subclasses. For example, here's how the `BaseClass` class can demand that its subclasses be granted unrestricted access to the filesystem:

```
[FileIOPermission(SecurityAction.InheritanceDemand,Unrestricted=true)]
public class BaseClass
{}
```

When inheritance demand is applied to a method, it verifies that the overriding sub-class has the requested permission. Inheritance demand takes place during load time, and no stack walks are involved.

 Neither programmatic nor declarative security can protect against untrusted code accessing public fields because no stackcalls are involved. Never provide public fields, and always use properties.

Permission Set Classes

Instead of constructing individual permissions and demanding them or using a permission to modify a stack walk, you can programmatically construct permission sets. In fact, the main reason for using a permission set is to install a stack modifier that combines multiple permissions (remember that you can install only a single stack walk modifier). Creating a permission set programmatically is similar to the way system administrators compose new permission sets using the .NET Configuration tool. You create individual permission objects and aggregate them in a permission set object. Using a permission set is an easy way to install a stack walk modifier that denies, permits, or asserts multiple permissions. Example 12-9 demonstrates composing a permission set with file I/O and UI permissions and denying it before accessing a questionable component.

Example 12-9. Creating and denying a permission set

```
public void SomeMethod( )
{
   PermissionSet permissionSet;
   //Create an empty permission set
   permissionSet = new PermissionSet(PermissionState.None);

   IPermission  filePermision;
   string path = @"C:\";
   filePermision = new FileIOPermission(FileIOPermissionAccess.AllAccess,path);

   permissionSet.AddPermission(filePermision);

   IPermission UIPerm;
   UIPerm = new UIPermission(PermissionState.Unrestricted);

   permissionSet.AddPermission(UIPerm);

   IStackWalk stackWalker = permissionSet;

   stackWalker.Deny( );

   QuestionableComponent obj = new QuestionableComponent( );
   obj.DoSomething( );
```

Example 12-9. Creating and denying a permission set (continued)

```
    CodeAccessPermission.RevertDeny( );
}
```

You can explicitly revert a stalk walk modifier set by a permission set using the static methods of CodeAccessPermission or wait for the method to return, as with individual permission modifier.

Permission Set Attributes

You can declaratively instruct .NET to take a security action, such as demand or assert a permission set, using the PermissionSetAttribute class. Unlike the programmatic composition of a permission set, when you use PermissionSetAttribute, you are practically restricted to use only the predefined named permission sets, such as the following:

```
    [PermissionSet(SecurityAction.Demand,Name = "LocalIntranet")]
    public void SomeMethod( )
    { }
```

The compiler is aware of the predefined, named permission sets and refuses to use any other name presently defined in the .NET Configuration tool. In addition, the compiler doesn't recognize the Everything permission set (probably because it's specific to the .NET Configuration tool).

If you want to declaratively use a custom permission set, you need to provide the attribute with an XML representation of that set. Please see the MSDN library for additional information.

Assembly-Wide Permissions

Instead of type-based or even method-based security configuration, you can declaratively apply security permission attributes to an entire assembly, affecting every component in the assembly. All the permission attributes can be applied at the assembly level as well, although the semantics of the security action taken is different from those of a type or method. In fact, you can't apply the values of the SecurityAction enum shown so far on an assembly. The SecurityAction enum provides three specific values, which can be applied only at the assembly scope:

```
    public enum SecurityAction
    {
        //Type and Method values,then:
        RequestMinimum,
        RequestOptional,
        RequestRefuse
    }
```

You can use these security action values with an individual permission, such as a request for full access to the *C:\Temp* directory:

```
[assembly : FileIOPermission(SecurityAction.RequestMinimum,All= @"C:\temp")]
```
or even a named permission set:
```
[assembly : PermissionSet(SecurityAction.RequestMinimum,Name = "Internet")]
```
You can apply an assembly permission attribute multiple times:
```
[assembly : FileIOPermission(SecurityAction.RequestMinimum,All= @"C:\temp")]
[assembly : FileIOPermission(SecurityAction.RequestMinimum,All= @"D:\temp")]
```
The SecurityAction.RequestMinimum value indicates to .NET that this assembly requires the permission or permission set to operate. Without it, there is no point in loading the assembly or trying to create the types in it. The SecurityAction. RequestRefuse value is useful when all the types in an assembly require denying permission or a permission set or when you explicitly want to reduce the permissions granted to the assembly. When .NET computes the permissions granted to the assembly, .NET subtracts the refused permissions from the administratively-granted permissions. The SecurityAction.RequestOptional value indicates to .NET what permissions this assembly wants in addition to the minimum permissions requested. Optional permissions also indicate that the assembly can operate without them and that no other permissions are required. Optional and refused permissions can prevent granting the assembly permissions it doesn't require. Although not a technical wrongdoing, it's always better to refuse any permission an assembly is granted but doesn't require. Doing so reduces the chance of abuse by malicious clients. The final permissions granted must therefore take into account the assembly attributes and the configured policy. If no assembly attributes are present, .NET grants the assembly the administratively configured permissions according to the security policies. However, if assembly security attributes are present, .NET follows the following algorithm: First, .NET retrieves the permissions granted by the .NET administrators. It then verifies that the requested minimum set of permissions is a subset of the granted policies. If so, .NET computes the union of the minimum and optional permissions, and intersects the result with the administratively granted permissions. Finally, .NET subtracts the refused permissions from the intersection. Figure 12-20 summarizes this algorithm by using formal notations.

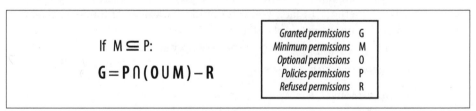

Figure 12-20. Computing assembly permission when assemblies permission attributes are provided

Principal-Based Security

As stated at the beginning of the chapter, .NET component-based security isn't a cure-all. There is still a need to verify that the user (or the account) under which the code executes has permission to perform the operation. In .NET, the user is referred to as the *security principal*. It's impractical to program access permission for each individual user (although it's technically possible); instead, is it better to grant permissions to roles users play in the application domain. A *role* is a symbolic category of users who share the same security privileges. When you assign a role to an application resource, you are granting access to that resource to whomever is a member of that role. Discovering the roles users play in your business domain is part of your application-requirement analysis and design, as is factoring components and interfaces. By interacting with roles instead of particular users, you isolate your application from changes made in real life such as adding new users, moving existing users between positions, promoting users, or users leaving their jobs. .NET allows you to apply role-based security both declaratively and programmatically, if the need to verify role membership is based on a dynamic decision.

Declarative Role-Based Security

You apply declarative role-based security using the attribute Principal-PermissionAttribute, defined in the System.Security.Permissions namespace:

```
[AttributeUsage(AttributeTargets.Class | AttributeTargets.Method)]
[Serializable]
public sealed class PrincipalPermissionAttribute : CodeAccessSecurityAttribute
{
    public PrincipalPermissionAttribute(SecurityAction action);
    public bool Authenticated{get;set; }
    public string Name{get;set;}
    public string Role{get;set;}
}
```

You apply the attribute to either classes or methods, specifying the security action to take and the role name. By default, a security role in .NET is a Windows user group. The examples in this chapter all use Windows user groups, but .NET allows you to provide your own custom role definition. Appendix B demonstrates implementing and setting such a custom mechanism. When you specify a Windows user group as a role, you must prefix it with the domain name or the local machine name (if the role is defined locally only). For example, the following declaration grants access to MyMethod( ) only for code running under the identity of a user belonging to the Managers user group:

```
public class MyClass

{
    [PrincipalPermission(SecurityAction.Demand,Role=@"<domain>\Managers")]
    public void MyMethod( )
```

```
    {...}
}
```

If the user isn't a member of that role, .NET throws an exception of type SecurityException. If multiple roles are allowed to access the method, you can apply the attribute multiple times:

```
[PrincipalPermission(SecurityAction.Demand,Role=@"<domain>\Managers")]
[PrincipalPermission(SecurityAction.Demand,Role=@"<domain>\Customers")]
public void MyMethod( )
{...}
```

When multiple roles are applied to a method, the user is granted access if it's a member of at least one role. If you want to verify that the user is a member of both roles, you need to use programmatic role membership checks, discussed later.

You can apply the PrincipalPermission attribute at the class level as well:

```
[PrincipalPermission(SecurityAction.Demand,Role=@"<domain>\Managers")]
public class MyClass

{
    public void MyMethod( )
    {...}
}
```

When the attribute is applied at the class level, only clients belonging to the specified role can create an object of this type. Note that this is the only way to enforce role-based security on constructors because you can't apply the PrincipalPermission attribute on class constructors.

By setting the Name property of the PrincipalPermission attribute, you can even insist on granting access to a particular user. This practice is unadvisable, however, because it's wrong to hardcode usernames:

```
[PrincipalPermission(SecurityAction.Demand,Name = "Bill")]
```

You can also insist on a particular user and that the user be a member of a role:

```
[PrincipalPermission(SecurityAction.Demand,Name="Bill",Role=@"<domain>\Managers")]
```

Enabling role-based security

Every app domain has a flag instructing .NET as to which principal policy to use. The *principal policy* is the authorization mechanism that looks up role membership. You set the principal policy by calling the SetPrincipalPolicy( ) method of the AppDomain class:

```
public virtual void SetPrincipalPolicy(PrincipalPolicy policy);
```

The available policies are represented by the values of the PrincipalPolicy enum:

```
public enum PrincipalPolicy
{
```

```
    NoPrincipal,
    UnauthenticatedPrincipal,
    WindowsPrincipal
}
```

By default, every .NET application (be it Windows Forms or ASP.NET) has the `PrincipalPolicy.UnauthenticatedPrincipal` for security policy. If you simply apply the `PrincipalPermission` attribute (or use programmatic role membership verification), all calls will be denied access even if the caller is a member of the specified role.

To use role-based security in ASP.NET, the caller must be authenticated. With authenticated callers in ASP.NET, there is no need to call `SetPrincipalPolicy()`, although it doesn't cause harm.

To enable role-based security in a Windows application, you must set the role-based security policy to `PrincipalPolicy.WindowsPrincipal`. You need to use this value even if you install custom role-based security mechanism, as in Appendix B. You need to set the principal policy in every app domain that uses role-based security. Typically, you place that code in the `Main()` method of an EXE assembly:

```
static public void Main()

{

    AppDomain currentDomain = AppDomain.CurrentDomain;
    currentDomain.SetPrincipalPolicy(PrincipalPolicy.WindowsPrincipal);
}
```

If you create new app domains programmatically, you also need to set the principal policies in them.

 When you experiment with role-based security, you often add users to or remove users from user groups. Because user-group information is cached by Windows at log-in time, the changes you make aren't reflected until the next log-in.

Role-based security and authentication

Role-based security controls user *authorization*—which users are allowed to access. Authorization is meaningless without *authentication*—verifying that the user is indeed who the user claims to be. In a Windows application, users have to log in, and are therefore authenticated. Internet applications (such as ASP.NET applications) sometimes grant anonymous access to users. It's therefore prudent to verify that users are authenticated when applying role-based authorization, in case your components are used in an unauthenticating environment. You can demand authentication by setting the `Authenticated` property of the `PrincipalPermission` attribute to true:

```
[PrincipalPermission(SecurityAction.Demand, Authenticated = true,
                                        Role=@"<domain>\Managers")]
```

Link-time role-based security

When you use the `PrincipalPermission` attribute and set the security action to `SecurityAction.Demand`, every time the code it protects is invoked, .NET verifies role membership of the client in the specified role. This may be an unnecessary performance penalty if your component is always being used by the same user. In intense calling patterns, you can mitigate the penalty by setting the security action to `SecurityAction.LinkDemand`:

```
[PrincipalPermission(SecurityAction.LinkDemand,Role=@"<domain>\Managers")]
```

Here the role membership verification takes place only once, during JIT compilation.

 Declarative role-based security hardcodes the role name. If your application is deployed in international markets and you use Windows groups as roles, it's likely the role names will not match. In that case, you have to use programmatic role verification and have some logic that maps the logical design-time roles to the local roles.

Programmatic Role-Based Security

As handy as declarative role-based security is, sometimes you need to programmatically verify role membership. Usually, you need to do that when the decision as to whether to grant access depends both on role membership and on some other values known only during call time. Another case in which programmatic role membership verification is needed is when dealing with localized user groups.

Principal and identity

A principal object in .NET is an object that implements the `IPrincipal` interface, defined in the `System.Security.Principal` namespace as:

```
public interface IPrincipal
{
   IIdentity Identity{get;}
   bool IsInRole(string role);
}
```

The `IsInRole( )` method simply returns `true` if the identity associated with this principal is a member of the specified role, and `false` otherwise. The `Identity` read-only property provides access to read-only information about the identity, in the form of an object implementing the `IIdentity` interface:

```
public interface IIdentity
{
   string AuthenticationType{get;}
   bool IsAuthenticated{get;}
   string Name{get;}
}
```

Every .NET thread has a principal object associated with it, obtained via the CurrentPrincipal static property:

```
public static IPrincipal CurrentPrincipal{get;set;}
```

For example, here is how to obtain the username from the principal object:

```
void GreetUser()
{
   IPrincipal principal = Thread.CurrentPrincipal;
   IIdentity  identity  = principal.Identity;
   string greeting = "Hello " + identity.Name;
   MessageBox.Show(greeting);
}
```

Verifying role membership

Imagine a banking application that lets users transfer sums of money between two specified accounts. Only customers and tellers are allowed to call this method, with the following business rule: if the amount transferred is greater than $5,000, only tellers are allowed to do the transfer. Declarative role-based security can verify that the caller is a teller or a customer, but it can't enforce the additional business rule. For that, you need to use the IsInRole() method of IPrincipal, as shown in Example 12-10.

Example 12-10. Programmatic role membership verification

```
using System.Security.Permissions;
using System.Security.Principal;
using System.Threading;

public class Bank
{
   [PrincipalPermission(SecurityAction.Demand,Role =@"<domain>\Customers")]
   [PrincipalPermission(SecurityAction.Demand,Role =@"<domain>\Tellers")]
   public void TransferMoney(double sum,long accountSrc,long accountDest)
   {
      IPrincipal  principal;
      principal = Thread.CurrentPrincipal;
      Debug.Assert(principal.Identity.IsAuthenticated);

      bool callerInRole = false;
      callerInRole = principal.IsInRole(@"<domain>\Customers");
      if(callerInRole)//The caller is a customer
      {
         if(sum > 5000)
         {
          string msg = "Caller does not have sufficient authority to" +
                     "transfer this sum";
            throw(new UnauthorizedAccessException(msg));
         }
      }
}
```

Example 12-10. Programmatic role membership verification (continued)

```
        DoTransfer(sum,accountSrc,accountDest);
    }
    //Helper method
    void DoTransfer(double sum,long accountSrc,long accountDest){...}
}
```

Example 12-10 demonstrates a number of other points. First, even though it uses programmatic role membership verification with the value of the sum argument, it still uses declarative role-based security as the first line of defense, allowing access only to users who are members of the Customers or Tellers roles. Second, you can programmatically assert that the caller is authenticated using the IsAuthenticated property of IIdentity. Finally, in case of unauthorized access, you can throw an exception of type UnauthorizedAccessException.

Windows Security Principal

In a Windows application, the principal object associated with a .NET thread is of type WindowsPrincipal:

```
    public class WindowsPrincipal : IPrincipal
    {
        public WindowsPrincipal(WindowsIdentity ntIdentity);

        //IPrincipal implementation
        public IIdentity Identity{virtual get;}
        public virtual bool IsInRole(string role);
        //Additional methods:
        public virtual bool IsInRole(int rid);
        public virtual bool IsInRole(WindowsBuiltInRole role);
    }
```

WindowsPrincipal provides two additional IsInRole( ) methods that are intended to ease the task of localizing roles—i.e., Windows user groups. You can provide IsInRole( ) with an enum of type WindowsBuiltInRole, matching the built-in NT roles, such as WindowsBuiltInRole.Administrator or WindowsBuiltInRole.User. The other version of IsInRole( ) accepts an integer indexing specific roles. For example, a role index of 512 maps to the Administrators group. The MSDN Library contains a list of both the predefined indexes and ways to provide your own aliases and indexes to user groups. The default identity associated with the WindowsPrincipal object is an object of type WindowsIdentity, which provides a number of methods beyond the implementation of IIdentity, including helper methods for verifying major user group membership and impersonation. When asked to verify role membership, WindowsPrincipal retrieves the username from its identity object and looks it up in the Windows (or domain) user group repository.

Custom Security Principal

There is a complete disconnect between declarative role-based security and the actual principal object type. When the PrincipalPermission attribute is asked to verify role membership, it simply gets hold of its thread's current principal object in the form of IPrincipal, and calls its IsInRole( ) method. The disconnect is true of programmatic role membership verification that uses only IPrincipal as shown in Example 12-10. The separation of the IPrincipal interface from its implementation is the key to providing other role-based security mechanism besides Windows user groups. All you need to do is provide an object that implements IPrincipal, and set your current thread's CurrentPrincipal property to that object. In addition, code that installs a custom security principal must be granted security permission with the Principal Control right.

Example 12-11 demonstrates installing a custom role-based security mechanism using a trivial custom principal.

Example 12-11. Implementing and installing a custom principal

```
public class MyCustomPrincipal : IPrincipal
{
   IIdentity m_OldIdentity;
   public MyCustomPrincipal( )
   {
      m_OldIdentity = Thread.CurrentPrincipal.Identity;
   }
   public IIdentity Identity
   {
      get {return m_OldIdentity;}
   }
   public bool IsInRole(string role)
   {
      switch(role)
      {
         case "Authors":
         {
            if (m_OldIdentity.Name == "Juval")
               return true;
            else
               return false;
         }
         default:
            return false;
      }
   }
}
//Installing the custom principal:
ICustomPrincipal customPrincipal = new MyCustomPrincipal( );
Thread.CurrentPrincipal = customPrincipal;
```

In the example, the custom principal caches the current identity because it doesn't want to provide a new identity. The custom principal returns `true` from `IsInRole()` only if the role specified is "Authors" and the username is "Juval". Of course, a real-life custom principal does some actual role membership verification, such as accessing a dedicated table in a database. Appendix B contains a fully implemented custom principal used in the context of an ASP.NET application. That custom principal uses a SQL table for storing roles and users, and you can use that solution in any other type of .NET application. But fundamentally, the custom principal in Appendix B isn't much different from the custom principal of Example 12-11.

Note that you have to repeat installing the custom security principal in every thread in your application that uses role-based security (either declaratively or programmatically) because by default, .NET attaches the Windows Principal to every new thread. You can provide .NET with a new default principal object to attach to new threads. To provide a new default principal, use the static method `SetThreadPrincipal()` of the `AppDomain` class, for example:

```
ICustomPrincipal customPrincipal = new MyCustomPrincipal();
AppDomain currentDomain = AppDomain.CurrentDomain;
currentDomain.SetThreadPrincipal(customPrincipal);
```

Note that the new default is app domain-wide, and that you can't call `SetThreadPrincipal()` more than once per app domain. If you call it more than once, .NET throws an exception of type `PolicyException`.

> Some applications can't use Windows user groups as roles and have no need for an elaborate custom principal. For such simple cases, you can use the `GenericPrincipal` class. Its constructor accepts the identity object to use and a collection of roles the identity is a member of. `GenericPrincipal`'s implementation of `IsInRole()` simply scans that collection looking for a match. By default, .NET uses the `GenericPrincipal` class for ASP.NET applications.

Addressing Other Security Vulnerabilities

This final section discusses a number of security issues, which encompass most of the security infrastructure discussed in this chapter. For the most part, you only need to be aware of them, but in some cases, you need to take specific actions to ensure proper secure execution of your application. This chapter ends with a rundown of these issues.

Link-Time Demand and Reflection

When you demand a security permission at link time using the `SecurityAction.LinkDemand` value for the security action, the demand applies only to early-bound code—that is, code that uses the compile-time (or actually JIT compilation time) linker. Malicious code can use reflection with late-binding invocation to avoid the link-time demand. To close this potential breach, when a method is invoked using late binding the .NET reflection libraries reflect the method, looking for a security permission attribute with link-time demand. If such attributes are found, the reflection layer programmatically demands these permissions, triggering a stack walk that verifies if a caller doesn't circumvent the demand for the permissions. As a result, code that works with a certain call chain that uses early binding may not work only when one of the callers uses late binding. This is because the reflection libraries convert a link-time demand (that affects only the immediate caller) to a full stack walk that affects all callers. This behavior is yet another reason to avoid late-binding invocation.

Link-Time Demand and Inheritance

Consider a subclass that uses a link-time security demand while overriding a base-class method. The subclass demand is security-tight only if the base class demands the same permission at link time. This is because a malicious client can cast the subclass to the base class and call the base class method, bypassing the demand at the subclass level. If you develop a class hierarchy that requires security, it's best to define an interface the class hierarchy implements and demand link-time permission checks at the interface level. This provides the demand for every level in the class hierarchy.

Strongly Named Assemblies and Full Trust

A strongly named assembly can easily be shared by multiple applications whose components come from a potentially untrusted origin. Imagine a component library vendor that produces an assembly and installs it in the GAC. That assembly is now available for use by any unknown, malicious client. To prevent even the potential for abuse, by default a .NET strongly named assembly can be used only by client assemblies granted the FullTrust permission set. This ensures that assemblies not properly secured can't be used by partially trusted clients. .NET enforces this default by placing a link-time demand for the FullTrust permission set on every public or protected method on every public class in the assembly. This is done automatically by the JIT compiler when it detects the assembly has a strong name. For example, if a strong name is specified, the JIT compiler converts this method definition:

```
public void SomeMethod( )
{ }
```

to this:

```
[PermissionSet(SecurityAction.LinkDemand,Name = "FullTrust")]
public void SomeMethod( )
{ }
```

A partially trusted assembly can still implement interfaces defined in a strongly named assembly because interfaces have no implementation to protect and the compiler doesn't change their definition.

In some cases, this extra precaution is a liability, especially if you intend for your assembly to be used by semitrusted assemblies. For example, if the client assembly is coming from the local intranet or from mobile devices, it can't access your code. If you want to allow partially trusted callers to your assembly, you can apply the attribute AllowPartiallyTrustedCallersAttribute to the assembly:

```
[assembly:AllowPartiallyTrustedCallers]
```

This instructs the compiler not to add the link-time demand for full trust to the public entry points.

Unsafe Code

C# (and potentially future .NET languages) allows you to use unsafe code to directly manipulate memory using pointers. Such C# code is called *unsafe* because it lets go of most of the safety of .NET memory management, such as bound-safe arrays. However, unsafe code is still managed code because it runs in the CLR, and it manipulates the managed heap. This can present a security breach because objects from multiple assemblies (with potentially different security permissions) share the same heap. A malicious assembly may not have permission to access assemblies that are more privileged, but it could use unsafe code to traverse the managed heap, and read or modify the state of objects. Worse yet, even if you try to isolate questionable assemblies in one app domain, and the trusted assemblies in another, it will be to no avail. Examine Figure 10-2 again. Because in the same physical process all app domains share the managed heap, a malicious component could use unsafe code to access the other app domains. Clearly, only trusted assemblies should be granted permission to use unsafe code. .NET doesn't have unsafe code permission, but it does have a security permission with the right to skip verification. Because unsafe code is unverifiable, you can use this permission to grant, in effect, permission for unsafe code. Note that the FullTrust permission set grants that permission, as does the dedicated SkipVerification permission set.

Security and Remoting

As long as the client and the object share the same physical process, .NET can enforce code access permission checks using stack walks, even when the call is made across app domains. It's possible because the cross app domain remoting channel uses the original client thread to invoke the call, so the stack walk can detect callers without the required permissions. However, in a distributed application that spans processes and machines, there are multiple physical threads involved every time the call flows to another location. Because each thread has its own stack, the stack-walk strategy as a mechanism for enforcing access permissions doesn't work when crossing the process boundary. Link-time permission demand is of no use either because the component is linked against the trusted host, not the remote client. In addition, each machine may very well have a difference code access policy. What is allowed on one machine may be forbidden on another. Principal-based security doesn't work by default in a distributed .NET application because .NET doesn't include the user identity as part of the information passed on the remoting channel.* While a message is in transit over the network, the information in the message isn't secure (although it's possible to use SSL when hosting with IIS). This is different from DCOM, in which the security call context was part of the information passed to the remote process or machine. DCOM also had the option of using secure channels. It's likely that future releases of .NET will provide secure channels and an easy way to propagate the security call context.

Serialization

Imagine a class containing sensitive information that needs to interact with partially trusted clients. If one client is malicious, it can provide its own serialization formatters and gain access to the sensitive information or deserialize the class with bogus state. To prevent abuse by such serialization clients, a class can demand during link time that its clients have the security permission to provide a serialization formatter, using the SecurityPermission attribute with the SecurityPermissionFlag. SerializationFormatter flag:

```
[SecurityPermission(SecurityAction.LinkDemand,
                        Flags = SecurityPermissionFlag.SerializationFormatter)]
[Serializable]
public class MyClass
{...}
```

Of course, as discussed in Chapter 9, if the class has sensitive state information, you may want to consider using custom serialization to encrypt and decrypt the state during serialization and deserialization. The problem with demanding serialization permission at the class level is that it precludes clients that don't have that permission but that don't wish to provide their own formatter from using the class. In such case, it's better to provide custom serialization and demand the permission only on the deserialization constructor and GetObjectData( ):

```
[Serializable]
public class MyClass : ISerializable
{
    public MyClass(){ }
```

---

* It's possible with some work and changes to the programming model to propagate the security call context by using the ILogicalThreadAffinitive and the CallContext types.

```
    [SecurityPermission(SecurityAction.LinkDemand,
                        Flags = SecurityPermissionFlag.SerializationFormatter)]
    public void GetObjectData(SerializationInfo info,StreamingContext context)
    {...}

    [SecurityPermission(SecurityAction.LinkDemand,
                        Flags = SecurityPermissionFlag.SerializationFormatter)]
    protected MyClass(SerializationInfo info,StreamingContext context)
    {...}
}
```

You can use the `SerializationUtil` helper class presented in Chapter 9 to automate implementing the custom serialization.

If all you need are the standard .NET formatters, there is a different solution altogether to the malicious serialization client. Use the `StrongNameIdentityPermission` attribute to demand at link time that only Microsoft-provided assemblies serialize and deserialize your class:

```
public class PublicKeys
{
    public const string Microsoft = "0024000004800000940000000602000000240000"+
                                     "525341310004000001000100007D1FA57C4AED9F0"+
                                     "A32E84AA0FAEFD0DE9E8FD6AEC8F87FB03766C83"+
                                     "4C99921EB23BE79AD9D5DCC1DD9AD23613210290"+
                                     "0B723CF980957FC4E177108FC607774F29E8320E"+
                                     "92EA05ECE4E821C0A5EFE8F1645C4C0C93C1AB99"+
                                     "285D622CAA652C1DFAD63D745D6F2DE5F17E5EAF"+
                                     "0FC4963D261C8A12436518206DC093344D5AD293";
}

[Serializable]
public class MyClass : ISerializable
{
    public MyClass(){}

    [StrongNameIdentityPermission(SecurityAction.LinkDemand,
                                  PublicKey = PublicKeys.Microsoft)]
    public void GetObjectData(SerializationInfo info,StreamingContext context)
    {...}

    [StrongNameIdentityPermission(SecurityAction.LinkDemand,
                                  PublicKey = PublicKeys.Microsoft)]
    protected MyClass(SerializationInfo info,StreamingContext context)
    {...}
}
```

Interface-Based Web Services

Web services carry with them the promise of the next information-technology revolution, allowing fast, cheap, and robust business-to-business interaction. At the heart of web services is the ability to develop such services and invoke their methods on a remote web site, with the same ease as conventional components. Web services allow you to connect middle-tier components on different platforms, across firewalls, over the Internet. The web services standard even provides for defining interfaces or a logical abstract service definition. In spite of the fact that .NET has superb support for developing and consuming web services, .NET doesn't (by default) support interface-based web services. As explained in Chapter 1 and demonstrated throughout this book, separation of interface from implementation is a core principal of component-oriented programming and is essential for application extensibility and reuse. This appendix presents you with a simple and elegant workaround for developing interface-based web services using Visual Studio.NET.[*] The source code accompanying this book contains the code presented here and the complete CalculationServices solution that uses it.

 The web services standard refers to interfaces as *ports*.

.NET Web Services Support

Consider the SimpleCalculator web service, which provides the four basic arithmetic operations (+, -, *, /), as shown in Example A-1.

---

[*] This appendix is based on an article I published in the *Visual Studio Magazine*, October 2001.

Example A-1. The SimpleCalculator web service

```
using System.Web.Services;

[WebService(Namespace="http://<Some URI>",
            Description = "The SimpleCalculator Web Service provides the
                           four basic arithmetic operations for integers.")]
public class SimpleCalculator : WebService
{
    public SimpleCalculator(){ }
    [WebMethod]
    public int Add(int num1,int num2)
    {
      return num1 + num2;
    }
    [WebMethod]
    public int Subtract(int num1,int num2)
    {
        return num1–num2;
    }
    [WebMethod]
    public int Divide(int num1,int num2)
    {
        return num1 / num2;
    }
    [WebMethod]
    public int Multiply(int num1,int num2)
    {
        return num1 * num2;
    }
}
```

Using .NET, all you have to do to develop a web service is add the attribute Web-
MethodAttribute to the methods you wish to expose as web services, and .NET will
do the rest. Note that deriving from WebService is optional, though it provides easy
access to common ASP.NET objects, such as the Application or Session state. Deriving from WebService has no bearing on the technique presented in this appendix, and
isn't present in subsequent code samples. The class attribute WebServiceAttribute is
optional as well, but you should use it. The attribute is defined as:

```
[AttributeUsage(AttributeTargets.Class)]
public sealed class WebServiceAttribute : Attribute
{
    public WebServiceAttribute();
    public string Description{get; set;}
    public string Name{get; set;}
    public string Namespace{get; set;}
}
```

WebServiceAttribute lets you specify a web service namespace that contains your service, used like a normal .NET namespace to reduce collisions. If you don't specify a
namespace, Visual Studio.NET uses *http://tempuri.org/* as a default. A published service uses a specific URI as its namespace, typically the service provider's URL. Web-

`ServiceAttribute` also allows you to provide a free-text description of the service. The description appears in the auto-generated browser page used by the service consumers and testers during development.

Producing client code for a web service is equally trivial. Select Add Web Reference from the client's project in Visual Studio.NET and point the wizard at the site containing the web service *.aspx* file. Once the wizard presents the available web services on the remote site, select the desired web service and click Add Reference. This causes Visual Studio.NET to generate a wrapper class the client uses to invoke the web service. Example A-2 shows the wrapper class for the service presented in Example A-1, with some of the methods and attributes removed for clarity.

Example A-2. The SimpleCalculator web service wrapper class

```
public class SimpleCalculator : SoapHttpClientProtocol
{
   public SimpleCalculator( )
   {
     Url = "http://<Some domain>/SimpleCalculator.asmx";
   }
   public int Add(int num1,int num2)
   {
     object[ ] results = Invoke("Add", new object[ ]{num1,num2});
     return (int)(results[0]);
   }
   //Other method wrappers
}
```

The `SimpleCalculator` wrapper class contains a public method for each of the methods exposed as web methods by the original web service. The wrapper class (sometimes called also a *web service proxy*) completely encapsulates the complex interaction with the remote service. The wrapper class is also coupled to the service's location, by means of the `URL` property of the `SoapHttpClientProtocol` base class.

The client code can use the wrapper class as if the `SimpleCalculator` object were a normal local object:

```
SimpleCalculator calculator;
calculator = new SimpleCalculator( );
int result = calculator.Add(2,3);
Debug.Assert(result == 5);
```

Problem Statement

With the programming model that was just presented, the client ends up programming directly against the service provider (`SimpleCalculator` in this case), instead of a generic abstraction of the service. A better approach is for the `SimpleCalculator` web service to be polymorphic with a service abstraction—an interface. Programming against an interface rather than a particular service implementation enables the client to switch between different providers, with minimal or no changes. This way, the client becomes indifferent to changes in the service provider. For example, imagine the client wants to switch from the SimpleCalculator to a different calculator web service, called the ScientificCalculator. ScientificCalculator supports the same interface as SimpleCalculator, but is perhaps more accurate, faster, or cheaper. Ideally, either the client or the service providers would agree to define a generic calculator interface, the ICalculator interface:

```
[WebInterface]//Imaginary attribute. Does not exist in .NET
public interface ICalculator
{
    int Add(int num1,int num2);
    int Subtract(int num1,int num2);
    int Divide(int num1,int num2);
    int Multiply(int num1,int num2);
}
```

If such a web interface were available, the client could code against the interface definition, not a particular implementation, as shown in Example A-3.

Example A-3. Web services client-side interface-based programming model

```
ICalculator calculator = new ScientificCalculator();

//or
ICalculator calculator = new SimpleCalculator();

//This part of the client code is polymorphic with any provider of the service:
int result = calculator.Add(2,3);
Debug.Assert(result == 5);
```

The only thing that changes in the client's code when it switches between service providers is the line that decides on the exact interface implementation to use. You can even put that decision in a different assembly from that of the main client's logic and pass only interfaces between the two assemblies. The client can also use a class factory to create the object and get back an interface. There are other benefits to interface-based web services; for example, the client can publish the interface definition, making it easier for different service vendors to implement the client's requirements.

Unfortunately, web services support in .NET is by default method-based, not interface-based, and there is no web interface attribute. There is no easy way to prove and consume services that are polymorphic with other services.

The Solution

The workaround presented next requires both the web service provider and the client to write their applications in a slightly different way, in order to gain interface-based web services. To create an interface-based web service, first expose the web service interface definition. For simplicity, assume the service provider is responsible for both defining and implementing the interface. There is a way for the client or any other third party to expose the web service interface definition and have anybody implement it, but that requires additional steps described in later sections.

Service-Side Steps

In a Visual Studio.NET web service project, right-click on the project, and select Add →Add Web Service from the context menu. This brings up the Add New Item dialog. Type ICalculator as the service name and click Open.

Visual Studio.NET then creates a skeletal web service called ICalculator. Open the *ICalculator.asmx.cs* file and change the ICalculator type definition from class to interface. Remove the derivation from System.Web.Services.WebService as well. Remove the constructor and the InitializeComponent( ) and Dispose( ) methods. Finally, remove the commented HelloWorld( ) method example. Next, add the interface methods: Add( ), Subtract( ), Divide( ), and Multiply( ). The interface should now look like any other .NET interface:

```
public interface ICalculator
{
    int Add(int num1,int num2);
    int Subtract(int num1,int num2);
    int Divide(int num1,int num2);
    int Multiply(int num1,int num2);
}
```

Although in principle you can simply decorate each interface method with the attribute WebMethod to expose the interface as a web service definition, in practice you shouldn't. The reason is the WebService attribute, which applies only to classes and is sealed, so you can't subclass it and change it. As a result, you can't assign a namespace and a description to the interface, which is an advisable step when defining a web service. To overcome this hurdle, you need to provide an *interface shim*— an abstract class that exposes to the world what looks like a pure interface definition. In the ICalculator.asmx.cs file, add the ICalculatorShim abstract class definition with abstract-only web methods and have it derive from ICalculator:

```
[WebService(Name = "ICalculator",Namespace="http://<Some URI>",
            Description = "This web service is only the definition of the
                           interface. You cannot invoke method calls on it.")]
public abstract class ICalculatorShim : ICalculator
{
    [WebMethod(Description = "Adds two integers and returns the sum")]
    abstract public int Add(int num1,int num2);

    [WebMethod(Description = "Subtracts two integers and returns the result")]
    abstract public int Subtract(int num1,int num2);

    [WebMethod(Description = "Divides two integers and returns the result")]
    abstract public int Divide(int num1,int num2);
```

```
[WebMethod(Description = "Multiplies two integers and returns the result")]
abstract public int Multiply(int num1,int num2);
}
```

By deriving from ICalculator, the compiler enforces that the shim class expose all the methods defined by the interface. Note that because ICalculatorShim is a class, you can use the WebServiceAttribute to provide a namespace and description. In addition, set the Name property of WebServiceAttribute to ICalculator. Doing so exposes the service definition as ICalculator instead of ICalculatorShim.

The combination of the WebMethodAttribute and the abstract class tricks Visual Studio.NET. On one hand, it agrees to expose the class as a web service, and on the other, it insists the class have no implementation because all the methods are abstract. Consequently, you actually end up with only a web service definition. To verify that all is well so far, set the *ICalculator.asmx* file as the start page and run the project. The autogenerated browser test page presents the ICalculator interface definition (see Figure A-1).

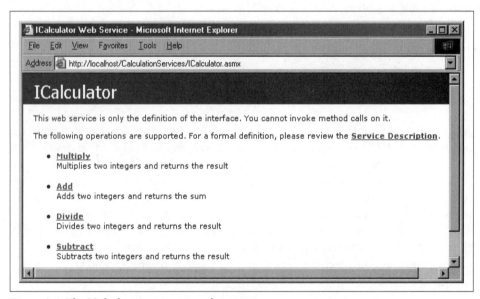

Figure A-1. The ICalculator auto-generated test page

If you try to invoke any of the methods, you will get an error because there is no implementation behind the service. Next, implement the ICalculator interface on web service classes. Doing so is like implementing any other interface in .NET: the class should derive from the interface and provide the implementation for its methods. For example, use the Add Web Service context-menu item again to add two web services, called SimpleCalculator and ScientificCalculator. Add to the classes a derivation from the ICalculator interface, and implement it. You must apply the WebMethodAttribute on all the implemented interface methods. Without the attribute, .NET

---

doesn't know it should expose a method as a web service, and the method will not be part of the service WSDL. Example A-4 shows the two implementations of ICalculator. Also note that the compiler insists the service provider implement all the methods defined by the interface.

Example A-4. Two different web services implementation of the ICalculator interface

```
[WebService(Namespace="http://<Some URI>",
            Description = "The SimpleCalculator web service implements ICalculator.
                           It provides the four basic arithmetic operations.")]
public class SimpleCalculator : ICalculator
{
   public SimpleCalculator( )
   {}
   [WebMethod(Description = "Adds two integers and returns the sum")]
   public int Add(int num1,int num2)
   {
      return num1 + num2;
   }
   //Other ICalculator methods
}

[WebService(Namespace="http://<Some URI>",
            Description = "The SimpleCalculator web service implements ICalculator.
                           It provides the four basic arithmetic operations.")]
public class ScientificCalculator : ICalculator
{
   public ScientificCalculator ()
   {}
   [WebMethod(Description = "Adds two integers and returns the sum")]
   public int Add(int num1,int num2)
   {
      return num1 + num2;
   }
   //Other ICalculator methods
}
```

Client-Side Steps

The client needs to have the interface definition so that it can program against it. The client can obtain that definition in two ways. The first uses the *WSDL.exe* command-line utility. Using the /server switch, you can instruct *WSDL.exe* to generate a pure abstract class matching only the definition of a web service. Assuming the interface definition resides at *http://www.SomeDomain.com/ICalculator.asmx*, run the utility with this command line:

```
WSDL.exe /server /out: ICalculatorDef.cs
   http://www.SomeDomain.com/ICalculator.asmx
```

The *ICalculatorDef.cs* source file will contain the web service definition only. Add the *ICalculatorDef.cs* source file to the client project. Unfortunately, even though .NET knows about interfaces, the /server switch generates a pure abstract class with abstract methods, instead of an interface:

```
//Some attributes omitted for clarity
 public abstract class ICalculator : WebService
 {
     [WebMethod]
     public abstract int Add(int num1, int num2);
     //rest of the ICalculator methods
 }
```

The client needs to convert the abstract class to an interface definition. Open the *ICalculatorDef.cs* file, remove the WebService base class, and change the ICalculator definition from abstract class to interface. Remove all the attributes (on ICalculator and its methods), and the public abstract modifiers from all the methods. You should now have the original ICalculator interface definition.

 Using the *WSDL.exe* command-line utility with the /server switch is how a service provider imports an interface defined by another party. The service provider needs to follow the same steps to convert the abstract class definition to an interface.

The second way a client can import the interface definition is by adding a web reference to the ICalculator web service. After adding the reference, the client manually extracts the interface methods from the wrapper class. To do so, point the Add Web Reference wizard to the site containing the interface definition. This generates a wrapper class called ICalculator, which exposes the original ICalculator's methods, as well as methods used for asynchronous method invocation, as described in Chapter 7. Each of these methods is implemented to forward calls to the web service. Of course, for an interface definition, you need only method definitions. Remove all the interface method bodies and the other methods completely, including the constructor. Remove the SoapHttpClientProtocol base class and the public modifier on the methods. Remove all class and method attributes. Finally, change the ICalculator definition from class to interface. The client-side should now have the original interface definition.

Regardless of how the client imports the interface definition, the client next needs to consume the web services that actually implement the interface. To do so, bring up the Add Web Reference wizard and point the wizard to where the implementations reside. Visual Studio.NET generates wrapper classes for the implementations (SimpleCalculator and ScientificCalculator, in this case). These machine-generated wrapper classes are the default wrapper class, and don't refer to ICalculator, looking just like Example A-2. It's up to the client to provide polymorphism with ICalculator by adding a derivation from the interface. The client-side wrapper classes are shown in Example A-5.

Example A-5. The client-side wrapper classes need to derive from the interface

```csharp
public class SimpleCalculator : SoapHttpClientProtocol, ICalculator
{
   public SimpleCalculator()
   {
     Url = "http://www.SomeDomain.com/SimpleCalculator.asmx";
   }
   public int Add(int num1,int num2)
   {
     object[ ] results = Invoke("Add", new object[ ]{num1,num2});
     return (int)(results[0]);
   }
   //Other method wrappers
}
public class ScientificCalculator : SoapHttpClientProtocol, ICalculator
{
   public ScientificCalculator()
   {
     Url = "http://www.SomeDomain.com/ScientificCalculator.asmx";
   }
   public int Add(int num1,int num2)
   {
     object[ ] results = Invoke("Add", new object[ ]{num1,num2});
     return (int)(results[0]);
   }
   //Other method wrappers
}
```

Finally, the client can write interface-based web services polymorphic code, as in Example A-3. Note that the only difference between the two wrapper classes is in the URL of the web service implementing the ICalculator interface. This leads to an interesting observation: in the web services world, from the client's perspective, the location of the service, the URL, is the object's type.

Also worth mentioning is that the technique described in this appendix works with other web services protocols besides SOAP, namely HTTP-GET and HTTP-POST. Using the *WSDL.exe* utility, you can generate wrapper classes that use these protocols and add the derivation from the web service interface.

APPENDIX B

Custom Security Principal

By default, .NET role-based security policy uses Windows user groups for roles and Windows accounts for security identities. There are several drawbacks to this default policy. The security policy is only as granular as the user groups in the hosting domain. Often you don't have control over your end customer's IT department. If you deploy your application in an environment in which the user groups are coarse or in which the user groups don't map well to actual roles users play in your application, or if the group names are slightly different, .NET basic role-based security is of little use to you. Roles localization presents yet another set of challenges because role names will differ between customer sites in different locales. Moreover, using Windows accounts for security identity means role-based security can work only if the users have accounts on the hosting domain or have a trust relationship with the domain that has the user accounts. This is obviously of little use for Internet applications, where it is often impractical to demand that every user have a matching Windows account.

This appendix presents a fully implemented alternative security principal mechanism. The custom principal class (simply called CustomPrincipal) addresses all the issues involved with using Windows user groups for roles; it allows you to define your own roles, at whatever level of granularity your design calls for, even if the application users don't have accounts on the hosting server. The roles used by CustomPrincipal are also locale-neutral because they are internal to your application. You can use CustomPrincipal in any type of application, but this appendix uses it in the context of an ASP.NET application.

Solution Architecture

Instead of using Windows accounts, passwords, and user groups, the custom security principal presented here uses a SQL server database to store the user information. The interaction with the database is encapsulated in the UserManager class, and no other class accesses the database directly. Thus, changes to the user information repository don't propagate up because no other class is coupled to the database structure. The ASP.NET application (called MySecureApp) uses ASP.NET forms authentication. The login page uses the `UserManager` class directly to authenticate the username and password. Once authenticated, a `CustomPrincipal` object is attached to the thread processing each user request. The ASP.NET pages can use custom role-based security, as can any middle-tier class they access. This is because `CustomPrincipal` implements `IPrincipal`. As explained in Chapter 12, both the `PrincipalPermissionAttribute` and `PrincipalPermission` classes simply access the current thread `IPrincipal` object and call its `IsInRole()` method. `CustomPrincipal` uses `UserManager` to implement `IPrincipal.IsInRole()`. Figure B-1 depicts the ASP.NET application security architecture.

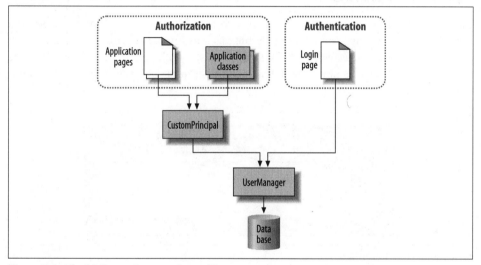

Figure B-1. The MySecureApp security architecture

The code accompanying this book contains the MySecureApp solution, with the source code presented in this appendix. The *MySecureApp.sql* script file creates the MySecureApp database and its tables.

Database Structure

The MySecureApp database contains a table called Roles. The Roles table has a username column and a column for each role users play in the application, such as Manager, Teller, Customer, etc. The username column (UserName) is the table's key. The username is stored as a string and the roles as single bits, allowing a user to be a member of multiple roles. The Roles table is presented in Figure B-2.

When you use a custom security principal, the motivation is to use it in the context of role-based security for user access authorization. With a real-life custom principal, it is likely the same database will also contain the user authentication

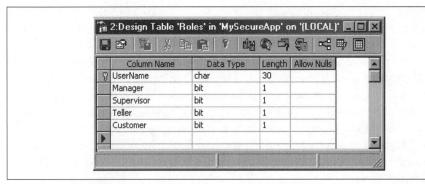

Figure B-2. The Roles table uses the User Name column as key; the roles are the other columns

information, meaning usernames and passwords. The database contains a second table called Passwords. The Password table has a username column (UserName) and a password column (Password), both strings, as shown in Figure B-3. The username is the Passwords table's key. The fields in the UserName column in both tables contain the same values.

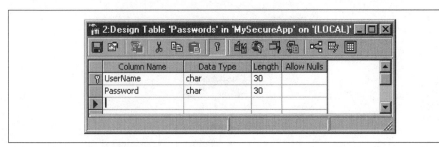

Figure B-3. The Passwords table

The Data Access Component

The UserManager class, defined as follows, uses ADO.NET to access the database:

```
public class UserManager
{
    public UserManager( );

    public bool Authenticate(string userName,string password);
    public bool IsInRole(string userName,string role);

    //Protected members and methods
}
```

The IsInRole( ) method queries the Roles table for a row matching the username. If such a row is found, IsInRole( ) looks for a column matching the specified role. If such a column is found, IsInRole( ) returns its value (one or zero, which are translated by ADO.NET to true or false).

The Authenticate( ) method queries the Password table for a row matching the username and compares the stored password with the specified password argument. If a matching record with the correct password is found, Authenticate( ) returns true.

The CustomPrincipal Component

The sole purpose of CustomPrincipal is to replace the default security principal and service the PrincipalPermissionAttribute and PrincipalPermission classes. To enforce and automate this design decision, CustomPrincipal doesn't have a public constructor, so its clients have no direct way to instantiate it. Instead, the clients use the Attach( ) public static method. Attach( ) creates an object of type CustomPrincipal, providing it with the security identity to use. CustomPrincipal has no interest in modifying the identity. Its constructor saves the identity provided in the m_User member variable. The saved identity is used in role-membership verification and in implementing IPrincipal.Identity:

```
public class CustomPrincipal : IPrincipal
{
    IIdentity m_User;
    public IIdentity Identity
    {
        get
        {
            return m_User;
        }
    }
    //rest of the implementation
}
```

The constructor replaces the default principal by setting the CurrentPrincipal property of the current thread to itself:

```
private CustomPrincipal(IIdentity user)
{
    m_User = user;
    //Make this object the principal for this thread
    Thread.CurrentPrincipal = this;
}
```

If Attach( ) is called in the context of an ASP.NET application, ASP.NET has already impersonated the user identity used during login and authentication. That impersonated principal is available in the User property of the current HttpContext object. Attach( ) retrieves that default principal's identity and creates a new CustomPrincipal object:

```
static public void Attach( )
{
    HttpContext context = HttpContext.Current;
    IPrincipal defaultPrincipal = context.User;
```

```
    IPrincipal customPrincipal  = new CustomPrincipal(defaultPrincipal.Identity);
    context.User = customPrincipal;
}
```

After creating the CustomPrincipal object, Attach( ) sets the User property of the current HttpContext object to the CustomPrincipal object because ASP.NET itself doesn't use the thread's principal.

CustomPrincipal's implementation of IPrincipal.Identity is trivial when using the UserManager class. CustomPrincipal retrieves the username from the cached identity and asks UserManager whether the user is a member of the specified role:

```
public bool IsInRole(string role)
{
    UserManager userManager = new UserManager( );
    bool inRole = false;
    inRole = userManager.IsInRole(m_User.Name,role);

    return inRole;
}
```

Example B-1 lists the full implementation of CustomPrincipal

Example B-1. The CustomPrincipal class

```
public class CustomPrincipal : IPrincipal
{
    IIdentity m_User;
    static public void Attach( )
    {
        HttpContext context = HttpContext.Current;
        IPrincipal defaultPrincipal = context.User;
        IPrincipal customPrincipal = new CustomPrincipal(defaultPrincipal.Identity);
        context.User =  customPrincipal;
    }
    private CustomPrincipal(IIdentity user)
    {
        m_User = user;
        //Make this object the principal for this thread
        Thread.CurrentPrincipal = this;
    }
    public IIdentity Identity
    {
        get
        {
            return m_User;
        }
    }
    public bool IsInRole(string role)
    {
        UserManager userManager = new UserManager( );
        bool inRole = false;
        inRole = userManager.IsInRole(m_User.Name,role);
```

Example B-1. The CustomPrincipal class (continued)

```
        return inRole;
    }
}
```

Using CustomPrincipal in a Windows Application

Using the CustomPrincipal class in a Windows application is very similar to using it in an ASP.NET application. The main difference is that Attach( ) needs to get the current user identity from the current thread because there is no HTTP context. In addition, you have to explicitly set the app domain principal policy. To ease using the CustomPrincipal class, encapsulate that step in Attach( ) and while you are at it, set the default principal object to CustomPrincipal, so that it will be attached to new threads automatically. Here's the revised Attach( ) method:

```
    static public void Attach( )
    {
        AppDomain currentDomain = Thread.GetDomain( );
        currentDomain.SetPrincipalPolicy(
                            PrincipalPolicy.WindowsPrincipal);

        IPrincipal defaultPrincipal = Thread.CurrentPrincipal;
        IIdentity defaultIdentity = defaultPrincipal.Identity;
        IPrincipal customPrincipal;
        customPrincipal = new CustomPrincipal(defaultIdentity);
        //Make sure all future threads in this app domain use
        //this principal
        if(defaultPrincipal is WindowsPrincipal)
        {
            currentDomain.SetThreadPrincipal(customPrincipal);
        }
    }
```

Finally, call Attach( ) in the Main( ) method of the Windows application:

```
    static void Main( )
    {
        CustomPrincipal.Attach( );
        //Rest of Main( )
    }
```

The Application

The MySecureApp ASP.NET application demonstrates using the database for both custom authentication and authorization. The application configuration file (*Web.config*) sets the authentication mode to Forms and designates *login.aspx* as the login page:

```
<authentication mode = "Forms">
   <forms loginUrl="login.aspx"/>
   </forms>
</authentication>

<authorization>
   <deny users="?" />
</authorization>
```

In addition, the configuration file allows anonymous access, so that users can try to log on. MySecureApp attaches the custom principal object at the global level. The Global class handles global events, such as application or session start. One of these events is the authorization request, and in its event handler, MySecureApp attaches the custom principal:

```
public class Global : HttpApplication
{
   protected void Application_AuthorizeRequest(object sender,EventArgs e)
   {
      if(HttpContext.Current.User.Identity.IsAuthenticated)
      {
         CustomPrincipal.Attach();
      }
   }
   //Other global event handlers
}
```

MySecureApp attaches the custom principal only after authentication to prevent using role-based security with unauthenticated callers.

By default, the ASP.NET application wizard doesn't add the authorization request event handler, so you need to add it manually.

Custom Forms Authentication

When you use Forms authentication with a designated login page, all requests by unauthenticated users to any page in the application are routed to the login page. The login page in the MySecureApp presents a simple username and password text boxes, as shown in Figure B-4.

The code behind the login page is the LoginPage class, shown in Example B-2. The core of the class is the OnLogin( ) event handler. OnLogin( ) is called by ASP.NET after a post back to the server is triggered by clicking the "Log in" button on the page. OnLogin( ) reads from the UI controls the value of the username and password and calls the Authenticate( ) method of UserManager. If the user isn't authenticated, OnLogin( ) writes an error message as response. If the user is authenticated, OnLogin( ) redirects the user to the original page he requested by using the static method RedirectFromLoginPage( ) of the FormsAuthentication( ) class.

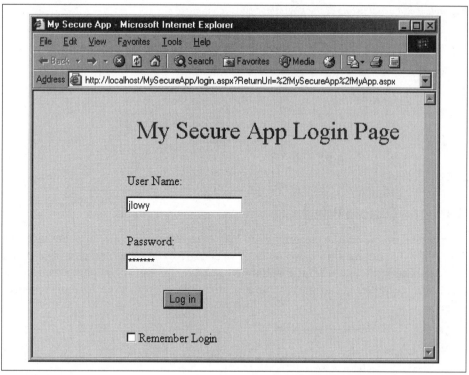

Figure B-4. The login page

Example B-2. Partial listing of the LoginPage class

```
public class LoginPage : Page
{
    UserManager m_UserManager;
    //UI Controls
    protected TextBox   m_UserNameBox;
    protected TextBox   m_PasswordBox;
    protected CheckBox m_RememberCheckbox;

    private void OnLoad(object sender,EventArgs e)
    {
        if(IsPostBack)
        {
            m_UserManager = new UserManager( );
        }
    }
    private void OnLogin(object sender,EventArgs e)
    {
        string userName = m_UserNameBox.Text;
        string password = m_PasswordBox.Text;

        bool userAuthenticated = m_UserManager.Authenticate(userName,password);
        if(userAuthenticated == false)
```

Example B-2. Partial listing of the LoginPage class (continued)

```
        {
            Response.Write("Incorrect user name or password. Please try again");
        }
        else
        {
            bool rememberLogin = m_RememberCheckbox.Checked;
            //will redirect to default.aspx if login page was requested directly.
            FormsAuthentication.RedirectFromLoginPage(userName,rememberLogin);
        }
    }

}
```

Using the Custom Principal

After attaching the custom security principal, there is nothing special about using it. The ASP.NET application can use both declarative and programmatic role-based security. The application can use declarative security directly on its pages' event handlers. For example, it can prevent unauthorized users from even loading sensitive pages:

```
public class SensitivePage : Page
{
    [PrincipalPermission(SecurityAction.Demand,Role = "Manager")]
    void OnLoad(object sender,EventArgs e)
    {...}
}
```

The problem with placing the security demand on the page-event handlers themselves is that unauthorized users will get a generic ugly page back, indicating a server error. You can get around this problem using programmatic role-based security and redirect the user to a dedicated error page if the user isn't a member of the required role:

```
public class SensitivePage : Page
{
    void OnLoad(object sender,EventArgs e)
    {
        IPrincipal  principal = Thread.CurrentPrincipal;
        bool callerInRole = false;
        callerInRole = principal.IsInRole("Manager");
        if(callerInRole == false)
        {
            Response.Redirect("AccessDenied.aspx");
        }
        //Rest of OnLoad( )
    }
}
```

However, programmatic security is much more cumbersome than declarative security. In general, ASP.NET pages should delegate all meaningful processing to middle tier components. This also prevents pages from knowing which request is sensitive and which isn't. The middle-tier components could insist on role-membership (or any other type of security permission), and the page class could catch the security exception and redirect the users to a page stating that access was denied. Example B-3 demonstrates this approach.

Example B-3. Using declarative role-based security by a middle-tier component

```
public class SomeMiddleTierClass
{
    [PrincipalPermission(SecurityAction.Demand,Role = "Manager")]
    public void SpecialOperation( )
    {...}
}
public class SensitivePage : Page
{
    private void OnSpecialOperation(object sender,EventArgs e)
    {
        try
        {
            SomeMiddleTierClass obj = new SomeMiddleTierClass( );
            obj.SpecialOperation( );
        }
        catch(SecurityException exception)
        {
            Response.Redirect("AccessDenied.aspx");
        }
    }
    //Other event handlers
}
```

Reflection and Attributes

Reflection is the programmatic act of reading the metadata associated with a type. You can read the metadata to learn what the type is and what is it made of (methods, properties, base classes). Reflection services are defined in the System. Reflection namespace. Reflection is most useful in conjunction with attributes—a way of adding information to a type and affecting the type's behavior. Reflection also has another esoteric feature not covered in this appendix: it allows you to define new types during runtime and emit the corresponding IL code and metadata (using the services found in the System.Reflection.Emit namespace). This appendix starts by reviewing some key .NET reflection techniques and then focuses on using and defining attributes.

System.Type

The abstract class Type defined in the System namespace is an abstraction of a .NET CLR type. Every .NET type, be it a .NET-provided type—from value types such as integers and enums to classes and interfaces—or a developer-defined type has a corresponding unique Type value.

 The ability to uniquely identify a type by means of Type object is analogous to the COM idea of identifying the type of a component by means of its unique CLSID.

The canonical base class of any .NET type is System.Object. Object (or just object in C#) has built-in support for retrieving the Type associated with any object by calling its GetType( ) method:

```
public class object
{
    public Type GetType( );
    //Other object methods
}
```

Having GetType( ) present in object allows you to call it on any .NET object:

```
public class MyClass
{...}

int num = 0;
MyClass obj = new MyClass( );

Type type1 = num.GetType( );
Type type2 = obj.GetType( );
```

Different instances of the same type must return the same Type value:

```
int num1 = 1;
int num2 = 2;

Type type1 = num1.GetType( );
Type type2 = num2.GetType( );

Debug.Assert(type1 == type2);
```

The typeof operator allows you to retrieve the Type associated with a type directly, without instantiating an object of that type:

```
Type type1 = typeof(int);
Type type2 = typeof(MyClass);
```

Type is your gateway to obtaining the metadata associated with the type you are interested in. To start, Type.ToString( ) returns the type's name:

```
Type type = typeof(MyClass);
string name = type.ToString( );
Debug.Assert(name == "MyClass");
```

But Type has a lot more to offer. It has more than 100 methods and properties that can obtain metadata about the type. For example, the GetMethods( ) method is defined as:

```
public MethodInfo[ ] GetMethods( );
```

GetMethods( ) returns an array of MethodInfo objects describing all the public methods of the type. Example C-1 demonstrates using GetMethods( ) to trace to the output window all the public methods of the class MyClass.

Example C-1. Using Type.GetMethods() to reflect a type's public methods

```
using System.Reflection;

public class MyClass
{
   public    MyClass( ){ }
   public    void Method1( ){ }
   public    static void Method2( ){ }
   protected void Method3( ){ }
   private   void Method4( ){ }
}
```

Example C-1. Using Type.GetMethods() to reflect a type's public methods (continued)

```
//Client code:
Type type = typeof(MyClass);

MethodInfo[ ] methodInfoArray = type.GetMethods( );

//Trace all the public methods
foreach(MethodInfo methodInfo in methodInfoArray)
{
    Trace.WriteLine(methodInfo.Name);
}
//Output:
GetHashCode
Equals
ToString
Method1
Method2
GetType
```

Example C-1 demonstrates a few other key points. First, GetMethods( ) returns all the public methods of a type (instance or static), including those defined in its base class(es). In its output, Example C-1 lists four public methods of object that are not part of the MyClass definition. GetMethods( ) doesn't return constructors. If you aren't satisfied with this behavior, you can use another version of GetMethods( ) that accepts a parameter telling it how to bind to the type:

```
public abstract MethodInfo[ ] GetMethods(BindingFlags bindingAttr);
```

Second, the BindingFlags enumeration is a bit-mask enumeration that lets you specify whether to return only instance methods, only static methods, nonpublic methods, methods defined only in this type (not inherited), and so on. Once you have obtained a MethodInfo object about a method, you can invoke it, even if it's a protected or private method. Example C-2 demonstrates how to invoke all the private methods of the MyClass class using the late-binding Invoke( ) method of the MethodInfo object. The Invoke( ) method is defined as:

```
public object Invoke(object obj, object[ ] parameters);
```

 Late binding invocation breaks every rule of encapsulation and type safety because the compiler lets you invoke private methods and pass in as parameters anything you want. Late binding is available for esoteric cases and for tool developers. In general, avoid reflection-based late binding invocation.

Example C-2 starts by obtaining a Type object from an instance (unlike Example C-1, which uses the class itself), and then it calls GetMethods( ), requesting back only nonpublic instance methods. Note that to invoke only private methods, further filtering is required after calling GetMethods( ) because GetMethods( ) returns both protected and private methods. The additional filtering is done by checking the IsPrivate property of the MethodInfo object. In the example, only Method4( ) is invoked. Invoke( ) accepts the object to invoke the method on, and an array of objects as parameters for the method to invoke. In the example, Method4( ) has no parameters, so a null is passed in to Invoke( ).

Example C-2. Invoking only the private methods of an object using reflection

```
using System.Reflection;

public class MyClass
{
    public MyClass( ){...}
    public void Method1( ){...}
    public void Method2( ){...}
    public static void Method5( ){...}
    protected void Method3( ){...}
    private void Method4( ){...}
}
//Client code
MyClass obj = new MyClass( );
Type type = typeof(MyClass);

MethodInfo[ ] methodInfoArray;
methodInfoArray = type.GetMethods(BindingFlags.NonPublic|BindingFlags.Instance);

//Invoke private methods only
foreach(MethodInfo methodInfo in methodInfoArray)
{
    if(methodInfo.IsPrivate)
    {
        methodInfo.Invoke(obj,null);
    }
}
```

 Use of the late binding Invoke() is similar to the old COM automation way of using IDispatch::Invoke( ) to invoke calls on objects.

Finally, in addition to GetMethods( ), Type offers numerous other methods. GetMethod( ) returns a MethodInfo object about a particular specified method. GetConstructors( ) and GetConstructor( ) return ConstructorInfo objects about the type's constructors. GetMember( ) and GetMembers( ) return all members or a type. GetEvent( ) and GetEvents( ) return information about the events the type supports, and so on. The general form of retrieving the reflection information is Get<Element Name>. Type also offers many properties dealing with what kind of type is reflected: if it's a class or an interface, what its base class type is, and so on. For example:

```
Type type = typeof(MyClass);
Debug.Assert(type.IsClass);
```

See the MSDN Library for a complete listing of the Type members.

Attributes

The ability to reflect methods and type information is a nice and intriguing technology, but reflection really shines and demonstrates its value when you use it in conjunction with .NET *attributes*. The idea behind attributes is simple: instead of coding functionality and features into your objects, you can add them by decorating your objects with attributes. The information in the attributes is added to the metadata about the objects that the compiler generates (its methods, base classes, etc.). .NET (or your custom tools) can read the metadata, look for the attributes, and perform the functionality they specify and add the features without the object's or its developer's involvement. Here's an example: when you want to combine enums in a binary masking value, you can use the Flags attribute:

```
[Flags]
public enum WeekDay
{
    Monday,
    Tuesday,
    Wednesday,
    Thursday,
    Friday,
    Saturday,
    Sunday,
}
```

When the compiler sees the Flags attribute, it allows you to combine enum/values with the | (OR) operator, as if they were integer powers of 2. For example:

```
const WeekDay Weekend = WeekDay.Saturday|WeekDay.Sunday;
```

Another example is the Conditional attribute defined in the System.Diagnostics namespace. This attribute directs the compiler to exclude from a build calls to any method it decorates if a specified condition isn't defined:

```
#define MySpecialCondition //usually DEBUG

public class MyClass
{
    public MyClass()
    {}
    [Conditional("MySpecialCondition")]
    public void MyMethod()
    {...}
}
//Client side code
MyClass obj = new MyClass();
//This line is conditional
obj.MyMethod();
```

Having the compiler do the method call exclusion automatically is of course a major improvement over C++. In the past, when developers did code exclusion manually, and wanted to put the method calls back in, they sometimes forgot to do it everywhere, thus causing a defect.

Attributes are used in every aspect of .NET programming: in asynchronous calls, in object persistence and serialization, in concurrency management, in remote calls, in security, in interoperability with COM and Windows, and in Enterprise Services.

Using Attributes

An attribute is actually a class in its own right. The attribute class should have the suffix Attribute in its name, and it must derive (directly or indirectly) from the class Attribute:

```
public class FlagsAttribute : Attribute
{...}
```

When you use attributes, you use square brackets [ ] (or angle brackets < > in Visual Basic.NET). However, the C# (and the Visual Basic.NET) compiler supports a shorthand when using an attribute. If the attribute name ends with Attribute, the compiler lets you omit the Attribute suffix (but you can add it if you like):

```
[FlagsAttribute] //same as [Flags]
public enum Color : long
{
    Red,Green,Blue,Purple = Red | Blue
}
```

You can stack as many attributes as you like on a type or a type member, as long as the attributes don't contradict each other. However, you can't apply any attribute to any type or type member. Each attribute has an attribute of type AttributeUsage associated with it that dictates which types the attribute is applicable to (class, interface, enum, etc.) and which level (constructor, method, parameter, returned value, etc.). The AttributeUsage also dictates whether the attribute can be used multiple times on the same target. (You will learn more about AttributeUsage in the next section.) Attributes can also have a default constructor and can accept construction parameters. If a default constructor is available, you can use the attribute with or without parentheses:

```
[MyAttribute()] //same as  [MyAttribute]
```

Attributes can also accept construction parameters and have public properties you can set. If you have both parameterized constructors and properties, the parameters to the constructor must be specified before setting the properties. There are limitations on the types of parameters the attribute constructors and properties can accept; for instance, they can't accept a class or struct as a parameter. The only permissible reference types are array, Type, and object.

Kinds of Attributes

There are three kinds of attributes in .NET. There are *standard attributes,* such as Flags and conditional. Standard attributes are available in .NET out of the box. The .NET compilers and runtime know about these attributes and obey their directions. The second kind of attributes are *custom attributes.* Custom attributes are attributes you provide. Custom attributes go completely unnoticed by .NET, expect that the compiler adds them as part of the metadata. You have to write the reflection code to make sense of the custom attributes. Such attributes usually have domain-specific semantics. The third kind of attributes are *custom context attributes.* Both .NET and you can provide custom context attributes. .NET is fully aware of them and will comply with their directions and influence the decorated object accordingly. Chapter 11 discusses context attributes at length.

Reflecting Assembly Version

The AssemblyVersion attribute presented in Chapter 5 is a special attribute; its value isn't recorded in the metadata, but rather in the manifest. If you want to programmatically reflect the assembly version, you can reflect the assembly version programmatically, using the GetName( ) method of the Assembly type. GetName( ) returns an instance of the AssemblyName class. The AssemblyName class has a public property called Version, of a class called Version:

```
public sealed class Version : ICloneable,IComparable
{
    // Constructors
    public Version( );
    public Version(int major, int minor);
    public Version(int major, int minor, int build);
    public Version(int major,int minor,int build,
                                        int revision);
    public Version(string version);

    // Properties
    public int Build { get; }
    public int Major { get; }
    public int Minor { get; }
    public int Revision { get; }
}
```

You can either access individual version numbers or just convert it to a string:

```
Assembly assembly = Assembly.GetExecutingAssembly( );
Version version = assembly.GetName( ).Version;
Trace.WriteLine("Version is " + version.ToString( ));
```

Implementing Custom Attributes

Implementing a custom attribute (and the accompanying reflection code to make use of it) is easy and straightforward. For example, suppose you want to provide a custom attribute that adds a color option to your classes and interfaces. The color is an enum defined as:

```
public enum ColorOption {Red,Green,Blue};
```

The color attribute should also have:

- A default constructor that assigns ColorOption.Red to the target class or interface
- A parameterized constructor that accepts the color to assign the target class or interface
- A property that accepts the color to assign the target class or interface

Example C-3 shows the implementation of the ColorAttribute attribute class.

Example C-3. Implementing a custom attribute

```
public enum ColorOption {Red,Green,Blue};

[AttributeUsage(AttributeTargets.Class|AttributeTargets.Interface)]
public class ColorAttribute : Attribute
{
    ColorOption m_Color;
    public ColorOption Color
    {
        get
        {
            return m_Color;
        }
        set
        {
            m_Color = value;
        }
    }
    public ColorAttribute( )
    {
        Color = ColorOption.Red;
    }
    public ColorAttribute(ColorOption color)
    {
        this.Color = color;
    }
}
```

Before walking though Example C-3, here are a few examples that use the Color attribute:

- Using the default constructor:

```
[Color]
public class MyClass1
{ }
```

- Using the parameterized constructor:

```
[Color(ColorOption.Green)]
public class MyClass2
{ }
```

- Using the property:

```
[Color(Color = ColorOption.Blue)]
public class MyClass3
{ }
```

- Using it on an interface:

```
[Color]
public interface IMyInterface
{ }
```

As you can see in Example C-3, there isn't much to implementing a custom attribute. The ColorAttribute class derives from the Attribute class and defines the public Color property to access the m_Color member variable. The AttributeUsage attribute indicates that the Color attribute can be applied only to classes or interfaces:

```
[AttributeUsage(AttributeTargets.Class|AttributeTargets.Interface)]
public class ColorAttribute : Attribute
{...}
```

As a result, trying to use the color attribute on any other target (such as a method) doesn't compile:

```
public class MyClass
{
    [Color]//This will not compile
    public void MyMethd( ){ }
}
```

The AttributeUsage attribute definition is:

```
public sealed class AttributeUsageAttribute : Attribute
{
    public AttributeUsageAttribute(AttributeTargets validOn);
    public bool AllowMultiple { get; set; }
    /* Other members */
}
```

Its constructor accepts an enum of type AttributeTargets, letting it know on which types this attribute is valid. The AttributeTargets enum offers a number of values such as AttributeTargets.Method, AttributeTargets.Assembly and so on.

The other interesting property of the AttributeUsage attribute is AllowMultiple. By default, AllowMultiple is set to false, so you can apply the Color attribute only once per class or interface. As a result, this usage doesn't compile:

```
[Color(ColorOption.Green)]
[Color]
public class MyClass
{}
```

However, if you explicitly set AllowMultiple to true, you can use the Color attribute multiple times on the same target:

```
[AttributeUsage(AttributeTargets.Class|AttributeTargets.Interface,
                                              AllowMultiple = true)]
public class ColorAttribute : Attribute
{...}
```

Reflecting Custom Attributes

When you write code to reflect attributes, it's often better to do so in the form of a static helper method that accepts the object to reflect and returns the information, as shown in Example C-4. That way, the method can be used by other parties in your application, without bothering with instantiating an object to call it or access instance state.

Example C-4. Reflecting a custom attribute

```
public static ColorOption GetColor(object obj)
{
    Type objType = obj.GetType();
    Debug.Assert(objType.IsClass || objType.IsInterface);

    Type attribType = typeof(ColorAttribute);

    object[] attributeArray = objType.GetCustomAttributes(attribType,true);

    //Only one color attribute at the most
    Debug.Assert(attributeArray.Length == 0 || attributeArray.Length == 1);

    if(attributeArray.Length == 0)
    {
        return ColorOption.Red;
    }

    ColorAttribute colorAttribute = (ColorAttribute)attributeArray[0];
    return colorAttribute.Color;
}
```

The GetColor() method in Example C-4 accepts a generic object as a parameter and constructs a Type representing the type of the parameter, verifying that it got either a class or an interface:

```
Debug.Assert(objType.IsClass || objType.IsInterface);
```

It then calls the GetCustomAttributes( ) method of Type to get an array of all the attributes of the specified attribute type. Note that GetCustomAttributes( ) returns all the attributes associated with the type, not just the custom attributes. A better name for it would be simply GetAttributes( ). After retrieving the array of attributes of type ColorAttribute, the GetColor( ) method verifies that the size of the array is either 0 or 1 because there can be only one color attribute associated with the object at the most. If no attribute is associated with the object, the method returns ColorOption.Red. However, if one such attribute is preset, the method returns its Color value.

What you choose to do with the knowledge of the color of the object is entirely domain-specific. All .NET provides is an easy-to-use and extensible mechanism for associating a custom attribute with a type and reflecting it.

Index

Symbols

< > (angle brackets), use with attributes (VisualBasic.NET), 417

[ ] (square brackets), use with attributes in C#, 417

... (ellipses), indicating code in this book, xvi

& (AND) operator, masking enum/values with, 115

+= operator
 adding target method, 101
 IntelliSense support of, 102

= operator, initializing target method list, 101

-= operator, removing target method, 101

| (OR) operator, combining enum/values with, 115, 416

A

Abort( ) (Thread), 155
 overloaded versions, 156
 reasons to avoid thread termination with, 158

aborting threads, 155–158

abstract classes
 interface shims, 397
 interfaces, differences from, 39
 similarity to interfaces, 38

accessors (event), 110

AcquireReaderLock( )
 (ReaderWriterLock), 192

AcquireWriterLock( )
 (ReaderWriterLock), 192

activating remote objects, summary of options for, 283

activation, just-in-time (JITA), 253
 (see also single call activation)

activation modes, 249–258
 choosing with Client application, 271
 client-activated objects, 249, 315
 client-type registration and, 270
 leasing and, 300–303
 client-activated objects, 300–303
 single-call objects, 300
 singleton objects, 300
 server-activated single call, 250–253
 server-activated singleton, 254–256
 server-activation mode, supplying for host type, 268
 synchronization and, 256
 client-activated objects, 257
 single-call objects, 257
 singletons, 257

Activator class
 CreateInstance( ), 269, 282
 GetObject( ), 269, 282, 290

ActiveX controls, 5, 211

activities (.NET Enterprise Services), 174
 (see also synchronization domains)

AddEvent( ) (Logbook), 332

AddHandler reserved word (Visual Basic.NET), 103

AddressOf operator (Visual Basic.NET), 103

adjusting security (Security Adjustment Wizard), 360

We'd like to hear your suggestions for improving our indexes. Send email to *index@oreilly.com*.

G

GAC (Global Assembly Cache), 15
  installing shared assembly, 83
  shared assemblies, 78
  verifying that assembly is loaded from, 86
GACUtil command line utility, 83
garbage collection
  client-activated objects, 316
  explicit, 63
  finalized queue, 63
  lease expiration on remote objects, 294
  .NET, 61
    COM vs., 12
  safe points, 152
  singleton objects, 256
  slots, named and unnamed, 197
GC class
  Collect( ), 63
  SuppressFinalize( ), 71
general-purpose components, 4
GenericPrincipal class, 388
GetActivationURL( ), 271
GetAvailableThreads( ) (ThreadPool), 200
GetClientContextSink( ), 322
GetConstructor( ) (Type), 415
GetConstructors( ) (Type), 415
GetCurrentThreadId( ) (AppDomain
    class), 149
GetCustomAttributes( ) (Type), 422
GetData( ) (Thread), 198
GetDomain( ) (Thread), 239
GetEvent( ) and GetEvents( ) (Type), 415
GetExecutingAssembly( ) (Assembly
    class), 34
GetFields( ) (Type), 232
GetHashCode( ) (Thread class), 148
GetInvocationList( ), 138
GetInvocationList( ) (EventHandler), 108
GetLifetimeService( )
    (RemotingServices), 298
GetMaxThreads( ) (ThreadPool), 200
GetMember( ) and GetMembers( )
    (Type), 415
GetMethods( ) (Type), 413
GetNamedDataSlot( ) (Thread), 198
GetObject( ) (Activator), 269, 282
GetObjectData( )
  custom serialization and base classes, 228
  ISerializable interface, 223
GetPropertiesForNewContext( )
  IContextAttribute class, 320
  LogbookAttribute class (example), 327

GetServerContextSink( )
    (IMessageSink), 322
GetType( ) (Object), 412
GetValue( ) (FieldInfo), 233
Global Assembly Cache (see GAC)
global custom policy, 91
global leasing defaults, setting before object
    registration, 296
GlobalAssemblyCache Boolean property, 86
globally unique identifiers (GUIDs), 12, 79
goto, aborting threads and, 156

H

handle to remote object, 242
Hash evidence, 343
heap
  compacting, 62, 152
  managed, 59
    garbage collection and, 61
    shared by all app domains in a
        process, 237
hiding information from clients, 3
hierarchies of classes (object-oriented), 5
high-level languages, transformation to
    machine code, 17
host app domains, 244
  access to server assembly, 244
  registering channels for remote client
      calls, 260
  registering to accept client-activated
      calls, 250
host channels registration, 264, 276
host pooling on Windows XP, 293
host type registration, 267, 278
hosts
  serviced components, .NET Enterprise
      Services, 293
  as system service, 291
    IIS, using, 292
HTTP
  client-side channel, configuring to use
      binary formatter, 277
  serialization formats and, 260
  web services, use of, 261
HttpChannel class, 263
  bidirectional nature of, 268
  SOAP formatter, use of, 266
HttpClientChannel class, 268
HttpContext class, 405
HttpServerChannel class, 268

About the Author

Juval Löwy is a software architect and the principal of IDesign, a consulting and training company focused on .NET design and .NET migration. He is a Microsoft Regional Director for the Silicon Valley and a frequent participant in Microsoft internal design reviews for future versions of .NET. Juval helped found Bay.NET, the California Bay Area .NET User Group, and he chairs its program committee. Juval is a frequent speaker at the major international software development conferences, where he talks about .NET, component-oriented design, and the development process. Juval has published numerous articles, on almost every aspect of .NET development. He is a contributing editor to the *Visual Studio Magazine* and a regular columnist at *CoDe Magazine*. He has also written for *MSDN* magazine. Microsoft has recognized Juval as a Software Legend—one of the world's top .NET experts and industry leaders. You can contact him at *http://www.idesign.net*.

Colophon

Our look is the result of reader comments, our own experimentation, and feedback from distribution channels. Distinctive covers complement our distinctive approach to technical topics, breathing personality and life into potentially dry subjects.

The animal on the cover of *Programming .NET Components* is a land hermit crab (*Coenobita clypeatus*). Land hermit crabs are found in tropical areas of the Indo-region, the western Atlantic, and the western Caribbean. They live close to the shoreline and must have access to land and water.

The front half of a hermit crab is covered with a hard exoskeleton. The long abdomen has a softer exoskeleton that can adjust to fit into a spiraled shell. The large left claw is used for defense, for holding onto tree limbs, and for balance. The smaller right claw and the next pair of appendages are used for collecting and passing food and water to the mouth. Hermit crabs have stalked eyes with acute vision and two pairs of antennae. The longer pair of antennae is used for feeling, the shorter for smelling and tasting.

The land hermit crab doesn't have a hard shell of its own; it uses old empty shells to protect its soft body. As it grows in size, the hermit crab must find a larger shell. When danger threatens, it hides in the shell and closes the entrance with its hard claw.

Hermit crabs are omnivores and scavengers. They eat worms, plankton, and organic debris.

Although land-based, these crabs must return to the sea to breed. Both males and females partially emerge from their shells to mate. The female lays her hundreds of eggs inside the borrowed shell. These eggs are safe and damp in the shell but, when they hatch, they must be released in the sea. The young are in danger until they find a shell of their own. When they reach adulthood, the crabs migrate to begin their terrestrial life. Land hermit crabs live about 10 years.

Mary Anne Weeks Mayo was the production editor and copyeditor for *Programming .NET Components*. Ann Schirmer proofread the book. Sarah Sherman and Claire Cloutier provided quality control. Matt Hutchinson, Derek DiMatteo, Emily Quill, Jamie Peppard, and Genevieve d'Entremont provided production assistance. Ellen Troutman Zaig wrote the index.

Ellie Volckhausen designed the cover of this book, based on a series design by Edie Freedman. The cover image is a 19th-century engraving from the Dover Pictorial Archive. Emma Colby produced the cover layout with QuarkXPress 4.1 using Adobe's ITC Garamond font.

David Futato designed the interior layout with Bret Kerr. This book was converted by Joe Wizda to FrameMaker 5.5.6 with a format conversion tool created by Erik Ray, Jason McIntosh, Neil Walls, and Mike Sierra that uses Perl and XML technologies. The text font is Linotype Birka; the heading font is Adobe Myriad Condensed; and the code font is LucasFont's TheSans Mono Condensed. The illustrations that appear in the book were produced by Robert Romano and Jessamyn Read using Macromedia FreeHand 9 and Adobe Photoshop 6. The tip and warning icons were drawn by Christopher Bing. This colophon was compiled by Mary Anne Weeks Mayo.